MW01002292

THE GREAT PHYSICIAN

THE
GREAT PHYSICIAN

The Method of Jesus with Individuals

By

G. CAMPBELL MORGAN, D.D.

FLEMING H. REVELL COMPANY
Old Tappan, New Jersey

FOREWORD

THE studies found in this volume were given for the most part in the cities and towns of the United States during my Conference work. Then returning to London, and resuming my work at the Westminster Bible School, they were given there, and prepared for publication.

The title reveals the purpose of the considerations. Our Lord referred to His work as that of the Physician. The statement that He went about healing "all manner of disease" applies to the spiritual as well as to the mental and physical. His own words in connection with a mighty work of healing, "I made a man every whit whole.", reveal the fact that He dealt with the whole of personality. Moreover the supreme concern of His heart was ever that of dealing with spiritual and moral malady.

Our purpose then is that of reverently watching Him at this work. As He went about, we are privileged to see Him, meeting in different places, and under varying circumstances, varied types of men and women, and to observe how He dealt with them.

Such a consideration must be of value to any who have committed to them the cure of souls, or in the terminology of today, who are doing personal work. The business of all such is not that of healing, but that rather of bringing the sin-sick face to face with the One Healer. To do this demands some knowledge of His methods, and these are most radiantly revealed in the records of His earthly ministry. He is the same, yesterday, today, and for ever.

The printed pages retain much of the roughness of the spoken word, but are sent forth with the prayer that they may be of some service in setting forth the glories of the Great Physician.

G. CAMPBELL MORGAN.

WESTMINSTER CHAPEL,
LONDON.

CONTENTS

CONTENTS—*contd.*

I

THE PHYSICIAN HIMSELF

THE description of our Lord as the great Physician is warranted by the fact that He Himself employed that designation illustratively in reference to the whole fact of His mission. Twice over He used it, once when He was referring to a possible criticism of Himself in His native town:

> " Doubtless ye will say unto Me this parable, Physician, heal Thyself."

This was, of course, a passing quotation, and might not be considered proof that we have any right to speak of Him in that way. The other occasion, however, recorded by Matthew, and also by Mark and Luke in almost the same words, does give us that right. Let us read the three occurrences. The narrative in each is the same. Matthew thus gives the record:

> " But when He heard it, He said, They that are whole have no need of a physician, but they that are sick. But go ye and learn what this meaneth, I desire mercy, and not sacrifice; for I came not to call the righteous, but sinners." (Matthew ix, 12, 13.)

The record of Mark is a little briefer, but essentially the same thing (ii, 17).

> " And when Jesus heard it, He saith unto them, They that are whole have no need of a physician, but they that are sick; I came not to call the righteous, but sinners."

Luke's report runs thus (v, 31, 32):

> " And Jesus answering said unto them, They that are whole have no need of a physician; but they that are sick. I am not come to call the righteous, but sinners to repentance."

It is perfectly self-evident that these words of our Lord uttered upon this particular occasion made a profound impression. Matthew doubtless heard Him, for it was in his house that they were uttered. Mark quite possibly was present at the time, though it is not said so. Luke, who gathered his information from eye-witnesses, has carefully recorded the utterance, thus further emphasising the fact that it had made a deep impression upon the minds of those who did hear it.

The occasion was the feast made in the house of Matthew, and the reason why these words were uttered was that of the criticism of Jesus by the religious rulers, because He was surrounded by sinning people. The meaning of His great declaration is clear. He was conscious of the sickness of humanity, of the fact that men were suffering from moral malady. The implicate of the declaration is equally patent that He was a Physician, confronting that malady, and able to deal with it.

We observe with what carefulness the three recorders have reported His words:

"I came not to call the righteous, but sinners."

Luke adds the words "To repentance." In the light of the story itself, these words cannot be read without a consciousness of an element of sarcasm for these men who were critical of Him. They did not understand their own Scriptures which revealed the fact that God desired mercy and not sacrifice. It was as though He had said to them, If you are righteous, then I have nothing to say to you. I came not to call the righteous. My mission has not to do with those who are whole and healthy in the spiritual and moral realms. Such have no need of healing. I came to call sinners. I am the Physician. The business of the physician is never with those who are in health. It is always with the sick. Here then our Lord was implicitly claiming that He confronts humanity in its deepest malady, and that He does so as the great Physician.

It is with that particular phase of His mission that we are proposing to deal in our present series of studies. We shall not be concerned in this attempt with His set discourses and discussions as they are recorded for us in the Gospel narratives. We shall rather attempt to watch Him at His work with individuals.

The purpose for such a series of meditations is twofold. It is first that of attempting to help those who in any sense have committed to them the cure of souls, and this, of course, means preachers and teachers, and all who in any wise are coming into contact with human life with desire to lead it to the place of healing and full realisation. That of course is the business of the whole Christian Church. The importance therefore of watching our Lord Himself doing this very work cannot be overestimated.

At the same time, such a continued study will constantly have in it the possibility of helping those also who are in need of such healing. Infinite, in the variety in many ways of expression, is this common malady of sin, and nothing is more marked, as we shall see again more fully, than the infinite variety of the methods employed by our Lord in dealing with it. In this opening consideration therefore we confine ourselves to general statements on the whole subject. Our knowledge of the New Testament reminds us at once of the very many different persons that are seen as we follow our Lord along the pathway of His earthly mission. By way of introduction to the more detailed study, therefore, we now notice first, the basis of His approach to the human soul; secondly, the universal recognitions in His method; and finally, that to which I have referred, and which is the whole theme, His varied methods.

As to His universal recognitions we may say that He always approached the human soul in the same way. As to varied methods, we may say that He never approached two human souls in the same way Such a paradoxical statement is of value, because it at once compels a little close attention. Nevertheless its meaning is surely self-evident. When our Lord approached a human being, there were great facts common to humanity, for ever present to His mind; whereas it is equally true that the infinite variety of human needs was so recognised that He never employed the same exact method twice over.

With regard to the first of these matters, the passage at the close of the second chapter in the Gospel of John is illuminative.

" When He was in Jerusalem at the Passover, during the feast, many believed on His name, beholding the signs which He did. But Jesus did not trust Himself unto them, for that He knew all men, and because He needed not that any one should bear witness concerning man; for He Himself knew what was in man."

The statement at the commencement is in itself interesting, declaring that many believed on His name, but He did not trust

Himself to them. It should be observed that the verb variously rendered there in our translation, is nevertheless the same concerning the attitude of the people, and our Lord's attitude. We might render, Many *believed* on His name, but Jesus did not *believe* in them. Or we might say, Many *committed* themselves to Him, but He did not *commit* Himself to them. Without dealing further with that, we now observe that John tells us the underlying reason of our Lord's attitude. He did not commit Himself to these people:

> " Because He knew all men, and . . . needed not that any one should bear witness concerning man; for He Himself knew what was in man."

Notice the declaration is that He knew all men, that is, individually; secondly, that He knew what was in man, that is, He knew human nature.

This declaration by John must of necessity be linked with his thought concerning the Lord Himself, and that thought is revealed at the opening of his story.

> " In the beginning was the Word, and the Word was with God, and the Word was God . . . and the Word became flesh."

His knowledge must always be thus interpreted. It was not merely that resulting from observation of men by another Man. It was the knowledge of One Who, in His humanity, bore the name Jesus, and Who in His essential Being, was the Word.

Thus we have the twofold fact, that He knew all men individually and universally; Simon as the son of Jonah; Nathanael as the watcher under the fig-tree; the woman by the well as having had five husbands, and so on, and ever on.

But He not only knew individuals individually, He knew humanity generically. He knew what was in man. On this twofold basis of knowledge He constantly proceeded, and this, let it be said resolutely, accounts for His unique ability in dealing with humanity. He knew perfectly what men are to-day seeking to understand. All the quest of the psychologist is a search for the ultimate truth concerning human personality or individuality. These things the great Physician knew perfectly. Reverently we may say in this connection, like God, He ever remembered that man is dust; and equally like God, He knew that man was infinitely more than dust. That was the basis of His approach, and of course, finally interprets His healing power, His ability to deal with all sorts and conditions of men. We are dealing in these studies with the records only. It is good, however, to remind ourselves at once that whereas they indicate the eternal principles, they do not exhaust the theme, for through all the running centuries that have come and gone, this Christ has been doing the self-same things, confronting human souls, knowing every one, knowing what was in man; and dealing with man according to the facts of his inherent nature, and of all the facts resulting from heredity and environment. Let it at once be said that when to-day men attempt to study the story of our Lord as of one among a number of teachers, they show they have never really seen Him. It is perfectly true that we may watch Him garbed with the simplicity of a peasant, growing weary in common with human nature, and yet He is seen for evermore coming into contact with other men and women and children, knowing completely not only the incidental facts concerning each, but the very nature and being of each. He was and is the great Physician, and the basis of His approach to human nature is that of His perfect knowledge.

Then as we observe Him at His work we discover what we have referred to as His universal recognitions. He dealt with men and women of differing temperaments and different situations, and in a very profound way He recognised certain universal facts. In that way He treated them all as being alike. We may at once cover the whole ground here by declaring that He treated all as spiritual in essence, sinning in experience, salvable by grace.

When we say that He dealt with man as spiritual in essence, we are not for a moment suggesting that He neglected either the mental or the physical. It is impossible to watch Him without realising that His words were ever characterised by intellectual depth and majesty, of such a nature that human intellect fails, even until now to completely apprehend. It was ever His method to compel men to the use of their mental powers. He was constantly asking questions, as though He would say, What is your opinion? What do you think? What is your mental activity in the presence of this matter?

He certainly was not unmindful of the physical. He cared for it. This was ever demonstrated by the wonders of His healing of bodily powers, and upon occasion in His feeding of physical hunger. Nevertheless neither the mental nor the physical

5

constituted His chief concern. He was ever dealing with the spiritual essence, which being at fault, everything else was at fault. The keynote of His preaching was found in the words:

> "From that time began Jesus to preach, and to say, Repent."

That is a call to a mental activity, but He was addressing Himself to the spiritual essence which had a mind. Or again, when He said:

> "Seek ye first His Kingdom, and His righteousness; and all these things shall be added unto you,"

the ultimate thought was undoubtedly that of the spiritual. As one of His apostles wrote later:

> "The Kingdom of God is not eating and drinking, but righteousness and peace and joy in the Holy Ghost."

One other illustration is climacteric in this regard. To His disciples He one day said:

> "I say unto you, My friends, Be not afraid of them which kill the body, and after that have no more that they can do."

On the level of much of our ordinary thinking, we should say that if the body is killed, there is no more to be said or done. The words of Jesus constitute a tender but definite mockery of that very stupid idea. If a man kills my body, he has paralysed his own arm, and can no further harm me, but I am still there. My body lies dead, but I am not dead. From that standpoint He for ever approached man, coming with a clear recognition that their chief glory, the central fact concerning them was not the body which dies, nor the mind that blunders, but the spiritual which is central.

Then it is equally self-evident that He dealt with man not only as spiritual in essence, but as sinning in experience. He saw humanity missing the mark, failing at the centre, and consequently suffering in all the circumference.

> "When He saw the multitude, He was moved with compassion for them, because they were distressed and scattered, as sheep not having a shepherd."

So He saw them, failing to be what God meant them to be, failing to be what was possible within the mystery of their own personality. In the words in which He spoke of Himself as the

6

great Physician, He made it perfectly clear that His mission was concerning such, and in dealing with man He treated him as sinning in experience.

The final word is that He treated humanity as salvable. That is a great old theological term, and is incapable of being improved. In spite of all the dereliction, He saw man as salvable, capable of the highest in spite of having passed to the lowest. It is impossible to follow our Lord upon the pathway of His service, and watch Him thus dealing with individuals, and then to speak of hopeless cases. All those who are engaged upon this selfsame sacred service are very conscious that there are occasions when we are inclined to feel that the case is indeed hopeless. Resolutely we declare He never did this. When no one else believed in the possibility of the recovery of a human soul, He did. We say, and we say correctly, that according to these records, men and women were saved or made whole through their faith in Him. It is perfectly correct to look more deeply, and if we do we find that their faith in Him was created by His faith in them. Thus He approached humanity, recognising it as spiritual in essence, sinning in experience, salvable by grace.

And so we pass to the other matter where the interest, of course, is enormous, and which is to occupy the whole of our subsequent meditations. Here we summarise briefly by saying that we never find our Lord dealing with two different persons in exactly the same way. To take one or two brief illustrations, to which, of course, we shall return for more careful consideration later. To Andrew and John He said, " What seek ye? " To Simon He said, You shall be Rock. To Philip He said, " Follow Me." To Nathanael He said, Before Philip found you, I saw you. To Nicodemus He said, You must be " born from above."

With that last illustration we pause a moment to remark that it is at least arresting that He is never recorded as having said that to anyone else. It is true that He so said it as to show that it applies to every human being; but it is equally arresting that He is not reported as having said it to anyone else personally. He was employing the method necessary in the case of the man, and this He ever did.

At the commencement of this meditation we declared that one purpose of this series would be that of helping those who have the cure of souls. We then showed that He proceeded upon the basis of His perfect knowledge. Here then for a moment we are halted, because we cannot, of ourselves, have any such perfect knowledge. It is, therefore, of the utmost importance that we should remember that all who are called to that work are called to a fellowship with Him in and through the Holy Spirit. It is only by such living, maintained fellowship, that we can ever do this work. That is a subject which surely needs no argument. It may be stated, however, with reverence and reticence, that the measure in which those called to this sacred business are living in true fellowship with Him, will be found to be the measure of their understanding of men and women, and their ability to deal with them, in order to their saving.

II

JOHN THE BAPTIST

OUR study this evening is concerned with the first man with whom our Lord came into contact in His public ministry, so far as the records reveal. Indeed, we have no account of any words passing the lips of Jesus apart from those uttered to His Mother at twelve years of age, until we find Him face to face with His great forerunner. In this case, as in all that follow, we shall attempt first to see the man, and then to watch our Lord's dealing with him. It should at once be said that there is something unique in this story, because John had a special and great function in the Divine economy. According to the records, he was a supernatural child, and he was born for this definite purpose, which he most gloriously fulfilled.

In considering the story of John there are three things which stand out pre-eminently. They are those of his essential greatness, his evident discontent, and his one great expectation.

As to his greatness, we are not left to speculation. In his case the portrait of the man is drawn for us by our Lord Himself. His estimate of John is recorded by Matthew and by Luke in chapters eleven and seven respectively. We will take that as recorded by Matthew, which is indeed almost identical with that of Luke. In referring to John on a memorable occasion, Jesus said:

"Verily I say unto you, Among them that are born of women there hath not arisen a greater than John the Baptist; yet he that is but little in the Kingdom of heaven is greater than he."

In passing, it is interesting to notice that Luke in recording those words of Jesus uses the phrase "the Kingdom of God," where Matthew says "the Kingdom of heaven." The terms are really synonymous in their deepest meaning.

This reference was unquestionably to what we may speak of as the natural ability and greatness of this man John, and declared that among all others "born of women," none greater

9

than John had arisen. The phrase, "born of women" is in itself suggestive and clear. We call to mind another phrase used by Paul of Jesus Himself, when he said:

"When the fulness of the time came, God sent forth His Son, born of a woman."

The Old Version read, "made of a woman," and our revisers in changing it, have not improved, but indeed, have hidden the suggestiveness of the Greek phrase. It is not the same word which our Lord used of John. That phrase literally meant, "born of a woman." That which Paul used of our Lord meant something preceding birth, namely generation.

Surveying the history of the human race after Adam, every member of which was born of a woman, our Lord declares that none greater had arisen than this man John. Another translation would be perfectly permissible here, which would read:

"I say unto you, Among them that are born of women there hath not been raised up a greater than John."

If that is the true rendering, reference is not so much made to the whole human race as to those specially raised up to fulfil some special function in the Divine economy. We need not discuss the different possibilities. It is enough to accept this estimate. It is, however, remarkably illuminated by the contrast suggested, as our Lord said:

"He that is but little in the Kingdom of heaven is greater than he."

In these words there was an implicit recognition of the greatness and finality of the mission of the Messiah, of which John was the herald. The reference is, in the last analysis, to the sovereignty of God, rather than to any particular territory. John announced that Kingdom as at hand. It was a reference to the new order to be ushered in by the work of our Lord Himself, that order which, according to John, was not available to men through the baptism of water, but through the baptism of the Spirit. The words of Jesus by no means excluded John from that Kingdom. As a man supernaturally born, and equipped for a mission, he was great; but the Kingdom which he announced included all such, himself also, who went beyond the prophetic hope to the practical realisation.

Further, concerning the man in the angelic announcement at his birth made to his father within the priestly office, this most remarkable thing was said concerning him:

"He shall be great in the sight of the Lord . . . and he shall be filled with the Holy Spirit, even from his mother's womb."

This necessarily bears further testimony to his greatness.

10

This is revealed, moreover, in the office which he held. One of the supreme glories of the Hebrew nation had been that of the prophetic gift. The true meaning of that gift may be gathered from the varied appellations by which those having it were designated. Sometimes the prophet was called a seer, quite simply, a man who sees. Sometimes he was called a man of God, that is revealing, of course, the sign of his authority. Once incidentally by quotation, he was referred to as a man of the Spirit. The prophetic order commenced with Samuel, and comprised within its sweep such men as Elijah and Elisha; and later on, of course, Isaiah, Jeremiah, and the rest, with whose names we are familar. Splendid as that succession was, none among all the prophets was greater than the last of the long line. Presently our Lord indicated that, when He said to the multitudes that they had seen in John " more than a prophet." Thus we are certainly looking at a remarkable man in human history, and the last fact which reveals his greatness was that of the coming to him of the Word of God. We remember how carefully Luke marks the date of that coming, by using a Roman emperor, a Roman governor, three tetrarchs, two high priests, to indicate the hour.

Having thus seen his greatness, we are next impressed with his discontent. By that we intend to emphasise the fact that his ministry was mastered by an almost overwhelming consciousness of the sin of his age, and of his people. He had lived a secluded life for many years. He was:

" In the deserts till the day of his shewing unto Israel."

There are different interpretations of the exact meaning of that statement. Personally I believe that it referred to a period of about ten years. We remember that John was a priest in priestly succession, and that his mother was also of the priestly line. In the ordinary run of events, he would have taken up the course of preparation for the priesthood at twenty years of age. Quite evidently, under a Divine call and announcement, and probably as the result of his earlier training, because his father and mother knew the purpose for which he was born, he turned aside from the priestly, and prepared for the prophetic office. When the moment came for him to emerge from his seclusion, and begin his public ministry, he spoke as one who, as we have said, was burdened with a sense of the sin and failure of his age.

This sense is specially manifested by his answers to individual questions. To the multitude he said:

" Begin not to say within yourselves, we have Abraham to our father."

He saw formalism covering corruption, trusting to fleshly relationship, and so negativing all spiritual values and moral results.

11

When the publicans came and asked him what they should do, he said:

> "Extort no more than that which is appointed you."

He clearly saw . dishonesty practising under the cloak of officialism.

When the soldiers asked him what they should do, he said:

> "Do violence to no man, neither exact anything wrongfully, and be content with your wages."

He saw the tyranny of the conqueror and rebuked it. All this proves that he conducted his ministry with an overwhelming sense of the sin and corruption of his time.

While this consciousness of sin is apparent, there is another note which is supreme. Hope was singing a great song in the soul of this man. He was conscious of an approaching crisis. He clearly saw the evil, but to employ his own figure, he saw the axe laid at the root of the tree. The axe at the root of the tree is the symbol of a process, that namely of pruning in order to the provocation to fruit-bearing, but it is also the symbol of judgment, for if the provocation does not produce fruit, the tree will be cut down. He saw the crisis centred in a Person whose activity was to be that of the fan and the fire. He clearly saw, moreover, that this One would exercise a power which he described as a baptism of the Spirit and of fire. He declared unequivocally that his baptism which was with water was not sufficient in itself to deal with the situation. It symbolised the necessity for repentance, and confessed the need for something more than repentance. In the coming One he saw One Who would supply that which was needed, namely a new life, which he spoke of as baptism with the Spirit. In John's account of those earliest hours in the ministry of Jesus, which were of course the closing years in that of John, he tells of how six weeks after the baptism of Jesus, he said:

> "In the midst of you standeth One Whom ye know not."

This was the One Whom he declared should baptise men with the Holy Spirit and fire.

Here, then, we see John, a man than whom none born of women was greater, greater in intellectual power, and greater in the high office that he was called to fulfil. As he himself declared, he was not the Messiah, not Elijah, not even the prophet that Moses promised should come. His own account of himself was that he was the voice crying in the wilderness, whose advent had been foretold by Isaiah the prophet, the voice preceding the Word, and declaring the near advent of the One for Whom that people had looked and longed and watched for long centuries.

We are now to observe how our Lord dealt with this man. It is really most arresting to remind ourselves that we have only one occasion on record when they spoke to each other, and that was at the baptism of Jesus. Six weeks later than this, the temptation in the wilderness having intervened, Jesus returning from it in victory, John had said concerning Him that already quoted:

"In the midst of you standeth One Whom ye know not;"

and on the next day he had singled Him out, and identified Him in the words:

"Behold the Lamb of God, which taketh away the sin of the world."

On the day following he had indicated Jesus Himself to two disciples as He passed by. Later in his ministry John sent to Jesus a deputation expressing, for the moment, his sense of bewilderment. I repeat, however, we have no record of a direct conversation between them.

The one occasion, then, when we see our Lord in contact with this man is at the baptism. When Jesus approached John it it important to remember that the herald did not know that He was the appointed Messiah. This he made clear in his declaration that he knew not who He was, save by the sign granted to him, of the Spirit descending upon Him. This was not given until after he baptised Him. Whether John knew Jesus as the Child of Mary, Who had been legally adopted by Joseph, it is impossible to say. Enough for us that when Jesus approached him and sought his baptism, John hesitated, not because he knew He was Messiah, but because John being a man of clear prophetic insight, and perchance because he had known something of Him personally, he knew there was no place for his baptism in the life of Jesus. He was calling men to repentance, and repentance always involves a confession of sin. John realised that there was no need for repentance on the part of Jesus; and in effect declared that he could not baptise the Sinless as he was baptising the sinner. It was then that our Lord spoke to him, and in these words:

"Suffer it now, for thus it becometh us to fulfil all righteousness."

It was a declaration that the only way in which sin could be dealt with, and righteousness established was by the identification of the Sinless with the sinning. He was indeed numbered with the transgressors in His baptism prophetically of His numbering with them ultimately, for dealing with sin, and bringing in righteousness.

Thus He dealt with John. The question naturally arises: Did John understand Him? The answer is that there is no doubt that he did. Whether that understanding was immediate, it is impossible to say. Be that as it may, John consented and baptised Him, and Jesus passed on His way. After six full weeks, He returned, and in the method of John's identification of Him we have a remarkable revelation of understanding.

" Behold, the Lamb of God, which taketh away the sin of the world."

He who had spoken of the coming of Messiah with a fan and a fire, and a baptism with the Holy Spirit, had said no word about the bearing of sin until then. At this point I am inclined to indulge myself in imagination, which may be received for what it is worth. I imagine John, after he had baptised Jesus, and had witnessed the identifying sign of the Holy Spirit, and after Jesus had passed out of his sight, taking down the roll of Isaiah, and looking over it. He had claimed that he was the voice of one, crying in the wilderness, Prepare ye the way of the Lord. Going on from that point in the prophecy, he would come to the chapter declaring the advent of the Servant of the Lord, and so on and on until he read what we call the fifty-third chapter. As he did so, probably he understood. When Jesus returned, therefore, he identified Him as Messiah, but he did not say, Behold One coming with fan and fire, and an axe. He was not contradicting all the truths contained in those figures of speech. The Messiah wields the fan, casts the fire, and uses the axe. He does lower the mountains and exalt the valleys, but the greatest fact is that which John now declared:

" Behold, the Lamb of God, which taketh away the sin of the world."

This whole story is the account of the merging of the old economy into the new, not the contradicting of anything of moral force in the old, but the proclamation of a new method of grace equal to dealing with the whole situation. In introducing Him John spoke of Him as " the Lamb of God." To that Syrian crowd listening to him the very word suggested sacrifice, and inevitably associated itself in their minds with the great Day of Atonement. Moreover, it may be mechanical and incidental, but it is at least suggestive that the first time we read the word " lamb " in the Old Testament, the spokesman was Isaac, who said to his father:

" My father . . . behold, the fire and the wood, but where is the lamb for a burnt offering? "

The first time we find the word in the New Testament is here in the announcement of John, " Behold, the Lamb of God, which taketh away the sin of the world."

The voice of the Old spoke, " Where is the lamb? " The voice of the New declared, " Behold, the Lamb of God."

Thus John, who had been burdened with a sense of sin, beheld in Jesus God's provision for dealing with it, and presently he declared:

" I have seen, and have borne witness that this is the Son of God."

The Lamb of God is the Son of God.

We have the record, then, of one brief sentence falling from the lips of Jesus directly spoken to John, and for John the whole outlook was changed. Nothing had been said which contradicted the great preaching of John, but the word illuminated the whole situation. Reverently it is as though Jesus had said, Yes, John, herald of Mine, voice sounding in the wilderness, sin must be dealt with, and there is only one way in which that can be done. Denunciation may be perfectly proper and necessary, but it cannot deal with the malady.

At last John said to his disciples:

" This my joy, therefore, is fulfilled . . . He must increase, but I must decrease."

Here our minds necessarily run on to that hour later when John sent to Jesus, asking the question:

" Art Thou He that cometh, or look we for another? "

With regard to this, it has been suggested that he was crystalising suggestions raised by his own disciples. That may have been so. It has also been suggested that it was a question arising out of a moment of depression, a doubting like that of Elijah beneath the juniper tree. F. B. Morton in his book, " The Steps of the Master," describes the situation of the castle in which Herod had imprisoned John, and the description makes us feel that it would have been no wonder if he had been depressed. I believe, however, that his question was not due to any flagging interest. It was born rather of perplexity created by the methods of Jesus. As reports of His work reached John in prison, it did not seem that He was doing the things that John expected would be done. His question was the question of intellectual perplexity. If we are inclined to wonder at John's question being raised at all, it is well to read again the story of the answer of Jesus as recorded in Luke. The first movement in that answer was that when the deputation arrived, our Lord was healing the sick, preaching the Gospel to the poor, raising the dead; and He left the deputation waiting while He continued that work, the very work which was puzzling John. Then, addressing the deputation, He told them to go back, and report to John exactly what He was doing. He was healing the sick, He was raising the dead; but the supreme thing was that He was preaching the good tidings of the Kingdom of

15

God, and thus leading men to the true franchise of their lives, by bringing them into relationship with that Kingdom.

This was followed by those words characterised by great tenderness, and yet by an element of rebuke:

"And blessed is he, whosoever shall find none occasion of stumbling in Me."

In effect this meant that He declared to John, if he could not understand, he was called upon to trust.

Moreover, it was in this very connection that Jesus had given His estimate of John, to which we referred at the beginning, and had declared his greatness, both as to natural equipment and as to the prophetic office.

Thus in that critical hour of the baptism He had spoken to John in such way as to illuminate all his ministry; and at the last He is found defending him against a possible misunderstanding, resulting from his own trembling in faith.

III

ANDREW

ANDREW is referred to eight times in the New Testament. His first meeting with our Lord is recorded in the first chapter of the Gospel of John. In Mark i, 16, we have the account of his call from his fishing nets, which occurred at least a year later than his first meeting with Jesus.

> "Passing along by the Sea of Galilee, He saw Simon and Andrew the brother of Simon casting a net into the sea, for they were fishers."

The record of the third occasion is found in Mark iii, 13, when it is said that our Lord went up:

> "Into the mountain, and calleth unto Him whom He Himself would,"

and He appointed them to be with Him, and to send them forth as apostles. Andrew was one of the number.

In John vi, we have the account of the feeding of the five thousand, and in it the next story of Andrew, who it was that told the Lord about the lad who was present, having the loaves and fishes. In John xii, 22, we meet with Andrew again, when at the end of the public ministry of Jesus the Greeks came and said to Philip, "Sir, we would see Jesus." Philip then consulted with Andrew, and they both came to the Lord. In Mark xiii, 3, we meet him again, when after the Olivet prophecy, when Jesus sat upon the Mount of Olives over against the Temple, he came with Peter, James and John to ask the Master privately to explain what He had been saying. His name is found next in the book of the Acts in the first chapter and the thirteenth verse:

> "When they were come in, they went up into the inner chamber, where they were abiding; both Peter and John and James and Andrew, Philip and Thomas, Bartholomew

17

and Matthew, James the son of Alphæus, and Simon the Zealot, and Judas the son of James."

Thus he is found in the apostolic company, and undoubtedly went with that company into the Temple. We find him, however, once more in the book of Revelation, xxi, 14, where describing the city of God it is said:

"And the wall of the city had twelve foundations, and on them the twelve names of the twelve apostles of the Lamb."

Necessarily Andrew's name was one. That covers the ground of our information concerning this man.

With these incidents in mind we will attempt to see the man himself. We know his father's name. We are not told this, however, in connection with himself, but in connection with his brother. When Andrew brought Simon to Jesus, our Lord said, " Thou art Simon, the son of John." It is quite evident that he was not a conspicuous man in the opinion of those who came into contact with him. Even John, when writing the story of his first meeting with Jesus, before he had named Simon at all, in order that we may know who Andrew was, calls him " the brother of Simon "; and we find he is constantly referred to in that way. Men who are known thus by their relationship to other men are almost always unobtrusive men, not strikingly impressive to others.

Then we turn to the more definite facts concerning him, and the first is that he was a disciple of John the Baptist, and was most evidently within the inner circle of those disciples. When we recognise that, we are face to face with some things concerning him. He was evidently a man who had become conscious of the act of sin, and of the fact of its abounding nature in the time in which he lived, and far more, of the fact of sin in himself. He had evidently become conscious of the need for repentance, and had submitted himself to the ritual baptism that indicated the confession of sin, and the desire for remission and renewal.

Moreover, as a disciple of John he was one seeking for the Kingdom of Heaven, or the Kingdom of God; for John had struck the key-note of his ministry with the great announcement, " Repent, for the Kingdom of Heaven is at hand." Andrew had heard that message, and had been obedient to it.

Moreover, John's whole ministry had been that of telling of the coming of One Who would bring deliverance with fan and fire, gathering out the wheat, and destroying chaff in all human affairs; lowering mountains and lifting valleys, thus ending all inequalities. Andrew therefore as a disciple of John, was living in expectation of the coming of the One Who should set up that Kingdom.

We may often know much about a man if we know his friends. We look at the friends of Andrew. John the Baptist was one, and John the apostle was another. We say this, of course, taking for granted there can be little doubt that John was the one with him when they saw and followed Jesus. Thus among his closest friends he numbered the man of stern, ascetic outlook upon life, and the man who was a poet and a seer. Moreover, Philip is found in that group, a man more unimpressive than even Andrew, quiet and retiring. Then necessarily there was his own brother, Simon.

In view of these few facts before us, we ask what sort of a man was Andrew? After pondering this narrative it seems to me that he was a singularly strong man. His name Andrew, Andreas, means manly. Necessarily nothing very much can be based upon that fact, but in all probability at his birth it might have been said of him as it was of Moses, that he was a proper child, and the name have been given in expectation of what he would become, and then the boy trained to manhood in keeping with the suggestion. I have a picture that I love of Simon and John hurrying to the tomb on the resurrection morning. In it Simon is represented as a strong, rough, almost dishevelled-looking man. I always feel that it might pass for a picture of Andrew also.

Moreover, he was a man marked by moral courage and insight, as is evidenced by the immediateness of the way in which at a critical moment, he left John, the herald, and followed Jesus.

As we watch him in his first meeting with Jesus, we see Andrew following quietly and reverently. He did not speak to the Lord until he was addressed. When the question was asked by Jesus, " What seek ye? " we notice Andrew's immediate reply, as he addressed Him as " Rabbi," and in the use of the title revealed the fact that he was putting himself under the instruction of our Lord. Jesus was no Rabbi according to the order of the times. He was a Galilean peasant. Nevertheless under the impulse of the conviction that filled him, as the result of John's words, he called Him " Rabbi."

Furthermore, his cautiousness is certainly manifest to the careful reader. Jesus said, "What seek ye?" and he replied, "Rabbi, where abidest Thou?" Thus he answered a question with another question, and with one that at first does not seem to be at all relevant. Pondering the story, it is impossible to escape from the conviction that what he meant was simply this: he realised at once the supreme importance of the question, and declared in effect that it could not be answered easily, and so he wanted time; that if he could only come to the place where Jesus abode, it would be possible to have such time.

Now we enquire how our Lord dealt with such a man. It is good to emphasise the fact that in Andrew we have no libertine, no man who had abused and debased himself by evil courses in life; or even if there had been such courses, there had also been definite confession and repentance; he had set his face towards righteousness, and was seeking the Kingdom of God. Andrew, therefore, is seen at the beginning as a man, repenting, questing after the Kingdom, expecting the coming of the Deliverer.

Our Lord's dealing with him began with His question, "What seek ye?" We pause to remind ourselves that that is the supreme question in any and every human life. Our Lord did not ask Andrew who he was looking for. There was no need to do that. It was quite evident that he was seeking Jesus. What He did ask him was, why he was doing that very thing. Why are you coming after Me? What is it that you really want? This question to Andrew becomes the more arresting when we remember that the words are the first recorded words of Jesus as He commenced His public ministry. The question was one that plumbed the very deeps of personality. Jesus was drawing him out by driving him in. It is at least probable that Andrew had seen Jesus when six weeks earlier He had been baptised. But yesterday he had heard John identify Him as the Lamb of God Who taketh away the sin of the world. He had come as far as that, and now Jesus said, Why are you coming? What do you want? What is the inspiration driving you along this pathway after Me? John had declared that He would come with His fan in His hand. At this moment He was using that fan in the soul of a man, driving away as chaff all secondary things, and taking Him down to the central matter of life. I cannot help believing that Andrew caught the suggestiveness of the question. It was the greatness of it that made him say, "Where abidest Thou?" In other words, Give me time, let me come closer before I talk.

The tremendous significance of the question cannot be over-emphasised. If at this moment we paused, and allowed our Lord to speak to us, there is a sense in which He would still say, "What seek ye?" When thus challenged, we pass to the master conception of life, and discover the inspiration of everything, we shall know the answer. Andrew had come a long way. He had heard John. He had obeyed. He was engaged in a quest after the Kingdom of God. He had confessed the fact of sin. He was longing for complete deliverance from all its effects. He had heard John say that This was "the Lamb of God which taketh away the sin of the world," and now he was asked why he was following. When he then enquired as to the abiding place of Christ, he heard the Master say, "Come, and ye shall see." This meant far more than that Andrew should see where He was abiding. It meant that there should come to him an answer to his quest, a seeing that would indicate the way by which it would be possible for him to find that which he sought.

The quiet day ran its course. How long they were together must depend on the view we hold as to the method of John in referring to time. There are those who believe he used the Hebrew method. Personally I am quite convinced that it was the Roman method he used. If it were the Hebrew method, then this meeting happened in the afternoon, and they were together until sunset. If on the other hand it were the Roman method, their meeting occurred about ten o'clock in the morning, and all the hours following to sunset were given up to these men. They found their way to the place where Christ was abiding, and we have no record whatever of the interview. We do know, however, what happened immediately that interview was over for we see this man Andrew hurrying away to find his brother, and to announce the fact that they had found the Messiah.

Whereas we have said we have no record of what took place between them, we can very reverently imagine much that happened. Andrew would probably talk to Jesus of the perplexity of the times in which he was living as seen through the ministry of the Baptist, and would ask Him what He had to say about these conditions. Possibly Andrew would ask the Lord to explain the mystery of Himself in regard to the prophecy, particularly desiring light on John's proclamation concerning Him as being "The Lamb of God which taketh away the sin of the world." All this is speculation and may be dismissed. The certain thing is that after the interview his heart was resting in the fact that he had found his Messiah.

We repeat that we have no particulars of the interview, but as we have reverently imagined things concerning Andrew, we may with equal reverence suggest that in His dealing with this man, He emphasised the necessity which later on to Andrew and others who listened, He put into clear and concrete form of command:

"Seek ye first the Kingdom of God, and His righteousness, and all these things shall be added unto you."

"What seek ye?" He had said to Andrew upon the highway, and later He had said, "Seek ye first the Kingdom of God." In each case we have the same word "seek," a word that suggests a quest for something hidden or lost. He used it again in that self-same Manifesto when He said, "Seek, and ye shall find." He used the same word, moreover, once of His own ministry when He declared:

"The Son of man is come to seek and to save that which is lost."

It was a word, therefore, in itself which indicated seriousness in quest. He thus Who had asked Andrew this question, in the quiet hours would surely emphasise the importance of the right quest, that, namely, of the Kingdom of God.

The issue was that this man who had enrolled himself as a disciple, and spent the day with Jesus, came to the great conviction to which we have already more than once referred. We see him finding his brother, and using to him the simple and yet sublime formula that revealed his position, as he said: "We have found the Messiah." The Messiah was to Andrew, the hope of his people, the hope that had become a hope deferred, and had indeed made the heart sick; the hope that had been rekindled as the result of the ministry of John the forerunner; and now Andrew declared, We have found Him.

It is good in this connection to be reminded that in all the prophetic foretelling, as in all the ritual'stic foretelling, the coming Messiah was shown forth as the One Who would merge in His Person the offices of priesthood and kingship. His authority of kingship would be vested in His redeeming and mediatorial work as Priest. We have found Him, said Andrew. In all probability at the moment Andrew by no means understood all involved in the announcement. It was three years later that his brother made the great inclusive confession. Nevertheless there had come to him the conviction of the fact even though he did not understand all its implications. He had found the Messiah, his King. He had found the One Who could answer the quest of his soul after the remission of sins.

Immediately this man became a missionary. Conviction in his own soul, followed by submission to that of which he was convinced, issued in an active, spontaneous, inevitable propaganda.

That is always so. It is impossible to find Christ in such relationship as Andrew did, without realising the birth in the soul of a missionary passion. No man can become a living follower of the Lord without immediately finding His compassion moving him, and driving him out after someone else. " He findeth first his own brother."

Then the great story runs on. He was called presently to apostleship, and later sent out as an apostle. Then we gain some suggestive glimpses of him. We first see him with venturesome faith when the multitudes were waiting to be fed. Philip the mathematician and careful man, was counting the cost. It was then that Andrew went a little further than Philip with his calculation, and spoke of the lad who was present with two loaves and some little fishes. But he qualified his venture as he revealed the fact that he had not very much hope, for said he, " What are, they among so many? " To him, then, was given the discovery that what seems worthless as our possession is abundance in the handling of the Lord. When at the end the Greeks came and told Philip that they would see Jesus, he, after consultation with Andrew, decided to take them into the presence of the Lord. Once more we have no details of the conversation between Philip and Andrew, and yet one can imagine that there flashed back upon the memory of this man the words that Jesus had spoken long ago to him and another, " Come, and ye shall see." He made up his mind if these men wanted to see Jesus, he had better get them face to face with Him.

The last glimpse, historically, that we have of Andrew is of him in the first chapter of the Acts. There he is not preaching, neither is he seen going out seeking some new follower of his Lord. His great occupation on that day was that of listening to the brother he had found preaching, and watching three thousand swept over the border line into the Kingdom of God. And to refer once again to something spoken of earlier, the last place in which the name of Andrew is revealed is on one of the foundation stones of the city of God. It is all poetic and suggestive, and notwithstanding the apparent bathos of the thing, I am

23

constrained to say that as you look at that city, you will find that Simon had no greater or more conspicuous stone than had Andrew. The tremendous significance of that simple and perhaps half foolish remark is that the building of the city of God will not be accomplished because of the notoriety of its builders, but because of their fidelity.

We close our meditation by reminding ourselves that Christ's first disciple was not Peter, but Andrew, and the first need of the Lord is still the strong, quiet soul who is content to remain largely out of sight. By saying this I am not undervaluing Peter. I am not undervaluing any man who in the Divine will is put in the forefront; but I am attempting to emphasise the fact that if the Kingdom of God had only the men whom we sometimes designate leaders, the work would suffer. It is by the host of those who, like Andrew, are strong, cautious, and faithful, that that work will be accomplished.

I repeat that all this is not to undervalue Peter, but it is rightly to estimate Andrew. The message of the study is pre-eminently for the man who has come far towards the Kingdom of God, who has not yet had personal, first-hand contact with Christ. There are multitudes of such men who see the glory of God, men who know their own sin, men who have gone so far as to seek release from that sin by an activity of repentance, but they have not found the Messiah.

What does the story say to such? Follow the lines along which you have been travelling, and they will inevitably lead you presently face to face with Christ. Having found Him, submit, enrol yourself as His disciple, obey Him. You certainly may not at the moment be sure of all the doctrines of the Christian Church. That need not affect your discipleship. Go after Him, and when He turns, and demands from you what you are seeking, take time to tell Him. As assuredly as you do so, you will find the Messiah, your Saviour and your King.

IV

JOHN THE APOSTLE

IN dealing with the subject of our Lord's methods with John the
Apostle, I shall proceed upon the assumption, which is a
reasoned conviction, that "the disciple whom Jesus loved,"
referred to in the Gospel, is John himself, and that he wrote this
story of Jesus. If these things be granted, one of the out-standing
facts in his narrative is that of his reticence in referring to himself
by name. As a matter of fact, he never names himself in the
Gospel. Moreover, his reticence in referring to those to whom
he was related, is equally marked. He never mentions his brother's
name, or his mother's name, or the name of the Virgin Mother.

From the synoptic writings we know that John was the son
of Zebedee and Salome. It is well to remember that while Zebedee
and his two sons, John and James, were fishermen, it does not
necessarily follow that they were poor men. Mark and Luke
both refer to the fact that Zebedee had hired servants (Mark i, 30,
Luke v, 7 and 10). It is also quite clear that Zebedee and his
sons were in partnership with Simon and Andrew.

Salome, the mother of this man, was the sister of the Virgin
Mary. This will be found by reference to Matthew xxvii, 55
and 56, and John xix, 25. Therefore, after the flesh, he was a
cousin of Jesus. It is equally evident that Salome, whether in
her own right or not we cannot tell, was a woman of means, if
not of wealth. Luke has given us (viii, 3) the list of a company
of wealthy women who ministered to the necessity of Jesus, and
Salome was one of such.

These references will help us to realise that John was not
a poor man in our sense of the term. Those times were simpler
and better times in that matter than those in which we live. It
is also to be remembered that John had a house in Jerusalem. It
was in that house he gave shelter to Peter after he had denied his

Lord, and surely it was to that house he first took the Mother of Jesus when she was committed to his care in the dark hour of the Cross.

We know one other fact concerning him, that he was a friend of the high priest. It is quite true there may be different interpretations of the reference. Mr. Morton in his remarkable book, "In the Footsteps of Jesus," has endeavoured to account for John finding access to the palace by saying that he probably sold fish, and knew the household. The only remark I have to make on that is that it is entirely gratuitous, in view of the fact that the New Testament distinctly tells us he was a friend of the high priest. This, of course, was the reason why he had access to the high priestly court.

Then, moreover, we are familiar with his intimate friends, his own brother, James, Andrew, and Simon; and as in other cases, this fact must be taken into account in thinking of the man.

In looking at him we may very rapidly follow in chronological sequence the places where he appears in the Gospel narratives. We first see him with Andrew following Jesus as they left John the Baptist. He is next seen about eighteen months later, when Jesus called him to leave Zebedee, and told him He would make him a fisher of men.

Then we find him among the number of the apostles, chosen by our Lord. Once more, we see him sent forth with the other apostles. These are the only references to him during the first three years of our Lord's ministry, except that he was associated with Peter and James in the visit to the house of Jairus.

In the final six months he is seen, first in the same company on the mount of transfiguration. Then we see him angry with one who had cast out demons in the name of Jesus, but who was not acting with the company of the apostles. Here it is worthy of note that we should not have known of this fact except that John himself had confessed it as a mistake made by himself. It was when the Lord had in answer to their enquiry about greatness, set a child in the midst, that John told this story.

Soon after that we see him going through Samaria with Jesus, and desiring to call down fire upon a village that had refused hospitality to his Lord.

Mark gives us an account of his coming with his brother to Jesus seeking the position of power in the Kingdom. Matthew in this connection shows that they made their request through their mother. Here, too, it is well to remember that however we may be tempted to criticise them for the request, it is arresting that they were asking it in dark days when our Lord was telling them that He was going to die, strangely perplexing them. Nevertheless they believed He was somehow coming into the Kingdom, and so preferred their request.

Again, he was one of the four who sought the explanation of the Olivet prophecy. He went with Peter to prepare the upper room for the Passover. At last we see him with the same two, Peter and his brother, taken into Gethsemane; and then presently following the Lord into the judgment hall. It is evident that while there he was watching Peter, and saw him in the moment when, with a broken heart, he went out into the night. It is equally evident that he followed him and took him to the shelter of his home. Then he was at the Cross, near enough for the Lord to address him directly, and commit to his care His Mother.

Beyond the Cross he is seen on the resurrection morning investigating the mystery of the empty tomb, and indeed, apprehending the full meaning of what had happened when he entered the tomb. Then, weary of waiting, he joined the company of those seven who went fishing, and was with Christ on the morning by the sea. Yet later he is seen in the upper room. After Pentecost we have a glimpse of him at the Beautiful Gate with Peter. Presently he is seen going through Samaria, the very region where he had desired fire to be called down, preaching with Peter. We have one other historic glimpse of him in the letter to the Galatians when Paul went to Jerusalem, John was one of those who interviewed him.

At last we see him in Patmos for " the Word of God, and the testimony of Jesus," and necessarily his name also is found upon one of the foundation stones of the city of God.

Now as we pass these incidents in rapid review in memory, I cannot help feeling that he was a man who, perhaps, as a fisherman was out of place. We might say that he was a dreamer, but we will change the word, and say he was a mystic. We may change that again, and describe him as a seer and a poet. These very words, dreamer, mystic, seer, poet, put him out of the realm of interest to multitudes of people. And yet we venture to say that there is not one of the disciples of Jesus named in these Gospel narratives in whom the common multitude of Christian people are more profoundly interested than in John.

John was a man who gained proof for himself by insight rather than by deduction. I am not suggesting that he undervalued deduction. His Gospel would contradict any such view, for throughout it, he is massing evidence from which deductions may be made. Nevertheless for himself, I repeat, that his proof came by insight. When we take up the first of the letters that bear his name, we mark the mystical qualities characterising them.

" That which was from the beginning, that which we have heard, that which we have seen with our eyes, that which we beheld, and our hands handled, concerning the Word of life . . . that which we have seen and heard, declare we unto you also."

Yes, he had seen, he had heard, he had handled; but when he saw, he saw far more than others did. When he heard, he heard what others did not hear. When he handled, he became conscious of matters not patent to the common crowd. John was a man who was ever looking for the invisible, and seeing it; listening for the inaudible, and hearing it; feeling after the intangible, and sensing it.

Moreover, John was a great lover, loving with ardour and force. The word " love " became the very keynote of his writings. The energy of this love created his dynamic. He was capable of being intolerant, as his statement concerning the forbidding of a man revealed. He might even be vengeful, as his desire to call down fire proves. He was self-confident, as his request for position and power shows. This request was not a desire for notoriety, but for the opportunity of the using of ability.

Now we enquire as to our Lord's methods with this man, so different from his friend, Andrew, and also from Simon. The first action was that taken when John was with Andrew. He challenged him as He did Andrew as to what it was he was seeking, and then gave Himself to him for the rest of that day. As we watch this man we can imagine how even then he was looking for the invisible, listening for the inaudible, questing for the intangible. There is a sense in which that question of Jesus was intensely poetic. To this man John, it would demand that he should investigate himself in all those inner promptings and desires of his nature. In reply to this word of the Lord, this man, in common with his friend Andrew, immediately enrolled himself as a disciple, as he addressed Jesus as Rabbi.

The next words of Christ again had a fuller meaning for John, " Come, and ye shall see." In this connection it is interesting to turn over to the book of the Revelation. There we read:

> " The Revelation of Jesus Christ, which God gave Him to show unto His servants, even the things which must shortly come to pass; and He sent and signified it by His angel unto His servant John; who bare witness of the Word of God, and of the testimony of Jesus Christ, even of all things that he saw."

Here we have the same word, the verb *eido* with reference to vision. Said Jesus, " Come, and ye shall *see* " at the very beginning of His ministry, and in the last writings he referred to the things that he " *saw*." Christ invited the seer to see, promised the questing soul of the poet that his quest should be answered, and now in his old age he says " I saw." This word, spoken to Andrew unquestionably had a differing interpretation for John, according to his own personality.

Presently we find our Lord calling this man to leave his fishing boats and his nets, and all the business of the common days. To him, in conjunction with Andrew, Simon, and James, He said, " I will make you to become fishers of men." This word, of course, applied to the four, and it had a distinct reference to their callings in life, our Lord making use of that calling to illustrate on the higher level, that which should be their business in the work of His Kingdom. For purposes of illustration I may say that our Lord never said to me, I will make you a fisher of men. In the year 1886 I sat at a teacher's desk, loving my work, teaching boys. There came a day when Jesus passed me at the desk, and said, Come after Me, and I will make you a teacher of men. I have no hesitation in making that affirmation. He called for the consecration of a natural capacity to His business. That is exactly what He did with John. He asked for the dedication of the skill and ability he had in his earthly calling to the higher business of the Kingdom which He was bringing in.

Presently John was among the number of the twelve whom the Lord called and set apart, first to be with Him, and then to be sent forth. It was in this connection that He surnamed him and his brother Boanerges. We are all familiar with the correct interpretation of Boanerges as sons of thunder. I think, however, we should not forget that when our Lord spoke of these men in that way He was referring to natural capacity unrealised and unfulfilled, but now to be realised and fulfilled. He had surnamed

Simon, Rock, the one thing which at the moment he was not, but the one thing he was capable of becoming, if a true principle were found and applied. So with John and his brother. There were within them dynamic forces revealed in the stories we have already considered in the action of John; and our Lord now used the descriptive name as intended to show that there should be a fulfilment of that natural capacity.

As we have seen in the story of John, there came three special hours when, in association with two others, his brother and Peter, he was with the Lord when the rest of the twelve were not present. In the house of Jairus, raising his daughter, at the mount of transfiguration, and finally in the garden of Gethsemane. Perhaps one may not be dogmatic as to the reason why these three men were taken by the Lord on these three occasions. Personally I do not for a moment believe that they were so taken because they were favourite disciples. I rather believe that they were taken to places of special revealing because of dynamic weakness within them. If we take the central one of the three occasions, that of the transfiguration, let it not be forgotten that He left nine men in the valley. Now I submit it takes more trustworthiness to remain in the valley and face the demon than go to the mountain to the place of vision.

However, to return, John saw his Lord on these three occasions in a special way. He saw Him first as Master of death as He laid His hand on the dead child, and said, " Talitha Cumi." He saw Him on the mount of transfiguration metamorphosed, the one Man Who came to the realisation of the fullest meaning of human nature, and Who might have left the earthly scene without dying. He saw Him then as the Realiser of life at its highest. Then he saw Him in Gethsemane, this Master of death, this Realiser of life at its highest, dedicating Himself to death.

Again we have an account of three occasions upon which our Lord sharply corrected him. He corrected his intolerance when he confessed it, as He said to him concerning the man whom he had forbidden:

> " Forbid him not; for there is no man which shall do a mighty work in My name, and be able to speak evil of Me. For he that is not against us is for us."

He was thus correcting his spirit which was that of complete loyalty to the Lord, but which conceived of his own position, and that of his fellow apostles as being so important that anyone else doing anything in the name of Jesus, but not in association with them, was to be forbidden.

He sharply rebuked him also when he manifested the vengeful spirit that would fain call down fire out of heaven. Again the action of John was that of loyalty to his Lord, but it was manifesting itself in an evil spirit. The Lord said, in view of this fact:

"Ye know not what manner of spirit ye are of."

Having said this, He gave John an example of the true spirit as He quietly passed on His way, without any manifestation of recrimination or action of revenge.

Once more He rebuked his self-confidence very beautifully and very tenderly, but none the less definitely when he and his brother sought positions of power. Said Jesus:

"Are ye able to drink the cup that I drink? or to be baptised with the baptism that I am baptised with?"

And then, amazingly, they replied, "We are able." He did not deny it, but admitted them to that fellowship, and told them that they should drink that cup, and be baptised with that baptism. That day He revealed to John that the way to the position of power in His Kingdom was the way of the Cross, of the passion baptism of suffering and of sacrifice. They had a good way to travel before they arrived, but what is noticeable is that He did not sharply rebuke them, but revealed to them the secrets of the power they sought.

Finally, in watching our Lord's dealing with John, we are impressed with the wonderful confidence which Jesus had in him. We have two illustrations of this fact, one which moves upon a very simple level, and is yet sublime, and one which is wholly sublime.

The first was that He trusted His Mother to his care. That in itself is full of suggestiveness as to the character of John.

The other is wholly sublime. When God authorised His Son to send to His bond-servants a revelation of Himself in glory, in grace, in government, this was the man He chose. He sent and signified it by His angel to His servant John. This, as we have already seen, John is careful at the beginning of the book to tell us.

As we thus pass over the record of our Lord's dealings with John we come to that final page, that postcript to his Gospel. Peter was still not understanding John. After his conversation with Jesus, in which following the miraculous draught of fishes He had challenged his love, given him his work, told him that he must go by the way of the Cross, Peter had looked at John, and had said:

" Lord, and what shall this man do? "

Sharply rebuking the interfering spirit of Peter He uttered words which are of the very essence of poetry, undoubtedly understood of John more than of any other. He said:

" If I will that he tarry till I come, what is that to thee? "

John, in his narrative, is careful to point out at this point that those hearing it did not understand it, and consequently a legend went out that John was not to die. This misapprehension John, who understood, corrected as he wrote:

" Jesus said not to him, that he should not die; but, if I will that he tarry till I come, what is that to thee."

Thus he made no attempt to explain the poetic reference, but simply corrected the misapprehension. John had heard the voice of his Lord speaking to Peter concerning himself, and he realised that whoever might misunderstand him, his Lord did not.

Thus, all through the history, we see Jesus dealing with this man, this seer, this poet, removing from him the elements that blinded, clearing the atmosphere, bringing the confused into focus, interpreting to him the deepest things, because he was ever a questing soul; using him at last for the interpretation of Himself in his Gospel, which leads men to the profoundest facts concerning Himself; and then commissioning him to be the writer of that Literature which unveils the Lord in His glory, His grace, and His government.

V

SIMON PETER

OF all the Apostles of our Lord, none seems to be better known than Simon Peter. He is conspicuous in the New Testament in the Gospel narratives, and in the first part of the Acts of the Apostles. He has been prominent in Church history, and remains to-day among the most fascinating of the band of men which surrounded the Lord in the days of His earthly ministry. This familiarity is both a hindrance and a help. It is a help because it obviates anything in the nature of detailed reference. It is a hindrance in that it may lead us to be more occupied with the man than with our Lord's method of dealing with him.

We need first to remind ourselves that his name was not Peter originally, but Simon. I never come to the study of this man without being reminded of something which Henry Drummond said concerning Dwight Lyman Moody, namely, that he was the greatest human that he had ever met. This characterisation seems to me to apply to Peter. Drummond did not suggest that in intellectual capacity or attainment Moody was the greatest man he had met, but rather to the fact of his essential greatness of human nature. This is clearly evident of Simon as we study him carefully. I should describe him as an elemental man. All the essential elements that go to the making of human personality were found in him.

We may fall back upon an old definition of personality that, namely, of Kant, who said that in it we have the union and the welding of intellect, emotion, and volition. Necessarily, as we look at Simon Peter, we see him in his relationships with Christ, and in the atmosphere therefore of Christianity. Nevertheless, through all these things we may discover the essential truth concerning him. Dr. MacInnis of California wrote a remarkable

33

book on Peter and his teaching, which he called " The Fisherman Philosopher." It was an apt and true description. He was a man of intellectual capacity, as is seen quite simply in the fact that the records speak of him as asking more questions than any of the disciples. The asking of questions is a sure sign of intellectuality. If a man never asks a question, it is because the intellectual side of his nature is stultified. As we follow Peter, we hear him saying, *inter alia*, " To whom shall we go? Thou hast the words of eternal life." " How often shall my brother sin against me and I forgive him? " " Who is it that betrayeth Thee? " " Whither goest Thou? " " Why cannot I follow Thee? " " What shall this man do? " A careful consideration of these questions will show that in every case they were really big questions, even though they may reveal a certain amount of ignorance.

That he was a man full of human emotion needs no argument. On the occasion when he cried out in the bitterness of his spirit, " Depart from me; for I am a sinful man, O Lord," he revealed that emotional nature. So also, when at Cæsarea Philippi he said to his Lord in anger, " That be far from Thee," the same thing is manifest. When he said, " I will lay down my life for Thee," it was a great emotional outburst. When later, amid the darkness, he went out into the night weeping bitterly, the same thing is seen. And again, it is clearly manifest in that conversation which he had with our Lord by the Sea of Tiberias.

Moreover, he was a man of tremendous will power. There are moments when that seems as though it were not so; and yet the whole outlook proves it. He left all to follow Jesus. He went over the side of the boat to walk to Him on the waters. He dared to protest against Jesus openly. He drew the sword and smote the servant of the high priest. Of course we are in danger of speaking carelessly about will. On more than one occasion a man has told me in excuse for some persistent sin, that he has no will power, as for instance when a man said concerning his drinking of whiskey, " I cannot help it. I have no will power." To such a man I replied, " You have great will power, as is proven by the fact that you will drink whiskey." Will power may be exercised in a wrong direction.

Thus all the elements of great personality were found in Simon, and yet he was a weak man. He lacked an element welding the elemental things into consistency and strength. Some years ago, Mr. Gardiner wrote a book, " Prophets, Priests, and Kings," and in the course of it, in a sketch on William Jennings Bryan, he said of him he was a great man, but he lacked preciousness. That statement showed Gardiner's Scriptural background, and may I say his familiarity with the writings of Peter. Peter later, speaking of relationship with Christ, declared that He was precious, and that to those related to Him the preciousness was communicated. What is preciousness? We speak of jewels as precious stones, and it is an apt word. Every true jewel is a combination of elements welded into strength. This is what Simon lacked. All this would mean that he was a trial to his friends, notwithstanding their love of him; and further, he was certainly a trial to himself. One can imagine a man like this, after the failure of the day, torturing his own soul with his weakness, and vowing never to repeat the follies over which he mourned; and yet on the next day probably repeating them every one.

Now we turn to observe our Lord dealing with him. Necessarily the story begins with the action of Andrew. An old Puritan writer once said that he thought the reason why Andrew hurried out to find his brother was that Simon had been such a difficulty in the family life. I do not know that I agree with this writer, or if I do, I would add something to it. If Andrew recognised what a difficult man he had been, if he knew, as he probably did, that there were elements of weakness in him, he also knew that there were elements of strength in him, and therefore he found him, and brought him face to face with Jesus.

The first thing we read, then, is that our Lord looked upon him. We halt here, because the word employed for that looking is not a usual one. It may be at once said that the same word is employed in describing His look at Peter in the judgment hall. The word indicates a look of penetration. The look was not a mere glance, courteous and attentive, but rather one that brought the consciousness of investigation and knowledge. The sense of it might be expressed by reading it, not, " He looked upon him," but He looked through him.

Then He told him in effect that He knew him, and knew his father, " Thou art Simon, the son of John." Then came the amazing word, " Thou shalt be called Cephas, thou shalt be called Peter."

It may be asked, what was there amazing about that? And the reply is that it is only as we recognise the truth about the man that we shall understand. Here one may observe at once that the remarkable thing in the story is that Simon made no reply. Anyone familiar with Simon will see how remarkable a fact that is. He was not given to silences of that kind. There can be no doubt that the reason of his silence was his utter astonishment. When the Lord told him that he should be called Rock, or Stone, it sounded incredible. It is well that we bear in mind that all geologists agree that rock is really the result of processes, and the exhibition of principle. Here was a man who lacked that very thing. The elements were there, but they were not mastered by principle. Our Lord looked at this man with all his intellectual powers, emotional force, volitional strength, still lacking that which made him dependable, that upon which men could build; and He told him he could become exactly what in that way, he was not.

The method of Jesus, then, was that of believing in the possibilities of this man, when no one else did, and when probably Simon did not. By this word our Lord captured him. It is a constant way of the Master. My mind goes back to an hour here at Westminster when a man came into my vestry and said, " I should like to shake hands with you as I pass, but there is no hope for me now, for I have gone so far, that even my mother does not believe in me." I well remember looking at him and saying, " That is indeed a terrible story, but I know Someone Who does believe in you, and He believes in you because He is able to make you exactly what you are not." That is the whole story of the beginning of our Lord's dealing with Simon. From that moment He never lost him. Even when it seemed as though he had almost committed spiritual suicide, He looked at him, and broke his heart. He prayed for him that his faith should not fail, and his faith never did, even though his courage did.

Presently we find He took Simon Peter to travel with Him, and serve with Him. Then in some moment of vacillation Simon went back to his fishing nets. Again our Lord found him, showed His ability in the realm of fishing, and then told him that he was called to a higher vocation, that of catching men alive.

Now we might go through these Gospel stories, dwelling upon every incident, which of course is not possible; but if we did, we should see how all the way our Lord was dealing with this man, and keeping him near to Himself. We will glance at four crises in the history.

The first came when He had been saying such things as they had never heard concerning the eating of His flesh and the drinking of His blood, and many had left Him, because of the difficulty of these sayings, Jesus had said to the group, " Will ye also go away? " It was Simon who uttered the words:

"Lord, to whom shall we go? Thou hast the words of eternal life."

Then at Cæsarea Philippi our Lord, after a general enquiry, asked His disciples, Who they said He was. Then came from the lips of Peter the great confession:

" Thou art the Messiah, the Son of the living God."

Immediately the third followed. when our Lord brought him face to face with the Cross. Peter was then brought suddenly face to face with something utterly beyond His comprehension. He protested, and he protested angrily, falling into language that was almost that of profanity. At this moment our Lord, shall I not say, in the most dramatic and drastic way, rebuked him. Peter had taken Him, that is taken Him aside to utter his protest. Then the evangelist tells us that the Lord turned, that is, turned from Peter, turned His back upon him, and uttered His rebuke.

We are driven here to enquire, What was wrong in Peter's action and speech? Let us remember that he saw the glory of the wonderful life of his Lord, had been completely possessed by His teaching, and all this so much so that he had come to conviction that He was the Messiah, and the very Son of God. Now he was told that He must fall into the hands of evil men, suffer, and be killed. It was against that he made his protest.

But let it be remembered that when our Lord had told him, and the rest, of these things, He had declared that they were inevitable, that He must go, and had added the words which quite evidently Peter had not apprehended the value of, that He must rise again. Seeing only the Cross, he put his intellectual conception over against the wisdom of the Lord; or as Jesus said, he was " minding the things of men," measuring what his Lord had said by human standards. It may be well to remember here that he never did understand until the Cross was accomplished, and he had found the risen Christ. That is proven when the opening sentences of his letter are read.

"Blessed be the God and Father of our Lord Jesus Christ, Who according to His great mercy, begat us again unto living hope by the resurrection of Jesus Christ from the dead."

When he protested, his hope was not living. For this setting up of his own thinking against that of his Lord, he was sternly rebuked in the words:

"Get thee behind Me, Satan; thou art an offence unto Me."

Then after eight days of comparative silence we see him again on the mount of transfiguration. There he saw his Lord transfigured, metamorphosed. In the presence of that vision he said:

"Lord, it is good for us to be here; if Thou wilt, I will make here three tabernacles; one for Thee, and one for Moses, and one for Elijah."

It is impossible to read that without calling to mind the last previous thing recorded as having fallen from his lips. When Jesus had spoken of the Cross, he had said, "That be far from Thee." Now, in the glory, he said, "It is good to be here." Not there in Jerusalem, in suffering, in death, but here in the glory and the beauty. Let it be observed that whereas he suggested building tabernacles for Moses and Elijah also, because he saw them there, they were talking to Jesus about the very thing that Peter was shunning, the decease, the exodus, which He was about to accomplish in Jerusalem. Here it was that he heard the voice of God saying:

"This is My beloved Son, in Whom I am well pleased, hear ye Him."

"Hear ye Him," an evident reference to what He had said concerning His Cross, which was the subject of His converse with the heavenly visitors.

Once more, at the very end, talking to this man in the upper room, our Lord told him of the still latent weakness that lurked within him, as He said:

"Wilt thou lay down thy life for Me? Verily, verily, I say unto thee, The cock shall not crow, till thou hast denied Me thrice."

But in close connection therewith, including the other disciples, but by no means excluding Peter, He said:

"Let not your heart be troubled; ye believe in God, believe also in Me";

and continuing, He told them that He was going to prepare a place for them, and if He went, He would come again, and receive them unto Himself. So far as Peter was concerned, it was a declaration that He was able to realise the best in him, in spite of the worst.

Then a solemn hush falls upon the heart as we think of what followed. Jesus was arraigned in the judgment hall, and Peter, first outside, until John gained him admission, and then within, is heard denying his Lord, and adding to his denial that false emphasis of language, profane swearing. It is here that once again our eyes are fixed upon the Master. He turned and looked at Simon. It is the same word that was used at the beginning, and means that He fixed His eyes upon him, and looked him through and through. He knew that in that hour of reflection there was the underlying desire to be true, in spite of all the cursing and swearing.

I wonder how that look might be interpreted. And yet perhaps there is no need to wonder at all. It is perfectly certain that it was not a look intended to prove the accuracy of the Lord's forecast concerning the man, as though He should say, "I told you so." Neither do I believe the look had in it anything of reproach for the wrong that was being done to the heart of Jesus. It was rather the look of eternal Love and compassion, a look which said in effect, "I told you, Simon, that you should be Rock. I also told you what would happen on this dark night. Trust Me now, and in spite of everything, the original word shall be fulfilled." The result is very clearly declared. The look broke his heart, and he went out into the night, weeping bitterly.

Then came the Cross, followed by the resurrection morning. We enquire, Where was Simon, and as we saw in dealing with John, he had been found by him, and taken to his home. There he received a message, telling him of the risen Lord. This message was given by special comment, " Go tell My disciples, and Peter." It is very suggestive and very beautiful. Would not the expression " My disciples " have been enough? No, he had denied his Lord, and at least it is possible that the disciples might be inclined to put him outside their fellowship. Therefore his Lord specially named him.

Further, we gather that he had a private interview with Peter, for when the two came back from Emmaus, the disciples said:

> "The Lord is risen indeed, and hath appeared unto Simon."

We have no account of that interview. We do not know exactly what was said; and yet we are sure that it was an interview in which there was complete forgiveness and perfect restoration. We can reverently almost imagine Him saying to him, "Simon, in spite of your protests, I have been to the Cross, and as I told you, I am alive from the dead, victorious over sin and death. Because of that, your sin is forgiven, and the fulfilment of your life is possible."

Once more, He met him by Tiberias, challenged him concerning his devotion, and his love, and gave him his work to do.

If we desire to know the issue, we glance on to Pentecost, and there we see this man unified, consistent; all the elements of his personality welded into consistency in his loyalty to Christ. We observe his courage as he faced the crowd, and are amazed at the clarity with which he sets forth the facts concerning his Lord.

Further on we have glimpses of him, and we find that while the principle was at work, bringing in the rock nature, there were still evidences of the old weakness. Paul had to withstand him once to the face, but there was that in him which was submissive; and in one of his letters he referred to Paul as "our beloved brother." As we see him in these varied other glimpses we observe a man of untiring energy, of unbending loyalty, an intellect supremely illuminated, an emotion completely yielded to his Lord, and a will that bore him onward in the pathway of fellowship.

VI

PHILIP

THE story of Philip is full of interest, because the man stands in contrast to any whom we have yet dealt with, and consequently there is a change in the method of the Master with him. It is a significant fact that all we know of Philip we learn from the Gospel of John. In a few sentences scattered over four chapters, we find these references. (John i, 43-46; vi, 5-7; xii, 20-24; xiv, 7-10).

Matthew, Mark and Luke all give his name as being one of the apostles, but beyond that say nothing about him. I am perfectly well aware of the fact that an argument from silence must always be used with care, and yet to me it is, as I have said, suggestive that neither of these three give us any details concerning this man. Believing that these writings are God-breathed writings, one still necessarily recognises the human element in them, and it is on this basis that it seems to me impressive that neither Matthew, Mark nor Luke make any reference to him. Necessarily they were compelled to include his name in the list of the apostles, because he was chosen of the Lord. To me it is quite conceivable that they may have wondered why he was thus chosen; but the fact remains, and therefore each of them names him in that connection. One may summarise by saying that the suggestion is that he may be described as an unimpressive man.

But John had eyes for his Lord, and a wonderful understanding of Him, and he saw that He was interested in Philip; and so, in the natural and proper course of his writing, he has given us the incidents to which we have referred.

Philip is first seen just after Andrew and John had followed Jesus, and Simon had been called. The day after these events Jesus found him. The reading here may possibly mean that Peter found him, but I think the whole context of the whole story

41

compels the other conclusion. Philip does not seem to have been with Andrew and John in the inner circle of John's disciples. We are told, the reference unquestionably being to our Lord, that:

> "On the morrow He was minded to go forth into Galilee, and He findeth Philip."

The result of that finding was that very soon, Philip, speaking to his friend, Nathanael, otherwise Bartholomew, is heard telling him that they:

> "Have found Him, of Whom Moses in the law, and the prophets did write";

and he gives His name, Jesus.

We do not see him again in the chronological sequence of our Lord's ministry until at least a whole year had passed away. He appears in John's sixth chapter, when in the presence of the multitude Jesus turned to him and said:

> "Whence are we to buy bread, that these may eat?"

All the disciples were there probably, and so it is significant that the question was addressed to this man. Reverently we may paraphrase Philip's answer. In effect he said, What is the use of talking about where we can obtain bread when we have not money enough to purchase it? To that protest our Lord made no reply in words. He did, however, answer by His action of feeding the five thousand without a reference to the two hundred pennyworth of bread.

We see him next in the final days in Jerusalem, when amid the turmoil, certain Greeks, proselytes of the Gate, but certainly Greeks, Hellenes not Hellenists, found him, and told him they desired to see Jesus. Evidently not quite knowing what to do, he found Andrew, and after consultation, they told the Lord, bringing forth from Him His remarkable reply.

We see him again in the upper room, in the company of those who were surrounding our Lord, as He talked to them about His going. It was Philip who then said:

> "Show us the Father, and it sufficeth us."

Now as we go over these illustrations, and look at the man, we enquire, what kind of a man was he? I am not now thinking of him as the result of his contact with Jesus, but of the man himself as he is revealed. The first thing that I should personally say, perhaps the superficial thing, and therefore I name it first, is that he seems to me to be a man who, to use a phrase which I think we owe to Scotland, was "slow in the uptake." For instance, at the very beginning he had to be found. He was not among the number of those who rapidly moved towards Jesus. He was not in the forefront of things. The two men who lived in the same town with him, did not find him.

Moreover, he could not argue. When Nathanael raised his question about Nazareth, all Philip could say was, "Come and see." Indeed we realise it was a fine thing to say, but it shows his disinclination for argument. Moreover, when he raised a question of the money for feeding the crowd, he is revealed as a man not sure. The thing comes out again when at the coming of the Greeks he sought consultation with Andrew.

But he was certainly a practical man. That also is proven by his reply to Nathanael. Knowing, as also Nathanael did, the corruption of Nazareth, it was not easy to answer. The practical solution was that Nathanael should himself come and investigate. His practical nature is equally manifest in his mathematical calculation. It is again manifest in the fact already twice referred to, of his consultation with Andrew at the coming of the Greeks.

But we have not said the greatest thing about Philip yet. Following the stories, we realise that he was a singularly devout soul. When speaking to Nathanael he said:

"We have found Him of Whom Moses in the law, and the prophets did write."

We have thus an incidental proof that he was a student of the Scriptures of his own people, specially familiar probably with the two first divisions of those Scriptures, the Law, and the Prophets. It is interesting, in passing, to remind ourselves that the Law referred to the Torah, that which we now describe as the Pentateuch, which constituted the first and supreme division of the Hebrew Bible. The term the Prophets, had a larger significance than we may imagine from our knowledge of our Old Testament. Under the heading, The Prophets, were two sections, the Former Prophets, and the Latter Prophets. The Former Prophets included the books of Joshua, Judges, Samuel and Kings. The Latter Prophets were Isaiah, Jeremiah, Ezekiel and the Twelve, commonly called Minor. These were the writings with which Philip was familiar. It is therefore interesting that he did not name the third division, the Kethubim, or Writings. This division contained all the Wisdom and poetic Literature. Again let it be remembered that an argument from silence is to be taken carefully, but it is at least suggestive that he does not seem to have been as interested with the poetry of his people, as with the Law and the Prophets.

As in other cases, we may gain some idea of the man from his friends. The one specially mentioned is Nathanael, the guileless soul, according to the estimate of Jesus.

It ever seems to me, however, that the man is most startlingly and clearly revealed in the cry that escaped him in the upper room:

"Show us the Father, and it sufficeth us."

In that final hour, and with the group of his fellow-disciples about him, at last he uttered the great cry which, in the last analysis is the ultimate cry of humanity.

This, then, was the man, a quiet, unimpressive man, but devout, and in the deepest of him, however difficult he found it to express himself, conscious of the supreme necessity of certainty concerning God.

We turn to watch our Lord's method with him, and in doing so, necessarily the first thing that impresses us is that Jesus found him. He went after him of set purpose, and with equal certainty in intimate knowledge, and with definite intention. He went after him because He needed him, because He knew him; and in all probability, knew it was not probable that other men would seek him.

Then it was to this man Philip that our Lord, according to the records, first used this formula, which I think we are warranted in saying He loved to use, namely, "Follow Me." Necessarily, the stories of Jesus are comparatively fragmentary, but they are perfect in their illustration of the whole fact of His ministry and method. As we trace the story, we find six or seven occasions upon which He used this formula. This was the first.

He did not say to Philip, "What seek ye?" He did not say to him, "You shall be rock." He approached this quiet, unimpressive man, this man steeped in the knowledge of the writings of the Law and the Prophets, this man with a great sense of the need for God at the centre of his personality, and He said to him, "Follow Me." It is important that here we should repeat what perhaps has often been said, that the words "Follow Me" hardly convey the strict meaning of the words which Jesus employed. If we used such an expression to-day we should immediately think that we were calling someone to follow us, as we led in the way. Now our Lord did use such a word, but here this is not it. The simple significance of this command is expressed by rendering it, Join Me in the way. Or we may put it more simply by saying that it meant, Travel with Me, Accompany Me.

Each of these two words is found in what our Lord said at Cæsarea Philippi.

> " If any man would come after Me, let him deny himself,
> and take up his cross, and follow Me."

Literally, If any man would follow Me, that is, come after Me, let him deny himself and take up his cross and travel with Me.

If the call was thus characterised by simplicity there were tremendous implications in it. It called Philip to surrender himself to the intentions of Jesus. He was no longer to choose his own pathway, but to walk side by side with his Lord. The call to accompany Him upon the way necessitated the surrender of him in the matter of the choice of the pathway, and the destination intended. But the beauty and the glory of it is that it shows that wherever one travels in the Divinely appointed pathway, the Lord Himself is with him.

Thus our Lord approached Philip, found him, and unquestionably gained him. Though we are not told so in so many words there is no doubt that he obeyed. Almost directly afterwards we find him telling his friend what travelling with Jesus meant, accompanying One Who had been foretold in the Law of Moses, and the Prophets.

Then after a little while, our Lord chose him as one of His apostles, appointed him with the others, first to be with Him, and then to send him forth as His representative and messenger.

Still later, we find our Lord asked him a question concerning the feeding of the multitude.

> " Whence are we to buy bread, that these may eat? "

Now it is significant that He did not ask this question of Andrew, or of John, or of Peter, but of Philip. It is the only occasion upon which we find our Lord seemed to ask advice of anyone, and John, who is telling the story, is careful at this point to insert the statement:

> " This He said to prove him; for He Himself knew what
> He would do."

He did not need advice, He did not need counsel; but Philip needed proving, needed to see more than he had yet been able to see. Asking the question Philip found his mind challenged. He gave his answer quite honestly, and in doing so, revealed himself.

Having thus expressed himself, he, in company with the others, received the command to make the crowd sit down, and evidently he obeyed. Then he saw his Lord take those loaves, and begin to break them, and as that exquisite couplet of one of our hymns says:

" 'Twas spring-time when He blessed the bread,
'Twas harvest when He brake."

Thus Philip was brought into the presence of the sufficiency of his Lord. Two hundred pennyworth of bread was not enough to give each a little. The Lord was able, with five loaves, to feed the multitude. One is reminded of the classic story of the pagan general, to whom one day in stress of war, an underling came and said, " Sire, we have only so many soldiers." The old general replied, " For how many do you count me? " A lad with five loaves and two small fishes is utterly inadequate. But the lad and the loaves and the fishes with Jesus, is enough. Of course, one is not saying that our Lord wrought the miracle for Philip; but knowing Himself what He would do, He made it the occasion of calling forth a mental activity on the part of Philip which was replied to by the revelation.

The next scene is that in which Philip was dealt with by our Lord, in the company of Andrew, at the coming of the Greeks. As we have said, these men were unquestionably proselytes, for they had come up to the Feast. We need not stay to discuss the reason of their desire to see Jesus. It is, however, well to remember that they had turned from paganism to Hebraism, and now, probably disappointed with what they had found, they had heard of the new Voice concerning which everyone was talking. After consultation with Andrew, Philip, possibly feeling gratified that these Greek proselytes were seeking their Master, told Jesus of the fact. I do not think the story can be read without the consciousness that the answer of Jesus must have been an almost staggering one to Philip. It is impossible here and now to fully go into that reply of our Lord, but we may with profit ponder some of its sentences.

" The hour is come, that the Son of man should be glorified . . . Except a grain of wheat fall into the earth and die, it abideth by itself alone; but if it die, it beareth much fruit. Now is My soul troubled; and what shall I say? Father, save Me from this hour? But for this cause came I unto this hour. Father, glorify Thy name."

This soliloquy of Jesus was answered by the voice from heaven, whereupon the Lord spoke again:

" Now is the judgment of this world; now shall the prince of this world be cast out. And I, if I be lifted up from the earth, will draw all men unto Myself."

The bearing of all this upon our study is the fact that Philip heard, and we may very reverently say that the answer of Jesus to Philip and Andrew in effect was this. These Greeks cannot see Me now. The only way in which they will ever see Me will be by the way of My death and resurrection. It may be at once objected that surely Philip and Andrew and the Greeks were then looking at Jesus. In that connection we may remind ourselves that very soon after Jesus was saying to Philip:

" Have I been so long time with you, and dost thou not know Me, Philip? "

The whole incident shows that our Lord was revealing to Philip, and of course to the rest, that the only way in which He could be seen in His glory was the way of the Cross.

A few hours passed, and Philip was in the upper room with the rest of the disciples and his Lord. There, in the midst of the conversation he uttered the tremendous word, to which we have already referred:

" Show us the Father, and it sufficeth us."

At this point our Lord rebuked him for his slowness, for his blindness, as He said to him:

" Have I been so long time with you, and dost thou not know Me, Philip? "

Philip had not responded as he might have done, or our Lord would never have addressed him thus. The point of value, however, is that if He told him he was blind, He did not leave him there. He uttered those wonderful words which in some senses may seem to be central to the Person of Jesus in human life and human history:

" He that hath seen Me, hath seen the Father."

Presently this man, equipped and illuminated by the Holy Spirit, and thus coming to full understanding of the One he had found at the beginning of his discipleship, is seen with the rest facing the future of responsibility.

We may thus summarise. Philip was obedient to the first call, and began to travel with Jesus, immediately bearing his testimony to the fact that he had found the Messiah. Through the years we watch a growing understanding through the patience of the Lord, and so ever on, until he saw the Father in the face of Jesus.

Beyond this, we know nothing of Philip. We have no record of any words he uttered, of any work he did, of any letter he wrote. We have no account of his journeyings. It may be necessary to point out here that he must never be confused with Philip the deacon, of whom we have some account in the book of the Acts. We repeat, therefore, we know nothing more about him, except that his name, as an apostle, is discovered upon the foundations of the city of God.

Unquestionably the message of this study is one to the slow man, and perhaps to the unimpressive man. There are many such. Andrew will not seek them, even though they live in the same town. Christ, however, is ever minded to pass their way. These are the people that He is ever seeking, and that because He wants them; and more, because He needs them. He has a use for such in that great fellowship of His followers through which He is carrying on His mighty work. Possibly enrolled among His disciples they will be slow to the end, but He will be patient to the end. The probability is that their biographies will never be written. In passing we may say that they may gain much by the omission. But their name will be written in the city of God. Let them then join Him in the way, and travel with Him, until that hour shall come in which He, in fellowship with His own, will " see of the travail of His soul, and be satisfied."

VII

NATHANAEL

THERE is practically no question that Nathanael and Bartholomew are identical. Matthew, Mark and Luke refer to Bartholomew, but do not mention Nathanael. On the other hand, John speaks of Nathanael, but never mentions Bartholomew. The synoptists, in dealing with Bartholomew, place him in relation with Philip. John puts Nathanael in relation with Philip. It may be said quite truthfully there is no proof that the two are identical, and further, that the view was not advanced until the ninth century.

In our study of Nathanael we confine ourselves to the one story which we have read in John (i, 43–51). He is also referred to again in the final chapter of John, as one of the group of seven who saw this special manifestation or unveiling of our Lord, as He appeared on that memorable occasion (John xxi).

The supreme revelation of the man, and our Lord's method with Him is found in the story in the first chapter. In attempting to see the man, our work is really simple, because we have a characterisation of him directly from the lips of our Lord Himself. When Philip found him and brought him to Jesus, we are told that our Lord saw him, and then said, not to him directly, but to the group standing around Him:

" Behold, an Israelite indeed, in whom is no guile ! "

Almost certainly Andrew and his brother, Simon; John, with perhaps his brother James, and Philip were present, and possibly others who are nameless.

We have no history of Nathanael, no account of whom his father and his mother were. We do know that he was a resident of Cana, but at this point he appears himself, and at once his story is revealed in these words of our Lord. In that original sentence there are two things, but closely linked together. The first was that he was " an Israelite indeed "; and the second that in him there was " no guile." Now as this is read, we become conscious at once of an Old Testament background of a remarkable kind. Let it at once be said that in the course of the story we find our Lord making two references to the Old Testament, and they were both concerned with Jacob. His name does not appear, but the references are none the less self-evident.

The first is found in this very description of the man by contrast. The second is found when presently Jesus said:

" Ye shall see the heaven opened, and the angels of God ascending and descending upon the Son of man."

The first of these references was to Jacob in his character, and specially his action when he was returning home, after an absence of long years, and a wealthy man; and received the name Israel. The second reference went further back to the hour when Jacob was leaving home, a wanderer and an exile through his own duplicity, and was given a vision of angels ascending and descending.

This arresting fact leads to the supposition, which is not more than a suggestion, that this man Nathanael had been specially interested in the story of Jacob, and possibly had but recently been reading it and pondering on its significance. Our Lord then when He met with him, took that story as the background of His words concerning him, and His words to him.

Let us consider, then, the estimate of the man revealed in the words of Jesus. We are first arrested by the term " Israelite." We might pause over it, quite naturally, thinking of it as referring to the fact that he was a Hebrew, and one of God's elect nation. But there is surely significance in the fact that he was described by this particular word. If we go back to the story to which we have referred, we find that the name Israel was given to Jacob on the night when God, in human form, wrestled with him, and he became through his defeat, a man, in a new sense, ruled by God. It is interesting in this connection to remember how constantly in the Old Testament the Hebrew people are designated the children of Israel. The real significance of the name is discovered by dividing it, Isra, El; the significance of which is, as we have already intimated, ruled by God. This was the name given to the man, Jacob, which meant the supplanter, the heel-catcher, when he had found the secret of strength in his mastery by God. Thus God had crippled him to crown him, had broken him to make him, had mastered him to give him majesty.

An Israelite, then, in the full significance of the term, was one living under the authority of God. By the use of this term our Lord described Nathanael, and that with emphasis when He said, " an Israelite indeed."

From the development of the story we learn that Nathanael had but recently been under the fig-tree, for our Lord said to him:

"Before Philip called thee, when thou wast under the fig-tree, I saw thee."

The fig-tree was often the natural summer arbour of the Eastern, the place into which one could go and find beneath its spreading leaves, both quietness and retirement. In such a place Nathanael had but recently been; and unquestionably he had been there for devotional purposes. It is possible that our Lord's reference to the fact was to some special experience through which he had passed, although, of course we cannot be sure about that. It may be he had been under the fig-tree reading the story of Jacob as the result of the preaching of John the herald of Jesus. All that being speculative, it nevertheless is clear that our Lord's description of him was that of his being a man fulfilling the purpose of God when He named Jacob Israel. "Behold an Israelite indeed."

It is of vital interest to our studies in the methods of Jesus to notice this remarkable recognition on His part of the truth concerning this man. He did not speak of him as a sinner, though undoubtedly such he was; but recognised his fidelity to whatever light he had possessed, and the fact that he was living the life of submission to the will of God.

That declaration our Lord then carried further as He said: "In whom is no guile."

Can it be possible to escape from the conviction that in this statement there was the memory of Jacob himself? I think we may dare to suggest for a moment, a change in the word which will not be of the nature of translation but exposition; and render the statement of Jesus thus:

"Behold, an Israelite indeed, in whom there is no Jacob";

no guile, no trickery, no double dealing in deceit. All that had been the story of Jacob before the night of wrestling, and indeed after it. It was a long time before he entered into full experience of all that was meant by his name. Seeing Nathanael, our Lord declared that he was a man who fulfilled the ideal without any qualification.

Nathanael, then, was a man sincere, straight-forward, transparent, all of which our Lord summarised in the phrase, "no guile." The word rendered "guile" is in itself a very arresting one. Peter employed it twice in his first letter, once when he said of the Lord Himself:

"When He was reviled, reviled not again, Who did no sin, neither was guile found in His mouth";

and once in his charge to those to whom he wrote:

> " He that would love life,
> And see good days,
> Let him refrain his tongue from evil,
> And his lips that they speak no guile."

This was the word, then, our Lord employed when referring to Nathanael.

We pause for one moment to notice the incidental evidences of the accuracy of that estimate. When Philip told Nathanael that they had found the One of Whom Moses and the prophets had written, the guilelessness of Nathanael is revealed in his immediate question, " Can any good thing come out of Nazareth? " This was the language of simple honesty. Nathanael did not belong to Nazareth, but to Cana, which was near enough to Nazareth for him to be perfectly familiar with the conditions obtaining there. A popular conception of the meaning of Nathanael is that he was speaking somewhat disrespectfully of Nazareth. Nathanael was not a Judæan, and therefore would not share the common Judæan contempt for Galilee, and perhaps especially for Nazareth. Living as near to it as he did, he was familiar with the facts concerning it. The most recent investigation has shown that it was a centre of corruption. It stood on the hill-side, at the foot of which there ran the great highways along which Roman soldiers marched, and merchant-men were travelling. It was a convenient stopping-place for the night, and it was notoriously rotten to the core. That is what Nathanael meant, and the guilelessness of the man is seen in this question, facing the truth, and expressing the wonder:

> " Can any good thing come out of Nazareth? "

The supreme proof, however, of his guilelessness is found in what he said when Jesus made the declaration:

> " Behold, an Israelite indeed, in whom is no guile."

Nathanael said:

> " Whence knowest Thou me? "

A tacit admission, without any mock modesty, that the thing was true concerning him. His problem was revealed in that question. Admitting the truth of the statement, what perplexed him was, how the fact was known to Jesus.

As we look at this man the question naturally arises as to whether he needed Christ at all. A man to whom, if we may use the very inadequate word, Jesus could pay so high a compliment, appears as though he did not need anything more, anything which Christ could bestow upon him. The answer to that enquiry will be discovered as we watch the method of Christ with him.

It was Philip's testimony that led this man to come to the Lord. Philip had answered his enquiry as to whether any good thing could come out of Nazareth by the simple words, " Come and see." As he approached, our Lord flung upon him the light which revealed him to those who stood listening. Nathanael knew the accuracy of the statement, and admitted it. When he expressed his wonder at how the Lord knew, Jesus uttered the word that showed His knowledge was not local and circumscribed, or dependent upon the testimony of others, and He said to him:

" Before Philip called thee, when thou wast under the fig-tree, I saw thee."

Thus Nathanael discovered that he stood in the presence of Someone Who knew him with a knowledge that was superior to all merely earthly understanding.

The fig-tree was the place of retirement, and no one of his earthly acquaintance, or of the company then standing around had been with Nathanael there. It is almost certain that he had gone there to escape from the eyes of men. It was there that the Lord had seen him. Thus Nathanael found that the knowledge of Christ was a particular one, completely beyond that of any other that he had ever known. This conviction brought from him the cry:

" Rabbi, Thou art the Son of God, Thou art the King of Israel."

Said Jesus, " Before Philip . . . I saw thee." Jesus is always ahead of Philip. He is ever before us, when we go seeking some other person. It is of the very genius of Christianity that this thing is done. Our own conviction becomes an urge to reach others. Let it never be forgotten that before we arrive, Christ is there.

In this connection it is well for us to be reminded that it is there, where human eyes are not watching, and we are away from all human investigation, that our Lord takes His measurements. Christ is not measuring us as we are gathered together in this assembly. Here we are all behaving ! Good behaviour in public may be hypocrisy. When we are alone, under the fig-tree, we are not thinking of behaviour, but are simply being. A memory comes back to me, to which I have often referred, of how once driving through the Northfield lanes with Dwight Lyman Moody, he said to me in his own characteristic way, quite suddenly, " What is character, anyhow? " Knowing that he had something in his own mind, I said, " Well, what is it? " And immediately he replied, " Character is what a man is in the dark." When the blinds are drawn, and nobody is watching, or when the mask is off, then the man is seen for what he really is.

" When thou wast under the fig-tree, I saw thee."

Then the truth was evident concerning thee, and thou wert seen as an Israelite indeed, in whom was no guile.

The effect of all this upon Nathanael is revealed in those words already quoted:

> " Rabbi, Thou art the Son of God, Thou art the King of Israel."

Jesus had called him " Israelite," and he replied, " Thou art the King of Israel "; and that to Nathanael meant something far more, and so he said, " Thou art the Son of God." It is evident that Christ had completely captured this man.

But He had not yet done with him. When he made the great affirmation revealing his surrender, our Lord replied:

> " Because I said unto thee, I saw thee underneath the fig-tree, believest thou? thou shalt see greater things than these . . . Verily, verily I say unto you, Ye shall see the heaven opened, and the angels of God ascending and descending upon the Son of man."

In these words our Lord had gone back to the story of Jacob, and the account of how he had dreamed that he had seen a ladder, with Jehovah standing by his side, while angels ascended and descended. He saw them ascending from their sphere of earthly ministry, and descending from the sphere of their heavenly responsibility. They were seen as going up with their reports, and returning to their service. Now, said our Lord to Nathanael, thou shalt see the dream of Jacob in the long ago translated into spiritual reality. Whatever was suggested in the dream was to be fulfilled in Him. The thing which Nathanael had been considering under the fig-tree, with all its mystery, was to come to full realisation through the Person of our Lord.

Nathanael had expressed his faith as the result of his first contact with Christ. Now the Lord lit the lamp of hope for him as He told him that there were greater experiences yet in store. The vision which had come to Jacob was confirmed to Nathanael in Christ. He, the Son of man, would be the Channel of prayer as typified in the ascending angels, and the Channel of answers as suggested by the descending angels. After the dream, when Jacob awoke, he had said:

> " Lo, God is in the place, and I knew it not."

This was to be ratified in the experience of Nathanael through his Lord. In Him he should discover the nearness of God, even though he had been ignorant of it.

In the old story, Jacob had added to the words already quoted:

> " This is none other but the house of God, and this is the gate of heaven."

All that was to be fulfilled in and through the Lord.

A little later on in His ministry, He said to a woman:

> " The hour cometh, when neither in this mountain, nor
> in Jerusalem, shall ye worship the Father . . . the true
> worshippers shall worship the Father in spirit and truth;
> for such doth the Father seek to be His worshippers."

Where the Christ is, there is the House of God. His presence
is the place of Divine revelation, and Divine subduing.

What wondrous things Jesus had thus said to Nathanael.
Though no record declares it in so many words, there can be no
doubt that added to the faith of Nathanael, there now came the
hope and confidence of fulfilment, and this created in his heart
his love for the Lord, and his loyalty to Him. If peradventure
we are right in considering that Bartholomew and Nathanael are
identical, we remember that he was one of the men whom Jesus
chose to be an apostle. Moreover, in that final scene where his
name appears at the shore of Tiberias, as he watched the Master
interested in fishing, and preparing for the physical necessities of
the tired toilers, and heard Him enforcing His claims, and commissioning His own to the caring of His sheep and His lambs,
he saw in a measure the fulfilment of the claims made in this
first interview.

We enquire what this story really has to say to us, and to
whom it makes special appeal? We may have friends in which
there is to be found much that is beautiful, but there is still a lack.
Our business is to say to them, as Philip said to Nathanael,
" Come and see." Come for yourselves. We do this, knowing
when we bring them, that He has perfect knowledge of them.
A man can be singularly alone in a great city, in the midst of
thronging multitudes. In bringing any such man to Christ we
are bringing him to One Who knows him individually, and in
loneliness, and in entire separation from the crowd. In this
sense it is correct to say He does not deal with humanity in
what we call mass movements. He deals with them one by one.
The preacher examines his congregation. Christ gathers it, and
knows every one who crosses the threshold of the sanctuary.
Oh, the comfort of it ! Oh, the terror of it ! Let those two
sentences suffice.

The story of Nathanael teaches us first that Christ fulfils
all that is most excellent in man. In Him, an Israelite finds his
King. An enquiring soul finds the One Who is able to answer
his questions. A devout soul finds the Son of God.

This contact also brings correction and enlargement. Nathanael
had said with perfect guilelessness:

> " Can any good thing come out of Nazareth? "

I think before his pilgrimage on earth had ended, he could have said, No good thing has come from anywhere except from Nazareth, because it was from Nazareth He came.

Finally, the words of Jesus to Nathanael show that the Incarnation of the Son of God is the basis of communion between man and God. Nathanael had said, " Thou art the Son of God." In close connection Jesus had named Himself, " the Son of man."

> " So heaven comes down our souls to greet,
> And glory crowns the mercy-seat."

He is the Son of man, close to my humanity. He is the Son of God, eternally related to Deity. Christ ever comes to enlarge the vision, to fulfil aspirations, to crowd the life with the gifts and the graces of the ascending and the descending angels.

VIII

THE VIRGIN MOTHER

EXTREMES have characterised the treatment which the Mother of our Lord has received at the hands of the Christian Church. On the one hand she has been worshipped, and on the other, largely neglected. In the rebound of Protestantism fron Mariolatry we have been terribly in danger of relegating the Virgin Mother to a position far inferior to that which she really holds in the counsel and purpose and power of God, and in the work of God in human history and human life.

I am not proposing to debate this matter, but make the statement as an introductory affirmation. There is no authority whatever in Scripture for worshipping her; but there is equally no authority for neglect. She certainly ought to occupy the place in our thinking that she does in Scripture. In the New Testament Mary is never presented as the principal figure. There is only One such, and that is the Lord Himself. All the appearances of Mary are directly connected with Him, and form part of the background, flinging Him up into brighter and clearer relief. Nevertheless the very fact that she is thus always associated with Him, gives her a place of prominence and importance. It is impossible, necessarily, to read all that is written concerning her, but we may, having familiarity with the New Testament, pass over the ground.

Let it be remembered that our purpose in this study is exactly what it has been in others, not merely to see Mary herself, but to watch our Lord's dealing with her. In the Gospel narrative she is presented to us as a virgin of the house of David, betrothed to a man named Joseph. Luke gives us her genealogy as descended from David, and consequently the genealogy of Jesus after the flesh, through her. In passing it may be said that much has been written concerning the difference between the genealogies of Matthew and Luke. Personally I cannot see any difficulty. Matthew has given us the legal genealogy of Jesus, due to the fact that He was legally adopted by Joseph, and consequently in

57

Jewish archives, according to Jewish law, He was entered in Joseph's line as his adopted Son. In Luke, on the other hand, as we have said, we have the genealogy traced through His Mother.

We see her then as a quiet, simple village maiden. Her parentage is obscure. We learn the name of her father through Luke's genealogy, where it is said that Joseph is the son, which means in this case the son-in-law of Heli. In this connection it is illuminative to remember that in Jewish writings concerning her subsequent to our Lord's life, she is referred to as the Mother of Jesus, and named directly as the daughter of Heli. Through this line of descent the royal blood of David was coursing in her veins. Joseph was also of that line, but coming from David through Solomon, while Mary descended through Nathan.

She is seen, dwelling in Nazareth, with all its limitations, its perils, and its advantages. Its limitations are self-evident. Nazareth was at that time a town of perhaps about ten to twenty thousand inhabitants. It was therefore a busy town, but a small one, and as distances then counted, suffering the limitation of being far removed from Jerusalem. The perils of the town were undoubted. Careful investigation during recent years has shown that Nazareth was a hot-bed of corruption. This is what Nathanael meant unquestionably when he asked, "Can any good thing come out of Narareth?" When I speak of its advantages, I am referring to the fact that it is advantageous to live in a small town in many ways. In the smaller towns people think more, personally and individually, than they do in a great city, where life is in danger of becoming too busy for any such activity.

The character of Mary is at once revealed in the angel's address to her. This commenced with the word "Hail." This is a translation of the Greek verb *Chairo*. We have a similar word Cheer; but the Greek word meant more than we do when we use the word. We have understood by the "Hail," a word of adoration, as for instance in the lines:

"Hail to the Lord's Anointed,
Great David's greater Son."

Now from the standpoint of strict etymology, Hail is right as a translation of Chairo, but it should be spelt Hale. It is a part of the old Anglo-Saxon word halig, which means whole. Hale therefore really means Good health to you. It is a wish expressed that the one addressed may know the blessings of health in every form and fashion. Thus the angel addressed Mary.

The following words reveal her character. Here, again, our rendering is at fault. "Thou art highly favoured." This would suggest that the angel was referring to the fact that a great favour was being conferred upon her. Now while that was true, the true rendering is, " Thou art endued with grace," which was a declaration of a fact concerning her. To this he added the further illuminative statement, " The Lord is with thee." A careful consideration will show how in this address of the angel we have a remarkable presentation of truth concerning this maiden in Nazareth. In that city, with its limitations, its perils, its advantages, lived this maiden of Jewish and royal blood. Living in the midst of impurity she was pure. Living in the midst of limitations she triumphed over them. Living in the midst of disadvantages she had the highest advantage of walking in fellowship with the God of her fathers.

As we follow the story, incidentally we are brought face to face with another fact revealing her character. Luke tells us that she was troubled at the saying of the angel, that is, perplexed by it, wondering what manner of salutation this could be. Mary was not alarmed or perplexed by the vision of the angel, but she was perplexed that the angel addressed her in this way. He had said to her, " Thou art endued with grace," and she was quite unconscious of the fact. This, in itself, is a revelation full of suggestive beauty.

We come then to the announcement made to her, and this was introduced by the words :

" Fear not, Mary, for thou hast found favour with God."

The word rendered " favour " here is the same as the one already used, when the angel said, " Thou art endued with grace". With perfect accuracy therefore, we may read so, " Thou hast found grace with God." " Thou art endued with grace," his declaration concerning her character. " Thou hast found grace with God" introduces the statement concerning her high office in the economy of God. That office was then declared in the words :

> " And behold, thou shalt conceive in thy womb, and
> bring forth a Son, and shalt call His name JESUS. He shall
> be great, and shall be called the Son of the Most High;
> and the Lord God shall give unto Him the throne of His
> father David; and He shall reign over the house of Jacob for
> ever; and of His Kingdom there shall be no end."

Every sentence, every phrase in that declaration is full of suggestive meaning. To summarise it all we may say that Mary was told by the angel that there fell to her the honour of becoming the Mother of the long-looked-for Messiah. It was a tremendous and almost overwhelming announcement.

Still further looking at Mary, we are brought face to face with her complete honesty. She said to the angel:

" How shall this be, seeing I know not a man ? "

In that question she expressed the biological difficulty, which, by the way, men are still discussing. It is well that we bear in mind when we hear such discussions, that it was Mary, according to the record, who herself first raised the difficulty.

She was answered with great simplicity, and sublime finali tyas the angel said :

" The Holy Spirit shall come upon thee, and the power of the Most High shall overshadow thee."

That is the one and only answer to this biological problem. It is an answer removing all difficulty to those who believe in the God of the Bible.

There was however another question which she did not ask, but which was involved. It is as to how the Child of a sinning woman could Himself be sinless. The angel messenger answered that deeper problem, even though Mary had not expressed it, as he said:

" Wherefore also that which is to be born shall be called Holy, the Son of God."

That is to say that by this self-same power and activity of the Most High, Jesus should be immaculately conceived.

To these stupendous statements of the angel, Mary replied, as bowing her head she said :

" Behold, the bond-maid of the Lord ; be it unto me according to thy word."

In this saying she submitted herself to the Divine purpose, programme, and power.

In the development of the story we may now follow her a little further as she took her journey into the hill country, a journey of at least a hundred miles. Why that hurried visit to Elisabeth ? The whole activity of human salvation has been wrought out through pain and misunderstanding. Imagine this maiden in Nazareth, with this awe-inspiring secret, tremendous in its significance, but which could by no means be explained to Nazareth. To recognise this is to understand why, for those first three months, she found refuge with someone else who knew something of the deep secrets of God.

There can be no escape from the conviction that Mary lived all her life under suspicion. The fact comes out more than once in the story. One day they said of Jesus, We know this Man, we know His father, and His mother. On another occasion they said, when putting themselves into contrast with Him, "We were not born of fornication." It was impossible for Mary to explain. There are things which are beyond the realm of explanation, except to those of like spiritual capacity.

When she arrived, she was greeted by Elisabeth as the Mother of the Lord, and she at once broke out into song. As we study the Magnificat, we find that it is pure Hebrew poetry. It was a weaving together of sentences found in the Psalter. In that hour they merged in her thinking, and she poured them forth in this great song.

The next view we have of Mary is in Bethlehem in the hour of the birth of Jesus. In that supreme hour we see her away from all that is dear and precious to the heart of motherhood; and so in the very circumstances of travail, she was in fellowship with the suffering of the One to be born. The appalling loneliness of it fills the heart with brooding sorrow. Away from home, no room in the inn, no woman by to help, *she* brought forth her First-born, *she* wrapped Him in swaddling clothes, *she* laid Him in the manger. Nevertheless the brightness and the joy and gladness of it is equally evident. The first sound of the voice of the Child turned all the discords of the wayside into harmonies for that Mother. The first gleam of light from His eyes, as He looked up into her face caused the shadows to merge into the infinite light. I shall always believe that Jesus was thinking of His own Mother very near to the end, when He said that unutterably beautiful thing:

"A woman when she is in travail hath sorrow, because her hour is come; but when she is delivered of the child, she remembereth no more the anguish, for the joy that a man is born into the world."

The shepherds arriving, told of the song they had heard, and the chorus that accompanied it, and of Mary it is said, she pondered these things in her heart. Here we have the first revelation of Mary's imperfect understanding. She had submitted herself to the will of God as the bond-maid of Jehovah. Nevertheless when she heard this story from the shepherds, she pondered these things.

She is next seen in the home when the rite of her people was administered in the case of her Son, and she gave Him the name which the angel had declared. We have no details of that ceremony, but simply the statement of the fact.

Next she is seen in the Temple, when Simeon took the Child in his arms, and uttered his great Nunc Dimittis. She heard him declare that a sword should pierce through her own soul;

and again her limitation is revealed in the declaration that she was marvelling.

In sequence there follows the story of the visit of the Magi, the flight into Egypt, the return to Nazareth; and then we know how for twelve years her life was devoted to the nursing and training of that Child, the little one, in Hebrew language, the *taph*, learning His first lessons in Scripture from her teaching.

When we turn to examine our Lord's dealings with her, we find that the first thing we are told is that after His presentation in the Temple at twelve years of age, He went down to His home, and was subject to His parents. He having now arrived at the age of twelve, and having become legally a Son of the law by His own choice, yielded Himself in submission to her, and to His adopted father.

In the Temple He had uttered to her the first words of which we have any record as falling from His lips:

"Wist ye not that I must be in the things of My Father?"

In that sentence He would seem to have been largely correcting something she had said, namely, "Thy father and I sought Thee sorrowing." While He was the adopted Son of Joseph, He evidently knew His true relationship, and revealed His sense of responsibility.

He is next seen in contact with her at Cana. Eighteen years had passed, and we have no account of anything that transpired during that period except that He

"Advanced in wisdom and in stature, and in grace by the side of God and men."

When we see Him at Cana we realise that the relationship between them had changed. He was not subject to her now in any sense. It was here that she said to Him, "They have no wine"; and to understand Mary we must come to a recognition of her meaning in the light of what He Himself said to her in answer to her declaration. Addressing her tenderly as "Woman," He said to her quite literally, "What is there to thee and to Me?" By which He evidently was reminding her that there were things which they had not in common. It is perfectly evident that when she told Him they had no wine, she was hoping for some action through which the profound secret of His Personality might be manifested in glory. To that He replied, "Mine hour is not yet come." It is evident that He did not mean that His hour was not come for a supernatural act, for He turned the water into wine. There was a deeper significance in the statement than that. He was declaring to her that not by the working of supernatural power in such a way as would accomplish this turning of water into wine would the true glory be manifested. The story of Mary at this point ends very beautifully as she said to the servants, trusting Him completely, even though she did not understand:

" Whatsoever He saith unto you, do it."

A later story concerning her, the full significance of which can only be gained by the study of it as it appears in Matthew and Mark, is a further revelation of her misunderstanding. They were crowded days. He was so busily occupied that He hardly had time to eat. She at the time, was evidently in Nazareth, and heard of these activities, and with a mother's heart, became anxious about Him. She had an awful fear that He was going out of His mind, and she journeyed from Nazareth to Capernaum to find Him, in order to take Him home, and this for very love of Him.

His dealing with her at this point may appear rough, but it was not really rough. Told that she was there, and seeking Him, He said, Who is My Mother, and My brethren and My sisters? that is, My real kinsfolk; and He declared in answer to His own question, They that do the will of God, My Father Who is in heaven. He revealed by that statement that there was a higher relationship than that which existed between Him and His Mother on the level of the physical. It was the kinship of those who were with Him in consecration to the Will of God. By this statement He was still dealing with her, rebuking an affection which would interfere with His own Divine purpose, and yet by the rebuke calling her into a higher kinship than that of Mother and Son on the earthly level.

We see her again in that unutterable hour when He hung upon His Cross. I sometimes am inclined to say that only a mother can understand that sorrow of Mary watching at the Cross. As she looked at Him, probably with breaking heart and in amazement, suddenly she saw His eyes rest upon her, and heard Him say, " Woman, behold thy son." Quite evidently His hands were transfixed, and only by the glance of His eye did He communicate the one to whom He was referring, as then looking at him, He said, " Behold thy mother." Thus in all the mystery of that hour of unfathomable pain, Mary found Him thinking of her on the earthly level, and providing for her for all the years to come.

We see her once more, on the day of Pentecost, mingling with the others of His waiting disciples. In that great hour when the Spirit fell upon all of them, Mary was one of the number, and in that act He enfolded her in His own life in a closer relationship than she had ever known, even though she had borne Him under her heart, and had been the instrument through which a body was prepared for Him, in which to carry out the mighty enterprises of God. She would surely remember in that hour how that long ago the angel visitor had said to her:

"The Holy Spirit shall come upon thee, and the power of the Most High shall overshadow thee; wherefore also that which is born shall be called holy, the Son of God."

Now again, that self-same Spirit came upon her, and He Who had formed in her womb the body of Jesus, now united her to Him for ever in spiritual life, and thus she came into the closest and final union with Him.

The personal values of such a story are in some senses difficult and unique, because the fact is lonely and unique. There are nevertheless great principles underlying the story. First of all it is a revelation of the fact that personal character does count with God. It was a woman endued with grace that was chosen for this high and lofty office.

Again we learn that highest service for God in this world must always involve pain. And finally, all such service is eventually in order to the glory of Christ, and His crowning. Mary is never named in the Apocalypse.

Perhaps the chief value of all this is its revelation of the sanctity of motherhood and childhood. It shows also that Christ can only be understood by the interpretation of the Spirit. Not even the Mother who bore Him ever understood Him until the Spirit came to her on the day of Pentecost.

We may fittingly close this meditation by the quotation of words which Dr. Burton wrote concerning her.

"The Virgin Mother takes her place in the focal point of all the histories. Through no choice, no conceit or forwardness of her own, but by the grace of God and by an inherent fitness she becomes the connecting link between earth and heaven. And, throwing as she does, her unconscious shadow back within the paradise lost, and forward through the Gospels to the paradise regained, shall we not ' magnify the Lord ' with her? Shall we not ' magnify the Lord ' for her, as, with all the generations we ' call her blessed ' "?

The blessed Virgin !

IX

NICODEMUS

THE account of our Lord's dealing with Nicodemus is full of vital importance because He said to him the thing which is true of every one. It is the only occasion upon which it is recorded that He revealed this fact in speech. His utterance, however, shows its application to all men. " Except a man be born from above " is a general statement.

We often hear it said to-day that there are many excellent people in the world who make no profession of Christianity. Here we have a man, shall we say, of that order, particularly so on the intellectual side; and it is an arresting fact that it was to this man, not to the publican in the parable, not to the woman taken in the act of sin, not to the thief in his death agony, He declared the necessity for the new birth.

Nicodemus is introduced to us by John in such a way as to reveal him in certain aspects very clearly. He says, " There was a man of the Pharisees . . . a ruler of the Jews." That he was a Pharisee proves that he was narrow, dogmatic, and bigoted. The first two of these words reveal excellencies. The latter marks the point where excellence becomes failure. The fact that he was a Pharisee means also that his outlook upon religious matters was supernatural, rather than natural, and traditional and ritualistic. Moreover, as Pharisee, he belonged to that order which was characterised by its patriotism. Yet again, the statement that he was a " ruler of the Jews " shows that he stood in high position among the ruling class, for it means he was a member of the Sanhedrim. That fact is proved further in the history as we find him raising his voice in the Sanhedrim.

In the course of this conversation with him, our Lord said something to him which is certainly significant. Our old Version rendered a question the Lord addressed to him, " Art thou a teacher? " Our Revised has more accurately rendered it, " Art thou *the* teacher? " The employment at this point of the definite article very powerfully suggests at least that at this time Nicodemus was, to use the phrase of our own age, a popular teacher. Being a Pharisee, he would belong to the School of Gamaliel, as did Saul of Tarsus. At the time he was the teacher of that School to whom men were giving special attention.

There is, however, a revelation of the man which the very division of the Gospel into chapters may hide. The second chapter closes with the statement that there were many who believed on Jesus, in whom He did not believe; that is, He did not trust Himself to them. Chapter three, which in John's writing is of course a continuation, begins, " Now there was a man of the Pharisees." That little introductory word suggests at once continuity and contrast. There were people to whom Jesus could not commit Himself. Now, or But, there was a man named Nicodemus, to whom He could and did commit Himself.

Moreover, he was evidently a man of discernment. When he came to Jesus, he said:

> " Rabbi, we know that Thou art a Teacher come from God; for no man can do these signs that Thou doest, except God be with Him."

Signs had their place and their value to the crowd. Their very unusual nature was attractive. To Nicodemus they were proofs that the One doing them was One through Whom God was acting. Thus his discernment is clearly revealed.

Moreover, he was a man of caution. He came to Christ by night. It has become quite a habit to abuse him on this ground, and to say it was an act of cowardice. I do not so understand the story. Here was a man, convinced that this new Teacher was from God, and he had a desire to get to Him in a special way that He might receive teaching from Him alone. He came in the night for quietness and privacy. He was familiar with the messages of the past. He knew the Torah, the Nebiim, the Kethubim, but here was a new authentic Voice, and he desired to be alone with Him.

Yet once more, the story cannot be read without a conviction of the honesty of the man resulting. He was sincere as he challenged the things that Jesus said to him, with great respect, and with pre-eminent logical insight.

We have two subsequent glimpses of him in John. One is found in the seventh chapter when the Sanhedrim had sent officers to arrest Jesus, and they came back empty-handed. The voice of Nicodemus then said:

" Doth our law judge a man, except it first hear from
himself, and know what he doeth? "
In that question was revealed his passion for justice.

We meet him once more in the nineteenth chapter where he
is seen carrying to the sepulchre " a mixture of myrrh and aloes,
about a hundred pound weight." These were the gifts of love
for the dead body of Jesus. Thus we see him as a man of emotional
nature, and of a great heart. The whole survey shows a man of
the finest type. There are three men in the New Testament
who always seem to me may be placed in that class; Nicodemus,
the young ruler, and Saul of Tarsus. Apart from Christ, they
were of the same type, intellectual, honest, upright.

We come, then, to the question of supreme importance as to
what Jesus has to say to such a man.

The first thing that impresses us is that upon which we have
already touched, that our Lord trusted him. There were many
that He could not trust, to whom He could not commit Himself;
but the whole story of His dealing with Nicodemus is that of
His yielding Himself to the man completely in the fullest and
most wonderful way.

The story recorded in John clearly reveals a three-fold
movement in our Lord's dealings with Nicodemus. Glancing
over it quite mechanically, observe these things. In verses one
and two, " Nicodemus . . . said." Verse three, " Jesus answered."
Verse four, "Nicodemus saith." Verse five, " Jesus answered."
Verse nine, " Nicodemus answered and said." Verse ten,
" Jesus answered and said." If we examine this conversation we
find very distinctly that there are three movements; and in order
to follow them we may state them thus. In the first we see Jesus
and Nicodemus face to face (verses 2–3). Then we see them mind
to mind (verses 4–8). Finally we see them heart to heart
(verses 9–21).

As we see them face to face we first hear Nicodemus'
estimate of Christ:

" Rabbi, we know that Thou art a Teacher come from
God, for no man can do these signs that Thou doest, except
God be with Him."

That is how Nicodemus saw Christ.

In Christ's answer we have His estimate of Nicodemus, as
placing him on the level of all human beings, treating him as
representing man He said:

" Verily, verily, I say unto thee, Except a man be born from above, he cannot see the Kingdom of God."

That was His estimate of Nicodemus. In these words He told him that his knowledge, which was quite correct as he had stated, " We know that Thou art a Teacher come from God," was discounted, because it did not carry him far enough. In order to clear vision, to correct apprehension of the Kingdom of God, it was necessary that man receive a new life, a life which in its essence, comes from above. He declared that investigation on the earth level would never lead a man into the Kingdom of God. That result could only be obtained by revelation and illumination, resulting from a new life element. Thus Jesus said to him in effect, Though I be a Teacher come from God, man cannot understand My teaching until he is born from above. He needs a new life principle. Thus our Lord uttered to Nicodemus His supreme message to the world, which runs counter to the pride of the human intellect, that no man can understand the Kingdom of God save as he is born from above.

Immediately proceeding, we find Nicodemus and Jesus mind to mind.

" Nicodemus saith unto Him, How can a man be born when he is old? Can he enter a second time into his mother's womb, and be born? "

These words need very careful consideration. The question Nicodemus asked was a tremendous question. We first observe that in it he tacitly admitted the wonder of the idea. He did not dismiss it, declaring that there was no necessity for such a birth. What he did say in effect was that such a thing was not possible. " How can a man be born when he is old? " means, If peradventure, a man could go back to the beginning, and live in the power of a new life, he might have his opportunity; but, said Nicodemus, How can this be? The question revealed his sense of the meaning of personality having arrived at maturity. It was as though he had said to Jesus, I am to-day the result of all I was yesterday, and the day before, and all the yesterdays since the day of my birth. I am not merely what I was when I was born. What I am to-day is the result of the accumulation of the experiences of the running years. Now this is true of every human being, and the question arises as to how these things which have become woven into personality, can be dealt with. How can a man be born when he is old? Then with daring, Nicodemus employed the physical to illustrate the whole fact of personality as he said:

"Can a man enter a second time into his mother's womb, and be born?"

That second question was not intended to be complete, for man is more than physical. It was intended to illustrate. In the realm of the physical, can a full grown man be pressed back into embryonic stage in his mother's womb and be born? The involved argument was that if it was impossible in the realm of the physical, it was equally so in the realm of the mental and spiritual. I repeat, it was a great question.

Now let us carefully observe our Lord's reply. He first repeated His declaration in fuller form.

"Verily, verily, I say unto thee, Except a man be born of water and the Spirit, he cannot enter into the Kingdom of God."

In considering this statement we must remember that Nicodemus was certainly familiar with the preaching of John, and knew that John had said:

"I indeed baptise you with water unto repentance, but He that cometh after me is mightier than I . . . He shall baptise you with the Holy Spirit and with fire."

The baptism of water was the symbol of repentance, the human condition necessary to the remission of sins. The baptism of the Spirit was the fact of regeneration, the Divine answer to the fulfilment of the human condition.

Thus our Lord declared that in order to enter the Kingdom of God there must be on the part of man repentance, and also on the part of God the regeneration of the spirit of the man.

Then our Lord referred to the illustration which Nicodemus had used in the realm of the physical, as He said:

"That which is born of the flesh is flesh; and that which is born of the Spirit is spirit."

The intention of the statement was to show that what is impossible in the realm of the flesh is possible in the realm of the spirit.

Continuing, our Lord made use of His great illustration of the wind, introducing it by the charge:

"Marvel not that I said unto thee, Ye must be born from above."

This charge called upon Nicodemus not to allow his intellect to hinder him. The illustration in itself shows that there are things beyond the grasp of the intellect as to explanation, which nevertheless are apprehended as facts, and must be acted upon.

" The wind bloweth where it listeth, and thou hearest the voice thereof, but knowest not whence it cometh, and whither it goeth; so is every one that is born of the Spirit." Thus our Lord recognised a mystery beyond the understanding of the intellect, but a fact so patent as an activity of the power of God that the only rational attitude is that of accepting and yielding to the fact, while postponing the interpretation of the mystery.

Then we come to the final movement.

" Nicodemus answered and said unto Him, How can these things be? "

Here let us not think this is the question he had already asked. Neither has it the same significance. The verb employed in the enquiry, " How can a man be born when he is old " is not the verb employed when he said, " How can these things be? " The question now asked may accurately be rendered, How can these things come to pass? His first enquiry revealed a conviction at the moment that the suggestion of Jesus as to a new birth, was impossible of realisation. Now, having received from the Lord the admission of a mystery, and the appeal to action, his perplexity was caused as to the method by which such a thing could come to pass.

For the answer to that question all the rest of the statement of Jesus is necessary, and what a marvellous answer it is.

First, with tender satire, Jesus, looking at Nicodemus with all his intellectuality and all his strength, recognising his popularity as a teacher, and certainly recognising his sincerity, said to him:

" Art thou the teacher of Israel, and understandest not these things . . . If I told you earthly things, and ye believe not, how shall ye believe, if I tell you heavenly things? "

He had told him the earthly things, the necessity for the new birth. Now He asked if Nicodemus had not believed that, how could he believe if He answered his enquiry as to how these things could be; in other words, if He told him the heavenly things. Yet let it be carefully noted that He did tell him the heavenly things. He began on the level where Nicodemus would be familiar, that is, his knowledge of the Scriptures.

" As Moses lifted up the serpent in the wilderness, even so must the Son of man be lifted up; that whosoever believeth may in Him have eternal life."

As we read these words the question naturally arises in the mind as to whether Nicodemus at the moment perfectly understood the illustration. I do not think he did, but I think the very form

70

of it, the very language of it did indicate to him that death was somehow referred to, and that the death of the Teacher was involved, the Son of man must be lifted up. The probability is that Nicodemus never understood until he wound the cloths around the dead body of Jesus, and left Him lying amid the myrrh and the aloes. And even then it is not likely that he understood. The final illumination would come to him when he found Him risen from among the dead. The lifting up of the Son of man was not merely His placing on the Cross. It included that resurrection. When at the last Jesus said to His disciples:

"I, if I be lifted up out of the earth, will draw all men unto Myself,"

we find the interpretation of His word to Nicodemus, including as it did, death and resurrection. At the moment, therefore, He suggested to this enquiring soul the idea of a death that should provide life. This was the first of the heavenly things.

Then our Lord passed to the heavenly fact which lay behind that.

"For God so loved the world, that He gave His only begotten Son, that whosoever believeth on Him should not perish, but have eternal life."

Thus He declared the heavenly truth that life should come through the lifting up of the Son of man, as the result of the love of God in thus giving His only begotten Son.

Continuing, He said:

"This is the judgment, that the light is come into the world, and men loved the darkness rather than the light."

As we read, we catch a remarkable mingling of great things, and so of great thoughts. They are those of life and love and light. Nicodemus had enquired, How can these things be brought to pass? and the reply summarised may be thus stated, They can be brought to pass by the liberation of *life* when the Son of man is lifted up, which lifting up results from the *love* of God for humanity; and in the *light* of this revelation men, walking and obeying it, come into the possession of life. These were indeed the heavenly things which answered the second " How " of Nicodemus.

When we turn to consider the result of this conversation we find that Nicodemus went back to his place in the Sanhedrim. For this we have no right in any sense to condemn him. Christ did not call him to travel with Him. He did not need him in that way, or He would have so called him. He passed back, as the majority of people have to do, to his ordinary position in life. Presently, as we have seen, we find his voice raised on behalf of justice for Jesus, and then at last we see him joined with Joseph of Arimathea in the fulfilment of the last offices of love.

Looking at that final scene it is impossible not to be impressed with a certain aspect of it. When Jesus was dead, when His body was laid in the tomb, all the other disciples for the moment had forsaken Him and fled. Then two secret disciples blazed into confession of love, Joseph of Arimathea and Nicodemus, and wrapped the cloths of death around that dead body, amid the aloes and the myrrh and the spices. At any rate as we watch that scene we are warned against undervaluing men who might seem to us to lack something in the matter of open and public confession. It may be that in some hour of crisis, such men will manifest a heroism greater than those who have made the loudest profession.

As we close the study we enquire what are the lessons the story teaches us? The first that suggests itself to my own mind is that Christ will always give Himself to honesty. If a man in his approach to the Lord, will state his difficulties, Christ is ever ready to receive him, and to commit Himself to that man. In proportion as such an one remains honest, there will come to him growingly, revelations, illuminations, and deliverances.

It is impossible, moreover, to read the story without seeing Christ's emphasis upon the limitations of the merely intellectual. He does not undervalue the intellect. His answers prove that. But He made it perfectly clear that in order to the apprehension of spiritual things, there must be something more than mere intellectual activity.

He reveals, moreover, the fact that the necessity is that a man should be born from above. It is only in the illumination that comes from this birth that there can be escape from darkness, and the realisation of life.

Finally, we have in all the teaching of Christ here a revelation that the way of life for man is the result of the love of God, placing it at human disposal as men come to, and walk in the light.

X

THE SAMARITAN WOMAN

THE story of our Lord's dealing with the Samaritan woman is in some ways full of surprises. When we consider it, we are first impressed with the fact that in beginning to deal with her He left so much unsaid that many of us would consider necessary in such a case. Knowing her and her history well, as events prove, in His approach to her He made no reference whatever to her sin, but did so on the level of common human courtesy. He offered her nothing, but asked for a gift from her.

We are further surprised that in the course of His conversation, He said so much to her that it is almost certain we should have felt her unready to receive, and consequently should have postponed the saying of to a later date. To her He uttered the profoundest things that ever fell from His lips on the subject of worship. This in itself is a revelation of His perfect knowledge of the human soul, and how that under the most apparently contradictory circumstances it has inherently a consciousness of spiritual realities. Indeed, is not that in part at least, what was in His mind, when speaking to His disciples presently, He said:

" Say not ye, There are yet four months, and then cometh the harvest? behold, I say unto you, Lift up your eyes, and look on the fields, that they are white already unto harvest."

That is, there are possibilities that are not apparent save to those who see most deeply into the mystery of human personality.

In studying the story, following our method, we will attempt to see this woman, and then watch our Lord's dealing with her.

If we take a general view of the whole story I think we shall see clearly that this woman had a definite religious background. In the course of her conversation with our Lord, she showed that she had a religious position as she said:

" Our father Jacob, who gave us this well."

Further, we see that subconsciously, perhaps, but none the less definitely, she had a religious problem which concerned the true place of worship. Finally we find that she entertained a religious hope, " We know that Messiah cometh." I do not say that as we meet this woman we are meeting with a religious woman, but that she was a woman with a religious background. It is possible that she had made no reference to her religious position or her problem or her hope for long years, but they were all present; and contact with Christ brought to her consciousness or remembrance these facts so long forgotten, ignored, dismissed. In dealing with Him they became vocal. She presents a picture of the condition of thousands of people to-day. They have a religious background, perchance some problem dismissed, and it may be some hope accepted, but having no practical bearing on life.

When she referred to " our father Jacob " she spoke, of course, as a Samaritan woman. The Samaritans belonged to the Northern kingdom of Israel, and the remnant remaining in Samaria of that Northern kingdom, found their centre of worship in Mount Gerizim. That fact takes us back in the history to the point when Jeroboam had created a new centre of worship around a calf. When he did this, he was breaking the second commandment. He did not desire the people to depart from the worship of God, but for political reasons he wished to prevent their going to Jerusalem. From that time, through the running centuries, Gerizim was their place of worship. They claimed relationship with Jacob, because the centre of their life was at the place where was the parcel of ground which Jacob had given to Joseph. In referring then to Jacob she revealed what we have described as her religious background. Everything points to the supposition that she had not lived at all in relationship with that background, but it had remained, and was thus stated in her conversation with Christ.

Moreover, when she submitted the question as to the true place of worship, she was referring to a problem which had often been discussed. There must have existed in the minds of these Samaritans through all the running years the consciousness of the contrast between Jerusalem and Gerizim; and consequently the very question which the woman raised. And once more, it is a remarkable thing that she referred, without any equivocation, to the hope that the Jew and Samaritan held in common, that, namely, of the coming of a Messiah.

Having recognised this religious background, we become of course, conscious that this woman was a woman of sin. There

74

is no need to dwell upon the details. The whole sad story is revealed in our Lord's words to her concerning her past. She was evidently a woman who had yielded to passion, and the history of the burning of that passion is found in the statement of Christ to her concerning her past. As she stood before Him her condition was that of one in whom passion had burnt itself out. She was degraded to the level of a common water-carrier, which was the occupation of a slave. Passion burnt out does not mean thirst quenched. That certainly remained, amid the tragedy that characterised her life.

Then it is impossible to read the story without being conscious of a certain flippancy and evasiveness that characterised her attitude. When Jesus said to her:

" Go, call thy husband, and come hither ";

she replied, " I have no husband." In the brief answer she was taking the position which to-day would be described as that of an emancipated woman, emancipated that is from all restraint and all responsibility. What business was it of this Jew to say such a thing to her? Because she refused anything like interference, she made this reply, dismissing the question.

So we see her, a really pathetic figure with a religious background, and yet, having yielded herself to the call of passion, all the deeper things had been submerged and trampled upon. Her relationship to Jacob had no meaning for her that was vital. The problem as to the place of worship was unimportant. The hope she shared with her people in the coming Messiah had no bearing whatever upon her life.

As we look at this woman the subject of how Jesus dealt with her becomes very vital. To begin with, let us summarise the whole story. He first appealed to her kindness. He then appealed to her curiosity. He then appealed to her feverishness. He then appealed to her sin. He then appealed to her sense of God. He finally fastened upon her hope of Messiah.

He first appealed to her kindness. He had travelled a long way, and as John tells us, was weary as He sat on the well; and when she arrived, He said to her " Give Me to drink." She protested with evident wonder at the request coming from Him. She said:

" How is it that Thou, being a Jew, askest drink of me, which am a Samaritan woman."

It is at this point that John inserts that revealing statement:

"For Jews have no dealings with Samaritans."

The woman knew that Jesus was a Jew, and that He had travelled up from Judea. That He, a Jew, should ask a favour of a Samaritan woman was a perplexing thing to her. At any rate she at once recognised there was something in Him different from other Jews with whom she had come into contact. This was His first approach to her. It was really a revelation of the vital difference between Himself and others.

This being accomplished, He at once appealed to her curiosity as He said:

"If thou knewest the gift of God, and Who it is that saith to thee, Give Me to drink; thou wouldest have asked of Him, and He would have given thee living water."

It may at once be said that curiosity is really a sign of intelligence. People who are never curious, have lost the first power of gaining knowledge. Thus He had said something to her which brought her beyond the consciousness that He was different from others, and produced within her the sense of bewilderment and wonder. She did not understand Him at all, and evidently thought He was still somehow referring to the water found in the well, for she said:

"Sir, Thou hast nothing to draw with, and the well is deep; from whence then hast Thou that living water?"

He then appealed to the thirst which He knew was a characteristic of her consciousness.

"Everyone that drinketh of this water shall thirst again; but whosoever drinketh of the water that I shall give him shall never thirst; but the water that I shall give him shall become in him a well of water springing up unto eternal life."

At this point we look at her again, a woman with a background of religion which had long been ignored, with a life in which the fires of passion had burnt themselves out, leaving nothing but ashes, and she herself a water-carrier, a mere slave. He knew, however much she might hide it, that in her life was a thirst that never had been quenched, and to that He made His appeal.

Her reply was at once an admission of that thirst and an evasion. She said:

"Sir, give me this water, that I thirst not, neither come all the way hither to draw."

Surely she had already grasped the fact that He was speaking of something far beyond the water that she was able to draw. And yet, owning to a thirst, she attempted to interpret it in the realm of the material as she spoke of having to come to the well to draw.

It was at this juncture that He appealed to her sin, approaching it with a command, which brought her face to face with it, whether she would, or no.

" Go, call thy husband, and come hither."

She was not aware of how perfectly He knew the facts of her life, and prevaricating, she said, " I have no husband." It was then that He flashed upon her a consciousness of His knowledge as He said:

" Thou saidst well, I have no husband; for thou hast had five husbands; and he whom thou now hast is not thy husband."

At this point we have a remarkable revelation of the attempt of the human soul to escape, as she said:

" Sir, I perceive that Thou art a prophet. Our fathers worshipped in this mountain; and ye say, that in Jerusalem is the place where men ought to worship."

We see her practically owning to the truth of the things He has said as she declares that He was a prophet; but she will not face the situation, and turns aside attempting to introduce a discussion in the realm of religion. It is a common device of the human soul, this turning from the challenge that brings it face to face with sin, in an attempt to discuss religion or theology.

Now perhaps the most amazing thing of all in the Lord's method is revealed. He consented to discuss the question she raised, and in doing so dismissed both Jerusalem and Gerizim as necessary centres of worship. He declared to her that worship consisted in the approach of the soul to God directly and immediately, providing it came in spirit and in truth. He thus showed that worship is not a mental matter finally, but a spiritual; but that the condition must be that of ceasing to attempt to hide anything, the very thing, by the way, she was doing at the time.

There would seem to be a wistful consciousness of the truth of what the Lord had said to her, as she replied:

" I know that Messiah cometh (which is called Christ); when He is come, He will declare unto us all things."

77

The advance in her thinking is revealed in the progressive description of Him. First He was " a Jew," then He had become " a prophet "; and now, wonderingly, and in the presence of what He had been saying, she did not declare Him to be the Messiah, but said that Messiah would tell them all things. It was then the Lord claimed the fulfilment of that highest conception that had come to the mind of the woman, as He said:

" I that speak unto thee am He."

We have no record of any reply that she made. Indeed John is careful to say that she went away, and went so quickly that she forgot the reason of her presence. She left her water-pot. Arriving, she said to the people:

" Come, see a man, which told me all things that ever I did. Can this be the Christ? "

He had claimed to be the Christ, and she went back with the wonder in her soul as to whether indeed this was so; and she called others to come, and see, and hear, and so she sought final assurance.

The result was that Jesus stayed in that city for two whole days. We have no record whatever of what He did during that period, or what He said, except as we learn the result was that they declared, " This is indeed the Saviour of the world." We may suppose that He emphasised more fully the things He had said to the woman with courtesy in His approach, the revelation of the fact that God was available to them without the necessity for travelling to Jerusalem, or the climb of Mount Gerizim; and that He had dealt with them concerning their sin, and had offered to them also the thirst-quenching water of life. In their confession they uttered the supreme and all-inclusive truth concerning Him, and that in itself is a remarkable fact, because these were Samaritans.

In what remains of the story we have a remarkable revelation of the underlying secrets of the life of our Lord, and of why it was, as John stated, " He must needs go through Samaria." Reminding ourselves that at that time orthodox Jews desiring to reach Galilee, would not travel through Samaria, but went the longer route, crossing the Jordan, and travelling up through Peraea, and so back into Galilee; He, however, must needs go through Samaria; and in His dealing with disciples, we have a revelation of the reason of the " must." These men had left Him, to go away and provide food. Coming back, to their amazement they found Him talking to this woman. Their respectful reticence is manifest in the fact that they asked Him no question as to the reason of His action. They were concerned for Him physically. They knew He was tired. They knew He was hungry, and they felt that He ought to eat, and they besought Him so to do. It was then that He said to them:

"I have meat to eat that ye know not."

In other words, He declared that He had sources of sustenance with which they were unfamiliar. When they, thinking wholly within the material, wondered whether anyone had brought Him anything to eat, He said:

"My meat is to do the will of Him that sent Me, and to accomplish His work."

In these words we have a revelation of the true meaning of what He had been doing in connection with this woman. He had been doing the will of God, and accomplishing His work. He had found in her one whose life had been one of dissipation, and who had reached the moment of complete disillusionment, a disillusionment which had rendered her flippant and callous. He had so dealt with her as to bring her face to face with her past as to its reality, and leading her forward had given to her unquestionably the thirst-quenching water of life. This was the will of God; this was His· work; and in the doing of the will, and the accomplishment of the work, He found the sustenance of His life.

Having said this, He indicated to His disciples that this also was their work, and in this connection said remarkable things to them. He told them that their work was to be that of reaping, not sowing; and the surprising thing to them was His revelation of the fact that the harvest was ready. Their calculations would lead them to believe that before the harvest there must be much ploughing, and sowing, and waiting. He said the fields were already white. The illustration was in the woman herself. The story of the life, with passion burnt out, and an unquenchable thirst, is the story of the very harvest which He had come to reap. We may summarise this by declaring that it is a revelation of the fact that wherever we find, according to the standards of human thinking, desolation and hopelessness, that is the place for the operation of the Saviour of the world, and for those who follow Him.

The story is full of wonder, teaching us many things. Let us close by summarising in the case of one or two of them. As we look at this woman we have the truth emphasised that the wreckage of human life is always the result of false attempts to satisfy its legitimate claims. What was the meaning of this wrecked life, this spoiled personality, this burnt out human being? It was all the result of an attempt to satisfy a perfectly legitimate claim of personality by false methods.

Again, we see that Christ, in spite of all failure, and all degradation, makes His appeal to the deepest things of the spiritual nature, talks to a woman like that about God being available to the human soul wherever that soul may be, independently of any special locality such as Jerusalem or Gerizim.

We learn further that when He deals with men or women He will be utterly faithful with them. He does not come to heal wounds slightly. He probes life, and makes men face it for themselves. He will reveal sin, but He will do it to the sinner, and not to someone else concerning that sinner.

The supreme glory of the story is the promise He made that He will give to the thirsty, burnt-out life living water, and give it in such fashion that it shall be within the life, a well, springing up. If we need the final statement of this truth we pass from what He said to the Samaritan woman to His great call in the Temple later on.

" If any man thirst, let him come unto Me, and drink. He that believeth on Me, as the Scripture hath said, out of his inner life shall flow rivers of living water."

XI

THE NOBLEMAN

THE story of Christ and the Nobleman is a very brief one, occupying only nine verses. It gives the account of His dealing with a nameless man. It is well to emphasise, in passing, the fact that this story must not be confused with Luke's account of our Lord's dealing with the centurion (Luke vii, 2-10). The term employed to describe this man by our translators is " nobleman," which quite literally means, a king's man, that is, one serving under the authority of a king. We know nothing of him except what we find in this story. There have been very interesting conjectures concerning him, one being that he was Chuza, who Luke mentions as the husband of Joanna, and Herod's steward. Some have sought to identify him with Manaen, mentioned by Luke in the book of the Acts. Yet others have argued that he was Herod's own foster brother. As I have said, these things are all interesting but not important. That which we do know is that he was connected with the court, and unquestionably the reference was to the court of Herod Antipas, who was then known as king by the courtesy of the Roman authority.

Thus the man was one who lived and served under the authority which was then being exercised in that region, and that would mean, in his case, that he was exercising this derived authority. I think we may say of him that, therefore, he was a man accustomed to having things done, which he desired; for with all the changes created by the passing of time, humanity remains very much the same.

John tells us that this was the Lord's second sign in Galilee, after He had come out of Judæa, and it took place in Cana, where, according to John's record His first sign had been given, that namely of the turning of water into wine. Thus we are brought face to face with the method of John, in speaking of these things

81

as signs. The only place in the Gospel of John where the word " wonders " which is the equivalent of " miracles " occurs is here, where our Lord made use of the word in addressing this man. This, then, is one of the group of such signs recorded by John, which taken together, and allowed to bear their united testimony, are intended as the writer himself declared at the end of his story, to prove that Jesus is the Christ, the Son of God. Necessarily therefore it is in that way that it must be considered.

In our present studies we are observing His methods with individuals; and the healing sign, whereas necessarily it has its bearing upon our study, nevertheless occupies a secondary position.

The remarkable thing about this second sign is that it was the operation of power at a distance, and the healing of the boy was not wrought by any physical contact with Christ at all. However, we fasten our attention upon the man himself, this king's man, in order that we may watch our Lord's method with him.

At once it may be said that the story appears to be a meagre one. There are very few details, and yet, as we ponder it we see that it is graphic and vivid, and very remarkable in many ways, differing from anything we have seen so far in the course of our considerations. As a picture it stands in striking contrast to those at which we have already looked, in which there has been much of light and shade, form and colour, and great variety. Here we have a picture which we may describe as one in black and white, a few bold strokes, in which the man is clearly seen, but in which the principal value is found in our Lord's dealing with him. Indeed, the method of Christ here is arresting in that He dealt with this man in a way that we do not usually associate with Him; and yet it was vindicated in a glorious result, namely, that the man himself, and all his household believed on Jesus. As a matter of fact, this is the first reference to any whole household thus submitting itself to His authority.

As we look at the man we remind ourselves once more that he was a king's man, under authority, and exercising authority. The whole story has to do with our Lord's dealing with him, and we can only see the man as we watch that process. We are first, however, impressed by the fact that whatever else may be said of him, he was a man of a great heart. He is seen making a desperate venture on behalf of his sick boy, who lay at the point of death.

He had come from Capernaum to Cana to find Jesus, a journey of at least twenty-five miles. Hearing that Christ had come into Galilee, and was at Cana, he at once took this journey. His boy meant more to him than anything else in the world, and he lay at the point of death. Therefore he made the venture.

When we speak of his coming as a venture, it is important that we understand what we mean by the word. He did not come because he was a disciple of Jesus, and as we shall see presently, from our Lord's address to him, he was not at all sure that Jesus could do anything for him. He went, as many another father has gone when his child lay at the point of death, and when skilled physicians had told him they could do no more. In such an hour a man will turn to anyone who has at least the repute of being able to heal. His attitude of mind is revealed in the words of Jesus:

"Except ye see signs and wonders, ye will in no wise believe."

In that saying the man is remarkably unveiled, but definitely so. Whereas He used the plural form in this saying, the man himself was included in what was said. He made no reference to the boy, but rather unveiled the deepest fact of the man's mental attitude, which he shared in common with others. It is necessary to glance ahead in this way, in order to see the man clearly. He did not know that Jesus could do anything, but he made the venture, He had heard that He had healed, and in his extremity, the extremity of his agony and wounded love, he came to Him.

When he heard this reply of Jesus, he said:
"Sir, come down, ere my child die."

It is impossible to read this without hearing in it the protest of an angry agony. He was not arguing with Jesus. He was not entering into any discussion as to whether the diagnosis of our Lord of the general mental attitude was correct or no. In effect, he said, Whatever the attitude of my mind may be, if there is any chance for my boy, come down ere he die.

Looking at him a little longer once more, the two sides of our study dovetail, and we see him as a man of courage, as he came, evidently quite suddenly, to a new vision and a new conviction. Here are two things which, when brought together, are found to be singularly dramatic. He said, "Come down, ere my child die." Jesus replied, "Go thy way; thy son liveth." The man said,

" Come " to Jesus. Jesus said " Go " to him. Then evidently something happened in the soul of the nobleman. It is one of those cases which indeed we are always face to face with when the mere letter of the story does not reveal all the facts. What made this man obey immediately? He wanted Jesus to come, and the Lord replied in effect, I am not coming; you go. Evidently in that moment a conviction seized him, upon which he acted. There came to him somehow a sense of confidence in Jesus, and the moment he arrived at that point, without any hesitation he left Jesus, and went. Here he is seen making a further venture, and it was the venture of courage.

Once more we see the honesty of the man in the final movement. When as he journeyed home his servants met him and said " Thy son liveth," he found a corroboration of the truth of what Jesus had said to him. In order to make doubly sure of the connection between the living of his son and the word of Jesus, he asked his servants at what hour did he begin to amend? In effect they said to him, It did not begin, but it happened:

" Yesterday at the seventh hour the fever left him."

In that statement he found his answer, and the ratification of his action when he had been obedient to the " Go " of Jesus. When he found his obedience thus vindicated, he did the only thing that was possible to an honest man; he surrendered completely.

Twice over we are told he believed. When Jesus said " Go," John declares that he believed His word, and then he made his venture; and now, in the fullest sense, he believed completely, so completely, that he swept with him into the realm of committal, all his house. In that hour the whole company of this king's officer became disciples of Jesus. He thus passed into the realm where he became the servant of another King, in a new Kingdom.

When we turn to examine the method of Jesus, necessarily we go over the story again. The first thing we observe is that our Lord, in dealing with this man, was that of ignoring apparently the trouble, even though the man's heart was wrung with anguish. He went to the very centre of his personality, and told him what his outlook really was. He classed him with his generation as He said:

" Except ye see signs and wonders, ye will in no wise believe."

In effect He declared to him that he was not an original thinker, that he was just one of the crowd, and one of the crowd by which our Lord was surrounded in His work. We are at once reminded of the statement of John at the end of his second chapter, that there were many believed who saw His signs, to whom He could not commit Himself. In these words our Lord referred to the same fact, that men were seeking signs, and would not believe except they saw them. This word of Christ was a sharp and incisive one; may we not say reticently and carefully, but resolutely, that it sounded a cruel thing to say to a man under such conditions. Just when his supreme consciousness was that of concern, and even agony about his boy, Christ talked to him about a general attitude of his life, his mentality, and told him that he was one of a crowd, more concerned in seeing signs than in anything else.

Yet what a revelation we have here of our Lord. There was no reserve in His own mind, in His own heart, in His own will. He loved that boy as much as his father did, and His ultimate intention was that of giving him healing; and in so doing, of bringing joy and comfort to the heart of the father. But for the moment He left all these secondary things, and declared the deepest truth concerning this man as one of the multitude. Their attitude was that which is revealed in a saying which we often hear to-day, When I see, I will believe. A moment's consideration will show what a foolish saying that is, which is so commonly employed—Seeing is believing. Seeing is not believing. Seeing is seeing. Belief is being sure when you cannot see. Our Lord was ever seeking for the quality of faith that was independent of signs, that quality of faith which must centre in Him, as apart from His works. This thing was declared by Him at the end of His ministry, when to the little group of disciples in the upper room He said:

"Believe Me . . . or else believe Me for the very works' sake."

In these words He made Himself the centre of confidence, and relegated the works to a secondary although admittedly important place. When therefore this king's man came to Him as a father, He halted, first to reveal to him what was the failing quality in his attitude.

Then when the man said in effect. I am not now prepared to discuss myself or my attitudes, I am in need of help, "Come down, ere my child die," our Lord replied to him, as we have

said in effect, No, I am not coming, " Go . . . thy son liveth."
In these words He laid upon the man an imperative command.
It was the voice of a King saying, " Go," and making an assertion,
" thy son liveth." It was as though our Lord said to him, You are
seeking a sign, and I will give you a sign, but not until you have
taken Me at My word, and acted upon that, without the sign.
John is careful here to declare that the man went because he
believed His word, not upon the basis of a sign. The sign was
offered, but it was postponed.

Here once more we are brought face to face with these things
that cannot be recorded, but which are patently present. What
made this man believe the word of Jesus? There can be but
one answer, and it is found in the Person of the Lord Himself.
There was something about Him, something in the glance of His
eye, something in the mien of His majesty, something perchance
undefinable, and yet convincing. The very quick obedience to the
word of Jesus on the part of this man is an evidence that there was
ever something about the Lord Himself which perhaps the only
word we can use that is adequate is supernatural. There was
something mystic, majestic, and merciful, in which all the com-
passions of eternity expressed themselves. It was this something
undoubtedly that captured the man, and made him act in
obedience to the word of the Lord.

Thus we see that first of all the Lord, in severe terms, expressed
His condemnation of that attitude which the nobleman shared
with others of his age. He then created for him an opportunity
to rise on to a higher level by uttering a word of simple authority,
coupling His imperative with an assertion which had no proof,
and could have no proof: " Thy son liveth." In uttering the
words, however, He had revealed Himself to that man in such
fashion as to give him the opportunity to exercise his will in
obedience to the conviction that had possessed him; and He
coupled His imperative with the promise of a sign.

Then the last thing in the method of Christ was that which
is patent. The boy was healed. Distance had no bearing upon
the question of the power of Christ. The sign was given, and
the activity of a daring and venturesome volitional faith in the
word, reinforced by the Person, brought to this man all he sought
of help, and such a conviction concerning our Lord, that he yielded
to Him completely, and carried his household with him.

As we ponder this story, brief as it is, there are certain great
truths stand clearly revealed. The first is that when any man

comes to Christ, he comes to One Who knows the truth concerning him. He understands that underlying attitude toward life that affects life powerfully, even when we ourselves may not be conscious of it. Here was a man, one of the crowd of his day, who was ever seeking a sign, in order to create faith. What our Lord did in revealing that fact to him is what He always does in every and any connection, when men come into contact with Him.

Having thus brought a man face to face with reality concerning himself, He immediately lays upon him some command, obedience to which must be dependent upon faith, even when there is no sign. Nevertheless He ever couples His command with some promise. The commands may vary, according to individual needs. In this man it consisted of an order to take a journey, to tramp back over the twenty-five miles that he had traversed. That was the command. It was necessary that he should obey. What the Lord's command may be to any individual can only be known to that individual. Personally I shall know His command, whatever it may be, and that it is for me, and for me alone. In the case of the young ruler He said:

" Go, sell all that thou hast and give to the poor, and come, follow Me."

He does not say that to everyone. The great truth is that He presents Himself to the soul as sovereign Lord, and lays upon that soul some command which claims obedience, right then and there, in the matter of something that is clearly in front of the soul. As in the case of this man, it is invariably the command which provides at the moment, no sign, but which, nevertheless promises some sign which shall come in the pathway of obedience. It would not be correct to say that there is no evidence of the fulfilment of the promise of the sign, for that, as we have already emphasised, is always provided in the Person of the Lord Himself. In the case of this man, he heard the announcement that his boy was living. There was no evidence that it was so, other than the tones of the voice, and the wonder of the Person. On the basis of these things he obeyed.

All this in principle is carried out in the case of every man or woman who comes thus face to face with Christ. He will rebuke weakness He knows, but at the same moment He will create an opportunity to overcome that very weakness, and to rise on to the higher level of life. He ever calls upon the soul to make a venture, based upon these two great evidences of His word and Himself.

If we obey, presently we may institute enquiry as did this man, and the result will ever be that we yield to Him in a new and more complete way. We may roughly say that if we will give Christ His opportunity, He will ever vindicate Himself. In His dealing with us, we may be conscious at first of the sharp incision of the surgeon's knife, that gets to the root of the malady, but that is ever followed by the healing that cures the trouble, and brings us into the full realisation of life.

XII

THE IMPOTENT MAN

A SUPREME interest attaches to this story because it gives the account of an activity of Jesus in connection with which He made a claim that, so far as human instrumentality is concerned, cost Him His life. It was what He did and said upon this occasion stirred the malice of the rulers against Him, and that hostility never ceased. John tells us:

> " For this cause therefore the Jews sought the more to kill Him, because He not only brake the Sabbath, but also called God His Father, making Himself equal with God."

If we glance on to chapter seven, which so far as the chronological sequence of our Lord's life is concerned carries us nearly two years on, we find that He, speaking to these same men in opposition to Him, said:

> " If a man receiveth circumcision on the Sabbath, that the law of Moses may not be broken; are ye wroth with Me, because I made a man every whit whole on the Sabbath? "

The reference was unquestionably to this healing of the man in Bethesda's porches. It was here and now that their determination was taken to slay Him, and they never rested until, again on the human level, they had accomplished their purpose.

The claim which He made, and which they resented, was that of co-operation with God, and He made it in such terms that whatever we might be inclined to think it meant, they clearly understood by the claim itself, and the form in which it was made, that He was claiming equality with God:

> " My Father worketh even until now, and I work."

The claim was perfectly distinct in the declaration that God was, to use their words, " His own Father." Thus He claimed that

89

in the thing He had done, which in itself did not raise their anger, but did raise their objection because it had been done on the Sabbath day, His vindication for His action was that of His equality with God.

When we turn to the story itself, we find that in the whole of our meditations on the great Physician, none is more dramatic and revealing than this, both in itself, and in His interpretation thereof.

The account of the man himself, and of those among whom he was found, when Jesus passed through Bethesda's porches, is a revelation of the people for whom He cared, and whom He came to seek and save. The story, moreover, reveals His method with such. These introductory considerations are intended to arrest attention, and to fix it upon the highest and true level of the story itself.

We look then first at the man. He passes before us nameless. He is seen as one of a crowd. John's description of that crowd is graphic in the extreme. He says that in the porches lay a multitude of " sick, blind, halt, withered." " Sick," that is, utterly strengthless; "blind," sightless; " halt," crippled; and finally that almost terrific word, " withered." Here we see a company of the unfit, the derelicts, the outcasts, and all this by reason of physical disability; and in all likelihood, in the majority of cases, such disability resulting from moral malady. These people are seen close to the pool which was near to the sheep gate, and is called the Pool of Bethesda. Opinions differ as to what that name really means, because it has been given in different forms. If Bethesda is the true name it means the house of mercy. In recent years it is claimed that a discovery has been made of the actual place of the pool, and if that discovery is correct, then the pool lay deeply down; and in order for this man, or any other, to get into its waters, he had to descend a steep declivity of steps.

If those seen there were derelict, it is nevertheless true that their very presence revealed their desire for recovery. The sheep gate was situated in the north. It was close to the market-place, the place of traffic, the place where the merchants were busily occupied, and business was conducted. It was not the usual entrance to Jerusalem for any other than those so interested. It is significant that Jesus chose upon that day to go that way. Ever and anon the waters of the pool were troubled. Our revisers have omitted what unquestionably was a gloss, concerning the

troubling of the waters by an angel. That was the popular interpretation as to the cause. It may be taken for granted that the
pool was fed by one of those natural springs still to be found in
the district, which ever and anon bubbled up. Attributing this
to angelic influence, men believed that to pass into those waters,
would be to find healing. Possibly, too, there were those who did
find healing.

Now as Jesus passed through, we are told that He saw one
thus referred to:

> "A certain man was there, which had been thirty and
> eight years in his infirmity."

Thirty-eight years! Let an attempt be made to realise what that
really meant. We do not know for how much of that period he
had been brought to lie near the pool, waiting for the troubling of
the waters.

Then, taking the whole story into account for a moment, we
discover that this man's physical disability was due to a moral
malady. In passing, we emphasise the fact that that is not always
so. In the last analysis all sickness in the world is the outcome
of sin, or broken law. That does not mean that those suffering
from disease are necessarily those who are guilty of the breaking
of law. The fact that in this case the man's malady was first moral
is revealed in the words that Jesus addressed to him later in the
day, when He said:

> "Behold, thou art made whole; sin no more."

The more accurate rendering of that word would be:

> "Thou art made whole; no longer continue in sin."

It is in this solemn word of Jesus to him later that we are brought
face to face with the fact that his physical disability was the outcome
of sin.

So he is seen, lying helpless, unable to do anything for himself,
apparently, a sufferer familiar enough to others, and indeed so
familiar that they have become careless about him. Moreover
he was utterly hopeless as is revealed presently quite clearly.
While still there near the pool, he had lost all hope of being able
to avail himself of its healing powers. It is indeed a tragic picture.

As we turn to consider our Lord's method with him, we go
back to the introductory things which have been said, and so pass
on to our Lord's words to the rulers:

> "My Father worketh even until now, and I work."

When these rulers dicovered the man carrying his mattress on the Sabbath day, they charged him with breaking the Sabbath. His reply was at once artless, and sensible, and natural:

> " He that made me whole, the Same said unto me, Take up thy bed, and walk."

The answer was simple enough, but it was sublime, for it claimed that the sanction for His action was found in the power of the One Who bade him do so, as vindicated in the wonder of his healing. It is certainly an arresting fact that this man did not know Who it was. The rulers, however, discovered, and then found Jesus, and charged Him with causing this man to break the Sabbath. They objected to the violation of a tradition concerning their Sabbath, while they were blind to the wonder wrought in the case of this derelict specimen of hnmanity. A broken tradition was more to them than a healed man. It was then that Jesus said to them:

> " My Father worketh even until now, and I work."

As we ponder these words coming out of the deep consciousness of our Lord, that is the consciousness of His whole personality, we discover in them His understanding of the things He was doing. He linked Himself with God in activity, and it was as though He said in effect to these rulers, You charge Me with breaking Sabbath. You do not realise that God has no Sabbath, nor can have while men are lying in this derelict condition.

If we take the whole sweep of human history as we find it in our Bible, we see man revolting from heaven's high decree and ordinance, and so bringing upon himself suffering. We see more-over, that in the moment when man thus revolted, the rest of God was broken in upon. We read in Genesis that God created everything, saw that it was good, and rested from His work; but from the moment in which man sinned, and so involved himself in suffering, God became active with a new activity. Thus in this profound utterance of our Lord, He declared the restlessness of God in the presence of sin, and all its consequent suffering; and revealed the fact of the activity of God to end sin and suffering, and so to give men rest. Thus the word of Jesus spans the running centuries and millenniums. So long as humanity is derelict, God is restless with the restlessness that is the inspiration of activity, an activity that moves toward the recovery of man from his sin and suffering, and giving to him cleansing and completeness. All that lies at the back of this story, and makes it so supremely significant.

As we turn to watch the details of the story, we are first impressed with the fact that passing through Bethesda's porches He saw the man. It is, as we said at the beginning, a dramatic story, for He only spoke to this man three times. If we set the three sayings out, these are they.

" Wouldst thou be made whole? "

" Arise, take up thy bed, and walk."

" Behold, thou art made whole; no longer continue in sin, lest a worse thing befall thee."

In these brief sentences considered in relation to the man, and their effect upon him, the whole method of God in Christ with derelict humanity stands vividly revealed.

He first addressed to him a question, " Wouldst thou be made whole? " The Old Version rendered it, " Wilt thou be made whole? " That is not necessarily wrong, but it may mislead us if we think of the word " wilt " as a part of the verb to will, as decision made. The Lord was not addressing the man's will, but rather his desire. We may give an accurate interpretation to the question if we put it in this form, Do you want to be made whole? Thus in His first approach to the man our Lord invaded and challenged him in the realm of the deepest thing in human personality. This is not intellect; it is not volition; it is not emotion; but it is that which perhaps results from all these in a way, namely, desire. He appealed to him as to whether he was content with his condition, as to whether he was satisfied, or as to whether he would rather be made whole. That is always Christ's first approach to the human soul. If it should be so that that man had answered Him, or that any should answer Him quite truthfully, declaring satisfaction, then He had and He has no more to say.

But the effect produced was that he replied, evidently in tones of protest. He said:

" Sir, I have no man, when the water is troubled, to put me into the pool, but while I am coming, another steppeth down before me."

This cannot be read without the fact becoming apparent that his difficulty lay in his helplessness. If we can put ourselves into the personality of that man I think we shall understand it. Here a passing Stranger, for we are told afterwards that he did not know Jesus, looked at him, and asked this question. By so doing, He would rouse in the man something that had been almost forgotten by himself. His answer in effect said, The question is superfluous.

Of course I do not choose to remain in this condition. Necessarily I would rather be whole. Thus our Lord had reached the very core of his personality.

Yet there is more in his reply than that. The Lord's question having thus made him face his actual condition, and recognise the deeper fact of his desire, brought him to an open statement concerning his hopelessness. That hopelessness was born of his helplessness; and yet in the very fact that he thus faced his sense of hopelessness, one cannot but see springing up within him, a new and wistful dawn of hope. Here, as is so constantly the case, we have to account for what happened not in the mere letter of the story, but in the facts concerning the personality of our Lord. There was something in the look of His eyes, something in the tone of His voice, which made the man wonder what He meant, and wonder along the line of hope. The question of Jesus drew him to speak of the deepest thing of his life.

Thus we see this man, a morally depraved, physical derelict, a withered soul, implicitly confessing that the deepest thing in his life was the desire for wholeness. He told this Stranger that his case was hopeless, and yet by the very fact of his speech, revealed something which he saw in the personality of Jesus which arrested him, and called forth his speech.

It was at that point that Jesus spoke again, and said:

" Arise, take up thy bed, and walk."

I never reach that stage in the story without wanting to imagine that I was there, and that as an on-looker. Perchance I had often passed that pool, and seen that man; it may be, ever and anon, flung him a shekel and gone on my way. But here to-day I see a Stranger speaking to him, and I am arrested; and now I hear this Stranger saying to this man, " Arise, take up thy bed, and walk." Watching this, my first inclination is to make a protest and to say to Jesus, What do you mean by this? Do You not realise You are telling this man to do the one thing he cannot do? Do You suppose if he could rise and take up his mattress and walk, he would be lying there? What do You mean by telling him to do an impossible thing? But that is exactly what Christ did, and what He always does. He brings the soul face to face with the one thing that seems impossible, whatever it may be, and commands him to act at that point. Watching the scene again, and imagining my own attitude that of protest, suddenly I see the man doing the very thing, and I look at him walking away, carrying his mattress. That is Christianity in an almost blinding flash of glory. That is what Christ has been doing through all the centuries, bringing men face to face with the one thing that paralyses them, and enabling them to do the thing they could not do.

In this whole command of Jesus there is contained a complete programme. The first thing is " Rise "; the second is, " Take up thy bed"; and the third and continuous, is " Walk." At this point we ask properly and necessarily, How do we account for this? He could not do it, but he did it. If we allow ourselves for a moment to enter into the consciousness of the man we may state the process thus. This Stranger has asked me if I want to be made whole. Of course I do, but there is no chance. Yet there is something about Him that enables me to tell Him of my helplessness. While I am wondering, He commands me to do something I cannot. He must mean something by that command. I will obey, because He commands. In that moment, when the will of the man touched the will of God in Christ, he made contact with healing power, and there flashed across that line of connection, health of spirit, mind, and body. Two years later, our Lord referring to it said, " Made every whit whole." All this may be said to be mystical. It certainly is out of the realm of the mechanical on the earthly level, but it is equally certain on the level of the heavenly activity. The moment in which contact was made between the will of Christ for the man, and the will of man in obedience, enablement came to him.

Then followed the command, " Take up thy bed." I never come to that without abandoning exposition, and accepting the exposition that came years ago from the pen of Dr. Marcus Dods. He said, Why did Jesus tell that man to take up his bed, and walk? and his answer was " In order that he should make no provision for a relapse ! " The whole philosophy of Christian life is there. This man, acting in obedience, might have said, Well, surely I have risen, I am healed, but I have acquired a vested interest in this place, and perchance it would be well to leave my mattress there, in case this thing is not permanent. Had he done so he would have found himself back ere much time had passed. One secret of continuity in power of the healing which Christ brings is that we burn our bridges behind us, and cut ourselves adrift from the things that had blasted us.

The final word of Jesus in this sentence was " Walk." The value of that may be expressed if we say that our Lord warned him against wanting to be carried. Let there be constant action in the power of the healing received.

It is to be carefully observed that this man thus healed, made his way to the Temple. His physical disability, if not his spiritual and moral, had excluded him from those precincts. Directly he was restored, he crossed this threshold again, and there Christ met him, and uttered the last word:

" Behold, thou art made whole; no longer continue in sin, lest a worse thing happen unto thee."

Christ never says to anyone " No longer continue in sin " until He first says " Thou art made whole." As we make contact with Him in an act of willing surrender, He gives us the power which enables us to live no longer under the mastery of sin. The whole story is indeed a matchless unveiling of God in Christ, unable to rest while humanity suffers, working ever in order that sin may be dealt with, and suffering end.

XIII

THE LEPER

IT is quite impossible to over-estimate the value and importance of this story of the cleansing of the leper. Taken as a separate story, it is full of light, and indeed presents the evangel in a picture. If, however, it be taken in connection with the ethical Manifesto of Jesus, it is even more suggestive, and more wonderful.

Necessarily there is some slight difference between this story, and some others which have occupied our attention, because here we see our Lord dealing with physical disability; but here as indeed in all cases, the physical disability was the result of human failure, or as we may accurately say, of human sin. When we were dealing with the account of our Lord's healing of the man in the Bethesda porches, we emphasised the fact, which now we may once more refer to, because of its importance. All disease is ultimately the result of the breaking of law; but this does not mean that every person suffering from physical disease is so suffering on account of his or her own personal sin. There are multitudes of people in the world to-day suffering from physical disability through no sin of their own; but such disability is always the result of the breaking of the law of God somehow, or somewhere. In the healing of the sick our Lord was never violating the true order of life, but rather restoring life to its true order, which is always that of health. Therefore in dealing with this story we are not for a moment to look upon the leper as a sinner above all others, but we do remember that leprosy was ever the outcome of broken law somewhere.

Now, as we have said, if this story be taken in very close connection with the ethical Manifesto, it is found to be the more arresting. In that Manifesto our Lord had uttered the ultimate and final and perfect Ethic of human life. It has often been pointed out, and it remains an arresting fact, that all students of human life, and the laws which condition it, are agreed as to the high idealism of what we speak of as the Sermon on the Mount. It is said that it is not practicable, that men cannot live up to the standard revealed in it; and there is no doubt that such statements are perfectly accurate, while man is under the mastery of sin. It is not possible for any man to live according to the ideal of the Sermon on the Mount until he is born again. Many years ago Archbishop Magee declared that England cannot be governed on the lines of the Sermon on the Mount. For saying this he was severely criticised. If, however, men who criticised him then had read the context of his statement they would have seen that he was perfectly right. He was insisting upon the fact that humanity cannot be governed on the basis of the Sermon on the Mount until it is regenerated.

Notwithstanding this recognition of the high idealism of the Ethic, it is found to be at once searching, severe, and sublime. As we listen to the enunciation, our attention is fastened upon the Lord from Whose lips these great words fell, and as we watch Him not merely as He delivers this utterance, but through all the story of His life as we find it in this four-fold Gospel, we find that in His own character, in His own Person, He realised and revealed the meaning of His Ethic. In Him we have a revelation of the ideals He presented, realised in the midst of ordinary human conditions.

We commenced our reading at the end of chapter seven (vii, 28, 29) in Matthew, and there find a declaration concerning the effect produced by the ethical Manifesto upon the listening crowds. A reference to the opening of this Manifesto (Matthew v, 1) shows that it was not spoken to the crowds, but to His own disciples.

"And seeing the multitudes He went up into the mountain; and when He had sat down, His disciples came unto Him; and He opened His mouth and taught them."

Nevertheless, it is equally evident that the crowds gathered round and listened, for Matthew declares that at the close of the Manifesto, "the multitudes were astonished at His teaching." Moreover, continuing, he reveals the nature of their astonishment, "He taught them as having authority." That is a sufficient declaration, but Matthew goes further, and employs these significant words, "and not as their scribes." Now the remarkable fact is that in those days the scribes, the order of which had arisen under Ezra, and had been highly developed in the Maccabean period, were the authoritative teachers. Our Lord ratified their authority when upon one occasion He said:

"The scribes and the Pharisees sit on Moses' seat. All things, therefore, whatsoever they bid you, these do and observe."

The "therefore" refers to the position, "Moses' seat." In so far as they were interpreters according to that authority, they were in authority. Continuing, He said:

"But do not ye after their works; for they say, and do not."

Now the authority of Jesus was put by the people into contrast with that of these scribes. Matthew gives us no further explanation, but it is self-evident that His authority was such as commanded the consent of the human soul, however depraved that soul might be. The question of obedience does not arise at the moment, but the consciousness that what He had said, could not be gainsaid.

This is a somewhat lengthy preamble, but it is important in our present consideration. It was as our Lord was descending from the Mount, surrounded by His disciples and the pressing crowds that this most arresting thing took place. We speak of it as arresting in view of the Eastern atmosphere. A leper is seen approaching Jesus, a leper who is separated by law from all contact with his fellow-men. The question at once arises : What then happened? We have just been listening to the law from His lips, a law infinitely beyond, and infinitely severer than the law of Moses. In His enunciation of it He has carried conviction. What will be His attitude towards this leper?

Matthew describes the leper as approaching in an attitude of reverence, "worshipping Him." It is not necessary at the moment to read into that statement all that we now properly associate with worship. It does, however, signify that he approached Him as One to Whom he rendered obeisance, One Who was evidently superior to him. Then we hear him speak:

"Lord, if Thou wilt, Thou canst make me clean."

There was not a moment's delay. The answer in words, and in an act synchronised. Jesus said:

"I will; be thou made clean,"

and His hand was stretched out and put upon the leper. Immediately the leprosy was gone.

It is evident that this carries us at once far beyond the presentation of an ideal. The presentation of an ideal is one thing, and the taking hold of a derelict human being outside the pale of religion and civilisation, and restoring him, is quite another matter. Here our Lord is revealed in an entirely new aspect. We heard Him enunciate the final ethic. Descending from the mountain we see Incarnate Purity and incarnate pollution brought face to face, and there we have an illustration of the whole Christian enterprise. Now while the story is simple, there are two ways of looking at it. The first is that of considering the Lord and leprosy, emphasising the contrast. The second is that of looking at the Lord and the leper, the contact made, and the result issuing.

As we look at the Lord Himself, to repeat the phrase already used, we know we are looking at Incarnate Purity. He had told His disciples that unless their righteousness exceeded the righteousness of scribes and Pharisees, there was no value in it. The righteousness seen in the Lord Himself did exceed the righteousness of scribes and Pharisees; and indeed, that of moral teachers of all kinds. His righteousness consisted first in His perfect knowledge of God, and secondly, in His perfect conformity to the will and the character of God. We remember how, later on in His ministry, He declared:

" The prince of the world cometh; and he hath nothing in Me."

He is seen, therefore, the One realising perfection of human life according to the Divine ideal. Thus He is the One, and the only One in Whom there is the realisation of Absolute Purity.

With that in mind we turn to consider leprosy. If we want to understand what leprosy meant in that Eastern country, and in the Hebrew economy, it is good to read and study technically the law of the leper as found in the thirteenth and fourteenth chapters of the book of Leviticus. For the purposes of the present meditation we may summarise that law. First, it demanded that if leprosy were manifested, there must be an investigation on the part of the priests. There was an actual leprosy, and there was that which often appeared to be such, but was not actually so. The first investigation of the priest was concerned with that fact. If that investigation proved that the appearance was false, that it was not the real thing, then the person was segregated for eight days, certain religious sacrifices were made, and the appearances vanished. But if the leprosy were found to be actual, there followed the segregation of the leper. He or she must be put outside the camp, away from the possibility of coming into contact in any way with any other member of the nation. This means evidently that leprosy was then considered quite hopeless. Nothing could be done for the leper. The only action possible in its presence was that of segregation, and that in order to the well-being of the community.

Moreover, a careful study of the chapters referred to will reveal that to the Hebrew people leprosy was the ultimate symbol of moral malady. The whole ceremonial law emphasised this fact. Because of its nature, of its insidious beginnings, of its slow processes, of its destructive power, and the ultimate ruin wrought by it, it became a powerful symbol of moral depravity. It was a disease that baffled human skill. It is very arresting in passing to note that those dealing with the disease to-day are beginning to find that if taken in its early stages it may be cured. It nevertheless was in the ancient economy, a type of the uttermost moral depravity. All this makes the contrast the most arresting. The Lord Himself, having delivered His ethic, stands confronting a man suffering from the disease which in itself is the supreme symbol of moral depravity. Holiness in the flesh is standing face to face with sin in the flesh in its most terrible manifestation. That brings us face to face with our consideration.

We pause once more to look at the man himself. In the presence of the Lord his sense of need was quickened. He knew that need, and he knew that so far as all ordinary skill was concerned, his case was hopeless. Nevertheless he desired cleansing. As he approached Jesus with that sense of need, and that consciousness of helplessness, his anguish became the more poignant. For some reason he came convinced that Christ could deal with him. This is evident in his saying, " Lord, if Thou wilt, Thou canst." One cannot help wondering as the story is pondered, whether this man had been on the edge of the crowd listening to the Manifesto. If so he, in common with others, must have been filled with a sense of its finality in authority. It may be that he had heard of Jesus. It may even be that he had seen Him before. Evidently he was familiar with His power, and came confessing it. In this his faith is seen in excess of some other cases. As for instance, a man came to Him once saying:

" If Thou canst do anything, have compassion on us."

This man did not come questioning the ability of the Lord, but wistfully wondering whether He would be willing to help. He came steeped in his leprosy. Luke, the physician, in his account, describes him as " full of leprosy," which means to say that he was in the worst and most terrible stage.

Yet observe that his approach was a venture, a venture of hope, a venture of wistful desire, a venture born of his consciousness of his own condition, and of his desire for cleansing. He came, making that venture, with the halting " If." As we have said, he was convinced of Christ's ability, but halted as to whether He would be willing. In the very form of address, however, we discover a submission to the authority of the will of Christ. It is certainly arresting that he did not ask to be cleansed. He did not prefer a petition, but flung himself out in all his misery and dereliction, knowing the ability of Christ, and recognising the authority of His Will.

Now we turn to look at the Lord in the presence of the man, and to watch carefully His attitude toward him. We are first arrested by the fact that there was no manifestation of fear in the presence of leprosy. It is evident that He knew perfectly what power was resident within Himself, and therefore there was no fear. Moreover there was nothing of contempt in His attitude, and certainly there was no suspicion of despair.

His answer to the cry of the leper was immediate. We referred a moment ago to the man who came and said:

" If Thou canst do anything, have compassion on us, and help us."

Jesus answered him:

" If thou canst ! All things are possible to him that believeth."

This leper came with an " If," but it had an entirely different emphasis. The one man questioned His ability. This man submitted to His sovereignty. In answer to that, in a moment the " I will " was spoken, and the hand was stretched forth and laid upon him.

Here we pause a moment to recognise that there have been, and perhaps still are, expositors who find difficulty with the story at this point. They recognise that the law of Moses forbad any one to touch a leper, and they declare that if Jesus touched the leper He broke the law. An attempt is made to escape from the difficulty by saying that the law did not apply to Him. But this cannot be affirmed. He was " born under the law." He kept the law. He obeyed the law. Whereas He broke resolutely all the traditions that men had superimposed upon the law as to the law itself, He was obedient to its every yod and tittle. Then how are we to explain the narrative? Quite resolutely I do so by declaring that He never touched the leper, that is to say that when His hand rested on him, he was already cleansed. Jesus said, " I will," and at once stretched forth His hand; but quicker than the movement of the human hand was the activity of the Divine power, and the leper was cleansed. The touch laid upon him was a sacramental symbol of the fact that he was now cleansed. He that a moment ago cried out as a leper:

" Lord, if Thou wilt, Thou canst make me clean,"

was now a leper no longer; and in proof of it the hand of Jesus was laid upon him.

It will at once be seen that this story is a most remarkable unveiling. When Christ comes face to face with a human being suffering from the leprosy of sin, He ever quickens the sense of need, and makes it possible for that need to express itself in His presence. The approach to Him may be made haltingly. The one coming may even come as figuratively on crutches, with an " If." That, however, is enough as long as the appeal is made to Him, and the venture made upon Him. As there was cleansing virtue resident in Him for that physical disability of leprosy, so there is cleansing virtue in Him for the polluted moral nature. If that be not so, then we have no Gospel, and the world has no Gospel. The whole story thus reveals the peculiar and lonely glory of the Lord.

A little later on John was in prison, and was strangely perplexed because he could not understand the methods of the Master. He sent two of his disciples to make an enquiry, which revealed his dawning sense of uncertainty. To that enquiry our Lord replied by naming the things He was doing, and among the rest " the lepers are cleansed." He thus gave as one sign of His Messiahship His power to deal with that which was the supreme symbol of sin. Here, then, at the foot of the mount of the interpretation of morality, we see Him confronting a derelict, and cleansing him.

All this has its present value and application. The world is full of lepers, lepers in the spiritual sense, lepers depraved through sensuality, through passion, through pride. Formal religion and external ceremony cannot deal with them. Social laws can only deal with them as the Hebrew law did, by segregating them. It is quite possible to take such men and women and incarcerate them in prison. We are doing that all the time. Moreover, it is necessary. Only let us never forget that when we have put men or women in prison on the basis of a righteous verdict of guilty, we have put them there for the sake of society, and not for their own sakes. Prison will not cleanse moral depravity, or cure it.

What then shall be done with such leprosy, and with these lepers? There is one inclusive answer:

> " In none other name is there salvation; for neither is there any other name under heaven, that is given among men, wherein we must be saved."

But we have that Name, and it is our business to proclaim it, and to affirm without any hesitation, that the leprosy of sin can be cleansed, and man can be purified by the infinite grace and power of the Christ of God.

XIV

MATTHEW

OF the identity of Matthew and Levi there can be no doubt. It is evident that his name was Levi, and that he was the son of Alphaeus. The name, Matthew, indicates the fact of a change. Possibly and personally, I would even say probably, Jesus made the change. He changed Simon's name. He surnamed James and John, Boanerges; and it is more than likely that He gave Levi his new name. At any rate the name is in itself significant, meaning the gift of God. It is conceivable that if the Lord did thus change his name, in the change He indicated the value of this man to Himself, the gift of God. Necessarily this was not true of Matthew only, because as we remember in the final words of intercession recorded in the seventeenth chapter of John, our Lord spoke of all the apostles as of those whom the Father had given Him.

This man is introduced to us by the three evangelists. They all tell us of the fact that our Lord saw him as He passed by. Matthew and Mark simply say that Jesus saw him, using the Greek word *eido*, which had two values. It is often used of the fact of casual seeing; but it is also used in the sense of seeing and understanding. Luke who, as we have so often pointed out, claimed that his record was the result of careful investigation, tells us that Jesus saw him, but he does not use the same word. Our revisers have rendered the word employed by Luke, " beheld." It is a word which suggests a close, penetrating look.

Again, Mark in introducing him, named him Levi. Luke described him as a publican, and also named him Levi. Matthew giving his own account, does not say that Jesus saw Levi. He does not say He saw a publican. He says " He saw a man," whose name was Matthew. Notice that he employed the name Matthew, not Levi. Moreover in the story, he did not refer to the fact that he was a publican. Writing at this point his own history, he went back in memory to the day when Jesus called him, and said that " He saw a man."

Perhaps it may be considered that that is an unnecessary emphasis, and yet to me it is very suggestive. That is what our Lord always does, He sees a man. He knew this man was a publican. He knew his name was Levi. He knew he was the son of Alphaeus, but that which attracted Him, as ever, was the fact that he was a man. It becomes the more significant when it is remembered that Matthew's calling brought him into contempt with his contemporaries. Despite all these limitations, Jesus saw him as a man, and that Matthew records. It is true that when presently he is giving the list of those called to the apostolate, he referred to the fact that he was a publican. In that connection it is at least interesting to notice that in the names of the twelve given by Matthew, by Mark, by Luke, and again by Luke in the Acts, this is the only man whose calling is referred to. We know that others were fishermen, and in the case of some, certain political predilections were referred to. This man, however, is placed in the list, and his calling is declared, and this by himself, not by Mark, or by Luke. We now follow our method of attempting to see the man himself, and then watch our Lord's dealing with him.

In some ways the account of Matthew is very meagre, although no name is more familiar to us to-day. That familiarity is undoubtedly due to the Gospel which bears his name.

We have only two incidents in which he appears, and they are recorded in close connection by each of the three evangelists. They are those of his calling; and of the feast in his house. Here again it is interesting to observe that Matthew does not tell us that this feast was in his house, except by implication. Neither does Mark. But Luke tells us distinctly that he made a feast for Jesus and his fellow publicans, and sinners. We see him then when he was called, and at the feast in his house. So, therefore, we hardly see him except through the fact recorded by Luke that he made the feast and that immediately.

Again it is remarkable that we have on record no single word that Matthew ever spoke. When Jesus said to him, " Follow Me," we are not told that he said anything. He gathered the company into his house evidently with a definite purpose, but we are not told that he expressed a welcome to Jesus in words, or to anyone else. Andrew was a quiet man as we have seen, and Philip a slow man; but we have the record of something Andrew said, and something Philip said. At any rate it is well to remember, whatever value there may be in the fact, that he seems to appear to us as a quiet man with very little to say. Yet he was a writer, and has become the chronicler of the King, drawing the portrait of our Lord for us in the terms of Kingship, in full and final authority.

We know then three things about him; first that he was a Hebrew; secondly, that he was a publican; and thirdly, that he was a deeply religious man.

First, he was a Hebrew. It is possible that he was a Jew, but I do not personally believe that he was. His name Levi suggests not membership of the tribe of Judah or Benjamin, but of the tribe of Levi. It is more than probable that he was a renegade Levite or priest. The fact that he was a Hebrew, however, means that he was characterised by a justifiable pride, and an understandable narrowness. These things were true of all the Hebrews. It is true of the Hebrew people to-day. Every Hebrew is proud, justifiably so, of his race, of his history, of all the marvellous past. It stands out as an amazing fact that whatever may be the tyranny employed against him, the neck of the Hebrew is never bowed or bent. Of all these things Matthew, in common with his people was justifiably proud. In view of his situation, and the situation of his people and race at the time, he was understandingly narrow. That, in certain ways, is an excellent quality. We are cursed to-day with a passion for breadth. A little more narrowness would strengthen the whole host of the people of God.

The fact that he was a publican had also a distinct bearing necessarily upon his character. As we look at him we see him " sitting in the place of toll," at the head of the Lake, by Capernaum. Day by day, there, he demanded and received the dues from the fishermen as they brought in their fish, and from the merchants as they brought their goods across the sea by boat. He was in the tetrarchy of Herod. Herod was a vassal of Rome. All the tolls collected were for him as tetrarch, but they were arranged by Rome itself. It was part of the Roman Empire, and this man, held in contempt by his fellow countrymen, nevertheless knew that behind him was the whole Roman government. That, of course, is the secret of strength in government, this knowledge that its meanest officer has behind him all the strength of the Empire. It may be said in passing that that is our element of strength. If you attempt the crossing of a road, and you see the policeman hold up his hand, you stop, not merely because one man is doing it, but because the British Empire is behind that uplifted hand.

Then his calling demanded that he should be a careful recorder and renderer up of accounts. These publicans, all under Roman rule, had to gather payments according to a fixed Roman tariff. It is quite evident that they often extracted more than their due, and by so doing became rich; but they had to be men who knew how to keep accounts, and give reports.

The question may be asked, What has all this to do with Matthew? In reply we may say that it has a great deal to do with him and his character. He was a man living in the atmosphere of government. We may use our more modern phrase and declare that he was familiar with things imperial. With his consciousness of the power of the Roman government behind him, it is probable that he was somewhat careless, in common with his class, about the hostility of his own countrymen. All these things entered into his mental make-up. A man's calling does react upon his outlook and character in a very remarkable way. Matthew then was a Hebrew, justifiably proud, understandably narrow, with a consciousness of an authority under which he served, and of responsibility for accuracy in the keeping of records.

But the supreme thing about this Matthew, which perhaps does not appear upon the surface, is that he was evidently a profoundly religious man. Saying this I am speaking of the man before Jesus called him. The proof of the fact is found in his remarkable familiarity with the Scriptures of the Hebrew people; more familiar, if we may argue from his method than either Mark, or Luke, or John or Paul. It is impossible to study his Gospel without noticing this fact. His quotations from the Old Testament were more, not only than that of any one of the evangelists, but more than that of all the other three put together. To make an approximate mathematical statement, we find in his Gospel no less than ninety-nine direct references to the Old Testament Scriptures. Moreover he quoted from every division of the Hebrew Scriptures, from the Torah, or the law; the Nebiim, or the prophets; and the Kethubim, or the writings. Further, we see as he traced the story of Jesus he applied this knowledge. He applied it to all the history from the birth to the death, constantly referring to the Scriptures of the Old Testament. He has a peculiar formula which occurs nine times in the process of the story, " That it might be fulfilled." At least it is worthy of note that Mark never used it, neither did Luke, nor John. In his writing he told the story of Jesus as the result of his own intimate relationship with Him, and all the way he puts that story against the background of Old Testament Scripture, showing his familiarity with the Hebrew religious writings. Thus, though he may have been looked upon by his contemporaries as a renegade, he was no renegade from the Hebrew religion. He had studied their writings in a remarkable way, and we may safely deduce the fact that he was a profoundly religious man.

The two incidents referred to reveal one fact about him. When Jesus called him he responded immediately. Having thus been called, and having obeyed, he, with equal promptness, began to gather together a group of his own calling to meet Jesus. He was therefore a man of quick and decisive action.

We turn, then, to watch our Lord's dealings with this man. We notice first that He found him " sitting at the place of toll " in the midst of his work. We can readily understand that all the brooding of his mind lay behind the outward activity of the tax collector. There is every reason, too, to believe that being there in Capernaum, or in close proximity, he knew very much about Jesus. Our Lord had made Capernaum the base of His operations at this time. We also know from the writings, that by this time all the countryside was talking about Him. It is quite conceivable that sitting there at the place of toll, he had listened to Jesus as He had talked from the boat, or to the crowds about the shore. As he listened, his trained mind in the Old Testament Scriptures would discover much in harmony with them. I cannot read the story of his immediate response without believing that there had been this previous mental activity and attraction. Then one day there came a critical moment. Jesus passed him, and as He passed, He said to him, " Follow Me." It is easy to believe that the crowd who, perchance, heard the words, would hardly understand them. Dr. Alexander Maclaren of Manchester once described that word of Jesus addressed to Matthew, as a command. It certainly was that. It was sharp, decisive, authoritative. He did not speak to him as He had done to others. He did not ask him as He asked Andrew, " What seek ye? " He did not declare to him that He knew him, and his father, and that he should become Rock, as

He had done to Simon. He did, however, use exactly the same formula He had employed in speaking to Philip. To Matthew the call meant that he must sever himself from his relationship with Herod and Rome, that he was to leave behind him his means of livelihood, that he was to yield himself in complete submission to Jesus. It is well to remember here as in other cases, that whereas the word " Follow Me " was a command; it was also an offering of fellowship. He called this man not only to leave everything, but to find a Comrade for the coming pathway. Submission undoubtedly was demanded, but fellowship was offered.

And yet it meant even more than that. To travel with Him was to enter upon His enterprise. In this formula of Christ addressed to the soul, all these things for ever merged. The call brought Matthew face to face with a sharp crisis, a crisis resulting not merely from the call itself, but almost certainly from the process that had been going on in his mind as he had pondered the Sacred Writings with their hopes and aspirations, their songs and their teaching, their history and their prophesying. In Matthew we have a man who almost certainly, had been thinking through these things; and then with the stories about Jesus coming to him, had been wondering whether in Him was to be found a fulfilment of the national hope, and the soul's deep need. Thus the first call of Jesus crystalised his thinking, and created for him a crisis.

The result is self-evident. He rose, left everything then and there, and went with Jesus. I do not hesitate to affirm that the story of the action of Matthew is dramatic, as without the slightest hesitation, in quick, decisive obedience, he abandoned everything in obedience to the call of Christ. He left his table and his shekels, left Herod and Rome, and ventured out upon the new way along which the Lord was leading.

As we have seen, it is Luke who tells us that Matthew at once made a feast in his own house, gathered together men of his own class. It was in the best sense of the word an adroit movement on the part of Matthew. We know to-day that men can often be gathered to a feast, who would not come to a Prayer Meeting. It is good, therefore, to have a feast, if we are ever careful in the motive behind the invitation.

In this connection we see our Lord first, accepting the invitation. He went into the midst of that unwashed crowd.

By unwashed, necessarily I mean now, as they were looked upon by the rulers, religiously and ceremonially unclean. He went to the feast in authority. He went in companionship and co-operation with the man who had left all to follow Him. How evident it is that Matthew had already discovered the straight highway into the Heart of Jesus. He knew that that Heart was set upon the depraved and the degraded. So with the quickest intuition, born, shall we not say, of his familiarity with the Scriptures that had fore-told the coming of One Who should preach release to the captives, set at liberty them that are bruised; the gathering of this company was the creation by Matthew of an opportunity for the carrying out of those great purposes of grace.

This, moreover, was the occasion when the Lord used for Himself the word which is the keynote to all this series of considerations, as He referred to Himself under the figure of the Physician. He was criticised by the rulers for violating the sanctions of their traditions, as He sat eating with these people, looked upon as polluted and depraved. It was in answer to such criticism that our Lord, under this figure of speech, revealed the whole purpose of His life and mission. He declared that He had not come on behalf of good people, or holy people, or righteous people. He had come to reach sinners, morally sick folk; and He had come as the great Physician. As our Lord uttered these words in vindication of His attitude and activity, Matthew must have been conscious of a great satisfaction, that he had indeed understood the heart of Jesus, and that in his action his discipleship was vindicated, as travelling on the way with his Lord, his action was in accord with His purposes.

We may then inquire what was the outcome of the finding of this man? The answer is found in his Gospel, wherein he became the Royal recorder, and wrote for his own people especially, and through them for all men for all time the story that tells of the Redeemer Who is King, of the King Who is Redeemer; of the One Who came to regain the territory that had been blasted by sin, and bring it back into the place of beauty and of glory.

In all these stories there are particular and peculiar applications, and it would seem to me that the first value of the story of Matthew is one for those who have been brought up in the atmosphere of religion, who have come to know very much about God and about Christ, but who have never committed themselves to Him and to His enterprises.

There are crowds of such people around us in the world to-day. They are familiar with all the great facts of religion, familiar with the story of Christ Himself; yes, and in very many cases more than familiar. They are reverent, and oftentimes more than reverent, they are wistful and wondering.

To such we declare that Christ is as actually passing by as He was in the case of Matthew. Moreover He is saying to every such halting man or woman, " Follow Me "; cease your wondering, cease your questioning, cease your intellectual debating. Come and travel with Me, and find the answer to all your questionings in My comradeship.

Thus the call of Jesus brings people face to face with all the processes of the past, which excellent in themselves, have yet led to nothing like finality of value or of power. It brings such processes to a crisis. When at the crisis there is quick and ready response, and obedience, complete surrender to the Lordship of Christ, then there follows such discovery as will lead on to an entirely new experience of life in all its power and all its glory.

XV

THE MAN WITH THE PALSY

THE account of our Lord's dealing with the man suffering with the palsy, and brought by his friends into the presence of Christ is given by Matthew, Mark and Luke. The stories are complementary, and help us to a right appreciation of the event. Perhaps it may be said that it is of arresting importance, because it is the first occasion on record in the ministry of our Lord on which we are told that He declared a man's sins to be forgiven, His authority for the pronouncement being immediately challenged by the scribes and Pharisees.

We may remind ourselves in passing that we only have one other instance recorded where He made the same pronouncement, and that was to the woman in the house of Simon. There also His authority was challenged.

The matter is important, because this whole subject of the forgiveness of sins is the central one to the Christian Gospel. In a sermon recently preached in the City Temple, in connection with the London Missionary Society, President Whale of Cheshunt College, put the questions in simple form, " What is Christianity? " " What is the distinctive thing that Christianity has to proclaim to men? " And he answered his questions by the simple declaration, " The forgiveness of sins." There is no question that the answer was right. Christianity has many applications and values; but as a distinct message of God to man, it is the announcement of the possibility of the forgiveness of sins.

The story we are considering is one full of charm. Jesus had arrived at His own city, that is Capernaum, and was there teaching within a house, which was so crowded that no more could enter. One of the evangelists says no one could get near the doors. Of course, we remember that those Eastern houses were built round a quadrangle. In many cases these quadrangles were open, but in other cases they were lightly roofed over. There is no doubt that it was so in this case. In Luke's account of the story we find that the occasion was a special one in that there was gathered together an arresting company of people. He says:

> "There were Pharisees and doctors of the law sitting by, which were come out of every village of Galilee and Judaea and Jerusalem."

The time had arrived when these men were becoming critical of Jesus, and they had gone to Capernaum from these scattered places. It was really a gathering of experts in theology and religion.

While He was talking to them the interruption occurred. Suddenly something was taking place, which must have attracted a somewhat startled attention. The roof was being broken up. The way to that roof would be by a staircase outside the building, up which this little company had passed, carrying the man sick of the palsy. We can imagine how, notwithstanding the crowded condition of the house itself, room was made as the man was lowered into the midst of the assembly. We seem to be able to see him lying on his bed, in the presence of Jesus. Let us not forget that these learned doctors were watching the whole proceeding.

Now, following our regular method, let us attempt to see this man, and then watch our Lord's method with him.

As we look at him of course we first see him suffering from that terrible form of physical disability described as palsy. On that side, he was, quite evidently, a derelict. He could not walk. He had to be carried. As we proceed with the story it becomes evident that this, as in other cases, is one of a man suffering disability as the result of moral malady. This is proven by the fact that the first word our Lord addressed to him had to do with this question of sin. I think we are absolutely justified in believing that as he lay there, a physical wreck, in the presence of Christ, he was profoundly conscious of the reason for his condition, and therefore he would be filled with a sense of fear. That further is substantiated by the fact that our Lord addressed to him a word that bade him dismiss his fear.

I think, further, any careful observation of the man will show that however weak and trembling he was, he was conscious of some element of faith in Jesus. Speaking of the fact that he was brought to Jesus, the evangelist says, " When He saw their faith." Much has been written about that as to whether it was the faith of the men that brought him, or whether his own was included. My own conviction is that in that plural pronoun there was included his own faith, together with that of the men who brought him. To me it is inconceivable that he was carried there against his will. He was surely brought with his own consent. We need to remember that Capernaum was now the very centre of the activity of Jesus. This man would have heard the accounts of what He had been doing; and conscious of his own disability, both physically and morally, there would spring up within his heart a desire to be brought into contact with this great Healer and Teacher. Whether he had any hope that his sin could be dealt with we have no means of knowing. Probably not. But there was some measure, shall we say, of wistful faith which made him give his consent to his friends to bear him into the presence of the Lord. This, then, is a picture of the man, as far as we are able to see it.

Then we turn our attention to the Lord's methods with him, and we notice in passing that He said three things to him. The first was " Son, be of good cheer "; the second and central, " Thy sins are forgiven "; and the last, a little later, " Arise, take up thy bed, and go unto thy house." Between the second and the third of these words spoken to him, Jesus had something to say to the critics surrounding Him, which becomes part and parcel of the story, and is full of vital importance.

The first word, according to Matthew was, " Son, be of good cheer." At least that is how we have rendered it. As a matter of fact, the word used by our Lord, *teknon*, is not " Son." It is a diminutive, and a word of infinite tenderness. It may be rendered " Child." It is the word that the Virgin Mother had used to Jesus in the long ago. This in itself is very revealing. There the man lay, derelict physically and morally, filled with fear, and yet perhaps wistfully wondering, and Christ's first word to him was this tender word, " Child." He looked into his eyes haunted with the consciousness of sin, and wondering what this great Healer and Teacher would say; and the first word that he heard was the word " Child."

Then, and of course in immediate connection, the words, " Be of good cheer "; and here again I am anxious to get the full force of that, and so accept the rendering at once, " Be of good courage." In our common use of the words "Good cheer" the real force of the idea is lost. The address of Jesus so rendered, carries the thought which we express when we say, Cheer up. Well let it be at once recognised that that is the language of those who do not understand the human heart. To say to a man trembling with physical weakness, and haunted with moral malady, Cheer up, is at once an impertinence and an insult. This was not the word of the Lord to him, but rather "Be of good courage."

And here once more we will halt, for perhaps technical and yet very important examination. There are two Greek verbs both of them quite accurately rendered courage, and yet having an entirely different significance. The Greek verb *tharseo* refers to courage, but refers to courage subjectively. The Greek word *tolmao* also refers to courage, but it describes courage objectively. *Tolmao* describes a form of courage which is a very real one, which a man exercises in order to master his fear. The Greek word *tharseo* describes the courage resulting from the utter absence of fear. This is undoubtedly the higher form of courage. I do not undervalue for a single moment the courage which, in spite of fear, and indeed, in order to its subjugation, goes forward in activity. That is certainly a real courage. The courage, however, suggested by the word *tharseo* is a subjective courage, the courage which consists in an absolute absence of fear, which is a far rarer thing than the courage, which, in spite of fear, goes forward in activity.

A simple and homely illustration of what I have described as objective courage may be gathered from my own experience as a boy. In those days I hated dark rooms. Indeed, I still do. I have a distinct recollection even until this hour, of a day when my father sent me into a room in which there was no light, to get something and bring it to him. Now I was brought up in the day when if your father told you to do something, you did it! Therefore I went, frightened half out of my wits at the darkness, and as I went I whistled. Probably this would have passed entirely from my memory but for the fact that I heard my father say to my mother while I was in the midst of the darkness, "That boy is proving his courage. Listen, he is whistling." Simple as it is, I still hold it is a good thing to whistle when you are afraid; but it is a greater thing when you do not whistle, because you are not afraid.

Now after this somewhat lengthened preamble, we turn to enquire which of these words did Jesus use to this man? It was not *tolmao*, which means get up and act, and master your fear;

116

but rather *tharseo*, which means there is nothing to be afraid of; banish your fear. We may pause here to remark that we find in the records five occasions when our Lord used that form of address. To this sick man then He said this amazing thing, Do not be afraid. He was addressing Himself to the man's immediate consciousness. Palsied, he was shaking in every part of his body, and unquestionably his whole moral nature was quickened with fear. To him, then, Jesus said in effect, There is nothing to be afraid of. We can imagine that the man at first would say within himself, Nothing to be afraid of? I am a derelict, I am ruined, I am blighted by sin. It was to that unquestioned consciousness that our Lord said, " Child, be of good courage."

Then, without any pause, He immediately gave the man the reason for the banishing of his fear. He did it in the words, " Thy sins are forgiven." It was a simple sentence, but full of significance. Our Lord used the plural number " sins ", referring to all failures, all comings-short in life spiritually, morally, and therefore physically.

These, said our Lord to him, are forgiven. Once more we are in the presence of an arresting word. By a very literal translation we may render it, " Thy sins are sent forth." That by no means contradicts the idea of forgiveness, but interprets it. Thus, if our Lord's first words were addressed to that which was uppermost in his consciousness, as He said, " Child, be of good courage," the immediately following and connected word was addressed to the reason of his fear. Once more, as so constantly here, we must interpret by the Personality of our Lord. In that Presence the man had become more acutely conscious of his sin than even of his physical disability. He found himself lying in the light of those eyes which even then on the earthly level were eyes of fire. He was conscious of the penetrating glance, and unquestionably conscious of his own sin as he had never been before.

The tremendous nature of the word by which the Lord had declared that his sins were dismissed, was immediately challenged. Matthew says that the religious watchers for the moment without question with perfect sincerity said, " This Man blasphemeth." We have been born and brought up in a Christian atmosphere, and so have been familiar through all our lives with the idea of the forgiveness of sins. This is so much so that we are hardly startled to hear a reference to it. If we go back and listen to it as these men heard it from the lips of Jesus, and listen from their standpoint, we shall understand their protest. They realised that ultimately

117

the dealing with sin was possible only to God. Mark and Luke tell us that they asked the question:

"Who but God can forgive sins?"

For a moment let us say that in their outlook they were perfectly right. Necessarily I am not suggesting that they were right when they charged Him with blasphemy. They certainly were right when they declared none could forgive sins but God only. That inescapable truth in the moral realm is acknowledged by the whole Church of God, whether Protestant or Romanist. It may be said that the Roman Church claims that the priest forgives sins. Ultimately that is not true. The Roman Church claims that the priest becomes the mouthpiece of God. We are not in agreement with that statement, but the fact remains that what we have said is true; none has the ultimate right or authority to tell a man that his sins are dismissed except God Himself.

The answer of our Lord to these rulers was a very arresting one. He asked them:

"Whether is easier, to say, Thy sins are forgiven; or to say, Arise, and walk?"

In other words, He enquired whether it was easier to perform a task in the moral or the physical. The implied answer intended by the form the question took, was that these men were incapable in either realm. In effect our Lord told them they were quite right, that God alone could forgive sins; but it was equally true that God alone could deal with that physical dereliction. No man was able to say to this derelict, "Take up thy bed, and walk," and immediately produce the result. It was only God Who could do this. It was only a question of observation. The forgiveness of sins could not be seen. It was an inward and spiritual action. The healing of the body could be seen. It came into patent observation.

Therefore, our Lord said:

"That ye may know that the Son of man hath authority on earth to forgive sins,"

He turned to the man, and said:

"Arise, and take up thy bed, and go unto thy house."

Immediately the thing was done. He rose, rolled up his mattress, and went home. Thus they saw in the physical that which was an act of God, and it demonstrated the possibility of the act of God in the unseen realm which was moral.

We pause there to point out that all healing in the physical, the records of which we have in the life of Jesus, were activities of God. The great summary referring to such action is found in the first sermon in the light of Pentecost, in which Peter declared:

> "Jesus . . . a Man approved of God unto you by powers and wonders and signs, which God did by Him in the midst of you."

Every wonder wrought in the realm of the physical was the act of God through Him; and whether men realise it or no, God was seen working through Him. So with this man. Our Lord was demonstrating the fact that He had authority from God, which operated through Him in the realm of the physical, which was intended to be a demonstration of the fact that He had similar authority in the realm of the moral; and therefore was able to say, "Thy sins are forgiven thee."

All this concerning His authority in the realm of the moral is found stated in His own words recorded in the Gospel according to John.

> "Therefore doth the Father love Me, because I lay down My life, that I may take it again. No one taketh it away from Me, but I lay it down of Myself. I have authority to lay it down, and I have authority to take it again."

In that saying we find the great secret of authority given to Him to forgive sins. It was because of that, that He had the right and power to say to a man, Thy sins are dismissed. The matter is so full of importance that we pause a moment with this question of authority. It is not one of power, but of authority. The references to this are full of vital importance in the Gospel according to Matthew. The word does not often occur. Its first occurrence is at the close of the record of the Sermon on the Mount, when a multitude were astonished at His authority. The next reference is one we have been considering, when He claimed to have authority to forgive sins. The final one is found in the last chapter, when He said all authority in heaven and on earth had been given to Him. If we take these three outstanding references, we find His ethical authority, His redeeming authority, His governing authority. At the centre therefore is this word of redeeming authority, His authority to say to the troubled soul of man burdened with sin, "Thy sins are forgiven.

We come in conclusion to the third word spoken to the man:

> "Arise, take up thy bed, and go unto thy house."

As the word was spoken, unquestionably the power was imparted. The man who had heard Him say, " Thy sins are forgiven," and at least possibly may have wondered whether it was so, heard the command in the realm of the physical, and discovering his power to obey, found a vindication of the words:

" Be of good courage; thy sins are forgiven."

He knew by the physical deliverance that he was indeed loosed from his sins.

We close by reminding ourselves of that which we said at the beginning of the meditation that this is the supreme wonder and value of the story. Necessarily there are many things which are not told in the story itself. For fuller teaching we pass to other words that fell from the lips of Jesus, and for final interpretation to the teaching of the Holy Spirit through the apostles, as we find that in the letters of the New Testament.

The supreme revelation is that of Christ's authority in the matter of sin. He has that authority now. He still can say to the soul of man, " Be of good courage; thy sins are dismissed." That is, He can say to the soul of man what no human being has a right to say under any conditions.

If we would have the final explanation of this authority, this central fact of our Gospel, this message to the world; we discover it in words written by an apostle later:

" God was in Christ, reconciling the world unto Himself."

If Jesus be Man, and none other than Man, I can wonderingly admire Him, but I know that as Man He cannot deal with my sin. If God be in Christ, and if that be the interpretation of the Cross, and it surely is, then I know that upon the basis of eternal righteousness, God can through Him, forgive my sins.

XVI

THE MAN WITH A WITHERED HAND

THE story of the man with the withered hand is told by Matthew, Mark and Luke, and they all tell it in connection with another, that of a Sabbath day in the cornfields. Reading in Matthew and Mark it might appear that the two things happened on the same day. Luke, however, points out that the happenings in the cornfield took place on another Sabbath. The fact that the three evangelists have thus placed the two events in close connection reveals a connection of ideas, and we shall certainly approach the story of this man with a withered hand more intelligently if we realise this connection

In the cornfields we find our Lord rebuking the rulers for their ignorance of God. He used two illustrations to show how there were occasions when the Sabbath day seemed to be violated. The first was when David, entering into the house of God, ate of the shewbread. The second is that of the constant habit of the priests in offering sacrifices on the Sabbath. His rebuke for the rulers was contained in these words:

> "But if ye had known what this meaneth, I desire mercy, and not sacrifice, ye would not have condemned the guiltless."

With that in our mind we come to the story of the man with a withered hand. The rulers did not know God, and when men do not know God they are always interested in trivialities, such as the tithing of mint and rue and anise and cummin. When men know God, they know that the passion of His heart is ever full of understanding and mercy. If David be hungry, he may eat of the shewbread, and the priests are warranted in doing things on the Sabbath, for in neither case was its real sanctity violated.

Each evangelist records the fact that it was in this connection of the rebuking of the rulers in the cornfields that our Lord also claimed Lordship of the Sabbath.

In this story of the man with the withered hand He was revealing and illustrating the activity of God in mercy, of which the rulers were ignorant; and He was interpreting His Lordship of the Sabbath by what He did. Had they had minds and hearts capable of understanding, they would have come to a new appreciation of the Sabbath and its value.

In this connection Mark tells us, what none other does, that His action in connection with this man was the outcome of His anger with the rulers. In passing it may be noted that in this Gospel more than in any other, we have a revelation of the capacity of our Lord for anger. Here He was angry, angry on behalf of the man, angry with the hardness of heart, and misunderstanding of the rulers, due to their ignorance of God.

Now with that background we turn to the story itself, and here we have to recognise at once that it is the account of the Lord's dealing with a physical disability. The way in which this statement is made is interesting. Literally the statement should be rendered, "A man who had his hand withered," and the participial form of the verb shows that it was not congenital disease. It was either the result of an accident, or of contracted disease. It was undoubtedly a case of disability resulting from some breaking of law in some way, at some time. All that has its bearing on the story; but we recognise at once that there is no reference here to moral or spiritual values. These facts may suggest a difficulty in dealing with the subject in our present series. Our supreme interest is in the work of our Lord as the Great Physician; and that work was always fundamentally and ultimately in the realm of the spirit. Nevertheless as we come to the story we come remembering a truth which many years ago I heard crystalised by Dr. Arthur T. Pierson, as he said, " Every parable of Jesus was a miracle of wisdom, and every miracle a parable of teaching."

Remembering that, as we approach an account of that which lay wholly within the realm of the physical, we nevertheless remember that in all our Lord's attitude He never divided between the physical and the spiritual. He never recognised our division of life into the secular and the sacred. All the things which we call secular became sacred when He touched them and dealt with them. Therefore, when He dealt with physical disability, He acted in conformity with the same laws, and observed the same principles which characterised His action when more directly and more evidently He was dealing with the moral and the spiritual. In this story then we may certainly say that spiritual law is illustrated in the natural world. As we watch Him, then, dealing with this disability, we shall see how He acts in the presence of spiritual necessity and moral turpitude. In that way we may consider the story, applying as we go.

Let me begin with a word of application. Let our consideration of the story make its appeal to any who may be conscious of some disability in the spiritual realm, or in the moral realm, conscious of some withered and atrophied powers.

Following our usual method of first of all endeavouring to see the man, there are only a few things which reveal him. The first arresting fact is that he was found in the synagogue, which really was unusual. He would not have been allowed in that condition to enter the Temple, and it was not easy to find a place in the worship of the synagogue. Nevertheless he was there. Possibly he had been a regular attendant, going quietly in from Sabbath to Sabbath, and therefore a worshipper, notwithstanding his disability. It is evident that he was known, or that he had been discovered by the rulers, and they would be familar with the fact that he was suffering from a withered hand. Without understanding the reason of it, it is quite evident that his hand was withered and useless. He could not extend his fingers. They could grasp nothing. He could not put his hand to a plough. He could not take hold of the tools of a carpenter. I repeat, these religious rulers were evidently acquainted with the fact, for this is revealed in that when Jesus entered the synagogue, they immediately connected Him in their thought with that man. They were opposed to Him. They were hostile. They were seeking for an opportunity to bring a charge against Him in the moral or the ritualistic life; but though they were ignorant of God, they knew enough of Jesus to connect Him with that man. If we may reverently say so, they paid Him that unconscious compliment as He entered the synagogue. They did not expect Him to be concerned with those who occupied the chief seats in the synagogue. They did expect Him to have something to do with that crippled man.

Two things, then, that we see in this man, are those of his disability, and of the fact that he sought the place of worship. We have no suggestion in the story that he was seeking healing.

There is no account of any appeal he made himself to Christ. He was certainly conscious of his own disability, but in some measure he was conscious of God, and found his place among the worshippers.

In dealing with this man our Lord spoke to him twice. His first word was a command, " Stand forth," or quite literally, " Arise, into the midst." Evidently the man was seated somewhere in the synagogue, and our Lord first of all called him to come into the place of observation. The second word was the personal, direct command, " Stretch forth thy hand."

It is an arresting fact that our Lord in this case separated the man from the crowd, and brought him, with his disability, into view. The man immediately obeyed. Here as so often, we are halted by things which are not recorded in so many words. It is evident that there was something in the very tone and manner of Christ which produced that obedience. Most likely also there was lurking in the mind of the man when he heard the command of Jesus, a wondering hope that the great Teacher and Healer was about to do something for him. There may be some element of speculation in these statements, but the fact remains that our Lord brought him into a place of visibility in order that what was about to take place might be seen by all.

Then came the quick, brief and definite command, " Stretch forth thy hand," which may be rendered quite literally, Extend thy hand. The Greek word here is very full of suggestiveness, revealing the fact that our Lord called for an activity in the hand that was quite limp and helpless. At this point in the story we find ourselves face to face with the same underlying principles that occupied our attention when we were considering the story of our Lord's dealing with the man in Bethesda's porches. If we place ourselves in imagination in that synagogue, we shall the better understand the thing that happened. Let us imagine that we were among the number of those attending that synagogue, and that we know the man, that we have seen him often enough; that it may be at times we have felt a passing pang of pity, as we have realised the helplessness of his condition. Now on this Sabbath day we hear Jesus tell this man to stretch forth his hand. Inevitably our first reaction, as we listen, will be a consciousness of the man's inability to do what he is told. To stretch forth that hand had probably been the desire of years, and with equal probability, the attempt had been made unnumbered times, perhaps especially in the earlier years of his suffering. He had felt the life forces of his body, and earnestly wished that they would pass into those fingers, but it was an impossible thing, and therefore simply on the level of human observation, we declare that because it was impossible, the command was unreasonable. Why should this man be brought out and placed in the midst of a watching company, and told to do what he is unable to do? The command appears to be a mocking of the man's impotence.

Now necessarily this line of argument raises a sense of impatience among us. Nevertheless it is good to face the matter in that way. As we do so, still using our imagination, we turn from a contemplation of a withered hand, and look at the face of Jesus. The moment we do this, we know that the command is possible because He commands it, however impossible it may appear. To look into that face must inevitably have meant to be perfectly certain that He was not there to reveal disability, save as He was also there to put an end to it. If He thus commanded the disabled man to stand in the presence of the crowd, that the crowd might see him, it was in order that presently he might return, seen of the self-same crowd, with his disability completely cancelled.

The thing so often insisted upon is once more evident here. and it is that behind the words of Jesus there is always the Person, Artists have attempted to portray Him, and as a rule have failed. But we know Him through sanctified and spiritual imagination well enough to be sure that when His eyes rested upon that man, and He commanded him to stretch forth his hand, there was shining from those eyes the very mercy of God, of which the rulers were ignorant. The pity and the compassion of God were focussed in the glance of the Son of man. While, therefore, we may be inclined to argue as to the impossibility and the unreasonableness of the command, we see the impossible become possible as the hand is stretched out.

That being so, then evidently the command was not unreasonable. It was reasonable to tell him to do what the Lord was enabling him to do.

If we lift all this, as we have the right to do, into the realm of the spiritual, we see once more the fact that Christ always brings men face to face with the impossible, and lays upon them a command that in their own strength, they cannot obey. But we see further the reasonableness of His command, because He is waiting to communicate the very power that is necessary for obedience.

We listen to the Old Testament command:

> "Let the wicked forsake his way, and the unrighteous man his thoughts";

and we say, we cannot obey. We listen to the words of the Lord Himself:

> "If any man will come after Me, let him deny himself."

and we say, That is what we are utterly unable to do. That is where Christian experience always begins. If men are endeavouring to be Christians by cultivating certain pleasant ideas which are involved in the Christian message, they have not begun to know what Christianity really is. Christ ever compels us to face our own disability, and that in the realm of the impossible, and commands us to begin there, in a moral action of power.

If we are perfectly honest we shall find that our inability to forsake our way of wickedness, or to deny ourselves, consists in our halting at some one thing in the life which has gained evil mastery over us, some habit, some propensity. If we are not Christian, the reason is to be found in ourselves; and as I have already said, almost invariably at some central point. I cannot stretch forth my hand, I say. He says, Stretch it forth. I cannot master this evil thing, I declare. He says, Master it. As long as I am looking at myself, His commands are impossible and unreasonable. But the moment I look at Him, I find they are both possible and reasonable.

The sequel to the story is evidence of all I have said. The man stretched forth his hand, and the people in the synagogue saw him do so. They saw that hand, which had been limp and nerveless and useless, restored; until as one of the evangelists puts it graphically, it was "whole as the other." The wonder had been wrought.

When we enquire how this is to be accounted for, we realise first of all the man was conscious of need, and never more so undoubtedly than on that Sabbath day, when he stood facing the Christ. Then as he heard the command, there was a venture, a venture of trust, something in the Person of our Lord that called forth a response of obedience; and he immediately found that in that act he was enabled to do the thing that was impossible. As he in obedience made contact with the power of Christ, that power became his enablement. It was not a case of waiting to obey until there was a consciousness of healing. It was obedience to a word of command, and it was in that action of the will that contact was made with power.

126

It is readily seen how all this illustrates spiritual values. To receive the benefits that Christ is ever waiting to bestow, there must first be a consciousness of need; or to use at once the old theological phrase, a conviction of sin. It is when the soul is saying, perhaps not in words but in the inner consciousness, I would do good, evil is present with me, that a man is coming into such relationship with Christ as will make possible His saving activity.

Then there must be within the realm of the will, determination to obey the command, however impossible it may seem. It is by that action that the power of Christ is communicated, and the shattered powers, the weak, nerveless longings, the atrophied forces all become instinct with life and power. Paul's final word in experience was not, " When I would do good, evil is present with me," but rather, " I can do all things in Him that strengtheneth me." The whole secret is that of disability making contact with ability, and thus ceasing for evermore to be disability. A homely illustration may be used, that namely of the electric cars that are operated by contact with an overhead wire. We look at the car standing perfectly still and in darkness. In that outstretched wire there is all the power that is needed to bring light and motion to that car. When presently we see the long arm move, until it makes contact with the wire, we see the car at once lit and empowered for movement.

Reverently we may say that in the Christ of God is all the power that is needed for the removal of moral and spiritual disability, and in the moment in which the will of man, in an act of obedient faith makes contact with Him, the results are assured.

Thus in all our consideration of the story we have seen its application. The trouble with us has so often been that we hesitate and fail to obey at the word of command, the word which calls for complete abandonment and obedience, in spite of all the consciousness of weakness and disability. There is a hymn which was very often sung in days that are gone, and may sometime still be sung, containing words which are most revealing:

> " I can but perish if I go,
> I am resolved to try,
> For if I stay away, I know
> I must for ever die."

That may sound like a counsel of desperation, but it is the very desperation that is needed. It is when we face the impossible, and dare to say as in the presence of Christ, I cannot do this thing, but I will at Thy command, then in a moment the " cannot " is cancelled, and the " can " becomes the mighty truth concerning life. " He stretched it forth, and it was restored whole as the other."

I am now venturing to add something that is not found in the story, but is nevertheless implicated and true. Once more imaginatively I look at the man with the hand made whole. Supposing he had looked at his own hand and said, It is indeed wonderful. I have not felt the pulsing power in these fingers for many years. I can now stretch them forth. I can use this hand. I am able to grasp something. It is all so wonderful that I had better take care of this hand in a special way. In order to do it, supposing the man had called for bandages, and had carefully enswathed that hand. Then supposing he had carefully placed it in his bosom, in order to take care of it. What would have happened? The answer is inevitable. It would have withered again. The only way in which the strength of that restored hand could be maintained was by using it.

Our Churches to-day are filled with men and women whose hands have been cured, and they are so carefully taking care of spiritual life that that life is withering. Let all such accept this added illustration, and learn that the new power which has been communicated to them has, as the secret of its maintenance, the activity of service.

XVII

THE CENTURION

THE story of the centurion is recorded by Matthew and also by Luke. In reading them there does at first appear to be some discrepancies between them. As we shall see, these disappear on careful consideration. So marked are they, however, that there are those who believe we have two separate occasions on which our Lord dealt with the same sick slave of the same centurion. That, however, is a most improbable solution.

As we read the story in Matthew it does appear as though this centurion came to Jesus himself, and preferred his request, and so received the answer of our Lord directly. On the other hand, Luke distinctly says that he sent elders, and did not come himself. Now there is an old Latin saying, which being freely translated reads, "What one does through others, one does himself." There can be no reasonable doubt that that is the explanation of these two accounts. We have to remember here as always, that Luke claims in his preface that he traced the course of all things accurately, which means that he sifted his material. In this case it is evident that he got particulars which by no means contravened Matthew's account, but in a sense explained it. We repeat, then, that Matthew says he came to Jesus, and Luke declares the same thing, only that he did so through others. In our consideration we shall take the story as given in Luke. That means that in all likelihood this man did not meet Jesus at all, but reached Him through others, and received an answer to his request in power, our Lord acting upon his suggestion, that He should not go into his house.

It is well to remind ourselves that all the scenes of the New Testament are revealed in the atmosphere of Roman government. The earliest stories are connected with Roman taxation, and the latest glimpse of the historic in the New

Testament is that of a house in Rome, in which there was a prisoner named Paul. We are conscious of the Roman empire all the way through.

It is also noticeable that we constantly come into contact with the Roman armies, as we read of cohorts, of legions, of bands, of officers, captains, centurions, and of soldiers. In passing we may remind ourselves that in our reading of the New Testament we are brought into contact with seven centurions, and the remarkable thing is that every one of them presented seems to have been of a fine type. I think there is a reason for this, which reason, by the way, emerges in our present study. They were all men living under discipline, and that in itself is a valuable thing.

The story is peculiar in some ways, because this man did not come to Jesus on his own behalf, but rather on behalf of another. Nevertheless it cannot be read without producing the conviction that what happened had a remarkable effect on the man himself.

If the stories as given by Matthew and by Luke are read with care, and combined, we have some arresting things revealed, concerning the centurion. We find first three opinions expressed. The first was that of the rulers of the synagogue, who said that he was " worthy." It is good to remember here that he was not a Hebrew, but a Gentile, this being proven by the fact that these elders said " he has built us our synagogue," showing that he was an outsider. This was further proven by the fact that when our Lord spoke of him, He said He had not found so great faith in Israel. Of this man the elders said he was worthy, because he had built them a synagogue. Thus we see a man outside the covenant, evidently attracted by what he had seen within the Hebrew religion and economy, so much so that he had built this synagogue.

The second opinion is his own opinion of himself, and we find that in a double statement. First, he said:

"I am not worthy that Thou shouldest come under my roof."

The word " worthy " in this case means sufficient; and he was declaring that he did not feel he could offer to Jesus the hospitality that was due to him. His home was not a worthy home for Jesus to enter. It was almost certain that this centurion knew a good

130

deal about Jesus, and in all probability was aware of the fact that He was constantly moving hither and thither. Possibly he had heard Him say, or had heard that He had said that He had no home:

> "Foxes have holes, and the birds of the heaven have nests, but the Son of man hath not where to lay His head."

Notwithstanding these things, peradventure he was familiar with them, he realised that his home was not good enough for such as Jesus.

Then immediately he used the same word the rulers had used when they said, "He is worthy," as he said:

> "Neither thought I myself worthy to come unto Thee."

In this two-fold opinion of himself as expressed, we have a remarkable revelation of the man himself.

Finally, we have our Lord's opinion of him, when presently He declared that he was a man of greater faith than He had found anywhere within the chosen nation.

Another incidental fact is really very revealing. This man was a Roman. That may not mean that by race he was, but nationally he was. Moreover, he was a centurion, that is, one who had under him one hundred soldiers, and this in all probability, in the court of the kingdom of Herod. Thus he was closely linked with the Roman empire, and its outlook on life. It was this man who said he had a bond-slave and that that bond-slave was dear to him. That is entirely foreign to the Roman outlook on slavery. Thus the man himself is seen to have been of higher ideals than the system in which he lived.

But now let us look a little more closely as he stands before us Christ-appraised. His incidental and certainly unintentional revelation of himself appears in what he said to Jesus. Christ's estimate of him is seen in the familiar words to which we have already referred, and to which we shall come back for a little closer examination.

Of himself he said he had:

> "Under myself soldiers, and I say to this one, Go, and he goeth; and to another, Come, and he cometh; and to my servant, Do this, and he doeth it."

All this he had prefaced by the declaration:

> "I also am a man under authority."

Over him were his superior officers, and over them the emperor himself, all the final authority of that system being vested in the emperor. This centurion therefore was dedicated to the cause of the State as it was personified in the emperor. When he said he was a man under authority, he meant that his life was completely submitted to a central will. Of course this was very absolutely so in the case of these Roman soldiers. A soldier was not permitted to say that he had a will of his own. His time was not his own. His dress was chosen for him. His food was chosen for him. By the law of Rome, no Roman soldier could hold any possessions. Indeed, he could have said he had no will of his own. He knew nothing practically about prosperity, and nothing about adversity. If he had kith or kin, they could make no claim upon him. Thus, when the centurion said he was under authority he was revealing the life he was living, and showing that such submission to authority fitted him for his work. Possibly he had never seen the emperor, and would never see him; but to him the emperor was the centre of life. Every march he took, and every action he performed he did under that authority.

Therefore he was able to say that he had soldiers under himself, over whom he exercised authority. He said to one Go, and he went; to another Come, and he came; and to another, Do this, and he did it. No question could be asked. His one hundred men yielded to him the same obedience as he yielded to the emperor. Thus we see the two facts merged in the life of this man. He was under authority, and therefore was in authority. The authority he exercised over his soldiers was the authority to which he was himself obedient. To state the whole case again with yet more brevity, it means that the secret of his authority over his soldiers was his submission to the authority over him. In the case of his life there was ever the upward look to the authoritative throne, and the downward look in the interest of that throne to those who were under his control. He made this statement of his own position the basis of his plea to our Lord.

Now we may at once turn to see how Christ dealt with him. And first we notice that He declared him to be a man of surpassing faith as he said:

"I have not found so great faith, no, not in Israel."

Now it is of the utmost importance that we understand that the nature of his faith was revealed in the very words we have been considering, and in his appeal to Christ on the basis of the facts concerning himself, which he had declared. That it was of an unusually intelligent nature is revealed by this appraising by Jesus.

Let us ponder the intelligence of it. This man did not say to Jesus, " I am a man under authority," but rather, " I *also* am a man under authority." In other connections I have often referred to the importance of the little word, " also," and here it is of supreme importance in order to an understanding of what he said to Christ. Implicitly it recognised the fact that Christ was under authority, and therefore was in authority. He had discovered somehow that our Lord was living by exactly the same philosophy of life as he was. His message meant then, Because Thou art submitted to authority, Thou art in authority, and therefore art able to deal with this difficulty of disease. We have surmised before that he may have known of Jesus before this time. We do not forget that Capernaum was the base of our Lord's operations during this Galilean ministry. This man in all probability knew how in earlier days Jesus had healed the nobleman's son without going to him, by a spoken word. He may have been familiar with many other facts concerning the work of our Lord. At any rate this word " also " shows that he had a remarkable apprehension of the truth concerning all that Jesus was doing. He recognised that He was in authority, and that all forces would obey Him, because he recognised also the nature of the authority to which our Lord was Himself submitted. Somehow this man had seen to the very heart of the truth concerning Jesus.

We may pause with this matter for a moment. Reminding ourselves that later on in the ministry of Jesus He said, " All authority hath been given unto Me," we declare emphatically that this was the case, because He had always been perfectly yielded to the one Supreme Authority. In all the account of His ministry we find manifestations of this fact. He ever acted and spoke in the consciousness of the Throne of God, and of His relationship thereto. He said, " I can of Myself do nothing," " As the Father taught Me, I speak . . . I do always the things that are pleasing to Him," " The things which I heard from Him, these speak I unto the world." Thus being for ever under that authority, He was in the place of complete authority, over demons, over disease, over all the forces of Nature. This centurion had discovered this truth, and he based his plea for the action of Jesus upon that abiding fact.

133

While his faith was thus characterised by his supreme intelligence, we notice how self-effacing he was in this connection. Said he:

"I am not worthy that Thou shouldest come under my roof."

This was the man who had spoken of himself as a man under authority, and in authority. Nevertheless in the presence of Jesus he realised that his dwelling was not a fit place in which to receive Him, nor he himself fit company for the Lord.

But again, this intelligent and self-effacing faith was active. He first sent the elders of the synagogue, which he himself had given to the people. It may be on the human level he imagined they would have more influence with Jesus than he personally could possibly have. Then when he found the Lord was approaching his dwelling, he sent some of his friends, most probably of his own kith and kin, with the request that He would speak the word of healing. All this was faith in action. We repeat, then, his faith was intelligent, self-effacing, and active; and of this faith our Lord said:

"I have not found so great faith, no, not in Israel."

Thus in observing the method of Christ with the man, we notice first that He recognised his faith, understood it, and appraised it at its full worth. Necessarily no appeal can be made against His finding. We have already seen the faith of Andrew, and the faith of Simon, the faith of John, the faith of others; but our Lord distinctly said among all these, He had not found faith so great as that of the centurion. It is in this connection that we are told He marvelled. We must not read into that word the element of surprise. He wondered with a wondering approbation. Here once more it is arresting to remind ourselves that we are only twice told in these Gospel narratives that Jesus marvelled. This, of course, is one of the cases where He marvelled at faith. The other is recorded by Mark when he tells us that in the synagogue at Nazareth He marvelled at their unbelief. Two things so stupendous that they created marvel in the mind of our Lord; the faith of this centurion, and the unbelief of His fellow-townsmen at Nazareth.

Then it is arresting that He not only recognised the greatness of this man's faith, but drew the attention of the crowd to it. He thus manifested His appreciation of the value of his faith, and proclaimed it. If as we have surmised, Luke's account is strictly correct, the man was not there as to bodily presence, but our Lord expressed to the people round about Him His appreciation of his faith.

He then laid a command upon the centurion. Matthew records His word to him as being:

" Go . . . as thou hast believed, so be it done unto thee.'

Here there is great significance in that first little word " As." The man's intelligent self-effacement and active faith was now called upon to rest in the assurance that what he desired was granted to him. Our Lord was accepting the man's estimate of His secret of authority. He called upon him to put that faith into practice. As he had confessed His authority as being vested in His submission to eternal authority, let him now carry out the philosophy of his belief, and seek for his servant as healed.

This is another of the stories in which the name of the man does not appear. We do not see him again in the narrative. What we do know is that Jesus acted, and because He was under authority He spoke with authority, and the disease from which the slave was suffering was dismissed.

The abiding value of a meditation like this is self-evident. Its first element is that of the philosophy of life which was revealed by this man as that of the Lord Himself. We see our Lord ratifying it, accepting it, acting upon it. We hear Him moreover calling upon the man who professed that philosophy, to an action harmonious with it; and upon the man's obedience, granting him the desire of his life.

Every man and woman is living by that philosophy. Each one is in authority in some degree. Each can say, Go, and be obeyed; Come, and thus command answer. Each can say Do this, and find it done, either to persons or ideas. We are all in authority.

But it is equally true we are all under authority, and ever behind the order Go, is the order obeyed. There is always the authorising Throne. It is of the utmost importance that we recognise this to be an explanation of life. We know that it applied to the whole Roman empire, and in the last analysis revealed the secret of the greatness of that empire. Then it may at once be said that the Roman empire proved at last to be a disastrous failure. What was the reason of this? The answer is self-evident. It was because the ultimate authority was rotten. However obedient the soldiers were, however obedient the centurions were, the throne was occupied by one who was self-centred, a tyrannical despot, lustful and impure. The authority of that throne ultimately percolated through all submitted to it, until the whole empire, living by a true and necessary philosophy, became corrupt and defiled, and was blasted and ruined.

Such consideration reminds us immediately of the fact that the true ultimate authority for human life, whether individually, socially, or nationally, is that of the Kingship of God. When men are submitted to that Authority, they remain in authority; but the authority they exercise will be the result of the authority they obey.

The question, therefore, that must ever confront us is that as to whether we are submitted to the Authority of that eternal Throne. It is not enough to hold it as an accurate conception. It is not enough to confess it theoretically. The question abides as to whether we are really under this Authority.

If we are not under the Authority of the Throne of God, we are still in authority, but the authority we are exercising over our children, over our friends, over those with whom we come into contact, is the authority that we obey. If that authority is debased, then ours is depraved. This is surely the clear light that is shining upon our lives from this narrative of the centurion. Let us ever bear in mind the words of Jesus concerning him:

" I have not found so great faith, no, not in Israel."

XVIII

SIMON, AND THE WOMAN, A SINNER

THE subject of our meditation this evening is peculiar to
Luke. In it we see our Lord in contact with two personalities.
We are compelled to consider them together, because His
method with each is revealed in that with the other. In some of
our studies, whereas two people are seen together, they are still
so separate as to our Lord's methods, that they may be considered
in separation.

The city in which these events took place is nameless, and so
is the woman. Reading the story, although we remember Luke
is never strictly chronological, it would appear that He had
recently been in Nain, which was twenty-five miles from
Capernaum. The city referred to may have been Nain, or He
may have gone back to Capernaum, and so it may have been
Capernaum. The namelessness of the woman is characteristic
of the Gospel stories, for no woman specifically a woman of sin,
is ever named.

Whatever the city may have been, the two persons presented
to us represent two remarkable extremes. They are the extremes
of social position, and almost surely also of the locality of their
residence. The fact that in our story we find them under the
same roof is wholly due to the presence of Jesus. Luke is careful
to tell us that when this woman knew that He was there, she
went in. I do not hesitate to say that she had never been in that
house before. Simon's dwelling would most probably be in a
residential quarter, and the woman's somewhere nearer the crowded
area of the city. Simon was a man who undoubtedly would be
careful never even to be seen in the district in which this woman
had lived and plied her trade.

As we look, we see these two under the same roof, with Jesus
between them. Simon would be on His left hand, at the head

137

of the table, acting as host. The woman, we are told, was behind Him. Kipling told us that West and East shall never meet. There may be an element of truth in that on the human level, but social differences constantly meet in the presence of the Lord. We are to observe Him, then, dealing with these two people from two entirely separated localities, of absolutely different social positions. Our business, then, is first to see the two persons, and then to watch the great Physician dealing with them.

As to Simon, we are told that he was a Pharisee. This oft-times repeated description in the New Testament it should be remembered, marks him as to his religious position, distinguishing him from the Sadducee. It means first of all that his religious conceptions were spiritual rather than naturalistic. If that tells the story of his fundamental religious position, we further know that he, in common with those of his order, was a ritualist, and withal a traditionalist, holding as our Lord said upon one occasion, the traditions of men rather than the commandments of God. Necessarily the Pharisees imagined that while thus holding the traditions of men, they were interpreting the commandments of God. This was their error, just as there are many people to-day, holding to some creed, and imagining that they are obedient to the commandments of God when they have no living relationship with them. There is no need to enter at all in detail into the matter; but we need to remember how tradition had been placed upon tradition in supposed interpretation of law, until the people were burdened beneath them. As our Lord said upon occasion, these men were binding heavy burdens upon others which they themselves did not lift with their little finger.

We notice that Luke tells us that he "desired Him that He would eat with him." Thus his invitation expressed a desire of his heart. When we read that he desired that He would eat with him, it appears that it was an entirely hospitable action on his part. As the whole story is considered, however, we discover that the very manner of his reception of Jesus lacked all the signs of common courtesy in the East. It was the habit of the East to meet on the threshold a visiting guest with water for his feet. This action was ignored. It was the common method of the East to greet the visitor with a kiss. Simon gave Jesus no kiss. It was the custom to bring to the visiting guest oil for the anointing of his head. This was not done. All these omissions show that his desire was either that of curiosity, or hostility. There is nothing definitely to prove that he entertained hostility, except that we know the attitude of these Pharisees toward Jesus. Evidently, however, as his actions prove, his invitation lacked cordiality.

But now something happened that must have filled this man with unutterable surprise and annoyance. When Jesus had entered, and taken His place at the table, without the water, without the kiss, without the oil, Simon saw a woman cross the threshold, swiftly pass round the board to the place behind Jesus. She was evidently a well-known character. Luke's method is ever characterised by clarity, and yet extreme delicacy. He tells the story of the woman when he says:

" A woman which was in the city, a sinner."

That phrase " a sinner " was not a general statement. It was at the time synonymous for a harlot. Simon saw this woman enter his house, and passing round to the place where the feet of his Guest were found, stand there as the tears rained upon those feet, then stoop down, and dry the feet thus wetted with her tears, with the hair of her head. Moreover, bending over, she kissed those feet, or as the Greek word has it, kissed them much. In our English language we can correctly convey the idea of that word by saying that she smothered them with kisses. Then she poured costly ointment upon them. All this Simon observed.

Now watching him carefully, and in the light of the narrative we understand exactly what he was thinking, and the reason for it. We may state the reason first bluntly by saying he saw a fallen woman fondling Jesus, and Luke tells us the result, " He spake within himself "; and our Lord knew exactly what he was thinking. This is revealed to us by Luke.

" This Man, if He were a Prophet, would have perceived who and what manner of woman this is which toucheth Him, that she is a sinner."

Let us carefully watch the process of his thinking. First of all his thought of the woman is expressed in that phrase already referred to, when he saw her as " a sinner "; and it is evident that there was contempt in the cool, calm, calculating soul of Simon. Then his thinking about the Lord took shape. He was convinced that He was no Prophet, or He would have perceived all the truth concerning this woman. Even though He had never seen her, He would have known what manner of woman she was. His conception, therefore, of a prophet of God was also a revelation of his conception of God. As a matter of fact, his thinking was a clear revelation that he did not know God at all. His thought of God precluded the possibility of his believing that any authentic representative or Prophet of God, would permit a woman of this character to shower upon Him evidences of love and affection. Thus we see the man, cold, self-centred, satisfied in his thinking, and in his conception of God, and so utterly contemptuous of this woman; and believing that in this attitude he was interpreting the Divine attitude. As we look at him, we are reminded of something which Jesus once said to some of these very men:

> " Go ye and learn what this meaneth, I desire mercy, and not sacrifice; for I came not to call the righteous, but sinners."

Of the tenderness of God, of His compassion, of His mercy, these men had no knowledge. Simon was of that company. He had a certain knowledge of God which was purely intellectual, and doctrinally conceiving of Him in His holiness and righteousness; but knowing nothing of the great fact of His grace and mercy. That conception of God created his conception of a prophet of God; and moreover, was the reason for his contempt for this woman.

From Simon we turn to look at the woman herself. As we have seen, Luke tells the dark and terrible story of her past in that simple and yet terribly revealing description of her as a sinner. That was the true account of her past. It was a dark and terrible one. There is no need to call that fact in question for a single moment. Yet if I may employ a personal word, based upon a somewhat lengthy experience, in which one has repeatedly been called upon to meet and deal with such a woman, I have found over and over again that behind the story of the sinning there was some tragedy. About this woman, of course, we know nothing, but we are compelled to recognise what Simon was conscious of, the story of her past. But let us look at her as she is seen on this occasion.

First of all we see her violating all Pharisaic traditions by coming into that house at all. It was contrary to such tradition that any woman should come uninvited into any house. It would seem that she either had no consciousness of these conditions, or at any rate for the moment they were entirely forgotten, as she resolutely entered. It is possible, and even probable, that she hardly saw the assembled guests, or Simon himself, having eyes for One alone, Whom she had learned was in the house, and Whose being there was the reason of her coming.

Further, she certainly trampled on her own personal feelings when she entered. There was no doubt whatever that she was aware of the feeling against her, and the house of Simon would never have attracted her. It is well that we should remember that if our character and attitude are those of Simon, this kind of woman will be as anxious to keep out of our way as we are to keep out of her way. Something, however, irresistibly attracted her, and made her forget, or made her unconscious of the glances of Simon, and the probable cynicism of his other guests. The reason for her going was that she was filled with adoring love for one Person. She entered, and that love was clearly seen in her falling tears, and expressed itself with abandonment in the kisses rained upon the feet of Jesus, and in the fragrant beauty of the ointment she poured upon His feet. Thus we see her, in the past a sinner, but at the moment a woman characterised by all the beauty and refinement of womanhood, when womanhood is love-mastered.

Now we turn to watch our Lord dealing with each in turn. As He talked to Simon we need carefully to remember that everything He said to him was an attempt on His part to reach and win the mind and heart of this man. Let it be bluntly stated that our Lord's love for this woman did not exceed His love for Simon. He was on His way to the Cross for the woman, and for Simon. He was in the world seeking to save that which was lost, and to Him Simon was as surely lost as was the woman. As we watch Him, then, we see Him going after the man, attempting to reach his heart, and bring him to an understanding of God.

First, let it be observed that He accepted Simon's invitation, in spite of His certain knowledge of the man and his attitude. As we have over and over again reminded ourselves by reference to our first meditation in this series, He needed not that any should tell Him what was in man, for He knew.

Further, He remained, in spite of the signal failure in the manifestations of hospitality. He noticed all this. He missed these tokens. Presently He said so, but these facts did not deter Him from sitting down at the board. He went into that house as surely seeking to save as He did at any time in any place.

The second stage in His dealing with Simon is that He spoke to him in answer to this thinking. Luke tells us that " Jesus answering said unto him, Simon, I have somewhat to say unto thee."

Up to this point, according to the record, Simon had not spoken openly, but our Lord knew his thinking concerning that woman, and concerning all that he saw happening. To the statement of Jesus that He had something to say unto him, Simon answered, with unquestionably a tone of superciliousness, " Master, say on." Simon had already made up his mind about Jesus that He was no prophet, or He would not have permitted that kind of woman to approach Him, but if He had something to say, let Him say it.

The next action of Jesus was that He told Simon a story, or if we choose, we may say He uttered a parable to him. He took him away for a moment from the things happening around him, and apparently from things more sublime and fundamental. He asked for the exercise of his judgment in the presence of a story so simple that it easily might have been told to and understood by a child. There was almost a touch of humour in the story, as a story, because it led to an inevitable answer. There was a man who had two debtors, one of them owed him fifty, and the other five hundred pence. The application which perchance Simon did not at the moment make, was concerned with the thinking of Simon about the woman, especially in comparison with himself. Being a Pharisee, his theology would not allow him to declare that he was not a sinner, but he was a small one by comparison, say, fifty pence. The woman was ten times more sinful than he, that is as five hundred is to fifty. Still, considering the story, if this creditor forgives both, which of the forgiven would love him most? Simon evidently followed the story, and was thinking; and moreover, was thinking accurately, for his answer was the true and inevitable answer. There would seem to have been some touch of superciliousness as he said:

" I suppose, he to whom he forgave the most."

We ask why he did not at once say, Certainly, he to whom he forgave the most. He was really dodging an issue with his own conscience. Nevertheless his answer shows that Christ had led his thinking to the point of a correct deduction. Our Lord at once declared this to be so, as He answered, " Thou hast rightly judged."

But the great Physician had not done with him. He now called upon him, in the light of that story, and his own finding concerning it, to consider the woman. Luke tells us quite revealingly, that He turned to the woman, while still addressing Simon. What He said first took the form of a question:

" Seest thou this woman? "

Certainly Simon saw her. It was seeing her that had aroused his criticism and his hostility to Jesus. Simon had said in effect that the Lord could not see her, or could not perceive her. The question asked him was as to whether he himself could see her. Then He proceeded by putting the woman into contrast with Simon, and revealing her. In effect He said, Simon, I will help you to see this woman by putting her into contrast with yourself, and that not on any high spiritual level, not even on the level of the morality in which you are confiding, I will contrast her with you on the level of common human courtesy. I came into your house. You gave Me no water. She has remedied your boorishness by bathing My feet with her tears. You gave me no kiss of salutation, but she has smothered My feet with her kisses. You gave Me no oil, the coarser material, for My head, the supreme member of My body, but she has brought ointment, the finer material, and anointed My feet. Thus as our Lord placed this woman by the side of Simon, He revealed the fact that Simon was coarse as sackcloth, and the woman fine as fine-spun silk.

He then declared that all Simon had seen in the woman was the activity of a great love, resulting from a moral cleansing. She loved much, because her sins were forgiven. Our Lord's meaning must never be interpreted as suggesting that she was being forgiven because she loved. Quite evidently she had met Jesus before, and was already a forgiven woman. This had been the inspiration of her coming into the house of Simon, and of all that had happened there. Simon could not see her as she was because he was looking at her as she used to be. That is a common trouble with Christian people. In dealing thus with Simon, He was surely, as we have said, seeking after his soul. He was showing him that a prophet of God was a representative of God, and that God's great concern was that the sinner should find forgiveness and freedom from pollution in order to the fulfilment of the highest ideal of life.

What happened in the issue we are not told. As I ponder it carefully I have it in my soul at least to hope that in some fair morn of morns, when I have crossed the borderline, I shall meet Simon in the Glory-land. I have no proofs of this, but at least we may wistfully wonder as to what the ultimate effect of the whole happening had upon the soul of Simon.

His dealing with the woman, of course, is self-evident throughout. First, He accepted her out-pouring of love. He welcomed her tears and her kisses and her ointment. He then proclaimed the reason for those tears, those kisses and that ointment. " Her sins which are many, are forgiven." That which had provoked the flow of tears was the moral cleansing of her nature which had taken place, and the out-springing of her adoring love as a result. Finally, speaking to her, He said:

" Thy faith hath saved thee; go in peace."

The Greek preposition there is *eis*, and I would like to render that word thus, " Go into peace."

The woman, that was a sinner, cleansed from her moral depravity, now mastered by an adoring and thoughtful love, evidenced in tears and kisses and ointment, was bidden to go forth into life in peace, peace with God, peace within her own soul, peace in spite of all human opinion.

XIX

THE THREE WOULD-BE FOLLOWERS

IN the six verses constituting the final paragraph in the ninth chapter of Luke, we find a very remarkable story. In it three men are presented to us. They are unnamed. We have no idea to what town they belonged, and yet they are presented to us in a series of three pictures clear-cut and graphic. In each case the man presented is seen quite clearly, and that the more so, as he is revealed in the presence of Jesus.

The time note here again is indefinite. The paragraph begins, "And as they went in the way." How constantly we read these words, or those having exactly the same effect. It is possible here that the reference should be taken in connection with the fifty-first verse of the chapter, which reads:

"And it came to pass, when the days were well nigh come that He should be received up, He steadfastly set His face to go to Jerusalem."

It may be that that fact was in mind when Luke wrote, "And as they went in the way." If so, we find ourselves here in the final period of our Lord's ministry, that following the confession at Cæsarea Philippi and the Transfiguration.

We find, however, that Matthew tells us the story of the two first men, but not that of the third. Matthew's account found in the eighth chapter of his Gospel, is characterised by the same graphic description of these men. It is brief and simple, and in it the first two are clearly seen.

Now it is well to remember at this point that neither Matthew or Luke was really careful about chronology. Matthew more than once grouped illustrations from the life of Jesus in their bearing on some great teaching. This is equally true of Luke.

In Matthew we have in chapters eight and nine so far as verse thirty-four a gathering together of incidents illustrating the power of Jesus. These are given immediately after the record of the Ethical Manifesto. At the end of the seventh chapter we are told of the effect His teaching had upon the multitudes who heard Him; and the question naturally arises as to what His power may be. His teaching was characterised by an idealism and perfection that astonished the men of His time; but there is ever a difference between high idealism and practical ability. It is evident that Matthew, therefore, in these two chapters, eight and nine, shows our Lord as able to deal with every form of human malady. It is in the course of that, that he gives the account of these two men. Luke's presentation of the men occurs at the beginning of his account of the final six months in the ministry of our Lord. Here he gives the story of the two men referred to by Matthew, and adds a third.

Personally, I believe that the first two incidents took place soon after the Ethical Manifesto, and the last as He was commencing that final movement with His face stedfastly set to go to Jerusalem. Thus when Luke recounts the story of the two, he adds that of the third man, undoubtedly grouping them for a definite purpose.

What we do see, then, is three men, each of them attracted to Jesus, but with differing mentality, and differing outlook, and we listen to our Lord, as in brief concise words, He deals with each of the three. It is well to say at once that we have no record of result in either case. There are those who seem to think that none of these men followed Him. We have no warrant whatever for coming to any such decision.

As to the first of the three. We know something about him that Matthew tells us that Luke does not, namely, that he was a scribe. It is important, because it helps us to see him the more clearly. As a scribe he occupied an official position in the life of the nation. We know what that meant, and so may refer to it in the briefest of statements. The order of scribes had arisen on the return of God's people under Ezra, and in process of time, it had become an official order. The work of the scribe was that of interpreting and applying the law. This man was one of that order. Then we remember that from the beginning of His ministry, and growingly, the scribes as a class, were antagonistic to Jesus.

Now, it was this man who here came to Christ and said:

" Lord, I will follow Thee, whithersoever Thou goest."
He did not come with a question. He indulged in no criticism as so many of his order were doing. He addressed himself in an outburst, which was surely the expression of an impulse created by what he knew. We may I think with accuracy refer to him as an impulsive man. It is well that we remember that is not necessarily an evil thing. It has been said that he was a man who, to use an expression of our own times, wore his heart on his sleeve. Possibly that is true, but it is always refreshing to meet a man who reveals the fact that he has a heart at all. It is quite evident that for the moment, for some reason, and in some way, he was captivated by Jesus, as he said to Him:

" Lord, I will follow Thee, whithersoever Thou goest."

Let us at once admit that it was a great thing to say. As I have already pointed out, we know nothing about the future, and for the moment that can be entirely out of mind. He is seen standing before Someone Whom he felt he could follow anywhere. I think the emphasis of his statement should be upon the word " Thee," " I will follow *Thee*, whithersoever *Thou* goest." Thus the man is seen, a scribe, accustomed to teach, and apply the law, knowing that those of his own order were antagonistic to Jesus; but seeing in Jesus something that made him feel there was nothing quite comparable to being in His company, and travelling with Him. How long he had been coming to this conclusion we have no means of knowing, or of the processes which had preceded it, we cannot tell. We simply see him confronting the Son of God, and speaking of the thing that was in his heart. He was impulsive. It cannot be denied that his impulse was a worthy one, created by his vision of One Who he felt was without peer, and with Whom he could travel anywhere.

When we come to the next of these three men, again we have something in Matthew that Luke does not tell us. Matthew tells us that he was a disciple. He was already enrolled among the number of the followers of Jesus. He is not recorded as having spoken to our Lord until our Lord had said to him, " Follow Me." Here, then, He is heard addressing to this man, already a disciple, a new command and charge, calling him to some yet more complete relationship with Him.

His reply reveals him, as he said to Jesus:

" Lord, suffer me first to go and bury my father."

It is in the light of this fact of his discipleship that we are compelled to consider this answer. That answer reveals the fact that he was a man devoted to high duty, and capable of earthly affection. So strong were these things that when the Lord called him to this higher and closer relationship, he replied that he could not obey awhile, because of present duty.

It is quite certain that this reply has often been misunderstood, and I think it well here to give an account of the moment when I personally came to understand it. Travelling back from the United States some years ago in the same boat as Sir George Adam Smith, he told me this story. We all know how intimate was his familiarity with those Eastern lands, and how he had travelled there, not only on the ordinary roads, but off the beaten tracks, and on the byways. He told me how that upon one occasion, desiring to go into a region unknown to him, he was very anxious to secure the services of a fine young Arab sheik, who knew the district where he desired to go. When he asked him to do so, the chief declared that he regretted he was unable to do so. As they conversed, sitting at the entrance to the tent was the young chief's father, a venerable man, still hale, but aged. As Sir George urged the young man to accompany him, he used the very words of this story as he said, " Sir, suffer me first to go and bury my father." Thus, the intention of the declaration was to show that he had obligations to his father as long as he lived. That undoubtedly is what this man meant when he said this thing to Jesus. He declared that he was not able to take the high adventure to which Jesus called him, because of his obligations to his father.

The third man is an entirely different one. We know nothing about him except as we learn it from what happened. He spoke to Jesus, saying:

"I will follow Thee, Lord; but first suffer me to bid farewell to them that are at my house."

Now here we have something entirely different from the second man. This man is characterised by the impulsiveness manifested in the language of the first man as he said, " I will follow Thee." Here we see a man attracted by Jesus, intending to go after Him, affirming his intention, but for the moment feeling a backward pull. Here we must necessarily interpret what he said by Eastern life and action. The business of saying farewell was not that of merely saying Goodbye. It would entail a long delay, accompanied by revelling. It was the desire for this that held him back at the moment.

Thus we see these three men, all attracted by Christ, all feeling the force of His personality, all desiring to follow Him, and yet how different. The first was an impulsive man, out of his own sense of attraction to Jesus declaring his intention. The second was a quiet, loyal man, putting off the great adventure in the interest of what seemed to him to be the call of duty. The third man is one who, similarly attracted by our Lord, felt the backward pull of social affairs, and wanted the great adventure postponed.

We now with great interest, listen to our Lord, and watch His method with these men. To this impulsive man who declared his readiness to follow the Lord anywhere, He replied:

" Foxes have holes, and the birds of the heaven have nests; but the Son of man hath not where to lay His head."

Now I am quite convinced that in our understanding of that word of Jesus, everything depends upon, shall I say, the tones of His voice, and the way in which the thing was said. How constantly we read it as though our Lord was speaking out of a sense of loneliness, almost sorrowfully. I think such interpretation is inaccurate, that He was really rather exultingly declaring to the man what His own position was. He was revealing the fact that He was detached from everything that would prevent progress, and so showing to him that travelling with Him meant the taking up of a similar attitude. Foxes have holes into which they can run. The birds of the heaven have nests in which they can tarry; and the attractiveness of such things are self-evident. Said Jesus, I have no such attractions. I have nothing that detains Me for a moment from the march I am taking. The statement was a clear revelation to this man of what following Jesus really meant. It meant, as we have said, detachment from everything that prevented progress.

To the next man He had uttered His command, " Follow Me." In so doing Christ had called this man to the highest, to an adventure such as he had never known, to a fellowship upon a pathway which he could not see or understand, but which would be taken in fellowship with the Lord Himself. What that pathway was is revealed in the final words of Jesus to the man:

" Go thou and publish abroad the Kingdom of God."
It was in the interest of that pathway that Jesus said to him, " Leave the dead to bury their own dead."

Let those who are dead, who lack vision, who do not see the glory of the Kingdom, attend to the burying of those who are also living life on that earthly level. He called this man to the abandonment of the closest earthly tie, and apparent duty, in the interest of the high adventure, upon which He Himself was engaged.

In this connection it must be carefully remembered that Christ does not call everyone in that sense to follow Him. The story is that of a man who had such a call, but was held back by some duty on a lower level. It is the word of command of the One Who had declared that there was something higher than earthly kinship. As He had one day said:

"Who is My Mother? and who are My brethren? Behold, My Mother and My brethren! For whosoever shall do the will of My Father which is in heaven, he is My brother, and sister, and Mother."

In that sacred kinship, obligations are created which transcend the call of every other earthly tie.

In the last man we see the same constraint, the same desire, the same admiration, the same intention. He wanted to go with Jesus, but he wanted to delay the matter as he went back to take farewell of those who were at home.

The answer of Jesus to this man does appear to be the severest of all. He said to him:

"No man, having put his hand to the plough, and looking back, is fit for the Kingdom of God."

The backward look proves a man unfit for that Kingdom, either in itself, or in its service; proves him to be unfit for the company of Jesus. It was indeed a word of the utmost severity, but it was revealing and necessary.

Now, for a moment let us listen to these answers of Jesus in a slightly different way. His reply to the first man proved the necessity for detachment from all that prevents progress. The word to the second man proved the necessity for the abandonment of the closest earthly tie, when it in any way interferes with the high imperial call of Christ. His answer to the third revealed the fact that true fidelity brooks no reluctance, no looking back.

So the scenes pass before us. In every case the word "Follow" occurs, spoken as we have seen, to such as desire to follow, to those who had seen Him in His beauty in some form or fashion, who had been impressed, possibly, by His teaching, possibly by His works. The one fact remains that they were all attracted, they all felt they would like to follow Him.

We return for a moment to remind ourselves of the placing of these three incidents in the narrative of Luke. Jesus was on the way, His face stedfastly set to go to Jerusalem, travelling resolutely towards the Cross. To Him one said:

" I will follow Thee whithersoever Thou goest."

Another,

" Suffer me first to go and bury my father."

A third:

" First suffer me to bid farewell to them that are at my house."

As He answered them, His face was set towards Jerusalem, and His whole attitude and activity proved that He was suggesting to them nothing that He was not Himself doing. There was nothing of earthly value which held Him back from that pathway of progress. There was no earthly tie, however tender and strong, even that to His Mother, that could deflect Him from that purpose. When upon occasion that Mother had sought to dissuade Him from continuing His action, because she believed He was in danger of losing His reason, He had declared that the will of God was supreme in His thinking, and in His purpose.

Finally, when He declared that a man looking back, was unfit for the Kingdom of God, He did so as One Whose face was stedfastly set to the goal of the Cross. The contrast between a face stedfastly set, and the backward look, is self-evident.

Therefore it was with all these men admiring and desiring to follow, He said in effect, "But Me no buts; come and travel with Me."

Let us end our meditation by considering something said at the beginning, but now to be perhaps a little more carefully considered. We are not told what happened in either case. What we do know is that in each case an alternative was presented. The first man either went back to his nest, or stepped out upon the highway of the march with Jesus, with nothing holding him back. The alternative was a return to the comfort and security of home, or that of marching out on the highway with the Son of God.

The alternative in the case of the second man was perhaps more difficult. It was as to whether he should take the pathway of the lower duty, or the higher; should he allow his loyalty to his earthly kin to prevent obedience to the voice of the King.

The alternative in the case of the last man was that of deserting the plough altogether, or cutting the straight furrow. The very figure of speech employed to him by the Lord suggests that his hand was already on the plough. It is only as the hand is kept there, and all energy concentred upon the business, that there is fitness for the Kingdom of God.

The revelation of this paragraph, and of the three men seen therein in their relationship with our Lord, is that of basic matters and high things; and the true contrasts of possibility within any human life. Let the attitude of our Lord be kept in mind, that of the face stedfastly set; and in the light of it, His answers to these men considered, as they reveal to us for all time what it really means to follow Him.

XX

THE DEMONIAC

THIS is the one instance, in our present series, in which our Lord is seen in contact and dealing with a demoniac. We shall have a glimpse of the same matter again when we come to the story of the boy in the valley; but there this subject will be of secondary interest. Here it is the principal matter. The whole subject of demon possession is often considered to be a difficult one, and it is important therefore that we give careful consideration to it as it appears here.

Matthew, Mark and Luke all tell this story, but Mark most in detail. There are glimpses of light, however, in the narratives of the other evangelists, which are all of value in a careful consideration.

This subject of demon possession constantly recurs in the Gospel narratives. I may say that I have dealt with it at greater length than is possible now, in my volume on Mark, where eleven pages are devoted to it. We shall condense our consideration now.

In approaching this subject it is necessary that we remember the fact that the testimony of the sacred writings to the existence of spiritual beings, who yet have dealings with men, is unequivocal. That applies equally to the Old and the New Testaments. The writers of the past, and the writers of the new dispensation all quite evidently took for granted this existence of spiritual beings having access to human life.

It is notably evident in the Gospel narratives, and they consistently bear testimony to the fact that our Lord in the course of His earthly ministry, exercised authority over these demons, and again and again cast them out of human life.

We are living in an age when all these things are called in question. I am not attempting to deal with the objections raised to these stories of demon possession. There are those who take up the attitude that our Lord was working within such human limitations that He accepted the views of His time. I do not propose to argue that position, as it involves our Christology; and any interpretation of Him which lowers the New Testament presentation of Him as God of God, and God's Son, involves a prior argument with which I am not now concerned. There are still others who do not deny His knowledge, but declare that He adapted His language to meet the low level of the intellect of those to whom He addressed Himself. Such a view would charge Him with giving countenance to superstition, in the interests of truth. This again is a misconception.

Once more, we are told that the language of the New Testament is really that of the recorders, who are giving their own explanation of things which Jesus did, which they at the time could understand in no other way. It is said that these people called demoniacs, were not in any way possessed by demons, but had lost their mental balance. That view destroys the authority of the writings in every particular, and if it is accepted, as the interpretation in this case, it may be applied to many other matters.

In any attempt to understand the matter, we should be careful to make an important distinction between a devil and a demon. This distinction is never revealed in the Authorised Version. Neither is it made in the text of the Revised, but constantly in the margin, in places where the text reads " devils," the word demons is substituted. The American Revisers have put the word " demon " in the text, and relegated the word " devil " to the margin. There is, however, a very distinct difference between the two. The devil is referred to thirty times in the New Testament, and in every case where the substantive is used, it is employed of the one who is head and front of all the spiritual underworld. The word demons is often used, and synonymous terms, " evil spirits," " unclean spirits."

The whole question of demons is too large for us to enter into at all fully. Enough for us to recognise that the New Testament refers to them as actually existing. The Greeks believed they were the spirits of departed men, and some of them good, and therefore in demonology, in Greek culture, was the worship of evil and of good in that sense. Even so remarkable a scholar as George Pember in a past generation, believed that these demons were pre-Adamic men. The older theology looked upon them as the angels that fell from their high estate under

Lucifer, the light bearer, when he rebelled against heaven's high rule. That view is the most satisfactory. However, realising that the final word cannot be said on this subject, the fact remains that their existence is recognised throughout the Scriptures, and that they have access to men.

The question may be asked, and indeed sometimes it is asked as to why we are not conscious of demon possession at the present time. The first reply to that is to ask another question, as to whether we are quite sure it does not exist to-day. Once again, we will not stay to debate the matter. To those interested and desiring to investigate more fully, I would recommend an old book, an American publication, on " Demon Possession, and allied themes," by Dr. Nevius. It is equally certain that missionaries in contact with pagan peoples, bear constant testimony to the fact that they have to do with this experience in a very definite way. Moreover, returning to something hinted at a little earlier, I cannot personally read my newspaper to-day without believing that there are still demon-possessed men in the world.

Turning to the subject as it is presented in the New Testament, I may say that I have already used an expression more than once, which may be permissible in a certain way, but which the New Testament never does use. I refer to the expression, demon-possessed. The New Testament never speaks of a man as being demon-possessed. It does speak of men as being demonised, as being demoniacs. I am not arguing that demon-possession is inaccurate, but simply pointing this out as a simple fact.

What is meant then by demon-possessed, or demonised, or demoniac, is that a man may be completely under the power and influence of an evil spirit. This fact, as we have said, is constantly recognised in the New Testament. Bernard, in his " Progress of Christian Doctrine," says that Mark seems to have been specially impressed with the matter.

We are told that out of Mary of Magdala our Lord had cast seven demons. The man in the story under consideration was asked, " What is thy name? " In his answer, in an arresting way he used first the singular and then the plural number, as he said:

" *My* name is Legion, for *we* are many."

As to how such mastery is gained over a man is a question open to some amount of speculation, because we have no definite information on the matter. It would appear that an evil spirit seduces a man, and the man yields, and that repeatedly, until presently he becomes completely mastered by the evil spirit. In that sense he is possessed by it. His thinking is under its mastery; His emotion responds to its impulses; and his will is dominated by the demon.

Here again we are in the presence of something which is suggestive, and yet perhaps difficult of explanation. It is quite evident that to these evil spirits, human beings become instruments. They are eager not to be dismissed from a man, but if they be, they choose swine, rather than no material instrument. The instrument is one through which they can exert an evil influence, beyond the being thus mastered or possessed. There is no illustration in the Old or the New Testament of any spirit taking possession of a man except it is an evil spirit, save only the Holy Spirit of God. They are all unclean. They suggest evil courses. They create the impulse toward evil. The effect of their mastery of any human being is that of the destruction of his personality, and so the complete ruin of the one possessed.

Much more might be said on the subject, and perhaps profitably. A remarkable fact, however, emerges, and it is that wherever the evangel has been widely preached, and peoples have passed under its influence, even apart from obedience to it, these manifestations seem largely to have ceased. This also may be a method of the arch-enemy, who now deceives men far more in the form of an angel of light, than in the form in which our fathers portrayed him, with hoofs and horns. Marie Corelli in her book, " The Sorrows of Satan," presents him as finally appearing as a cultured person, coming out of the House of Commons. Necessarily we are glad he was coming out!

In the case of the man before us we have one of the worst it is possible for us to imagine. Demon possession had brought him into the place of complete isolation from his fellow-men. He was dwelling among the tombs, as far away from his fellows as he knew how to get.

He is seen also in his appalling lawlessness, breaking through every attempt made by others to restrain him. They put chains upon him, they put fetters upon him. He snapped the chains, and rent the fetters. He refused to be governed.

Added to this isolation and lawlessness, he is seen cursed by a fearful restlessness, crying out night and day.

And yet, once more, and as a result, he is seen suffering, lacerating himself with stones, and so being a menace to others, for none could pass that way.

All these things reveal the result of mastery by evil spirits. Somehow, somewhere, somewhen, we know not how, or where, or when, he had listened to the voice of evil, had submitted to the domination of its suggestions, and continuing so to yield, had come to the hour when he had neither will nor choice of his own, no emotion moved him towards higher things, and there was no clarity in the realm of the intellect. This is the man who is seen coming into contact with our Lord.

As we observe this we first of all notice the fact that the man is presented, the man as possessed. The man himself spoke, and yet as he uttered words in human language, the evil spirits were speaking. That is the force of the fact already referred to. He began by saying " My," and continued by saying " we."

Then we see this very arresting thing that when he saw Jesus he made towards Him, and fell down and worshipped Him. Admittedly the phrase here may merely mean that he made obeisance in His presence; but it is significant that he did that.

In reply to the command of Jesus that the evil spirit should come forth, the man said:

" What have I to do with Thee, Jesus, Thou Son of the Most High God, I adjure Thee by God, torment me not."

Now there is a sense in which no language of mine can interpret the horrible and terrible significance of that cry. It is the cry of the man. But it is evidently the cry of the demon through the lips of the man. He knew Who it was, Who was confronting him. He knew His name, " Jesus." He knew His nature. He was " The Son of the Most High God." He was conscious that the only thing that befitted his own being was torment. He knew moreover that there was a time fixed for that final experience, for Matthew records the fact that the demon said:

" Art Thou come hither to torment us before the time? "

As we read these Gospel narratives we see how constantly these evil spirits said that which revealed their knowledge of the deepest truths concerning the personality of our Lord. They spoke through human lips, but their language was demon language. Here they besought Him that if they must leave this man, they might find some material instrument, if they were only swine. Thus we see the merging of a man with evil spirits, and hear these evil spirits speaking through the man. The man's language had become their language. His thought had become their thought. He was mastered by them, and this mastery was revealing itself in these strangely amazing words.

In turning our attention to our Lord, and the method with this man, we notice that even before the evil spirits spoke at all, He had spoken. That is made clear by the way in which Mark tells the story:

"Crying out with a loud voice, he saith, What have I to do with Thee, Jesus, Thou Son of the Most High God? I adjure Thee by God, torment me not. For He said unto him, Come forth, thou unclean spirit, out of the man."

The word of Jesus was the word of authority, a command that brooked no argument, "Come forth, thou unclean spirit, out of the man."

In this connection we need to recognise the remarkable and arresting fact that after the temptation in the wilderness, the Lord is never recorded as having entered into any argument with evil spirits, or as having spoken in any other way than of full and august authority. In the wilderness He had answered the repeated temptations that came to Him, and had gained complete victory over them. Luke in recording this temptation ends by saying,

"When the devil had completed every temptation, he departed from Him for a season."

That phrase " for a season " is in itself very suggestive. We have a more literal translation in the margin, which would make the statement read, "leaveth Him until." We ask naturally, Until when? A reference to the apostolic writings reveals the fact that in the hour of His Cross the principalities and powers of the unseen world of evil came up against Him, and in that connection it is declared that He triumphed over them openly, making a show of them in it, that is, in His Cross. It was until then that the devil departed from Him. Demons never came into His presence if they could escape Him. Whenever they did, they recognised His authority, and He exercised that authority by casting them out from their possession of human beings.

Addressing the man, the Lord asked him, "What is thy name?" As I read it I am convinced there was a great tenderness in His question. In answer to His authoritative command, the man was being dispossessed, and so was coming back to a sense of personality. The Lord asked him for his own name, but the evil spirits gave the name of "Legion," for they said, "We are many." To their request that they might enter into the herd of swine, our Lord consented. Matthew graphically says that in response to their appeal He said " Go." Mark and Luke both say " He gave them leave."

There is an old controversy on the subject of the destruction of those pigs thus permitted by the Lord. Some fifty or sixty years ago there was a great controversy between Gladstone and Huxley over this matter. There is one simple fact which seems to have been entirely missed in the discussion. It is that the Lord was in the first place a Jewish Messiah, and was exercising His ministry among Jewish people. If Josephus was right that this took place in a Greek city, that does not for a moment affect the fact that He was dealing with a people under Hebrew law. No Hebrew had any right to the possession of two thousand pigs. It was a strictly forbidden traffic. By this very permission then, our Lord not only set the man free from demon possession, but cleansed a people from an unholy traffic.

The story ends so far as the man is concerned, with the wonderful picture of him sitting, clothed, and in his right mind. It closes, however, with a very dark and sinister kind of action of those who had owned the swine. We are told they besought Him that He would depart from their borders, and Matthew says He entered into a boat and crossed over.

What a revelation of the condition of the community. Our Lord had landed on their shore, had taken hold of a man who was the curse of the countryside, and had restored him to his right mind, had given him back to society, a blessing rather than a menace. Nevertheless they besought Jesus to go away, and He went away.

If we should travel through that district to-day, we should find it desert, and inhabited by people called troglodytes. Troglodytes are dwellers in tombs, a wild and savage people. The old Persian proverb is indeed true, " If the mills of God grind slowly, they grind exceeding small."

Why did these people ask Him to leave them? We have a remarkable revelation of the truth in an incidental word in Matthew's record. It says:

" They that fed them fled, and went away into the city, and told everything, and what was befallen to them that were possessed with demons."

That statement is an amazing one as it says that " they told every thing, and." Is it possible to tell everything, and something else?

159

What, then, we enquire, did they mean by everything? Quite evidently they were referring to the fact that their pigs were destroyed. Then the " And," and that referred to the man freed from possession, clothed, and in his right mind. How many a person there is in the world to-day would welcome Jesus but for the fact of the pigs, some illegal, illicit vested interest.

When we enquire what value such a consideration has for us, we reply that the incorporation of this story, and other similar stories in the records has indeed great value. They unveil for us the fact of the underworld of evil spirits which still exists. It unveils for us, moreover, the Lord's authority and power over that underworld.

It may be objected, as we have said before, that there are no such cases now; and I repeat that such a statement needs very careful consideration. Admitting, however, that in some senses it may be true, that we have around us no such manifestations as thus described in the Gospels, it abides true until this hour as the apostle declared,

> " Our wrestling is not against flesh and blood, but against the principalities, against the powers, against the world rulers of this darkness, against the spiritual hosts of wickedness in the heavenly places."

But it is equally true to-day that

> " Jesus is stronger than Satan or sin,
>   And Satan to Jesus must bow.
> Therefore we triumph without and within,
>   For Jesus is saving us now."

In view of the existence of these evil forces, oftentimes hidden, and largely camouflaged by the false culture of a decadent age, it behoves us to:

> " Put on the whole armour of God, that we may be able to stand against the wiles of the devil, and having done all, to stand."

XXI

JAIRUS

THE story which constitutes our theme in this study is again told by Matthew, Mark, and Luke. We base our consideration principally upon Luke's account, making passing reference to matters revealed by the other writers.

In this story two individuals are seen in contact with Christ practically at the same time. In a previous study, considering the story of Simon and the woman who was a sinner, we took them together. We change the method now, and look first at Jairus, and in a subsequent study at the woman.

Here once more we find two persons widely separated socially. The man held a position of honour. He was a ruler of the synagogue. The woman was an outcast in a way that we shall consider more fully presently. Moreover they differed in their need, and in the reason that prompted their approach to Jesus. The need of the man was relative: his child. The need of the woman was purely personal.

The story of Jairus is a very remarkable one in many ways. At first it would seem as though very little exposition is needed. Nevertheless, it is radiant in beauty, in its revelation of our Lord, and of His dealing with this man in this supreme hour of his need.

Looking at the man, we begin with the things that are accidental. As we have said, he was a ruler of the synagogue, which meant that he held a position of responsibility and power. These rulers were not priests, but to use a word common in our speech to-day, they were laymen. Nevertheless, they had under their control all the sacred possessions of the synagogue, and the ordering of all matters concerning therewith. The position of such a man was one of responsibility, trust, and power. When we refer to this as being accidental, I mean that all this would certainly have been considered by him both accidental and unimportant in the presence of the need that drove him to Christ. It was for him an hour when he was face to face with life as he had never been before, because he was face to face with death. For the moment every matter faded into the realm of insignificance in the presence of the one, overwhelming and terrifying fact of death, and that coming to him in its most appalling form. When Temple Thurston wrote " The City of Beautiful Nonsense," he said a very illuminative thing when he declared that we are inclined in early days, and in days of prosperity to treat life as though it were a circus. Each one imagines that he or she is master of ceremonies in the circus ring. We come out into the ring in broadcloth, and buckskin breeches, and a silk hat, and cracking a whip. Everything seems to go to our order until one day, a lion breaks out of his cage. Then, said Temple Thurston, " life gets up and looks at us ! " This was surely a day when life got up and looked at Jairus.

Matthew says that his coming to Jesus took place at, or immediately after the feast in his house. Mark and Luke do not refer in this connection to that feast, and yet place it in the same period as Matthew does. Matthew, referring to what Jairus told Jesus, says that he declared her to be " Even now dead," which was a superlative way of referring to the apparently hopeless nature of the case. Mark says she was " at the point of death " Luke says " she lay a-dying." Evidently the child was beyond the reach of human aid.

Luke tells us that she was " his only daughter." It is a simple statement, but most revealing. A sympathetic imagination will help us to understand what all this meant to Jairus. The child was twelve years of age, which meant that he had had twelve years of sunshine in his home, twelve years of the music of the feet that had pattered, and twelve years of the sweeter music of the lips that had prattled. Now the feet were still, and becoming icy, and the lips were silent, soon to utter no further word. The child lay dying. It is evident that nothing mattered to Jairus that day but the terror of the situation. A ruler of the synagogue, he held a position of honour and power, but these things were of no value as his child lay dying. The uttermost gloom had settled upon his life. The lion had broken loose from its cage, and life had got up and looked at him. To-morrow, and the day beyond, and all other days were to Jairus unthinkable with the child gone.

It was under such stress of the consciousness of the agony of life that he made his way to Jesus. Evidently also, in spite of the darkness, he came to our Lord in confidence. All ordinary help had failed. He had done everything he could in the matter of physicians and nursing and care, without any doubt. All had been useless. She was " even now dead," " at the point of death," " she lay a-dying."

It goes without saying that he must have known about Jesus. It may be that he had seen Him work wonders before. Certainly he had heard about Him; and on the basis of what he knew, he made his way to Him, and he did it in confidence. This is shown by his words:

> " My little daughter is at the point of death; I pray Thee that Thou come and lay Thy hands upon her, that she may be made whole and live."

He was sure of one thing, that if Jesus came into his house, and touched his child, all would be well. The confidence may have had in it some tinge of superstition, but it was confidence. It did not reach the level of that of the Centurion, who with a faith that had called forth words of approbation from Jesus, had declared that there was no need for Him to come into the house, and implored Him to speak the word only, in order to produce the result of healing. But it was the language of assurance. Thus we see this man, coming in a day of deep darkness, and hopeless from the standpoint of ordinary human aid, and desperate; nevertheless feeling sure that he was approaching One Who could help him.

To us the rest of the story is concerned with what Jesus did. The first thing that impresses us is that of His immediate response to the appeal of Jairus. Each evangelist shows this in differing ways. Matthew says that when the story was told Him at the feast " Jesus arose and followed him." Mark says that when the appeal of Jairus was heard, " He went with him." Luke reveals it in the little phrase, " As He went," used in connection with the coming of the woman. Thus we see that such an appeal from the agonised heart of the father reached the heart of Christ, and He immediately responded.

The next thing is in some ways an amazing one, that is, it would be amazing if it were not for the Person of our Lord. He had been told, according to these recorders, that the child was so sick she could only be described as " even now dead," or as " at the point of death," as one who " lay a-dying." Under such circumstances there would seem to be the necessity for immediateness of action. We watch our Lord. He rose, He went, He followed Jairus. He Who was ever calling men to follow **Him,** now, drawn by the agony of a man's heart, went after him. Then suddenly we see Him pause. Some other needy soul had reached Him, and there was no hurry in His action in the case of Jairus. He stood long enough to raise a question as to who it was that touched Him. He listened to the woman's story, and spoke words of strength and comfort to her. We can only gain the significance of this as imaginatively we look at Jairus. Jairus was waiting. He had come to Jesus with a sense of terrific urgency. He had come knowing that his lassie was beyond all ordinary human help. So far as that was concerned, she had even now crossed over. Nevertheless, he had appealed to Jesus, and believed that if He came, He could put His hand on the child, and she would be made whole. His heart had been gladdened by the immediate response of Jesus. Then suddenly this pause, this waiting, this delay.

After the delay, Jesus moved on toward the house of Jairus. How far it was we have no means of knowing, but the picture is presented to us of this man walking by the side of the Lord towards the house of darkness.

Then suddenly there was an interruption. There came from the house messengers saying to Jairus:

" Thy daughter is dead; trouble not the Master."

Here again we need sanctified imagination to understand what that message meant to Jairus. He had left the child as good as dead, at the point of death, dying. He had come to Jesus, and found His response immediate, for He had started with the father directly He heard the story. But He had stopped on the way, just too long apparently; and therefore His coming was just too late.

With that statement concerning his child, the last gleam of hope probably faded from the sky. It was such a message as would shake him to the very foundations of his being. His faith was shaken. His love was wounded. His hope was destroyed. All this must have been, inevitably, for the moment at least, the experience of Jairus.

Then was heard immediately the voice of Jesus:

" Fear not, believe only. She shall be made whole."

No comment in certain ways is needed upon that. It was so simple, so plain. It was the word of Jesus to this man at the moment of his uttermost despair. He had not said this thing to Jairus when he first came to Him with his appeal. He had not said it to him when He started on His journey with him. He had not said it to him to hold him in courage when he waited, as the case of the woman was dealt with. He said this only when the news came that killed hope, " Thy daughter is dead, worry not the Master."

Now let it be at once recognised that from that moment Jairus had nothing to depend on but the word of Jesus. As we read the story at a distance we recognise that that word was all-sufficient. If, however, we can put ourselves into the place of Jairus, into that hour in which the light had gone out, and darkness had settled, we shall understand what it meant. It called for an activity of faith far exceeding that which had brought him to the Lord in the hour of his distress.

And yet had he not something more than the word of Jesus to depend upon? In that very moment of delay, when probably his soul was in revolt against it, he had seen something which must have had its effect upon his thinking. In that hour Jairus would certainly have hastened the footsteps of Jesus if he could, and have left the woman in her need. Then he heard the story which the woman had to tell, and which he, as a ruler of the synagogue, would perfectly understand. She had been twelve years in her infirmity, exactly as long as the period in which he had lived in the sunshine of his child's presence in his home. Yet she was healed, and in that fact he had evidence of the power of Jesus.

On the basis then of that word which Jesus spoke to him, " Fear not, believe only," and of what he had seen, he continued his journey with the Lord. The word of Jesus was a call demanding that he banish fear, and that he exercise his faith. This very call was at least a suggestion that there was reason for hope. All the circumstances were against faith, and against hope. The Lord called upon him to take a wider outlook, demanded that he should not measure the present by the apparent. The victory of our Lord is seen in the fact that on the basis of that spoken word, reinforced by the thing he had seen on the way, he continued his walk to the house where the child lay dead. As we have said, we cannot tell how far it was, but what we do know is that Jairus walked by the side of Jesus in a faith that may have been very trembling, very imperfect, very questioning; but he went, and on the way saw the victory of the Lord.

So we come to the wondrous ending of the story, with which we need not tarry, save to glance at it. They arrived at the house, and as had been affirmed, the child was dead. Mourners had already gathered within the house, and were wailing and beating upon their breasts in the presence of death. Into that house, and into the midst of that crowd Jesus entered.

As He did so, He cast upon the whole scene the light of His own outlook. Those gathered round saw a dead child, and in that the end of life, the passing to dust and nothingness of the sweet and beautiful personality. And than that, there is nothing more terrible in this world. Charles Kingsley in one of his writings declared that the death of a soldier is touched with heroism, the death of an old man is surrounded with the glory of completion; but the death of a child demonstrates something wrong somewhere. Jesus saw the dead child, but revealed what His outlook was upon that fact. He said, " She is not dead, but sleepeth." That sentence illuminates the whole universe. The child was surely dead from the human standpoint, but as Jesus looked He said in effect, That is not the child. We remember that concerning Lazarus He said, " This sickness is not unto death." He also said, " Our friend Lazarus is fallen asleep "; and when those listening to Him were perplexed, He used their language and said, " Lazarus is dead." His outlook, however, was that of the persistence of personality beyond what we call death. On the earth, yes, they are dead. In the whole of the fact of personality they are not dead. So He said to this stricken father, " She is not dead, but sleepeth."

It is perhaps not to be wondered at that when men heard such words, they felt how absurd they were, and laughed Him to scorn. It was in the presence of that laughter that He rose in quiet majesty, and put the whole company outside. He did not argue with them. He knew perfectly well that no human argument could demonstrate to them the accuracy of His vision. There was only one thing to do, and that was to exclude them.

Then, when apparently only father and mother were present, and the three disciples who had accompanied Him into the house, He bent over the mattress where the little lifeless clay was laying. He put out His hand, and took that cold little hand in His. " He took her by the hand "; that was His act.

Then He spoke, and said, " Maiden, arise." That may be in some senses, perfectly accurate translation, and yet, as a matter of fact, it has missed something of infinite beauty. Mark tells us that He said, " Talitha cumi." Now that is not Greek; it is not Hebrew, but it is Aramaic. It was the language almost unquestionably of His home, the common language of the common folk, in the common things of life. We render the saying with supposed dignity as "Damsel, arise." Let us look at it a little carefully. The word "Talitha" is a diminutive. It means "Little lamb." It was a word of infinite love and tenderness. We are looking and listening, and we see God manifest in flesh put His hand, the hand that guides and governs the movement of all worlds, upon the dead hand of a little lassie, and we hear Him call her "Little lamb." With this address He uttered the word of authoritative command, "Arise."

Then we are told in beautiful language what happened. "Her spirit returned." Her spirit had never been dead. Her essential personality had passed beyond the earthly sphere, had gone beyond the tenement of clay. Our Lord addressed her in that essential personality, using this tender and endearing term "Little lamb." He knew she could hear Him, because His voice apparently confined within the walls of a house, would penetrate beyond, and reach to any place where she might be. She heard that voice. She knew it, and knew it in that spirit world, as she would not have known it in any other; and at once she obeyed, "her spirit returned."

Then follows the further statement, "She rose up, and walked."

As she did so, Luke tells us something of infinite beauty and interest. To me it is the more remarkable saying that it was written by Luke, himself a physician. He tells us that Jesus commanded that they should give her something to eat. Thus He recognised that she had returned to the earthly level, and needed sustenance of her earthly existence.

In thus calling her back, He had indeed called her back to the world, and all its circumstances. In this connection we may remind ourselves of that which we know, that it is a matter which gives us cause for thought, that in all the story of His ministry we only have the record of three people He raised to life. Lazarus, the son of the widow of Nain, and this child. Lazarus was an only brother. The boy at the gates of Nain was the only son of his mother. This was the only child. The question may arise as to why He was apparently so reticent in the exercise of this supreme power. Perhaps we ought hardly to attempt to answer, and yet I cannot think of it without believing that He saw the whole of life, and knew where these were that men called dead. He knew that in calling them back into the earth life, He was calling them back to the place of sorrow. Hence His reticence. However, we have the three illustrations, and all of them show Him in the tenderness and understanding of His heart towards those in such sorrow.

It is indeed a wonderful story, and it has tremendous value for all of us. I do not hesitate to say that the supreme value is to be found in the word that Jesus uttered to Jairus in the moment of his uttermost extremity, " Fear not, believe only."

The rest of the saying is not needed. It was local, it was incidental. He said to Jairus, " She shall be made whole." He does not always say that. He does always say " Fear not, believe only."

I can hardly speak of this matter without becoming personal, and reminiscent, remembering a time about forty years ago when my own first lassie lay at the point of death, dying. I called for Him then, and He came, and He surely said to our troubled hearts, " Fear not, believe only." He did not say, She shall be made whole. She was not made whole on the earthly plane. She passed away into the life beyond. He did say to her, " Talitha cumi," " little lamb, arise "; but in her case that did not mean, Stay on the earth level. It meant that He needed her, and He took her to be with Himself. She has been with Him for all those years as we measure time here, and I have missed her every day; but His word, " Believe only," has been the strength of all the passing years.

Faith, however, cannot triumph unless it has some reason for doing so. Faith that does not start from reason is credulity, superstition. What, then, is the basis of faith in Jesus that brings triumph? The answer is in a word: Himself. He was there, walking with Jairus to his house. That day has not passed. He is still with us, going wherever we are going; and for evermore saying to us, in the consciousness of His nearness, " Fear not, believe only." There is only one song that is fitting, and it is the one we all love:

> " Begone, unbelief, for my Saviour is near,
> And for my relief He will surely appear."

XXII

THE WOMAN WHO TOUCHED

WHILE the story of this woman is closely related to that of Jairus, the two personalities are so distinct, and their circumstances so different, that we are taking them in separation.

In the case of Jairus we watched our Lord dealing with a man of standing and position, a ruler of the synagogue. In this we have a very striking contrast. He is here seen dealing with a woman of no standing, of no position at the moment; as we shall see more distinctly presently, she was an outcast. In the case of Jairus He was dealing with a man who in his home had had twelve years of gladness in the life of his child. In this case we see Him dealing with a woman who had had twelve years of sadness and suffering. The period of her trouble had been as long as that of Jairus' joy. In the case of Jairus we saw Him dealing with a man who, in the hour of desolation, sought the help of Christ, and found it. In this case we see Him dealing with a woman who made a great and daring adventure in coming to Christ, which venture was rewarded.

Our attention, then, is first fixed upon the woman herself. The story is in some senses a technical one. Matthew, Mark and Luke all tell us the fact concerning her, which it is easy for those of us who may be in health and strength to read, without grasping its significance. She was suffering from an issue of blood. In the fifteenth chapter of the book of Leviticus, in verses nineteen to twenty-seven we find careful instructions as to how any persons suffering from any form of that malady were to be treated. They were to be segregated from the company of worshippers so long as it continued. That was not a punitive provision, but rather a hygienic arrangement. This woman had suffered from such a malady for twelve years, and therefore had been for that period segregated in certain ways. The law as given to Moses had been overlaid by attempted interpretations and traditions. There was a popular misconception concerning that particular form of disease that it was always the result of sin. The view was based entirely upon the medical opinion of that day, interpreted by Rabbinical interpretation of such cases. There is no warrant whatever for adopting such a view, but it was held at the time. That her case was a serious one is proven, of course, by the fact that she had suffered for twelve years. Luke, himself a doctor, declares its hopelessness as he says, she " could not be cured of any." The doctors had, in all probability, done their utmost for her, but had failed. It will be remembered, too, that Mark, in telling the same story, tells it in a different form as he says:

> " She had suffered many things of many physicians, and had spent all she had, and was nothing bettered, but rather grew worse."

Necessarily, no doctor would state the case in that way, but it agrees perfectly with the doctors' finding.

Now, as a consequence of this false view, this woman's segregation was first of all excommunication from the Temple and the synagogue, with their religious rites. Moreover, by the law of the Rabbis, for the same cause she was divorced from her husband, and shut out from family life. All this inevitably meant that she was ostracised by society.

We know nothing more concerning this woman than what appears in this story. Legendary lore has been busy with her, and as is so often the case its suggestions are full of beauty. Legend has it that her name was Veronica, and that she handed to our Lord her handkerchief to wipe his face when He was on His way to the Cross. Of course we have no means of knowing, and possibly it is only a legend. We know concerning her definitely, only the things that we have been considering, and those may be summarised by repetition of our earlier statements, that she was an outcast.

The twelve years had been years of struggle, which had ended hopelessly. She had spent all that she had, which necessarily means that at the time she was reduced to poverty. As we look at her, we, therefore, unquestionably see a woman not only helpless but hopeless after these long and agonising years. This is the woman whose life for twelve years had been ebbing away, weak and wan and emaciated, who we see coming to Jesus.

Mark says, " Having heard the things concerning Jesus." That was the inspiration of her great adventure. We are not told that she had ever seen Him before. Possibly she had, but Mark's suggestion would lead us to think otherwise. She came, " having heard the things concerning Jesus."

Now we may enquire, What had she heard? We must remember that by this time His fame was spread abroad through all the countryside. Everyone was talking about Him. If we glance back for a moment chronologically, there are certain things that had taken place, of which in all possibility, she had heard. He had entered the house of Peter, and raised from the bed of fever his mother-in-law. He had come face to face with a leper, and had communicated cleansing to him. He had raised from the dead the son of the widow of Nain. He had cast the demon forth from a demoniac. He had stilled the storm on the lake one day, and again had cast forth the evil spirits from a man terribly possessed. She may have heard of all these things. This woman, then, ostracised, divorced, excommunicated, probably through no sin of her own, but through widespread misconception and misunderstanding, this woman who, having tried everything, and spent all her money in doing so, heard about Jesus. On the basis of the reports concerning Him there came to her a conviction that if she might make contact with Him, there might be hope even for her. Matthew and Mark tell us that that conviction within herself was a very clear one, for they tell us that she said:

" If I touch but His garments, I shall be made whole."

This woman was amid the thronging crowds. These crowds were surrounding Jesus, and moving with Him as He passed on His way to the house of Jairus. In the movement of the story the disciples referred to these crowds as thronging Him and pressing Him. It is impossible to read this story without being amazed in some senses how a woman in so weak a condition managed somehow, borne along by the new hope springing within her, to get near enough to reach Him as He passed.

Then the narrative tells the story of the contact she made, and Matthew, Mark and Luke use the same word. We have rendered it in each case, " touched." Now I want us to realise that that word gives an entirely wong impression of what she did. The idea conveyed by our translations is that she merely touched the edge of His robe. To begin with, the Greek word does not mean a touch of that kind. Whereas it may not sound so euphemistic, the force of the Greek word would be far more accurately rendered clutched, or grasped. This is what the woman had been saying in her heart, that if she might grasp His garment, she would be made whole. Her word suggests an action of force and of desperation.

Again, the word rendered " border " has a definite signification, and it is not that of a hem or edge. It is the word *kraspedon*. In the book of Numbers, chapter fifteen, verses thirty-seven to thirty-nine, we find instructions in the secondary law, which was nevertheless obligatory, which provided that the members of the nation should wear upon the fringe of their garments a tassel bound with blue. It is that word which in the Septuagint is rendered *kraspedon*, and one was found at each corner of the garment worn. This garment was flung across the shoulders, so that one of these tassels hung in front, one on the left, one on the right, the last falling at the back of the wearer. Now there can be no question that our Lord wore such a garment, and that He Who was born under the law, was obedient to its commandment, concerning the wearing of this *kraspedon*, with its cord of blue. It was that which the woman grasped as He passed her by. According to the law, that kraspedon was indicative of the loyalty of the wearer to the requirements of God; and in His case had its superlative significance. She grasped the *kraspedon*, and that was the act of a great adventure, a great daring, a great resolution. She had been saying to herself, If I grasp but His garments, I shall be made whole. Now He was close at hand. She saw Him passing. She saw His garment. She saw the cord of blue in the tassel, and somehow forcing her way through the thronging, jostling, crowds, she grasped that *kraspedon*.

Immediately she found her confidence vindicated, for the trouble of the long twelve years was over. Her blood was staunched, and she knew it. She endeavoured to slip quietly away. She had gained that for which she came.

So we see this woman, an outcast and helpless, hearing about Jesus, coming to the conviction that if no-one else could do anything for her, He could; seizing her opportunity as He passed her way, grasping the *kraspedon*, and immediately finding the healing she sought.

Then, as we turn our eyes upon the Lord, to observe His dealing with her, we see that His action, unseen of the crowd, but realised by the woman, preceded any word that He uttered. His first answer to her coming and her confidence was that, to use His own words, strength, power, dynamic, which is the Greek word, had passed from Him. He had responded to the approach and the action in the way that vindicated her confidence, and gave her healing.

But He had not done with her. In His walk with Jairus He halted, and asked what we may accurately describe as a divisive question, and we see as we proceed that the question implicated ᴝ requirement laid upon the woman herself. When she had heard the question, and replied to its implication, He uttered to her His final words.

The question which we have described as divisive, was the question, " Who grasped Me? " for He employed the same word which we are told she had used as she had thought of Him. In effect He declared that someone by an act of definite faith, had fastened upon Him, and had immediately found the response of power coming forth in healing from Him.

It may be said that the woman's thought was a somewhat superstitious one, that she had heard of the great Healer, and of the wonderful things He had done, that she had felt that there was some mystic power upon Him, with which if she could but make contact, there would come healing to her. Even if it be admitted that there was an element of superstition in what she was saying within herself, it is well to remember that at the heart of superstition there may be faith. And where that is so, our Lord will ever answer the faith, and correct the superstition.

When this question was asked by our Lord, Peter and the rest made an astonished protest. Whereas probably Peter was the spokesman, Luke makes it perfectly clear that in their opinion the disciples were unanimous. All they said was apparently most reasonable and sensible. They asked Him in effect what He could mean when He suggested that someone in that jostling crowd had made contact with Him. The probability was as they intimated, that during the period of that walk, with these people thronging and pressing upon Him, many had made contact. Nevertheless His question revealed that someone had done far more than press upon Him and crush Him. Someone had made such contact with Him as to draw the answer of power from Him. His question proved that He knew the difference between the jostle of a curious mob, and the contact of a soul in need and in faith.

But His question was also a requirement. The woman was quietly slipping away, having gained the healing she sought.

Of the healing she was certain, but perchance desired to get away from the crowd, in order to realise the fulness of the thing that had been done. When, however, she heard His voice asking this question, she knew that something more was necessary. She came in front, and she came trembling. We must remember that she was already healed, and she knew it. She felt the healing power pulsing through her body, and overcoming her weakness. When Jesus healed He did it perfectly. Her healing was complete. As we see her in obedience to His enquiry, coming before Him, we see her trembling, and we are inclined to ask the reason of that trembling. We may at least suggest one answer to such enquiry. She knew that according to Rabbinical law, her touch had defiled Jesus. The law provided that no person, with that particular form of disease, must touch any other person. Any such contact was supposed to convey defilement to the one so touched. Nevertheless she had dared the action, dared the Rabbinical law, and had grasped the *kraspedon* on the robe of Christ. She had thus made contact with Him. Necessarily we know that her contact had not defiled Him. His purity was never negative; it was positive. When the enemies of our Lord said upon occasion, " This Man receiveth sinners," they were complaining, because their view was that in such contact with sinning men, He would contract their defilement. The wonder of His personality is seen in the fact that in such contact He never contracted defilement, but rather communicated purity. The touch of the woman, therefore, had communicated none of her defilement to Him, but He had communicated to her the cleansing and life-giving power. This she knew, came forward, and openly confessed.

Such confession was and always is necessary. It is possible that someone in a great crowd may make contact with Christ, and receive the very spiritual health that they are seeking. They may even at the moment slip away; but sooner or later it is essential that they should bear witness to the fact.

It was, however, important in this case, among other reasons because Jairus was standing there, probably feeling impatient at the delay. The value to him we saw in our study concerning him. When immediately after the journey was resumed towards his house, and the news was brought to him that on the human level it was too late because his child was dead, surely there would come to him the memory of the confession made by that woman, that she had received healing.

So we reach the final words of Jesus to her. These need studying from the records of Matthew, Mark, and Luke. They all tell us that He addressed her as " Daughter." It is the only occasion on record when we are told that He used such an expression. Matthew tells us that He said, " Be of good courage." Mark and Luke tell us that He said, " Go in peace."

Now let us remember that her circumstances were still very doubtful. The healing was sure. She was made whole, but she was still penniless, she was still friendless, she was still divorced, she was still excommunicated by Rabbinical law. Whether for the moment she herself was conscious of these things we are not told, but the Lord knew and understood. He knew how difficult it was for one who had fallen under suspicion to be received back into respectable society. As in the case of the woman in the house of Simon, we saw that Simon could not see the woman as she then was, because he was looking at her as she had been; so it would be in the case of this woman. She was penniless, still ostracised notwithstanding the fact that she was healed. How would society treat her? How would her family look upon her? How would the religious rulers contemplate her? So far as they were concerned, she was still outside. But Jesus had said " Daughter," and by the use of that tender word He had recognised her adoption into the family of God. We have no further authentic account of her, but it is impossible not to realise that in coming days, all other considerations would be insignificant by the fact that He had called her " Daughter."

Moreover, He had charged her to be of good courage. Whatever fear might possess her, concerning her uncertain future, and on account of human opinion concerning her, and doubts toward her, He told her that there was no reason for fear.

He then pronounced the word of healing. She was already healed, but in His pronouncement He perchance corrected any superstition that had lurked in her mind, prompting her to come to Him. She had said, If I fasten upon His garments I shall be made whole. He said in effect, No, it was your faith which made the contact and was answered by healing. The physical was only the sacramental symbol of the spiritual, and that spiritual attitude and activity is the secret of healing.

He then used the same formula that He had used to the woman in the house of Simon. Not as we have rendered it, " Go in peace," but " Go into peace." Even though for the moment it may be that her consciousness was that of healing rather than that of complete peace, He indicated the fact that she might enter into peace on the basis of all that had happened. She was still excommunicated, still divorced, still ostracised; and in all probability she would not find it easy to find restoration to these realms. But she was now His adopted daughter. She had received from Him complete restoration, and she heard from Him the word that made her gloriously independent of all minor considerations.

These stories all constitute definite history, but their chief glory and value is that they give us age-abiding illustrations of the attitudes and activities of Christ. This thing that happened so long ago as a matter of history, is probably being repeated in this very congregation. We may say, without any question, that the multitude is thronging and pressing upon our Lord. That is why we are gathered together here. Our presence proves our interest, and there is absolutely nothing wrong in such interest. But it may be, hidden away in the crowd from all other than the Lord Himself, someone is stretching out the hand of faith conscious of great and over-whelming need. That man, that woman, whatever may be the spiritual or moral malady, can find healing as instantaneously and perfectly as the woman found when the issue of her blood was staunched.

> " She, too, who touched Thee in the press,
>   And healing virtue stole,
>   Was answered—' Daughter, go in peace,
>   Thy faith hath made thee whole.'
>   Concealed amid the gathering throng,
>   She would have shunned Thy view;
>   And if her faith was firm and strong,
>   Had strong misgivings too.
>   Like her, with hopes and fears, we come
>   To touch Thee, if we may;
>   O send us not despairing home;
>   Send none unhealed away."

XXIII

THE SYROPHŒNICIAN WOMAN

THERE are two matters which arrest us in the story of the Syrophœnician woman. The first is that the event took place on the occasion of an excursion of Jesus outside strictly Jewish territory. Tyre and Sidon was a region outside the economy of the ancient people, resting even then, as it had done for centuries, under the curse of God. The journey which Jesus took to reach the region was one of at least fifty miles over mountainous country, and almost impassable roads.

The second impressive fact in the story is that this was an occasion upon which He deliberately sought rest and retirement. This Mark makes perfectly clear:

> " From thence He arose, and went away into the borders of Tyre and Sidon. And He entered into a house, and would have no man know it."

If we consider this statement in the light of the context, we find on the human level, the reason. Hostility to Him had become more and more bitter. The days were crowded days, and so for a while He left the country of the privileged people to whom He was commissioned as the Messiah. Necessarily, we remember that in the ultimate meaning of that commission all the world was included; but He began at Jerusalem with the ancient people of God. Here was an occasion upon which He sought retirement and quietness, by crossing the border-line into Tyre and Sidon.

The woman to whom the story introduces us was an outcast from the Jewish standpoint. We read that she was a Greek, which simply means in this connection that she was a Gentile. Her actual nationality was Syrophœnician, and therefore her religion was pagan. We see our Lord then taking a long journey with His disciples, leaving for the moment the people to whom He was first specially sent, and coming to this region beyond the boundary line, He was brought into contact with this woman.

It is quite evident, however, that even in this region He was known, for we read that:

"He entered into a house, and would have no man know it."

However the statement of Mark which we have already quoted, is ended with the declaration that "He could not be hid."

This is a most arresting statement. We are led to enquire at once why it was that He could not be hid. The declaration is not a reference to the crowds of people that may have been surrounding Him. We know from other stories that He could always be hidden if He so desired. For instance, we read in the eighth chapter of John how, when hostile crowds were thronging round Him, and they were attempting to arrest Him, Jesus hid Himself. On this day, however, "He could not be hid."

I am emphasising this statement by way of introduction because the answer to our enquiry as to why He could not be hid becomes self-evident in the story itself. He knew the facts concerning this woman, and although He had sought retirement, He could not remain therein, while that woman was outside in her agony and need. In such cases He could not be hid. In that connection we may remind ourselves of the situation already referred to as recorded by John, when it is written He hid Himself. From intellectual pride and opposition He ever hides Himself. In the presence of human agony, when it makes its appeal to Him, He cannot be hid.

In looking at the woman we take first the accidental things, that is, the things of her circumstances and condition.

As we have said, she was a Gentile, which means of course from the standpoint of the writings of these evangelists, she was outside the covenant of Israel. We remember that Paul divided the human race into Jew and Gentile, for the purposes of his argument. So did all these writers in their thinking. This woman, then, was outside the privileges created by covenant relationship with the ancient people of God.

Then she was a Syrophœnician. That tells the story of her religion. The Syrophœnicians were all worshippers of Asherah, sometimes called Asheroth, and sometimes referred to as Astarte. Astarte was the moon goddess. The worship of the moon goddess began in the admiration of beauty, for all these false religions had something underlying them in the matter of their beginnings, which was worth while. Astarte was ever conceived of as the goddess of beauty. We have to bear in mind, however, the fact that at this period the whole idea had degenerated. These Syrophœnicians were affected by, and indeed, to a large measure, shared the Greek philosophy and outlook which declared that three things were of supreme importance. First, emancipation from all restriction; secondly, a complete expression of whatever may be found within human nature; and so, finally, all those experiences resulting from these two matters.

Many years ago Dr. Hugh Black, then of Edinburgh, wrote a book called " Culture and Restraint." In that book he contrasted the Hebrew ideal with the Greek. The Greek ideal was that of culture, the cultivation of anything and everything within human personality, without any restriction whatever, that is, without restraint. To put it in the common phraseology, it was the philosophy of letting oneself go, independent of all opinion and all law. The ideal of the Hebrew was that of restraint, that is government of personality by law. Dr. Black showed how in Christ the two ideals merged, culture, but under restraint; and consequently, restraint in order to culture. The religious atmosphere in which this woman had been born and brought up, declared that instinct and passion were perfectly right, and were to be indulged in, without any restraint whatever. The worship of beauty had become the worship of everything thought desirable, within human personality, of which life was capable. All that is undoubtedly suggested by the declaration of the evangelist that this woman was a Syrophœnician.

Turning from these matters, and looking at the woman as she stands revealed in the story, necessarily our first impression is that of her love. Here was something inherent in her motherhood; and in itself it was quite independent of her religious position. The story pulsates with the revelation of the suffering of this woman in the presence of her afflicted child. As she said, " My child, afflicted with an unclean spirit," we hear the wail of a mother's love. Thus we see manifested in this woman what I do not hesitate to call the universal good. We find it everywhere in humanity, however degraded that humanity may be. In passing one has to admit there do seem to be exceptions not alone in what we speak of as pagan countries, but in our own land. One does meet mothers who seem to have no love for their children, and who abandon them. I am not speaking of some distressed woman who abandons a baby on a door-step. That may not prove the absence of love. I am thinking rather of supposedly refined women who abandon their children to the care of servants and others. In spite of these exceptions, however, it is true that the love of motherhood is universal in human life. It was clearly manifested in the case of this woman. She was outside the covenant of Israel, but she was a mother. There was no one to whom she could turn among the privileged people, whose conception of motherhood was holy, but she was a mother, and was consumed by the love of her heart for her child.

The next thing that we observe about this woman is her faith. Perhaps we should hardly have seen this had it not been that presently we hear Jesus saying to her, " O woman, great is thy faith." How she knew Him we are not told. Mark does tell us earlier in his story, in chapter three, that people had come to see and hear Jesus from Tyre and Sidon. Evidently some of these people now knew Him. The way the story is told would suggest that she had not been among the number of such, because we are told she had heard about Him. Her faith is manifested in an activity, based upon conviction. That is always faith. If there be no conviction, faith is impossible. If conviction, however, produces no activity, then there is no faith. When conviction compels an activity, we have the evidence of faith.

Again, watching the whole process, we discover that she was a woman of tremendous will power and persistence. This is seen in the way in which she refused to be deflected from the purpose that had brought her to seek the Lord.

And once more, it is evident that in this hour of her dire necessity, she was entirely disillusioned as to the value of her own religion. Her child was possessed by an unclean spirit. She knew the hopelessness of Astarte in the presence of such a condition. Beauty meant nothing to her now, for ugliness was incarnate in her own offspring. She was conscious that the expression of passion was of no avail.

We do not know, but it is at least possible that the existence of the child was due to her own conception of life, that of giving expression to passion, and gaining experience. Be that as it may, the fact remains of her consciousness of helplessness in the presence of her need. It is an arresting picture, because there are thousands of people living in that realm to-day. Experience and expression, passion allowed to have its full fling; no restriction. These people often speak of their condition as being one of emancipation. Well, it may sound and seem excellent so long as the sun is shining. When the storms gather, there is no value in it. This woman had lived in that atmosphere, but now in the hour of her dire need, because of the suffering of her child, as Mark says, she had heard of Jesus, and now she heard that He had crossed the border-line, and was in the region of Tyre and Sidon.

When we turn to the contemplation of our Lord's dealing with this woman, let us honestly say that we find it a very startling story. Our first feeling as we read it, is that it does not seem to harmonise with all we know of Him. His first speech concerning her approach to Him does not sound like Him. That feeling, however, is the result of superficial understanding of the story. If we watch Him carefully, we shall understand what He was doing, and the ultimate result proves the intention that He had in the whole of His attitude. It is often a good thing to look at a result in order to understand a process. That I think will be true of life in its entirety presently. When we reach the life that lies beyond, we shall understand the processes through which we have passed, as we cannot understand them now. The ultimate result in the case of this woman is found in His final words to her, and His act of power through which the deliverance came that she sought. When that is borne in mind we find the interpretation of the method He adopted in dealing with her.

In His method we are conscious of what appeared to be His hesitations. I am not suggesting that there was any hesitation in His mind as to His ultimate intention; and, of course, there was no hesitation really, but His method seems to suggest it. The first thing we read was that when she first came:

" He answered her not a word."

Then His disciples besought Him to interfere and to send her away; and to them He replied:

" I was not sent but unto the lost sheep of the house of Israel."

So far He had addressed no word to the woman. The request of the disciples is in itself an interesting one. It may be that they were conscious of His desire for retirement, and therefore pleaded with Him to grant this woman's request, in order that she might go.

Then, when the woman made her appeal more urgent, " Lord, help me," He replied to her:

" It is not meet to take the children's bread and cast it to the dogs."

That does, to our ears, sound a harsh thing to have said. Even here, however, let us remember that the word He used for dogs was not the common one, but a diminutive, and one that had in it something of the note of tenderness. In those Eastern lands the dog was ever looked upon with contempt, that is, the wild, marauding dogs that were a positive menace to society. But in all those houses there were little dogs that had their place. When our Lord spoke thus to the woman, He did not use the word that described the ferocious dog, but that which referred to dogs admitted to the household.

What then, we enquire, was our Lord really doing? And we reply at once that by the very apparent harshness He was creating an opportunity for the complete activity of her faith. Presently He said to her, " O woman, great is thy faith." He knew that faith through all the processes. I declare without any hesitation that if He had not known it, He would not have adopted this method. We have really a remarkable illustration of how He adapted His method to the need of those with whom He was dealing. Here was a woman, a strong character, and great faith. He knew her. He was giving her the opportunity to proceed along the line of her own confidence, until she reached the point of full and complete expression. His silence when first she came was not refusal. Indeed, He had come outside the house, because she was there. He might have refused to see her. He needed retirement, but could not be hid.

Matthew tells us that she said in her approach:

"Have mercy on me, O Lord, Thou Son of David."

He made no response to her, but speaking to the disciples, He said:

"I was not sent, but unto the lost sheep of the house of Israel."

That statement in itself was remarkable, that He was sent, not to the house of Israel, but "to the lost sheep of the house of Israel." As we consider this statement we may call to mind a later hour in His ministry, when after controversy with the rulers in the case of the man born blind, He had instituted a new order of things, and had said to the listening Jews, possibly to their unutterable surprise:

"Other sheep I have, which are not of this fold; them also I must bring, . . . and they shall become one flock, one Shepherd."

It was to these lost sheep that He was sent. Here the objection may be raised that this woman was not of the house of Israel; and at once we recognise that this is true so far as the relation of the flesh is concerned. Presently, however, we see her receiving from Him in an act of power, a blessing that proved that spiritually she did belong to the house of Israel as the result of faith. She was one of the lost sheep.

In addressing her, what He said would seem to number her among the "little dogs." Let us bear in mind that these were the playthings of the children; and were constantly found around the tables in the homes. He told her that it was not fitting to take the children's bread and give it to these little dogs. Now we observe how His method was vindicated in the victory He gained. It may be said that it was her victory, and that is so; but that is what He was aiming at; and when she gained the victory of her persistence, He had gained His victory.

Against His silence she persevered. Against His apparent exclusion of her by what He had said to His disciples, she still persevered. When addressing her, He had seemed as though He was putting her out of the realm of the possibility of receiving help from Him, she still persevered. When He said:

"It is not meet to take the children's bread and cast it to the little dogs,"

she said:

"Yea, Lord; for even the dogs eat of the crumbs which fall from their master's table."

That was the point when her faith reached its ultimate, and gained its victory. An old Puritan writer says of her answer that it was

182

characterised by the wit of faith. She had come to Him against prejudice; she persevered against silence. She persevered further against apparent exclusion; and at last, with scintillating wit, which means with a vision to the heart of truth, she had consented to be numbered among the little dogs, under the master's table; but declared that even they partook of the crumbs. Thus all His method was vindicated as her faltering faith had persevered, until it had become victorious faith.

It is worthy of note that when she first spoke to Him she addressed Him as "Son of David." That was the peculiar Messianic description of Him. Evidently she was familiar with this, although herself not of the Hebrew people. It was to that application He made no reply. Presently she dropped that designation, and put the ultimate plaintiveness of her appeal into the word, " Lord, help me." That was not Messianic; that was universal. It was the cry of a human soul to One in Whose presence she recognised the presence of the Lord.

To that cry He gave the answer of power, and revealed the secret of it, as He said:

" O woman, great is thy faith; be it done unto thee even as thou wilt."

At that point this woman passes out of sight, but we see her travelling home, and watch her as she found the reward of her faith in the evidences of the power of Jesus. She had left her child possessed by an unclean spirit, twisted and contorted, and possibly in the paroxysms of passion. She returned to find her lying on the bed, resting, the demon gone, her life one of quietness and peace.

In this story we see our Lord turning from the infidelity of traditional orthodoxy to a faith found in pagan surroundings. The rulers within the covenant people were in opposition to Him. They lacked faith, and remained infidels in the presence of the wonders and signs of His mighty works and words. Turning from them, He found in pagan surroundings, a faith that drew from Him the commendation, " O woman, great is thy faith."

This remains a revelation for all time. Our Lord is ever doing this self-same thing, and will continue to do it when orthodoxy is cursed by infidelity. Over and over again He finds faith in surroundings that orthodoxy condemns.

The great teaching of the story is that faith is the principle of life, and not race. She was not of the chosen race. She lacked all the things of privilege. Nevertheless she made a venture upon the basis of a conviction; and by the activity of that faith came into vital relationship with the Lord and His power. It abides true that wherever men or woman make that venture on the basis of that conviction, they too enter into such relationship

183

with Christ which makes them of the seed royal, of the race eternal, of the very people of God.

Surveying the story, we remember that He had said to His disciples:

"I was not sent but unto the lost sheep of the house of Israel."

His action in this case was no departure from that high commission. Outside the fold of Israel He had found a member of the flock of God. He had fulfilled the function of His office in its wider sense.

When He had said to her, "It is not meet to take the children's bread and cast it to the dogs," and she had replied:

"Even the dogs eat of the crumbs that fall from their master's table."

He did not give her the crumbs, but the children's bread.

Whenever a soul, whatever its background may be, however pagan, and apparently contrary to past revelation, in its agony seeks Him, "He cannot be hid." That is the lesson of this story. Let it sing its song in every heart.

XXIV

THE FATHER, AND HIS BOY IN THE VALLEY

IN this story we see our Lord in contact with a father, and with his boy. The principal revelation is that of our Lord's dealing with the man, whereas of course, deliverance was wrought in the case of the boy.

This story is told by Matthew, by Mark, and by Luke, Mark giving the more detailed and vivid account. It is, however, important to observe, because of its bearing on our study, that the three evangelists place the incident at exactly the same point in the ministry of our Lord. This is significant. We are all fully aware that the chronology of the Gospel stories is not easy of arrangement. Matthew and Luke especially, wrote their Gospels from a definite standpoint of revelation, in the case of Matthew of the King, and in the case of Luke of the Son of man as the Saviour of the world. Therefore each of them introduces some story at a given point, which may not be in chronological sequence. Here, however, is the record of something that happened, and they all place it in direct connection with the account of the transfiguration. It is, as I have said, most important that we keep that in mind, because of the bearing of the fact upon the matter under consideration.

Before examining the story in detail, it is well to reconstruct so far as that is possible, the whole scene presented to our view. In order to that we need necessarily, not only the more detailed account found in the record of Mark, but those also of Matthew and Luke, adding as they do, some details not given by Mark.

It is so wonderful a picture that is presented to the mind that I have often wished that some artist would put it on canvas, and have connected it in my mind with my friend, Frank Salisbury, whose mural work is so well known. Simply as a scene it is unquestionably an amazing and most remarkable one. In the background is Mount Hermon. Without entering into any argument concerning it, I am assuming that of which I am

185

quite convinced, that the transfiguration of our Lord took place on Hermon, and not as so often stated, on Tabor. It was there that Peter made his great confession, and from there they had descended to the valley where this incident took place. Consequently, in any painting of the picture, Hermon should be seen, snow-capped, in the background.

Then as we look at the picture we are necessarily arrested by the central figure, that of our Lord Himself. In depicting this Figure in this particular picture I am inclined to think an artist would have somehow to represent some of the after-glow of the Mount of Transfiguration still resting upon Him. That is how I understand the statement of Mark:

"Straightway all the multitude, when they saw Him, were greatly amazed, and running to Him, saluted Him."

I am well aware that many reasons have been given for that amazement, but to me the simplest, and therefore the most satisfactory, is that which I have now suggested. While it is true that the disciples who had been with Him on the mountain, had been charged not to talk about what they had seen, I think the amazement caused was created by some unusual appearance of the Lord. When Moses came down from the Mount, his face shone, and he wist it not. The declaration that they were greatly amazed is an arresting one. In passing we may say that the Greek word here used for " amazed " only occurs four times in the New Testament, and they are all in the Gospel of Mark. This is the first occurrence. We find it again in the fourteenth chapter when it is said that Jesus was amazed in Gethsemane. The third occurrence is in the sixteenth chapter, when we are told that the disciples looking into an empty tomb, except for the presence of an angel within it, they were amazed. The last occurrence is found in the words the angel spoke to them, when they were in that condition, as he asked them, Why are you amazed? The real significance of the word is not that of surprise. It is rather that of an ever-haunting fear, as of the vision of something so unusual as to be appalling. As the crowds looked at Jesus when He had thus descended from the Mount of Transfiguration, and stood in their midst, they were amazed. I repeat, I cannot help believing that some after-glow of the mountain experience was still visible in Him.

Turning from our observation of the central Figure, we see two groups of people gathered there, opposed to each other. First we see a group of the scribes, and these were questioning and discussing quite evidently, with the disciples. The word questioning may be most accurately rendered disputing. As we look at these men, it is inevitable that we see in their very countenances something of cynicism. This is created by their view of the disciples on this particular occasion. We turn to look at these disciples, and we find them to be a company of defeated men. A case of demon possession had been brought to them, and they were quite unable to deal with it. It goes without saying that their defeat had produced in them a sense of dejection. The scribes hostile to Christ and to His followers, were seizing upon this opportunity of the defeat of the disciples of Jesus to dispute with them. These two groups must be clearly seen.

Then we come to the very centre of everything, and there we see two human beings, a father and his boy, the former filled with a terrible sorrow by reason of the suffering of his boy, and the boy quite helpless and undone. I repeat, that the scene in itself is a great subject for an artist.

Now to summarise the whole story as it is revealed in the scene. It presents to us helpless and defeated humanity. That is focussed in the picture of the boy and his father. In the presence of that the scribes themselves are defeated, though they certainly would not have described themselves in this way. They are defeated in the sense that they are quite unable to deal with the situation presented by this father and his boy. All they can do is to enter into some discussion with the disciples of Jesus. They could not do anything to help the boy or his father.

As we have seen, the disciples were also completely defeated. The boy had been brought to them, and they were unable to exercise any power that would set him free from his evil case.

The father is utterly helpless. It is impossible that we should be merely drawing upon our imagination when we say he had done everything he knew how to help that boy. Moreover he would willingly have given his own life if it had been possible by so doing, to set the boy free from demon possession. But he was quite helpless.

Necessarily the supreme illustration of helplessness is that of the boy himself. Thus the whole picture is that of defeated and helpless humanity in the presence of evil. But we look again, and we have the vision of the victorious Lord as He appeared on the scene. We might spend much time in attempting to see Him in His own Person. All that must, however, reverently be taken for granted, and we watch Him in connection with the situation. His first words were those of rebuke:

> " O faithless generation, How long shall I be with you? How long shall I bear with you? "

The words were general, and included in their sweep His own disciples, the disputing scribes, and the suffering father and his boy. He spoke out of the consciousness that He was living in a generation without faith. The cry constituted a soliloquy coming out of the very heart of Jesus, revealing His consciousness of the difficulties in the midst of which His work was being done. We may turn aside for a moment here to remind ourselves that all the ministry of our Lord was conducted in the midst of difficulty, which appeared all the way to be too great, and to produce continued defeat. When to-day I hear people talking of the failure of the Church, I am ever inclined to remind them that by all human standards and measurements from beginning to end, the ministry of Christ was characterised by failure. Necessarily we know now that what appeared to be failure was a continuous progress towards an ultimate victory. This is true of the Church also.

After this word spoken to the generation, our Lord turned to the father, asking him a question, and receiving his answer. He then addressed the underworld with absolute authority, which not only set the lad free from his evil case for the moment, but commanded and secured the continuity of that freedom, for He said:

" Come out of him, and enter no more into him."

Thus the authority of the Lord was revealed in the presence of that which had defeated the father, His own disciples, and the scribes. He did what none other could, and that with quiet authority and power.

Now let us turn to observe this man and his boy a little more carefully. As we look at the father we first necessarily are impressed by his suffering. The case of the boy appeals to us because of its entailment of suffering, but in the last analysis it is the suffering of the father that is the most outstanding fact. Luke tells us that he referred to his boy as " mine only child," which phrase might be most accurately rendered " mine only begotten son." This description is, in itself, arresting, in view of the Person of our Lord. He was the only begotten Son of God, and here He is seen in the presence of a demon-possessed only-begotten son of a man. The reference is made here, however, to emphasise the fact of the suffering of this man in the presence of the madness and physical torment of his child.

Then as we look at him, and listen to him, we know of his sense of bitter disappointment. He had brought his boy to the disciples, and they were beaten. The arresting fact is that while they were beaten that day, they had in the past accomplished the very thing they were unable then to do. When Jesus had sent them out, He had given them authority to cast out demons, and they had done it. But here was an hour in which they were helpless and paralysed. Hence the sense of bitter disappointment filling the heart of the father.

Once more it reveals his mind, as he employed the language which expresses a forlorn hope. It is the language of hope, but it is forlorn, as the result of his disappointment. He had told

Jesus about the child, and his terrible sufferings. He had thus revealed to Him the agony of his heart; and then he cried out:

"If Thou canst do anything, have compassion on us, and help us."

When he first spoke to our Lord he had said, "I brought unto Thee my son," and then he said:

"I spake unto Thy disciples that they should cast it out; and they were not able."

Evidently the first intention of the man was not to bring him to the disciples, but to the Lord Himself. When he arrived, Jesus was not there. His representatives were there, but they were helpless. Now he said:

"If Thou canst do anything."

In the very saying there is revealed the wonder or fear in his heart, created by the failure of the disciples. One can almost imagine the working of the man's mind. It is as though he were thinking, 'I came with the boy. I brought him in hope. I felt that if I brought him to Thee, there might be hope. But Thou wert not here. Thy followers were here, but they could not do anything. Does that mean that Thou hast lost Thy power, or that all the stories I have heard were not true?' All this seems to lie within that expression, "If Thou canst." In that sense, therefore, it was a definite appeal, and an appeal of hope, and yet hope that was struggling against fear, and almost mastered thereby.

Then when Jesus replied to him in words which we shall consider presently, he cried out:

"Lord, I believe, help Thou mine unbelief."

It was a venture made with the consciousness of its weakness. Thus we see the man suffering, disappointed, having a forlorn hope in the midst of his sorrow, and then making the venture of a faith which he himself was conscious, was characterised by weakness.

Turning from our contemplation of the man we look at the boy. In this connection it is an arresting fact that the Lord asked the father how long the boy had been in that case. Necessarily we know that He did not need information. There was, undoubtedly, however, a reason for the enquiry, and the reason was that there should be clear understanding of how desperate a condition he was in. The father answered, "From a child," which quite literally means from his birth. Thus we see that the possession of this boy by an evil spirit, with all its terrible consequences, was not the result of his own personal sin. For the moment I am attempting no explanation of the fact, but am facing it. In that boy in the valley we stand in the presence of suffering, not resulting from the wrong-doing of the sufferer. We may say that our world is full of this kind of experience. Nevertheless we may say in passing, that all such suffering has some explanation in racial relationships. Thus the boy is revealed utterly beyond the reach of human effort, suffering mentally and physically through no wrong of his own; while behind it all the mystery of evil, having this terrible manifestation.

As we turn from our contemplation of the father and his boy to watch Christ, we necessarily return for a moment to the point at which we began our meditation. The significance of this event in the valley following immediately the experience of the Mount of Transfiguration is related thereto in a remarkable way. As we look at the Lord we see the One Who had reached the experience of transfiguration. No other human being had ever been transfigured. It is quite true that we make use of this word in other ways, and there are senses in which this may be permissible. We see someone who perchance has endured suffering, passing into the place of restoration, and we speak of them as transfigured. It is a beautiful poetical word, but inadequate to express the experience through which our Lord had passed. I repeat none other had ever been transfigured. In the Old Testament we read that Enoch walked with God, and he was not, for God took him. He was translated by an act of God, not transfigured. We read of Moses whose face shone after communion with God, but he was not transfigured. There never has been any other transfiguration in the full sense of the great word than that of our Lord Himself. To understand the meaning of the experience we may quite properly change the word transfiguration, and do so by transliteration. To do this is to read that He was metamorphosed; the whole of the form was changed, and in that change God's second Man had come to the perfect realisation of human nature, according to the Divine ideal. Immaculately conceived, innocent in the true sense of the word in childhood, holy as against all temptation, He at last reached the true consummation of human life according to Divine intention; He was metamorphosed. From that mountain top Jesus might have passed into the life that lies beyond, without dying.

He it is Who is now seen standing in the midst of the crowd. He had left the mountain, and so far as it is possible in human language to express the truth, we may say that He Who had been metamorphosed, had resumed the form which had been changed, the form in which death was possible. The One we look upon, therefore, was not only the Man of the mountain height of transformation. He was the One Who had turned His back upon it for some great purpose. On the mount we see Him talking with Moses and Elijah, and the subject of conversation was that of the exodus He was about to accomplish in Jerusalem. Even there in all the glory of the perfect victory and realisation of His humanity, His face was set towards the valley and the Cross. He was the only begotten Son of God even in His human nature, that is the only One Who had realised the Divine intention in His Sonship, and He is now seen confronting the only begotten son of man demon-possessed. He was the One Who had reached the mountain height, but Who had left it with His face set to the valley.

In dealing with the father He first asked the question to which we have already referred, emphasising the appalling condition of the boy as He received the answer that told Him he had been in that case from a child. Then when the father cried out in his anguish:

> "If Thou canst do anything, have compassion on us, and help us,"

our Lord replied:

> "If thou canst! All things are possible to him that believeth."

It will be observed that I have slightly altered the emphasis as is revealed in the changed punctuation. Our Lord was not now telling the man that all things were possible to him if he believed. But He was declaring the profounder fact as to why things were possible to Him, when they were impossible to others. The man had said, "If Thou canst," to which our Lord in effect replied that the principle of ability in this universe is that of perfect faith in God. At the beginning of the incident He had cried out "O faithless generation." Now He said, "All things are possible to him that believeth." It was because He Himself believed in God in the full sense of the word, that there was no wavering, no failing, no halting, no hindrance. He was in contact with Almighty power. We call to mind the fact that these miracles, or wonders, or powers that Jesus wrought were wrought by God through Him, and that is because of His perfect faith. On the day of Pentecost this truth was declared by Peter, when he said:

> "A Man of Nazareth, approved of God unto you by powers and wonders and signs which God did by Him in the midst of you."

He did not say He did these things, but declared that God did them, acting through Him. It was by the power of God that the demon was cast out of this boy. That power operated through His Son to Whom all things were possible because of His faith in God.

It was then that the father cried, "Lord, I believe"; and knowing that his faith was by no means complete, he added, "Help Thou mine unbelief." He had seen something of the truth of the principle declared by Jesus, and in reply, in effect, he said, If that be so, then I venture, I believe; and yet I am conscious that the belief is imperfect; there is something which is holding me back, something which is still raising questions. Therefore, help Thou mine unbelief.

Our Lord's reply to that was immediate. He turned to the boy and dismissed the demon. The word was one of full and complete authority, accompanied by victorious power, so that the thing was done for the boy, which could not be done by father, disciples, and certainly not by critical scribes.

Then we are told He stretched forth His hand, and took the boy by the hand. Very beautiful is the way in which Luke tells what happened. "He gave him back to his father."

The whole story is supremely wonderful in that it is not only matter of history, it has microcosmic value. It is something far more than the narrative of an occurrence in the long ago. In itself it is an unveiling of the reason for and the exercise of perfect power by our Lord. The inter-relation of the mountain and the valley here is clearly marked. Jesus is seen as the Man of absolute perfection, Who came to the fulness of humanity's stature in transfiguration. He is seen, however, there as not counting His realisation something to be taken and held to His own advantage. There in human life as in the mystery of His Deity, He emptied Himself denied Himself, and set His face to the valley. Herein is the eternal secret of the power of Christ. He is the sinless One as the mountain testifies. He is the redeeming One as the valley witnesses.

XXV

THE CONDEMNED WOMAN

R EADERS of the King James Version, commonly called the
Authorised, will see nothing unusual in the arrangement of
the text in the Gospel according to John at this point of his
story. Those reading from the Revised Version will observe
that the paragraph, John vii, 53, to viii, 11, is printed within
brackets. That applies both to the English and American
Revisions. Moreover, if the reader is using the Greek New
Testament, Westcott and Hort's text, he will find the paragraph
is omitted, but is put in at the end of the Gospel. If on the other
hand, Nestle's text is used, the paragraph is in the place where it
is found in the translations, but in brackets. I pause to refer
to these facts because naturally young folk reading, will ask the
meaning of them. That may at once be stated by saying that
the weight of external and internal evidence is considered by the
most competent and devout scholars to be in favour of the view
that this story did not form part of the Gospel as John wrote it,
that it is an interpolation added, probably at a later time.

The questions may further be asked as to when and why it
was inserted. The probability is that we have here an extra-
illustration in the life of Jesus from the pen of Papias. Of Papias,
Eusebius says that he was a bishop in the first half of the second
century, and that he collected traditions illustrative of " The
Oracles of the Law." His intention was to throw further light
upon the history contained in the Gospel narrative   It is therefore,
more than probable that Papias committed to writing this story
of oral tradition, and intended it to be an illustration of the
statement found in viii, 15, in its spiritual values. What was a
marginal reading, so far as Papias was concerned, was at some
period embodied in the letter of the text. In that sense it is
looked upon as an interpolation.

Nothing can be dogmatically asserted concerning it. If, however, this suggestion is correct, there is no reason to doubt the authenticity of the story, for doubtless many true stories were not committed to writing, but transmitted orally; and the work of Papias was valuable in retaining them. In our consideration we shall proceed upon the assumption of its accuracy, and in doing that I feel that its authenticity is stamped upon its character, for there is no more beautiful story in the record of John than this.

Our first business, then, is to see the woman as she is presented to us here, and in this case, as constantly in such cases in the New Testament, her name is not given. Neither is the city to which she belonged named. It is evident that this took place in Jerusalem, and there she had been found guilty of sin, and had been arrested. Necessarily there is one thing to be said concerning her, which sounds almost banal, but which nevertheless must ever be remembered in considering this story, and all such stories. She was some mother's child.

As we look at her as she is presented here, we first of all find ourselves in revolt against the men who brought her, and the methods of their speech. In passing I may say their successors are not all extinct. They represent a class and an attitude whose only effect could be that of hardening sinners in their evil courses. On the other hand, as we read the story we are thankful that they are clearly seen, for they help us in what they said, to see the woman, and their action helps us to see our Lord as He dealt with her.

Now we realise first of all that the whole truth at the moment concerning the woman can be told by declaring that she was criminal, she was caught, she was condemned. There is no question whatever about her criminality. The very indelicate and almost indecent way in which these men told the story reveals that fact. Their account of the matter was not challenged. There was no question as to her crime. Then she had been caught, and at that time as now, in the eyes of men that is the supreme sin. We have no further details than this statement that she had been taken in the very act of sin. Consequently by the law of God as it had been enunciated to the people through Moses, she was condemned. So much the literal account reveals.

Then we come to the place where, with all these things in mind, if the imagination be quick, and the heart illuminated, we can see things that are not stated. It was early in the morning when they brought her into the Temple. Jesus had returned there after retirement in the Mount of Olives through the night. There is pathos in the statement with which chapter seven ends and chapter eight beings:

" They went every man unto his own house; but Jesus went unto the mount of Olives."

From that place where He had spent the night, He came back to the Temple, and the people thronged round Him, and He taught them. It was then, while He was thus occupied, that these men brought this woman to Him. John is careful to tell us she was placed in the midst, that is, in the midst of the crowd. This would constitute a disturbance. While the people were listening to Jesus, something happened which broke in upon' the crowd, and upon the teaching. A company of men, with a woman, disturbed the occasion, and found their way to the very midst of the crowd, and into the presence of Jesus. Necessarily there would be cessation in His teaching, while the people who had been attentive, became interested in what was happening.

Now with that quick imagination to which I have referred, look at the woman as she comes in. Do not forget that she had been caught in the act of sin. There was no escape from the fact of her guilt, and these moral rulers have arrested her, and for purposes of their own, have brought her into the presence of Jesus. It is impossible to look at her without seeing that in the hands of those men, and under those conditions, her attitude was that of a woman sullen and defiant. The men in whose charge she was, could do nothing to help moral dereliction. The finer possibilities of her womanhood were submerged under the influence of their hard, cold legalism. She was caught ! Very well, then, let them do what they like. Under the circumstances she was calloused. The question which arose at the time undoubtedly in the mind of the watchers, and which recurs as inevitably to us is, as to what Jesus will do or say under these circumstances. The woman before Him is criminal, caught, condemned, and for the moment calloused.

As thus we wait and watch and wonder, we see the Lord doing an apparently strange thing. Without uttering any word, He stooped and bending over, He wrote with His finger upon the ground.

These men had brought this woman to Jesus, and had enquired from Him what He had to say in view of Jewish law. According to that, her condemnation was that she should be stoned. Their enquiry was concerned with His opinion on that matter. They were really attempting to place Him on the horns of a dilemma. The law according to Moses had definitely said that a woman guilty in that way was to be stoned to death. The Roman power had taken away from the Jewish people the right to inflict the death penalty. In passing we remind ourselves that that was why at last they went to Pilate concerning Jesus. When later on, in madness, they took Stephen and put him to death, they were breaking the Roman law. In view of all this it will be seen that if Jesus said that this woman must suffer the penalty Moses had commanded, they could charge Him with running counter to Roman law. If on the other hand, He said that such penalty was not to be executed, they might charge Him with lowering the standards of morality.

It was under these conditions that He first of all maintained a silence, and bending over, wrote with His finger on the ground. As once more imagination helps one, the woman can be seen watching this procedure, and in all probability there was some change coming over the look of callous defiance which had been there when they brought her.

These men, however, were determined to have an answer. They kept on asking the same question. Then He rose, and spoke to them. In doing so He compelled them to the supreme matter of their act of bringing this woman; and its possible issue according to Mosaic law. Standing between competing laws, the Roman and the Jewish, He referred neither to the one nor the other, but in the presence of them He enunciated an eternal principle. He did not contradict the law of Moses. He did not suggest that tenderness of heart might be a reason for abrogating its requirements. He uttered this statement:

"He that is without sin among you, let him first cast a stone."

Now it is of vital importance that here we pause in order that we may accurately apprehend the thing that our Lord had done. The woman was before Him, standing, watching, and almost surely wondering. He did not discuss the Roman law. He did not discuss the Mosaic law. But He declared that there was only one condition upon which any should have the right to ultimate judgment and the infliction of punishment; and that condition was that of sinlessness. We need to remember that the word our Lord employed here was one which we translate by two. Our translation reads " He that is *without sin*." That phrase,

" without sin " is one word in the Greek, and it is the only place in the New Testament where it occurs.   It suggests far more than freedom from committing sin.   It means freedom from sin in nature as well as in experience.   These men who had brought this woman to Jesus were far more interested in trapping Him in some way than they were in catching her.   To them then He said in effect, in answer to their enquiry; If according to Moses this woman should die by stoning, then let the sinless among you first cast a stone.   Thus, though He did not discuss the law, either the Mosaic or the Roman, He declared an eternal principle, namely, that sinlessness is the condition of exacting a penalty.

There was ever something in the very presence of Jesus, and in the way in which He spoke that brought men face to face with reality.   By His enunciating of this principle these men were impaled.

We turn to look at the woman, and find her still there waiting, and almost surely wondering.   If when He spoke of being sinless His application was intended only in the particular moral realm involved in the sin of the woman, then these men were called upon to face their own history and experience.   In His enunciation of His own ethic He had said:

" Ye have heard that it was said, Thou shalt not commit adultery; but I say unto you, that every one that looketh with desire hath committed adultery."

One can imagine the effect produced upon these men by such a judgment.   Then at the risk perhaps of criticism I cannot help saying the fun began.   If objection be taken to the statement, then it seems to me that those objecting, lack all humour.   Personally I cannot follow this story without being filled with merriment. Suddenly I see a procession of men passing out of the Temple in single file.   The account declares that they:

" Went out one by one, beginning from the eldest, even unto the last."

That may mean that they were still standing upon the dignity of precedence, granted to age.   Personally I am inclined to think that the eldest went first because he had most sense.   As they went, the Lord is seen once more bending over, and writing on the ground.   There is an old legend that He wrote the name of some town, or some woman, and that these men seeing it, were brought face to face with His full and intimate knowledge, and therefore they hurried forth. Necessarily there is no proof of this, but it is at least a suggestive story. The one definite fact is that their exit was their own confession of unfitness to carry out the sentence upon this woman.

At this point the story definitely says:

" And Jesus was left alone, and the woman, where she was in the midst."

This is a revealing way of saying that the crowd was still there, but that for all vital purposes, Jesus and this woman were alone. As we look at them we are conscious of an almost appalling contrast. He, absolute and incarnate Purity. She, confessed, incarnate impurity. He was the only One Who, according to His own principle, had the right to cast the first stone at her. These arresting men dared not do it. They had gone. He was sinless. We wait almost breathlessly for what will happen next.

He asked her two questions, I think in quick succession, for they are in their entirety, one. He said:

" Woman, where are they? did no man condemn thee? "

As we listen, the first word arrests us, " Woman." We find other occasions on record when our Lord used that word, but always in the accents of respect and tenderness. He used it to His Mother in Cana. He used it in addressing the woman of Samaria. He used it again to His Mother on the Cross. He used it to Mary on the resurrection morning. He used it now. By all the laws and opinions of men she had forfeited the right to that very name. We can think of all sorts of objectionable epithets that might have been applied to her. He used the word that invested her with beauty and dignity, in spite of the fact that He knew exactly her condition.

There was surely a touch of playful irony in His first question, " Woman, where are they? " He was drawing attention to the fact that she was alone with Him. He had excluded her accusers. Then in that loneliness He referred to these men who had gone, when He said, " Did no man condemn thee? "

Then there fell from the lips of the woman the only words she is recorded to have uttered. They had brought her in in sullen silence. All these things had happened, and now in answer to His second enquiry, she said, " No man, Lord." It is perfectly true that the word " Lord " might oftentimes be accurately rendered Sir. Here, I think, however, it may be taken with its fuller value. She realised at any rate that she was standing in the presence of One infinitely superior. It was then that He uttered His final words:

> " Neither do I condemn thee; go thy way; from hence-forth sin no more."

Two things were involved in these words of Jesus, and the second follows the first.

The first was, " Neither do I condemn thee." The word here rendered " condemn " is a very strong one not often found in the New Testament. Indeed, its only places in the Gospel narratives are when our Lord used it concerning the generation, when placing it in contrast with Nineveh, and the Queen of Sheba; when He was anticipating His own death, and when the sentence actually passed upon Him, was referred to. It is further used by New Testament writers to describe the penalty of unbelief in Him. The idea of the word includes the finding of a verdict, and the passing of a sentence.

The one absolutely certain thing is that in uttering this word, our Lord was not lowering the standard of moral requirement, or in any sense condoning sin. As an aside I am ever inclined, when I read this sentence, to put an emphasis upon the word ". thee " " neither do I condemn *thee*." They had brought this woman to Jesus, and declared that she had been caught in the very act of sin. If this were true, then another was involved. Where was he? They had no right to bring her alone into the presence of Christ. I do not desire to over-emphasise that application, for it certainly is not a final one. Nevertheless it is a question that may very pertinently be asked to-day, when over and over again, the woman is condemned, and the man is dined.

But what He said meant infinitely more than that. It was the refusal of the sinless One to condemn the sinful one, and that can best be explained by quotation from the pen of an inspired apostle. In the letter to the Romans, Paul wrote:

> " There is therefore now no condemnation to them that are in Christ Jesus."

If perchance it should be objected that when our Lord spoke, the sacrificial work of the Cross was not accomplished, that view should be corrected by a recognition of the fact that in the mystery of the Godhead and its redeeming activity, the " Lamb was slain from the foundation of the world." I have not come, said Jesus, upon another occasion, to condemn the world, but that the world may live through Me. In that moment our Lord put

Himself between that woman and her sin on the basis of that eternal fact:

"'No condemnation,' Oh my soul,
'Tis God Who speaks the word."

But God never speaks that word idly. Behind the action of God and the speech of Jesus is all the mystery of His mission as finally manifested in His Cross.

Then followed the second word:

" Go thy way; from henceforth sin no more."

He was indicating the fact that a new pathway was open before her, and again if we turn to the letter to the Romans we find the secret revealed. Not only was it true that there was no condemnation, it was equally true that there was given a new empowerment, a new life, which was that of ability to overcome sin. We do not know anything about what subsequently happened to her on any documentary evidence. We cannot tell where she went when she left those Temple courts. This we do know that wherever she went, she went out a new woman, the sullenness gone, and the defiance at an end; she passed forth to the future pardoned, cleansed, forgiven, empowered for the coming days.

The story is full of perpetual value. If some shall read it knowing themselves to be criminal, caught, and condemned, let them remember that they can be alone with Christ. He excludes all others from any right of interference. Such souls may receive His word of absolution, and receive His power for life.

Perhaps someone reads the story who is not caught, not condemned by the laws of man, who yet is criminal. Let such an one also stand in the presence of Christ, and facing the truth concerning his or her condition, yield to Him as Saviour and Lord, and receive from Him the word of freedom and the word of power.

XXVI

THE LAWYER

THE parable of the Good Samaritan, which is peculiar to Luke, is radiantly beautiful. Indeed, so wonderful is it that we may lose sight of the reason of it. Expositors have often treated it as setting forth the mission and method of our Lord, and that quite permissibly. It is well, however, to remember that when our Lord uttered it, His intention was not to interpret His own mission, save as there was in Himself the fulfilment of all the great things revealed in the parable. The parable in itself constituted part of our Lord's method of dealing with one man. It is in that way we approach it now, and shall only touch upon the parable as it applied to the case under consideration.

The man appearing before us, then, is a nameless lawyer. A careful consideration of the whole narrative will reveal that he was a very interesting, and indeed, a remarkable man. We may even describe him as a fine character, save as revealed at one point of moral breakdown, to which we shall come presently.

The simple fact, as we have said, is that he was " a lawyer." We remember that there are three terms employed in the New Testament which are synonymous in their application to persons. We read of the scribe, of the doctor or teacher, and of the lawyer. Here we have three distinct Greek words, *grammateus*, rendered " scribe "; *didaskalos*, rendered " doctor " or " teacher," and *nomikos*, rendered " lawyer." Whichever name is employed, the reference is to the same office or position. At the time of our Lord, these men constituted an order well established in the life of the Hebrew people. No provision was made for them in the Mosaic economy. The office and the order emerged in the time of the return of these people from captivity under Ezra and Zerubbabel. Ezra was the first to institute the order of the scribes.

We are told of them in the time of Ezra that they read the law and gave the sense. This means more than that they read clearly and properly. It indicates interpretation. These men were expositors of the law. As time had gone forward, the order had continued; and in the story of Jesus we constantly meet members thereof.

We may say, then, that the lawyer was an expert in law. He had three duties devolving upon him. One was to study and interpret the law. The second was to give definite instruction especially to the youth of the nation in the law. The third was the exercise of judicial capacity. The lawyer was called upon to decide questions in law. Now this man was one of this order.

We see at once, then, that he was not an ordinary man, but one trained in one particular subject, the law of the Hebrews as given to them through Moses. Moreover, at the time of our Lord, as we are well aware, there had been super-imposed upon the law of Moses traditions intended to explain them. It was the work of the scribe or lawyer to interpret and apply these also. So much for the man and his position.

We now attempt to see him by carefully and critically reading the story, and watching him. First of all it is evident that he was seriously enquiring. Luke introduces him by saying:

"And behold, a certain lawyer stood up and tempted Him."

Here it is most necessary that we halt and consider what is meant by that word "tempted." It is not the usual word employed. It does not mean that he was endeavouring to entrap Him. It is indeed a strong word, and we may quite accurately render it:

"A certain lawyer stood up, and put Him thoroughly to the test."

There is no reason for thinking that there was any hostility manifested in this case. It is perfectly true that we do find over and over again hostility revealed in attempts to entrap Jesus. There is no evidence of anything of the kind here. He was rather suggesting a question, the answer to which would inevitably be a revelation of the mind of the Master.

We notice further that he was seeking the highest, and that with rare intelligence. The question he asked was one which must put any man thoroughly to the test:

"Teacher, what shall I do to inherit eternal life?"

There are many things in our holy Faith with which we have become so familiar that unless we keep constant watch, we miss their full value. I am thinking now of this term " eternal life." Rightly apprehended, we shall find that the question the lawyer asked was the supreme question for all life. It is a question which to-day may be asked of any teacher, of any philosopher; and upon the answer given will depend the knowledge or lack of knowledge of the one so questioned.

Let it be at once said that eternal life means something far more than long life. Its continuity is dependent upon its nature. The question might be framed, What shall I do to inherit the life of the ages, life that is abiding, life that is full, the life that lacks limitation, life which is as broad and as deep and as high, as it is long? We remember at this point that the young ruler asked exactly the same question. Wherever a man is found seriously asking this question, he is thinking on high levels, and is engaged on the highest possible quest.

He was conscious of his own deficiency as the form of the question proves:

" What shall I do to *inherit* eternal life? "

His enquiry was a revelation of his dissatisfaction with any experience he had so far had of life. He knew life. He had been born. He had played as a child. He had grown up as a young man. He had come into a position of influence as a lawyer. But his question proved that he was still seeking that life which could only be described as eternal, or the life of the ages.

We see him, then, as a man dissatisfied, but aspiring to something higher. With this greatest of all questions he approached Jesus, and by asking it, determined to put Him thoroughly to the test.

Still watching him through the story, we are arrested by his answer to our Lord's first question:

" What is written in the law? how readest thou? "

As we have already said, technically he was expert in the matter of the law, but it is evident that he had a spiritual apprehension of it which was correct. He answered our Lord in the declaration:

" Thou shalt love the Lord thy God with all thy heart, and with all thy soul, and with all thy strength, and with all thy mind; and thy neighbour as thyself."

It will be observed that our Lord did not ask him only what was written, but how he read it, that is, understood it. It is an arresting fact that he said nothing in his answer about sacrifices, nothing about duties, nothing about social obligations; and yet he summarised all these in the answer he gave. We need not argue its excellence because our Lord approved the answer, as He said:

" Thou hast answered right; this do, and thou shalt live."

In these words He declared the accuracy of his intellectual conception, and declared to him that in obedience to it, the secret of life is discovered.

It was at this point that we see the moral breakdown. Luke very carefully tells us:

" He, desiring to justify himself, said unto Jesus, And who is my neighbour? "

He was evading an issue. He had answered correctly as to the text of the law, and as to its spirit. When he was commanded to act upon his understanding obediently, he made an answer that revealed him as desiring to justify himself.

Directly a man seeks to justify himself, he is admitting that he is arraigned before some tribunal. What was the tribunal before which this man found himself suddenly arraigned? It has been suggested that it means he was desirous to justify himself before men. Others have said that he desired to justify himself before Jesus. Personally I believe there is a deeper meaning in the declaration. He desired to justify himself to himself. He knew at once that while his thinking was correct in the matter of law, his actions were not in accord therewith, and he would evade the issue of this question as to who was to be looked upon as his neighbour. It was a refusal at the critical centre of his being to face the challenge that had come to him from his own answer, and the Lord's approval of it.

We have a further revelation of this man's rare intelligence in the apprehension of truth, in that when our Lord had uttered to him the parable, and asked him a question upon it, his answer was again correct. Having portrayed the wretched condition of the man on the highway, He had told the lawyer of three men, who passed along the road. They all had vision of the man. The priest saw him. The Levite saw him. The Samaritan saw him. The vision in the case of the first two brought no result of helpfulness to the man. They passed by on the other side. In the case of the third, the vision appealed to his heart, and stirred his compassion. When Jesus asked the lawyer which of the three was neighbour to the wounded, bruised, half-dead man; he immediately gave the right answer, " He that shewed mercy on him." Thus we have in him a picture of a man questing for life, knowing he had not found it, desiring it, putting Jesus to the test, and then evading a moral issue.

We now turn to watch our Lord dealing with this man. His first enquiry was one which turned him back upon himself, and called for an opinion in a realm in which he was unquestionably a specialist. Jesus said in effect to him, Why do you come to Me asking about life? You are a lawyer, that is, an interpreter of law. Let Me, therefore, approach you, and ask you the very question that scores of people have asked you in other matters, What saith the law? How do you read it? The very method of these questions was remarkable. First, " What is written in the law? " Secondly, " How readest thou? " The two were necessarily interdependent. The " How " depends upon the " What " as to the actual statement of law. The " What " depends upon the " How " for moral value. It is possible to answer the " What " with perfect accuracy, and yet discover that the reply to the " How " is a revelation of failure.

The question, " How readest thou? " was a common question put to the Rabbis. Men and women in difficulty about law would often quote to the Rabbis its terms, and then ask for an interpretation of it. Thus the man found himself flung back upon his own calling in life, and upon the things with which he was supposed to be, and undoubtedly was, an expert. The question was such as to produce a revelation of his correct understanding. It is noticeable, however, that he gave no answer to the second question, except as that might be involved in his first answer. It is an arresting fact that he did not quote from the Decalogue. He linked together two passages found in different positions in the ancient law. So far, then, he had replied to both questions. The " How " was answered in the method by which he summarised the written requirements. Then followed the evasion on the part of the lawyer, and the parable, in which our Lord dealt with the evasion.

The outstanding fact in the parable is that in employing it our Lord completely changed the emphasis of the lawyer's question. The lawyer had said, " Who is my neighbour? " And now let it be observed that our Lord did not answer that question; but to gather up the whole impact of the parable we find that its purpose was to say to this man, The question is not so much, Who is your neighbour, as, To whom are you prepared to be a neighbour? Here we pause to listen to the parable in itself. Our Lord took the supreme case of a bruised and broken and half-dead man lying upon the highway. A priest is seen looking upon that man, but at once passing him by. That is also true of the Levite. Neither priest nor Levite was a neighbour to that man. They both saw him, were cognisant of his condition, but did nothing for him. Then came this Samaritan. The question was not as to whether the half-dead man was a neighbour to the Samaritan. It was a necessary question, was the Samaritan a neighbour to the man? With a fine satire our Lord excluded all official religion as it then existed in the Hebrew nation, and He excluded priest and Levite because of what they were in themselves, and of how they had acted in the presence of such a case. If He excluded them, He included a man outside the covenant people, a man held in contempt for that reason by both priest and Levite, and Jewish nation—a Samaritan. The Jew had no dealings with the Samaritan nationally or religiously; and it was equally true that the Samaritan had no dealing with the Jew. Nevertheless this Samaritan is seen acting without any reference to these hostilities in the presence of human need. Our Lord used of him that great expression so constantly employed concerning Himself, " He was moved with compassion "; and, therefore, he acted the part of neighbour to the man in need. It is possible that he was at the time returning along the road, after he had been to worship in Mount Gerizim; but something deeper than mistaken conceptions of worship, and its true place, was found in the compassion of his soul.

The picture is Eastern and beautiful, of what he did, using the remedies of the time, he poured oil and wine in those gaping wounds. He lifted the man, and placed him on his own beast, and evidently walking by his side until they came to the inn, he placed him in charge of the host thereof, and undertook responsibility for him. Moved with compassion for him, he bound up the wounds, carried the man who could not carry himself; put him in a place of safety, and thus acted as a neighbour.

The story told, the challenge of our Lord was uttered:

" Which of these three, thinkest thou, proved neighbour unto him that fell among the robbers? "

In this enquiry we have the vindication of what we have already said, that while the lawyer had asked, " Who is my neighbour? " Jesus was showing him that that was a secondary question, the first being whether he himself had the heart of a neighbour. If so, then the one to whom the heart goes out, becomes a neighbour. If this had been a man living by the law he had quoted, really loving God and loving man, he would have been a man capable of feeling compassion in the presence of wounds and weariness, and of such action as would bring healing and help to the distressed.

In the answer he gave to the enquiry of Jesus, " He that shewed mercy," he rose for the moment at least, above all the nationalism of his pride and his prejudice, as he owned that this Samaritan outside the covenant, revealed the true neighbour heart.

In that answer we discover the victory of our Lord in the case of the man intellectually at least. He had touched in him that finer consciousness of compassion, and compelled him to own that even one outside the covenant could be a neighbour. He then left him with the words, " Go, and do thou likewise."

We may here pause for a moment to notice the recurrence of that word " Do " in the story.

" What shall I *do* to inherit eternal life? "

" This *do*, and thou shalt live."

" Go, and *do* thou likewise."

Here we have the quest for life, and the revelation of the secret of its possession.

And there we have to leave the story. We know nothing definitely beyond. We may be permitted, however, reverently to indulge in some speculation.

All this happened very soon after the experience of the Mount of Transfiguration. It took place in the early days of those final six months in the ministry of Jesus, all o'ershadowed by the Cross. This being borne in mind, we see how this story of the Good Samaritan as to all the principles it contains, does find its full interpretation in our Lord Himself. Lifted on to the highest level of spiritual application, we see how everything here suggested is fulfilled. We can indeed say:

" He found me bruised and dying,
And poured in oil and wine."

As to this particular lawyer, as I have said, we know nothing more, but it is at least suggestive that about six months later, as Mark tells us, close to the end, when all the storm-clouds were gathering over the head of Jesus, and all His bitterest enemies

were surrounding Him like wolves, " One of the scribes came,"
that is, a man of the same order:

" And heard them questioning together, and knowing
that He had answered them well, asked Him, What commandment is the first of all? "

To that enquiry Jesus answered:

" The first is, Hear, O Israel; The Lord our God, the
Lord is one; and thou shalt love the Lord thy God with all
thy heart; and with all thy soul, and with all thy mind, and
with all thy strength. The second is this, Thou shalt love thy
neighbour as thyself. There is none other commandment
greater than these. And the scribe said unto Him, Of a
truth, Master, Thou hast well said that He is one; and there
is none other but He; and to love Him with all the heart,
and with all the understanding, and with all the strength,
and to love his neighbour as himself, is much more than all
whole burnt offerings and sacrifices. And when Jesus saw
that he answered discreetly, He said unto him, Thou art
not far from the Kingdom of God."

Was that possibly the same lawyer? The question cannot be
answered. If it were not the same man, he was one of the same
order, and he enquired not concerning life, but concerning law,
" What commandment is the first of all? " The intention of the
enquiry is as to which is the first in the way of being chief. Our
Lord answered him by quoting him the same commandments
that the lawyer of our story had declared was his reading of law.
It is further noticeable that the scribe of this later occasion agreed
with that answer, as he said, " Of a truth, Master, Thou hast
well said," and our Lord, seeing that he had answered discreetly,
said to him, " Thou art not far from the Kingdom of God."

XXVII

THE MAN BORN BLIND

WHEN the apostle John wrote his Gospel he selected from the ministry of the Incarnate Word eight signs in the realm of His works. All those selected were in some sense superlative in their revelation of the power of God operating through His Son. This one stands out as peculiar, for it is the only one on record of our Lord's dealing with what to-day we describe as congenital disease. It is possible there were other cases, but this is the only one definitely recorded.

In order to a correct apprehension of the story, the whole of chapter nine, and chapter ten so far as verse twenty-one should be read. There is really no break between these chapters. The discourse of our Lord runs to the verse named (x, 21).

In that discourse we find His great statement, "I am the Good Shepherd," and His declaration concerning other sheep that must be gathered, that there may be one flock. That discourse of Jesus has its distinct bearing upon the story of this man. It was indeed the outcome of what He had done for him, and the interpretation of His final action in connection with him.

The time notes of this story are not very clear, and there are different opinions concerning them. Personally I think it is to be linked very closely with chapter eight, and indeed contains a continuation of the story of how, at the Feast of Tabernacles recorded in chapter seven, He had declared Himself to be the Source of living waters. I think the connection is very close. He had been in the midst of those opposed to Him, whose opposition had been characterised by great bitterness. They had listened to what He had said to them, and then with a touch of supercilious disdain they had said, " Thou art not yet fifty years old." I never read that without wondering whether it is not a revelation of His appearance. He was not 33 years old, but probably looked much older. He had told them that their father Abraham had seen His day, and had rejoiced so to do. This led to the words:

"Thou art not yet fifty years old, and hast Thou seen Abraham?"

It was to them a most absurd suggestion. It was in that connection that He uttered that great claim, "Before Abraham was, I am." Then they took up stones to cast at Him, but He hid Himself, and went out of the Temple, and as He passed by He saw a man blind from his birth.

As we read on in the story, we find that the man was a beggar, that he obtained his livelihood by sitting and receiving alms from the passers-by. Such men were almost invariably gathered in the Temple precincts. Jesus, Who had made His great claim, "Before Abraham was, I am," now passed from the Temple, and as He did so, He saw a man blind from his birth.

As we attempt to look at this man, there are two things of importance, first an outstanding and arresting fact, and then some incidental things, not unimportant, but taking a secondary place.

The arresting central fact, then, is that here is a man sitting as a beggar, seeking alms. Moreover, a man born blind, that is blind from his birth, a man who had never looked into his mother's face, had never seen the face of Nature, and had never beheld the Temple courts. He may have been strangely familiar with them by touch, that marvellous new sense that ever comes to people deprived of sight. Nevertheless, as we have said, he had never seen the Lake, had never seen the hills, had never seen the flowers. He was a human being, apparently and almost certainly in possession of all his other powers, lacking this supreme gift of sight.

We are brought face to face with the centrality of this matter, and its superlative nature by the problem raised in the mind of the disciples as they looked at the man.

Evidently our Lord drew their attention to the man, if only by His own looking at him. John carefully tells us that He saw a man, and the disciples asked Him their question. As they looked upon the man, upon whom they saw Him looking, a problem was at once suggested, which it is quite possible that they had often discussed, perhaps in the presence of the man himself. It was the problem of a man born into this world with a limitation and disability, lacking this great gift of sight. Their question was:

"Who did sin, this man, or his parents, that he should be *born* blind?"

It was an enquiry as to the relationship between this disability and sin. Their thinking is at once revealed. They were sure that there was some connection between human disability and sin, and they were right. That was their philosophy, and so far, they were perfectly correct. No man is ever born blind in this world except as the result of something wrong, some breaking of law somewhere. It is not the will of God that a man should be blind. I am not for the moment saying, of course, that limitation is the result of personal sin, which it certainly is not in every case. Indeed, here is the problem. We emphasise the fact that when God created a man in His own image and likeness, He gave him the marvellous gift of sight. Here is a man lacking that gift. The question arose as to why. The belief was that there must be sin somewhere to account for this.

Then they made their half-suggestions, which seemed to cover the ground for them. Either he had sinned, or his parents. Their question really suggested first that he might have committed some sin before his birth; or on the other hand, that his parents had been guilty of sin. Thus they made two propositions. They were convinced that there was a connection somewhere between this frustration of the Divine intention, and sin. The first suggestion would seem to admit the possibility that the man had had a pre-existence. Now let me at once say I am not proposing to enter for a moment into a discussion of that matter, and for the simple reason that our Lord made no reply to it other than to dismiss the idea that the man's sightlessness was the result of his sin before birth. It is quite true that many Jewish teachers of the time believed in the pre-existence of personality, and some even accepted the idea of the transmigration of souls.

Thus, as we look at this man, we find ourselves face to face with the problem which is continuous in human history. At some time or other, almost invariably, we have to face and discuss it. A human being is seen suffering from a limitation that is a terrible handicap, frustrating the highest purposes of life, and that from life's beginning. We may employ a very familiar phrase in this connection, and say that we are confronted by the problem of evil, and its relation to some moral depravity. These disciples, conscious of such a problem, and knowing that they were with their Master, Who they believed could give light and explanation of problems, asked Him the question:

" Who did sin, this man, or his parents, that he should be born blind."

Now, let us observe quietly and remember clearly that our Lord gave them no solution of the problem. He dismissed their suggested solutions, declaring that the man was not suffering as the result of any sin committed by him, neither was he suffering as the result of sin committed by his parents.

Now we come to the point in the narrative where there are differing interpretations, and we need to proceed with reverent care. In doing so we will first observe the statement made exactly as it is printed in the Revised Version, following the punctuation:

" Neither did this man sin, nor his parents; but that the works of God should be made manifest in him. We must work the works of Him that sent Me while it is day; the night cometh, when no man can work."

The punctuation there which places a full stop after the word " him " is misleading. Let us change it, and again examine the change carefully.

" Neither did this man sin, nor his parents. But that the works of God should be made manifest in him, we must work the works of Him that sent Me, while it is day."

The change looks slight, but it really is radical. The old punctuation has led expositors into a most curious region of difficulty, and attempted explanation, in which they all and always break down when they attempt it. That punctuation would mean that our Lord said, This man did not sin nor his parents, but he was born blind to give God the opportunity to manifest His power. I admit that that is a brutal interpretation, but that is exactly what it means. The inference is that this man had been born blind, had lived through the years without a sight of his mother's face, of Nature, or of the Temple courts, had gone through life with frustration of his personality, in order that God should have this opportunity of revealing His power. To me that view of God savours of blasphemy. God does not bring a man into this world, and allow him to suffer for thirty years the frustration of personality, in order to show His power to remove that limitation.

If we read the paragraph with the amended punctuation, which I have suggested, we shall find a great difference of opinion. It may be well at this point for me to say that nearly thirty years ago this paragraph gave me great pause. I translated it, and introduced the punctuation I now suggest. I then submitted it to a most eminent scholar, and he replied that:

" He would be an exceedingly bold scholar who would undertake to prove that the punctuation should be one way

212

or the other on the mere ground of the Greek itself. It seems as if the question would have to be finally decided on doctrinal grounds, for it is plain that the difference in punctuation would change the meaning altogether. If one rendering would be more in spirit with the tenour of Christ's teaching, as seems quite probable, that would be quite naturally preferable."

Upon the basis of that opinion I adopt the new punctuation. Thus our Lord did not solve the problem suggested, but proceeded at once to do the work for which, as He said, He had been sent, and that was the work of removing the disability which caused the problem.

This story, therefore, is vital because in it we see a man who is an abiding type of individual suffering, not the result of personal wrong-doing, or even of wrong-doing of immediate ancestors. Unquestionably such disability is the result of a violation of law somewhere. The whole point that we would emphasise is that our Lord gave no solution of the problem, but did remove its cause in the case of the individual.

Still looking at this man, and turning from this essential fact to those which are incidental, we find him to have been a simple soul, who was prepared to do what he was told. He made no appeal to Jesus except as the fact of his necessity was an appeal. Our Lord approached him evidently on His own initiative, and forming clay, He anointed his eyes, and said, " Go, wash." Simple as it is, we cannot avoid being arrested by the immediate obedience of the man. Necessarily there was something in the presence and the voice and the touch of Jesus, although the man could not see Him, which produced an effect. He immediately arose and went. He started as a blind man, perhaps feeling his way to the pool, or gaining help from someone to lead him there.

As we watch him through the story, we see that he was an honest soul. He refused to be deflected from the facts. When he came back with his sight, it was to his own people, to his home, and to his neighbours. We can imagine their amazement as they looked at the man they had known so long asking alms, and never seeing them as they passed by, now looking at them. It was so amazing a sight that some doubted his identity. He, however, was perfectly sure, and asserted the fact. He told the story quite simply that a man that is called Jesus had made clay, and anointed his eyes, had told him to wash in Siloam. He had been, and had returned, and was able to see them.

At this point the incubus of tradition is manifested. They at once became concerned that the thing had happened on the Sabbath day, and I think with no hostile intention, they nevertheless took the man to the rulers, those in charge. Before these also he adhered to his statement concerning what had actually happened. When they tried to perplex him, he grew satirical, and asked if they also would become His disciples. Still watching him, we see him yielding to light as it broke upon him. He first affirmed the fact. He had received his sight. Later he said, that he did not profess to know the Person Who had wrought the wonder, and so did not profess to know whether He was a sinner or not. The one thing he did know was that having been blind, he was now able to see. While he was telling his story, evidently there dawned upon him the consciousness that the One Who had wrought the wonder was a prophet, and obeying that growing light he declared that it was so. They urged him to give glory to God, by which they did not mean, attribute the wonder of his sight to God, but, Be truthful; and declared that they knew nothing about Jesus as to who He was, or how He gained His authority. The light was still growing upon the man, and he said that it was a marvellous thing that they did not know whence He came, that from the foundation of the world it had not been known that a man born blind had received his sight, and he was now convinced that He must have been from God. The final light broke when presently our Lord revealed Himself to him, and he said, " Lord, I believe," and worshipped Him.

As we turn to watch our Lord's dealing with this man we are arrested by that which is a commonplace thing, and yet a wonderful thing. " He saw him." The Greek word employed is *eido* which has a twofold significance. It may be used quite simply of the fact of sight, but it may also be used to describe perception and understanding. It was surely so in this case. Our Lord saw, perceived, understood the whole of the facts of the case. Everything resulted from that vision.

It is quite evident, too, as we have already said, that there was something in that very look of Jesus which attracted the attention of the disciples to the man. Then they raised their question, and as we have seen, our Lord offered them no solution, but declared that He was in the world as its light; that He was in the world working the works of Him Who had sent Him. He then did that very thing. He wrought the wonder by which the disability which had caused the problem, was removed, as He gave this man

214

the boon of sight. It is an interesting fact that He employed clay, and the anointing of the eyes. Unquestionably the method was rendered necessary by something in the man, of which we are ignorant. He gave sight on other occasions without anointing clay. By this method, therefore, He reached the will of the man, and brought him to the place of obedience.

The value of the story lies within the fact that we are constantly faced by problems that baffle all our thinking as we look out upon conditions in this world. In the light of this story we enquire, What has Christianity to say to these problems? And the reply is that it attempts no solution, but that it is its mission to remove the cause of the problem. It may sound an almost banal thing to say, but I say it with great deliberation, we shall have more time in eternity to consider these problems, and more intelligence.

The one sure thing before us at the moment is that the work of Christ and His Church is to approach disability with relief and release. It might be said in passing that we find nothing in the Old Testament about the opening of blind eyes except prophetic words. We read of the healing of the body, of the cure of leprosy, but what the man said was perfectly true:

" Since the world began it was never heard that anyone opened the eyes of a man born blind."

It is the very superlative nature of this sign which creates its value.

But there is more in the story. As the result of this man's testimony they cast him out, which means far more than that they put him outside the synagogue. It was an act of excommunication. It was when Jesus heard that they had taken this action, that by the old order of things, and by the will of those in authority the man was excommunicated, that " He found him."

Finding him, He at once challenged him:

" Dost thou believe on the Son of God? "

Here we pause simply to say that there are those who believe that the question should read, " Dost thou believe on the Son of man? " There is no question about it that some of the old MSS. have the question in that form, and it may be that it was so. But even in that case it must be interpreted by our Lord's use of the phrase; and the form, in the last analysis makes very little difference. He had said to His own, " Who do men say that the Son of man is? " Peter had made the answer, " Thou art the Christ, the Son of the living God." Now He asked the man this question either in the one form or the other. Personally I am inclined to believe that it was the form found in our text:

"Dost thou believe on the Son of God?"

for the man was evidently arrested, as probably he would not have been had the other form been used. This is proven by his reply:

"Who is He, Lord, that I may believe on Him?"

Then it was that Christ revealed Himself completely as He said to him:

"Thou hast both seen Him, and He it is that speaketh with thee."

Immediately the man replied, "Lord, I believe."

And "he worshipped Him." That was an act following belief, and it was the act of complete surrender and submission. Thus our Lord is seen receiving this man into a new economy, and a new relationship. The full interpretation of it all must be discovered by that which is not possible to us in detail now, namely the examination of all the discourse of our Lord which ensued. In the course of that He said "I am the door," "I am the Good Shepherd." He was instituting a new economy which was to supersede the old. This man had been put out of that old economy by the action of the authorities, and Jesus found him, asked him the testing question, received his confession, and thus opened the door into the new fold where there is one and only one Shepherd.

Thus the whole story is indeed, as we said at first, singular and central. It is revealing in the matter of the problem of evil, and the revelation of the fact that the mission of Christ was not that of solving problems, but that of removing disabilities. He is seen as having come to banish our blindness and open our eyes, and receive us into the new economy of the Kingdom of God on the basis of our submission to Him.

XXVIII

THE COVETOUS MAN—AND HIS BROTHER

OUR subject consists of a story in the Gospel according to Luke which begins abruptly. It is the account of an interruption in the teaching of Jesus, which at the time He was giving specially to His own disciples, and that under remarkable circumstances. In order to a correct apprehension of the value of it we need to take a little time with some verses which do not at first arrest our attention, but which have a very distinct bearing on the whole matter.

If we glance back, we find that the chapter (xii) opens with these words, "In the mean time." It is important that we understand what that phrase really suggests. It is the translation of the Greek words *en ois*, which means quite simply, in which; so that we may render, "In which the many thousands of the multitude were gathered together." We see at once that some explanation of the phrase is needed, and our translators have adopted our phrase, "In the mean time." I think that we may get nearer to the intention of it if we render, "During which things." That necessarily raises the enquiry as to what things were referred to; and going back into the previous chapter we find in verse fifty-three the words:

"When He was come out from thence."

Once more, that reference raises a question, From whence? and we are introduced to the account of how He had been talking not to His own disciples, but to the rulers and the lawyers, and that in terms of the severest denunciation. It was then that " The scribes and the Pharisees began to press upon Him vehemently." That statement is a very forceful one, and it has been truthfully said that it presents a scene of violence probably unique in the whole record of the life of Jesus. They jostled

Him, they pressed upon Him. It was a physical contact of a hostile nature. As they did so, they attempted:

> " To provoke Him to speak of many things; laying wait for Him, to catch something out of His mouth. During which things when the many thousands of the multitude were gathered together, insomuch that they trod one upon another, He began to say unto His disciples."

And then followed the teaching given to the disciples, to which we have made reference.

These, then, were the circumstances, the rulers so angry that they were literally jostling Him and badgering Him with questions, the vast multitude of people around, and He speaking, in the midst of the tumult, to His own.

The first thing He did was to warn them against the leaven of these Pharisees which He defined as being " hypocrisy." The main burden of His teaching was that of charging His disciples to trust in God in the midst of all opposition, even unto death. It was in this connection that He said to them:

> " Be not afraid of them which kill the body, and after that have no more that they can do. But I will warn you Whom ye shall fear; Fear Him, which after He hath killed hath power to cast into Gehenna."

He then interpreted the nature of fear as being that of an absolute trust in that God Who numbered the hairs of their head.

At that point, one of the multitude said:

> " Master, bid my brother divide the inheritance with me."

Thus the story is seen to be an interruption on the course of His teaching of His disciples, which He resumed immediately afterwards as we find in the twenty-second verse:

> " And He said unto His disciples, Therefore, I say unto you, Be not anxious for your life, what ye shall eat; nor yet for your body, what ye shall put on."

The interruption consisted, then, of a request preferred to our Lord by a nameless man. As we listen to it we at once see that two men are to be recognised. We know the names of neither, and we see one of them through what he said. He was unquestionably observable in the crowd, and was vocal. The other man is not seen. Possibly he was not present. Probably, however, he was. The request which was preferred was one employing the very speech of the Jewish law, and it has an interesting aspect in the place where it is found. The Jewish law of inheritance had to do with a man having a plurality of wives. It provided that if a man had two wives, one whom he loved and the other whom he did not, when he died, the law did not permit him to leave the whole of his inheritance to the son of the woman he loved, while the other son remained unprovided for. He must "divide the inheritance." It may be that behind this request of the man to Jesus lay a story of this kind. Be that as it may, this man became vocal, and treating Jesus as one of the scribes, remitted to Him the case, and asked for a decision, which would compel his brother to divide the inheritance.

Now as we look at these two men we see quite enough for our purpose. In the case of the man who spoke we hear a cry for justice, and possibly there was justification for his appeal. If his brother who is out of sight and non-vocal were violating the law of inheritance, then there was justification for what this man asked. Even if this were not so, we still see the silent, hidden brother, grasping something which the man appealing felt an action of injustice. It is a saying with which we are very familiar to-day that possession is nine points of the law. As a matter of fact such a statement is subversive of justice. However, here was the case of a man in possession, and of a man desiring to share the possession.

As we look at these brothers again, then, though we may grant the probable justification of the plea for justice, we notice that in both cases the supreme subject was the inheritance. One held it. The other wanted to share it. One held it because he wanted it. The other wanted it because he did not hold it. Whether we think of the case of the one or the other, we see that both were concerned with this matter of inheritance. Thus here are two men, both desiring, that is, coveting possession of things on the earth level.

As we think of these two men thus revealed, we certainly are inclined to say that their desire does not seem to be a very dreadful one. It is common. The fact, however, that it is common does not redeem it from its ugliness, and that becomes evident when we turn to consider our Lord's dealing with the matter.

The first response of Jesus was that He sharply refused to do what the man requested, and that in a completely repressive manner. It is impossible to read this, either in our English translations, and even more so in the language in which it was written, without hearing a note of definite sternness, something sharply forbidding in our Lord's abrupt dismissal of the request:

"Man, who made Me a Judge or a Divider over you?"

He addressed the one who had preferred his request by the title that reduced him to the plane of common humanity, and by so doing lifted him to the level of the greatness of that humanity, as He called him "Man." In this very method of address our Lord revealed His recognition of the nature of the being preferring the request. He was not an angel. He was not a fiend. He was a man, with all that ever meant when Jesus used the word, and all that it ever ought to mean when we use it. All the possibilities and the dignities and the glories of human nature were thus compressed into a word. One almost feels as though in the very employment of this method of address, He was calling this man away from the low level upon which he was living and thinking and desiring; and compelling him to a recognition of all the truth concerning his personality. That becomes very self-evident as we proceed with the story.

In this question of Jesus, moreover, there was a recognition of His own authoritative appointment. He said:

" Who made Me a Judge or a Divider over you? "

The implication is that He was made or appointed to some office and work. By His question He eliminated an activity to which He was not appointed. This man was appealing to Him on a certain level, as One having authority in such a matter of law as he raised. Our Lord declared explicitly that He was not sent to interfere directly in such matters. It was as though He had said, I am not a scribe, balancing between paltry things. I repeat, there was a recognition underlying the question of His appointment to some definite mission and work, but it was not for this.

Then, continuing, He uttered the words of solemn and searching warning:

" Take heed, and keep yourselves from all covetousness."

It is noticeable that He employed the plural, and thus included both the brothers, and His disciples, and the listening crowd. The ugliness of the position was that this man and his brother evidently were mastered by this very form of evil. Both of them were coveting.

Then came the statement:

" A man's life consisteth not in the abundance of the things which he possesseth ";

and covetousness in the realm of such things is destructive of all the highest elements in human life.

It remains even until this time that men have an inadequate sense of the destructive nature of covetousness. Nevertheless the Old Testament has warning after warning of the danger of it. We see there how this very sin cursed and blasted men. Balaam's sin was the sin of covetousness. Achan's sin was the sin of covetousness. Gehazi's sin was the sin of covetousness. Necessarily we are not pausing to tell these stories. We are familiar with them, but they all reveal the same fact. If we turn into the New Testament, we find that the sin of Judas was the sin of covetousness. The sin behind all the opposition of the Pharisees and the rulers was that of covetousness. On a later occasion when our Lord was dealing with the subject of Mammon, it is said that they were covetous, or as the Revised Version has it, " lovers of money." The sin of Ananias in the Acts of the Apostles was the sin of covetousness.

We go over these facts in order that we may be reminded of the true nature of this sin. We are in the habit of labelling sins as great or little. We speak of terrible sins and little sins, which we attempt to dignify by the term peccadillos. Well, if we are inclined so to do, it is well that we remember covetousness is no peccadillo. It is one of the most blasting and damnable sins of which the soul of man is capable. When Paul in his letter to the Romans was speaking of his own spiritual experience, he made what is really a most arresting, and even amazing, declaration. It is that when in the presence of law he came to the commandment, " Thou shalt not covet," he became convinced of sin. In another of his letters he declares that touching the righteousness that is in the law, he was found blameless, that is, that he had been obedient to all the enactments of the Decalogue, and the general laws of Moses. Nevertheless as the Roman letter shows, there came a day when he found one sin of which he was not guiltless, and that was the sin of coveting. All this lends emphasis to this tremendous word of Jesus:

" Take heed, and keep yourselves from all covetousness."

This He then interpreted and emphasised by His great declaration:

" A man's life consisteth not in the abundance of the things which he possesseth."

That translation of what our Lord said is excellent for purposes of interpretation. It is, however, an interesting fact to observe that our Lord did not Himself use the word " man " in that connection. He did use it when asking the question, " Man, who made Me a Judge or a Divider over you? " But in this statement the word is not present. It is perfectly true that its equivalent is found here, but actually it is a pronoun, and a peculiar pronoun that marks personality, a pronoun which is adversative and diffusive, which is to say it applies to any individual; so that we may render:

" For one's life consisteth not in the abundance of the things which he possesseth."

It is, therefore, as we have said, a pronoun laying emphasis upon individuality, personality. It harmonises perfectly with the word " man," but it singles the individual out as a person. Whereas this is not translation, we might with perfect accuracy for the sake of interpretation, render the declaration, " Personality consisteth not in the abundance of the things possessed."

Still pausing to attend to these words a little critically, we enquire, what is meant by the word " consisteth? " Whereas we cannot say that the word " consisteth " is incorrect, we do say that it is capable of being misunderstood. The intention of the word here is not that of holding together. There is such a word, and there is such a thought, but the real intention of this may be rendered thus, One's life existeth not in the abundance of the things possessed. That is to say, the secret of personality, the essence of it, the main truth concerning it, is created not by the abundance of things possessed.

Covetousness, then, is the desire to possess something or things. Against that Jesus solemnly warned those who heard Him. The question may be asked, Have we not the right to possess? That question is dismissed by our Lord's declaration that He was not made a Judge or Divider. His mission was not to deal with these accidental things of possession, but rather with the mystery and the majesty of personality. That does not exist in possessions.

And yet once more, we pause with the word "life," as it occurs in this declaration. In doing so we find that it was a common Greek word for life, *zoe*; not *psuche*, not *pneuma*. Now this word was the simplest word for life in itself, essential life, the life of a butterfly, the life of an arch-angel, or the very life of God. In the Greek language they had another word for life, *bios*, and in their use, *bios* was supposed to describe something higher in the scale of being. We have adopted both words into our language in certain applications, as for instance in our employment of the terms zoology and biology. We have, however, made use of the former in application to the beasts; and the latter, biology, for all life. In doing this we have reversed the Greek idea. Now the arresting fact is that uniformly in the New Testament, when life is spoken of on its highest level, as eternal life, the term used is not *bios*, but *zoe*. *Zoe*, therefore, is essential life, life in itself, with all its mystery and its marvel, its possibility, and its power. So here our Lord employed that word, and declared that a man's life, his essential life, does not exist in things possessed.

Here once more we pause to say that the word "things" is not found in the original text, but it is quite necessary to insert it for our understanding. We say, therefore, that in this very word "things" there is something of severity, and even of disdain, in such a connection as this. In the course of our studies we have often made reference to the varied accents and tones in the voice of Jesus. It may be heard throbbing with the depths of infinite tenderness, thundering with the wrath of infinite anger, and sometimes filled with the tones of sarcasm. There can be little doubt that there was sarcasm in this reference. Life does not consist in things, whatever their abundance may be. As our Lord said this, both brothers were involved. The thought of each was moving in the realm of things. It was this attitude which created the almost severe terms of His first question:

"Man, who made Me a Judge or a Divider over you?" As though He had said, Why put Me down as a Trifler? My purpose is that of dealing with life, and men never enter into life through things.

It was in this connection that our Lord uttered that matchless parable with which we need not deal at any length now, save to glance over it, and catch the force of its application.

It presents the picture of a man who would have passed current at the time, and even to-day, as a straight, upright, honest, far-seeing, hard-working man. On the earth level there would appear to be nothing wrong with him. He possessed land, and his possession had proved a good investment. It "brought forth plentifully." Then he reasoned within himself. That seems to be a rational thing to do, and yet, as the story shows, he was prostituting his own personality by confining his reasoning to that personality. We listen to him, " My fruits," " my barns," " my corn," " my goods," " my soul." We at once ask the question as to where, through all this reasoning process, God is found? He is not referred to. For all practical purposes He is not counted upon. God is ignored. I do not say that He was denied. There is no proof that this man denied God. There is no suggestion that he definitely and openly rebelled against God. He was successful, and he was thoughtful. He was a good business man, but in his outlook and his calculation there was no place for God.

Therefore he was entirely self-centred, and being self-centred, he was utterly mistaken concerning himself. We hear him say:

" I will say to my soul, Soul, thou hast much goods laid up for many years; take thine ease, eat, drink, be merry."

When we thus pause and think, we are driven to the conclusion it is almost impossible to find a more appalling conception of life than that. The idea that the soul can be fed with goods is disastrous. Moreover, the whole outlook was limited by the phrase, " for many years." For how many? That was not considered, for, of course, it was not known. The outlook, however, was that however long or short the period, it was to be a period for eating and drinking and being merry.

Then across the story the words come with a crash, " But God " ! God is introduced after a conjunction. That is the tragedy of all tragedies.

" God said unto him, Thou foolish one, this night is thy soul required of thee."

The " many years " contemplated are cancelled. The end is " this night." Therefore, the " much goods " trusted in are dealt with by the satire of the question, " Whose shall they be? "

I sometimes am inclined to think that there is nothing much more tragic in human life than the reading of a will. Gone is the man or the woman who possessed. The border-line has been crossed. The summons that brooks no refusal has been obeyed, and now those left are gathered together to consider whose shall these things be?

Thus, these two men are seen, both living on the earth level, concerned about "things." One has them. He is determined to hold them. The other wants them, and is appealing for them. In all the majesty of eternity, with the weights and balances of the ages in His hand, Jesus shows these men life, and how that it is independent of things. By the use of the parable He does that, ending everything with the words:

"So is he that layeth up treasure for himself, and is not rich toward God."

The sequel of the story is not on record. What happened to these men we are not told. The revelation of the story, however, abides in all force. We see in it men concerned with things, with possessing, while God is ignored. But God is present throughout. He was in the land that produced the fruit. It was by His government and activity that the barns were filled with corn. The man living in forgetfulness of God, and occupied with his grain, was guilty of the degradation of his own personality. Such an outlook puts life on the level of the beasts. As we listen to our Lord, we learn that the secret of the glory of personality is that of being rich toward God. God recognised, God seen in all the processes of Nature, God taken into account in the calculation of the years, and the dealing with possessions means the cancellation of the merely animal desire to eat, drink, and be merry. It is God alone Who lifts the soul into the place of the everlasting riches.

XXIX

MARTHA

IT may be admitted at once that it is not easy to consider the story of Martha in separation from that of Mary. There are three pictures in the New Testament of these women, and in each case they are seen together. The contrast between them constitutes part of the revelation concerning them. Nevertheless they are so distinct, and our Lord's methods with them were so different, that we are taking them in separation. Necessarily in looking at Martha, we shall have to glance at Mary, and when we come to consider Mary, we shall have to glance at Martha.

These women are named by neither Matthew nor Mark. Of the three pictures one comes from the pen of Luke, and two from the pen of John.

Let us first glance at the three pictures. The first of them is found in the final paragraph of the tenth chapter in the Gospel according to Luke; the second in the eleventh chapter of John; and the third in his twelfth chapter. As we look at the three we see that they present three days, and it may be well first of all to describe the days in themselves. The first was a day of prosperity and gladness and sunshine, over which certain shadows are seen creeping. The next is a day of gloom and of anguish, and of calamity, but a day upon which wonderful light breaks forth. The third day was a strange day indeed, in which we are conscious of a mingling of light and of darkness. Terrible darkness is there, but the most wonderful light is shining also. We may roughly describe the three days as, first a day of sunshine, then a day of gloom, and finally a day of mystery.

As we look at Martha on the day of prosperity and of gladness and of sunshine, we see her busily occupied as the hostess. Luke tells us with artless simplicity that:

"A certain woman named Martha, received Him into her house."

No reference whatever is made to Lazarus, and it is quite evident that Martha was the householder. If we had been passing through Bethany at the time, and called, it was not Lazarus who would have received us. It was not Mary who would have interviewed us first, but Martha. Trespassing a little on our meditation on Mary, it is interesting to notice that whereas Luke makes it clear that the house belonged to Martha, John, referring to the two women, puts Mary first, as he says, " the village of Mary and her sister Martha." So that while the house belonged to Martha, there is a sense in which Mary had first place in the possession of a village. Perhaps that cannot be carried too far, but it is at least suggestive.

Let that be as it may, what we do see as we look on the first picture is that of Martha as a loving hostess, determined to do everything that lay in her power to make the visit of Jesus bright and beautiful. Most of us have been familiar with this woman or her type. We watch her moving swiftly round, attending to many matters. Each succeeding moment becomes more filled than the preceding one with activity, and all this in order to make her Guest welcome. Luke described this activity by declaring that she was " cumbered about much serving." Quite literally the Greek word there employed means she was dragged round. If peradventure no mere man understands that, I venture to affirm that every woman does.

Now watching closely, we find that as the result of this very activity as a hostess, she becomes disappointed. She cannot overtake the promptings of her heart. She cannot get done all that she desires to see done. Suddenly she became aware of Mary, who, but a little while ago was by her side, helping, but now has left her. It is important that we observe carefully how she herself stated the case. She

" Did leave me to serve alone."

Martha now saw Mary sitting at the feet of Jesus, and she became angry first with Mary, and then—mark it well—angry with the very One Whom she was trying to welcome.

That is the picture of Martha presented to us on this first day, the disappointed hostess, whose love has been thwarted, because it has been attempting to express itself in activity, and is unable to do so satisfactorily. So we see her coming into the presence of Jesus, and saying:

" Dost Thou not care that my sister did leave me to serve alone? bid her therefore that she help me."

We turn now to the second in this triptych of pictures. It is a day of agony, and a day of that agony which follows, when the possibility of service is at an end. Martha is seen bereft of her brother. One can imagine that in the days of the sickness that ended in his death how ceaselessly active she had been in service. Now the hour had come when such service was useless. Nothing more could be done. Her brother was dead.

Then she had added to that awful pain of bereavement the deeper anguish of feeling that she had been neglected by her Friend. She and Mary had sent a message to Jesus Who was away on the other side of Jordan, telling Him:

" He whom Thou lovest, is sick."

When they sent that message their feeling undoubtedly was that Jesus would come immediately. He did not come. The message that they received in answer to their appeal was that He had said:

" This sickness is not unto death."

But now he is dead, and Martha learns that Jesus is coming, as it must have appeared to her, too late. Then we see her violating all the conventionalities of her religion and her nation, in that when she heard of His approach, she did not wait in the house as was the custom of mourning women; she crossed the threshold, and meeting Him, said:

" Lord, if Thou hadst been here my brother had not died."

There can be no doubt that in her case it was the language of protest, because He had not come.

Then we turn to the third picture. The atmosphere was hushed and tense. Calamity was at hand, and the disciples knew it, though they were perplexed beyond measure. Their outlook was baffled and beaten. They knew that the enemies of their Lord were closing in upon Him. As we look we see a supper in a house, with at least sixteen people present. When our eye falls upon Martha, we see her revealed in a sentence of two words, " Martha served." Here, however, there is no reference to her being cumbered. With a quiet and fine dignity John tells us she served. Probably that day her feet went faster and her fingers moved more swiftly than ever before, but there is not a word about distraction. So we see Martha in the sunshine, Martha in calamity, Martha in the presence of mystery.

As we look at her we are first of all impressed with the fact that she was a woman of great affection. Love was the inspiration of her service on the first occasion. Love was the reason of her tumultuous grief at the death of her brother. Love was the inspiration of her quiet service on the day of mystery.

Moreover, in her we see a woman of unquestioned honesty. She dared to utter the criticism of Jesus and Mary, of which she was conscious on that first day. She was equally honest when in the day of calamity, when our Lord had made her the stupendous declaration, He challenged her, " Believest thou this? " she replied, " Yea, Lord "; and then immediately qualified her answer as she said:

" I have believed that Thou art the Son of God." She had already said to Him:

" Even now I know that, whatsoever Thou shalt ask of God, God will give Thee."

In saying that she was honest, although she did not quite understand her own attitude; for when presently Jesus commanded that the stone be removed, she protested that it was too late. This whole conversation reveals her, as we have said, as a woman of transparent honesty, refusing to affect a faith which she does not possess.

Moreover she is seen as a woman characterised by reasonableness. In the day of sunshine it seemed to her unreasonable that Mary should leave her to serve alone. Her reasonableness is manifested in every point in her conversation with her Lord on the day of calamity. It was also evident in the day of mystery, when she was content to serve in quietness and stillness. Thus is she seen, a woman of great affection, perfectly honest, reasonable and constantly active.

We turn now, then, to observe our Lord's dealing with this woman. We remind ourselves at once that we have no story of His method of winning her to Himself. It is rather an account of how He dealt with one who was His disciple. We have no account of the beginnings. It is impossible, however, to read the story which Luke tells us without realising that the home at Bethany was a place of refuge for Jesus. I have no hesitation in saying that that home was the one place in the public ministry of our Lord where He, to use our familiar phrase, could be perfectly " at home." The phrase suggests the casting off of all restraint, and the perfect restfulness of the realisation that there can be complete relaxation. We realise that the life of Jesus was in very many ways an unutterably lonely one. As I have said in other connections, so I would repeat, we could almost write the story in brief sentences. Chapter one, " There was no room for them in the inn." Chapter two, " The foxes have holes, and the birds of the heaven have nests, but the Son of man hath not where to lay His head." Chapter three, Burial in a charity grave. Into this house at Bethany He came as into a harbour of refuge.

There He found Martha busily occupied in a loving attempt to give Him a worthy welcome. He found her baffled and cumbered by that very attempt, and at last she appeared before Him making her complaint. The first thing we notice is that He had no word of rebuke for her. Yes, there was a word of reproof, but there is a great difference between reproof and rebuke. He was not angry with her. There was no resentment on His part. He listened to what she had to say, and then in tenderest way addressed her, " Martha, Martha." We notice on several occasions how when Jesus had some reproof, and His heart was full of tenderness, He introduced it by twice using the name.

" Simon, Simon, Satan hath desired to have you ";

" O Jerusalem, Jerusalem, how often would I have gathered thy children together, even as a hen gathereth her chickens under her wings, and ye would not."

So here He said, " Martha, Martha." In the very repetition of the name there was something of reproof.

Then He proceeded to show wherein her mistake lay. He saw her condition, and explained it to herself. She was divided, disturbed, distracted. Life for the moment had become broken up for her, and this because she had been so occupied with " many things " as to become forgetful of " one thing."

Here we need care as we listen to Him saying, " One thing is needful." We may be tempted at first to put into contrast " many things " with " one thing." As a matter of fact our Lord was not objecting to the " many things," but He was showing her the effect produced upon her by " many things " was that " one thing " was lacking. He was revealing to her the fact that she needed concentration at a centre, and where this was so, activities could still be carried on in peace and poise and quietness. Mary was conscious of this, and was observing it. She was taking time to sit in devotion at His feet. She was seeking at the fountain head, and finding the secret of peace. Martha was cumbered and distracted not by the " many things," but because they were not held in right relationship with the " one." Our Lord was not declaring that the " many things " were unimportant. Let love do its "many things," but let its activity be under the mastery of the "one thing," that of discipleship, and taking time for the practice of it. Necessarily if this "one thing" be done, there are "many things" that may be omitted. Martha needed this "one thing" in order to quietness and freedom from distraction.

Turning to the day of calamity, we first observe that there can be no escape from the conviction that when Martha came to Him, she came protesting. It is perfectly true that she and Mary said exactly the same thing, and yet the difference was marked. It was a difference of tone, of temper, and consequently of accent. Martha was perfectly honest, but she was angry. Once again, as in the day cf sunshine, she uttered a word of complaint.

Here again we observe that there was no rebuke on the lips of Jesus. He looked upon that hot, troubled, tempest-tossed soul, and He uttered in her hearing words of the sublimest majesty in which He made a supreme claim for Himself. He first declared to her:

"Thy brother shall rise again."

Her answer is very revealing. Before quoting her actual words, we may express the thought of them by saying that her answer meant, Do not try and comfort me with theology just now. That is seen as we ponder her actual words:

"I know that he shall rise again in the resurrection at the last day."

Quite evidently Martha was no Sadducee. She believed in resurrection, but an ultimate resurrection did not heal the wound of an immediate bereavement. The protest again was characterised by spontaneous honesty. My memory travels back some years to a day in New York when I dropped into the office of a friend of mine, and I found him smitten, stricken, afflicted, because his wife had died not many days before. He was hot and angry. I but refer to it, because I so well remember something he said to me. "People are sending me books about the Second Advent and the resurrection. All may be true, but I don't want them. I want my wife!" There is no doubt that that is exactly what Martha meant when she said:

"I know that he shall rise again in the resurrection at the last day."

Then there fell from the lips of our Lord those wondrous words, which surely she could not fully understand at the moment. Yet He uttered them to her, and so flooded her with light, the light that has been shining down the ages ever since, the light that transfigures every graveyard. He said:

"I am the Resurrection and the Life; he that believeth on Me, though he die, yet shall he live."

Here let us very carefully observe that He did not say, Yet shall he live *again*. We may with reverence put the great statement in another form. It simply meant that if a man believes on Him, though he die, he is still alive. The death is very real on the earth level, but the man is not dead. Necessarily the emphasis is on the condition.

"Whosoever liveth and believeth on Me."

Thus the method of Jesus with Martha on the day of darkness was that He gave her light such as had never shone in human history before, light which might have been challenged by the men who heard Him speak, but which has been vindicated through the passing centuries as the only definite word that proves immortality. The measure of His victory is demonstrated by the fact that when He challenged her, "Believest thou this?" she fell back upon the conviction she had as she said:

"Yea, Lord; I have believed that Thou art the Christ;"

and that confession then made, implicated her approach to conviction concerning the strange things He had now said. He knew that what Martha needed that day was not sympathy so much as light, illumination in the midst of the darkness.

Thus we come to the last picture of her revealed in the simple statement, "Martha served." Somehow or other as the result of previous experiences, she had certainly found her Lord in a new way. She was still doing "many things," but in the power of "one thing"; and by that "one thing" she was held in peace and balance and poise for the "many things." We are not told of a word that He spoke to her on that day, but we see Him receiving her hospitality, and His very silence was that of His accomplished purpose in the case of this strong and wonderful woman. He had brought her to the place where she served in quietness and in peace.

When we enquire what this story has for us, we realise how many things there are in it. Perhaps, however, the simplest of all is the realisation that Christ is seen seeking hospitality in the day of sunshine, and finally receiving it in the day of mystery, even when His own Passion was approaching. May we not declare that He is still seeking for homes into which He can pass and be perfectly at home. He is still seeking for active service which makes Him welcome.

But as we examine the story, with Mary in the background, inevitably we learn the truth that hospitality can only be rendered to Jesus by those who are also His guests. If I would be His host, I must be His guest.

What a mystical and wonderful word that is, found in the letters to the Churches in Revelation:

" Behold, I stand at the door and knock. If any man hear My voice and open the door, I will come in to him, and will sup with him."

That is to say, I will accept his hospitality, I will be his Guest; and he shall accept My hospitality, I will be his Host, he shall sup with Me. That is perfect idea of fellowship with Him. First, we must be His guests. Then we can be His hosts.

The other simple and yet searching and comforting lesson we draw from the story is that He is never angry with honesty.

" I tell Him all my doubts, and griefs, and fears."

And that may be perfectly true. We can say to Him things that we cannot to any other. When we are with Him, accepting His hospitality, and offering Him our hospitality, we may say whatever is in our heart. The one thing that ever stirred His anger in the days of His flesh, and still does, is hypocrisy. We may pass into His presence as Martha did, and by absolute honesty give Him the opportunity to talk to us, and reveal to us the secrets of life.

XXX

MARY

A S we come to the story of Mary we must remember that, as in the case of Martha, we are observing our Lord's methods of dealing with His own. These two women, in common with their brother, were friends of Jesus, and certainly were His disciples. Again, we have the same difficulty as we experienced in dealing with Martha, namely that it is not easy to look at either of these women, losing sight of the other. There is a sense in which it is not only difficult, but impossible. Therefore, while our business is to see Mary, we shall be conscious of Martha throughout the study, and shall have to refer to her, as in the last study we did to Mary, when dealing with Martha.

As in the case of Martha, then, we have three pictures in exactly the same connection. We may describe them as we did in the last study as constituting a triptych, presenting to us three days in the lives of these women. In the first the principal impression made upon the mind is that of sunshine and joy, a little overshadowed in certain ways. The second presents a picture of shadow and darkness and trouble, in the midst of which a wonderful light breaks forth. The final picture may again be referred to as one of mystery and darkness. As we have looked at Martha on these three days, so now we turn to look at Mary.

Now as we look at Mary the old comparison with Martha with which we have long been familiar, almost inevitably comes to mind. This comparison often suggested that Martha was the busy housewife, alert and active; and too often we have looked at Mary as though she were somewhat anæmic, that is, the kind of woman we sometimes are inclined to describe by the word clinging, that is, one whose nature was such that she was quite prepared out of affection, to sit quietly down, forgetful of duties, which were being carried out by another.

Now such a contrast shows that we have not carefully considered the story as it is written for us. We observe Luke, in his account, after having told us of Martha, and that she had received Him into her house, added the words:

" And she had a sister called Mary."

Reading those words and those that immediately follow, let me first render them as they seem to have been constantly understood:

" And she had a sister called Mary, which sat at the Lord's feet, and heard His word."

Now if we look carefully at this, it will be seen that that rendering has omitted a little word. Probably we should not omit it in reciting it, but we are in danger of omitting it in our thinking. The word I refer to is the word " also." Let us read it then in that way.

" She had a sister called Mary, which also sat at the Lord's feet, and heard His word."

That word " also " changes the whole meaning of the statement. If we ponder it we see that it can only mean one of two things. It either means that Martha sat at the Lord's feet, and Mary also; or it means that Mary had already rendered service in the house, and also sat at the Lord's feet. It cannot possibly mean that Martha sat at His feet, for the whole point of the story is that it was exactly that which she had failed to do.

Mary, therefore, having rendered service, and taken her part in the work of the house in providing for the Guest, also sat at the Lord's feet.

This is borne out as we carefully consider how Luke tells the story of the approach of Martha to Jesus when she said:

" Lord, dost Thou not care that my sister did leave me to serve alone? bid her therefore that she help me."

Thus it was not the case of complete neglect on the part of Mary against which Martha complained, but that in her judgment she had not done enough. She had left off too soon. Mary is thus revealed as one who knew however important service was, it was not enough. Life demanded something more than that, in order to its full realisation.

What that something was will be best understood if we bring to bear upon this story the light of Eastern custom. Sitting at the feet in the East had two distinct significances, both of them merging in one. To sit at the feet was first of all an activity of worship, a revelation of subservience, the taking up of the attitude of one who stood in awe, recognising the superiority of the One at Whose feet she was sitting.

Then also sitting at the feet is a synonym for discipleship. To take that position was to do so in order to learn, to receive

234

from the One at Whose feet she sat, the instruction which He had to give, and that she was conscious that she needed. Thus Mary recognised on that day, that it was of supreme importance that she should take time to render homage to her Lord, and in that attitude to receive from Him what He had to give her of instruction. Thus she would give to Him in adoration, and receive from Him instruction. Martha, with love prompting her, was attempting to fill the opportunity in service, and by doing so was becoming distracted. Mary in that day of sunshine, having taken her part in the service of the home, sought the full realisation of life as, ceasing activity, she sat a disciple, rendering adoration, and waiting for instruction.

We now pass to the second of these pictures, and once again we see these two women equally in the midst of trouble. Their brother Lazarus was sick, and disease was rapidly increasing, mastering all their attempts to cope with it. It was then that they together sent a message to Jesus in those arresting terms:

" He whom Thou lovest is sick."

It was evidently a most confident message. They were sure that if He knew of the sickness of His friend, He would be with them; and therefore they sent to tell Him.

Then came what must have appeared at the moment to be strange and inexplicable. He did not come. Hearing of the sickness of His friend, He had remarked, " This sickness is not unto death."

But now to all human seeming, and as a definite earthly fact, Lazarus was dead. The solicitous care of the sisters had failed to hold life within that body, and he lay in the house an inanimate corpse. Then the news reached them that Jesus was arriving—and again I use the words as expressing what they must have felt at the moment—too late. Martha is at once seen breaking through all conventionality, and leaving the house in order to meet Him, and pour out to Him her complaint. Now Mary is seen still sitting in the house. He was on the road, and she knew it, but she remained quietly where she was, until the message was brought to her by Martha that her Lord was asking for her. John tells us that after Martha's wonderful conversation with Jesus, in which He had flooded her soul with those astounding statements concerning life and resurrection, she came into the house and said:

" The Master is here, and calleth thee."

Although John does not record in process the fact that Jesus had called for her, there can be no doubt that it was as Martha declared.

Now we see Mary, in obedience to that call, rising from her place in the house, and passing down the road to meet Jesus. Carefully notice that when she arrived, she fell at His feet, and

235

there uttered the words which expressed her sense that had He been present, the ultimate calamity would not have occurred. It it most arresting to observe that these two women used the same words in addressing their Lord·

" Lord, if Thou hadst been here, my brother had not died."

Nevertheless it is evident that if the words were the same, the tone was entirely different, and therefore the meaning was different. Martha standing erect, spoke to Him. Mary falling at His feet, spoke to Him through her tears. Martha was saying in effect, Why did You not come? as though challenging His friendship. Mary was saying in effect, I wish You could have come, and regretting His absence.

Then to return to the contemplation of the last of the three pictures. At least sixteen people are seen, and Martha is revealed as serving, creating hospitality. The supreme Guest is Jesus Himself, and He is surrounded by His disciples. Suddenly Mary enters, and now she violates all the conventionalities. In the day of her sorrow she, a quiet, retiring woman, still sat in the house until she was sent for. She who had made time to sit at His feet when the sun was shining, now breaks in upon this gathering, and does that which at once arouses the attention, and indeed the criticism of the onlookers. She brought with her costly spikenard, and pausing at His feet, poured it out in full view of those assembled. It was such an unusual act as to call forth protest. As we read this matchless story we have a feeling that we would like to leave out the account of that protest. But we cannot leave it out, for it is needed as background to the beauty of the thing which Mary did. The voice of Judas was heard.

" Why was not this ointment sold for three hundred pence, and given to the poor? "

It is to be carefully noted that while Judas uttered the words, they all were in agreement with him. They were looking upon something the meaning of which they could not understand.

It is of the utmost importance that we should attempt very carefully to examine the incident, and to see what it really meant. Going a little ahead of any line of proof, I have no doubt that as Mary had looked into the eyes of her Lord, she had seen Him as none other of those surrounding Him saw Him. She saw the shadow of the coming Cross and tragedy. He had certainly long told these disciples that this would be so, but Mary that day was the only one keen and sensitive to the sorrow of His soul. It was as though she said within herself, If only I can get near enough to touch the fringe of His garment of sorrow, and show Him something of sympathy ! It was then that she became what the disciples designated as wasteful. That she was successful is proven by the fact that our Lord, in referring to her action, connected it with the day of His burial. She had indeed touched the fringe of the garment of His sorrow, and He understood.

As we look back over these three scenes we enquire what is the key to the character of Mary? It is undoubtedly found in words which we have already emphasised, to which we return for the discovery of the secret. They are the words, " His feet." In the day of sunshine she went to His feet, and in the doing of that there was a revelation of love expressing itself in worship and discipleship. In the day of her own sorrow, when He had sent for her, she returned to the same place, " His feet." And now in the day when His sorrows were manifest to her love-lit eyes, she went back to His feet, and in an act that appeared only wasteful to less illuminated watchers, passed into the fellowship of His sufferings. On this last occasion she was supplying that for which love is ever seeking, that which can only be supplied in silence, and in those acts that demonstrate understanding and fellowship.

We glance over the ground once more, perhaps to say the same things, but they are full of value. In the day of prosperity and joy she sat at His feet in adoration, and in the reception of revelation. In the day of her anguish, with Lazarus dead, and already in the tomb, she waited for His call, and then found her way to the old trysting-place, and unlike Martha, who in honesty challenged His friendship, she expressed only her regret that it had not been possible for Him to be there. The attitude was the same as in the day of sunshine, that of submission and worship. In this final day while Martha is blessedly occupied in serving, and the disciples perhaps were busy discussing the situation with trembling hearts, Mary hurries past them all, back to the same place, and that in order that she might somehow show the fellowship of her soul with Him in His suffering.

In this meditation there is not very much to be said as to the Lord's methods, because they are so self-evident. As we watch Him with Mary we are inclined to repeat the verse many of us know so well and love.

> " He knows, He loves, He cares,
> Nothing this truth can dim.
> He gives His very best to those
> Who leave the choice to Him."

That tells the story of His dealing with Mary. She left the choice to Him in sunshine and in shadow, and He gave her the best. In the day of sunshine when she sat at His feet, He gave her His teaching. As Luke puts it, she

> " Also sat at the Lord's feet, and heard His word."

That is all Luke says, but with reverent and sanctified imagination we can listen. He would talk to her of love, His supreme message, of love that was stronger than death. He would speak to her of

237

light, light that was ever shining, and which no darkness could extinguish. He would talk to her of life, life in that fulness which never can be destroyed by death. These were ever His great themes. As Mary sat at His feet and heard Him speaking of love, she would realise that all round about her light was breaking such as she had never dreamed of. She would find life, not as a brief space of happiness that knew an ending, but as an age-abiding quality and quantity. These would be the things that she heard falling from His lips.

When we come to the day of darkness, we notice how careful John is to declare, that Jesus loved Martha and Mary and Lazarus, and in connection with that statement, continuing, he said:

> " When therefore He heard that he was sick, He abode at that time two days in the place where He was."

Surely if this was an imagined story on the human level at that point, the case would have been stated quite differently. We should almost inevitably say, that when He heard that Lazarus was sick, He hastily arose and went to the sisters. As a matter of fact He did not come until it was—as we have said, from their standpoint, at the moment—too late.

Then when Mary came to Him, the story of what He gave her is told in that one shortest and perhaps sublimest verse in the Bible, " Jesus wept." Nothing now is said of her listening to His words. He gave her now no teaching. To Martha He had spoken about the resurrection, for that is what Martha supremely needed. To Mary He gave His tears.

Expositors here have seemed to be in some reverent difficulty. Some say that the tears were tears shed on account of the Jews, and their hardness of heart. But that fact had been revealed a little earlier, when it is said that in the presence of the last enemy He groaned in the spirit, and was troubled.

As I ponder the marvellous story, I see Mary weeping, and Jesus weeping also. Now at first there is a sense in which it is not easy to understand this. Supposing for the sake of argument, that someone had a loved one lying ill, yes dead, and I came to the home, knowing that within a few swiftly passing moments, I could bring your loved one back, I do not think it would be possible for me to weep. But there at once is the difference between my heart and the heart of God. To me there is no sentence more radiantly revealing the heart of God than that brief declaration, " Jesus wept." The keen, quick, great sensitiveness of the heart of the Lord went out to meet the broken heart of Mary, and His tears fell in sympathy. I feel that that can only be understood as we understand God, as He is revealed in Christ. As a matter of fact it is always God's attitude toward suffering. The ultimate consummation of God's love is that He will wipe away all tears from human eyes. Nevertheless, knowing that that is so, He also knows the anguish suffered by the human heart, and even though it is ultimately to be removed, He suffers with humanity. Thus He gave to Mary on that sad day the very best, the sacramental symbols of the sympathy of the loving heart of God.

We glance finally at that hour of mystery, so full of poignancy, and we enquire, how did He then respond to Mary? We notice carefully in the first place that He appreciated her motive. He knew that she had done what she did for the day of His burial. Then He defended her against misunderstanding and misconception. Accepting her gift, He made it the inspiration of similar devotion through all the running centuries. First He appreciated her motive. She had come to Him, seeing in His eyes the haunting pain, the evidence of which she only was capable of understanding. He was the only One Who understood, but seeing that He did understand, Mary would care little or nothing for the criticism of Judas and the rest.

He sharply rebuked them as He said, " Let her alone." Do not insult that kind of devotion and love by mechanical and evanescent criticism. In this connection Matthew and Mark tell us not only what John records, but that He said:

" Wheresoever this Gospel shall be preached in the whole world, that also which this woman hath done shall be spoken of for a memorial of her."

That has happened over and over again, for nineteen hundred years the story has been the inspiration of all sorts of actions of love in the bringing of gifts to be devoted to the Lord Himself.

In our meditation on Martha we emphasised the need for taking time to sit at His feet, on the negative side, as watching Martha, we saw the reason of her failure was that she had left out that one thing which was supremely needful.

In this meditation on Mary, the lesson is stressed on the other, the positive side. She took time to sit at His feet in prosperity, even though her action was misunderstood. She returned to His feet in her adversity. And now at the last, she is seen going to His feet in the fellowship of His sufferings. Surely these stories are speaking to us very powerfully if we will but listen to them. Is not one great cause of our trouble and restlessness to-day that we take so little time to sit at His feet? We are all so busily occupied, quite honestly, in service, forming committees and organisations, even exhausting the alphabet in our attempt to show how wonderful they are. And yet how appallingly we lack the one thing really needful, time for sitting at His feet in devotion and discipleship.

In the day of prosperity we must make time for this. If we do so, we shall grow so familiar with Him that when some shadowed hour closes in upon us, we shall hear Him calling us, and we shall know the true place to which to go to find love and strength.

That leads us to the final matter. I do not care to over-emphasise this, but with life's experiences behind me, I am very much inclined to the conviction that the only way of entering into fellowship with His sufferings is through some suffering of our own, in which at His feet, we have discovered the sources of strength and comfort.

So to those in the hey-day of health and strength, let the stories make their appeal, that we make time to sit at His feet, accounting any activity as weakened where this is neglected. To those who suffer, the stories tell us that the Master is ever calling us to come to Him, and to find in Him keen and quick and powerful sympathy, which is our deepest need. And so, finally, we may find our way into that closest fellowship with Him, which brings to Him the sense of our fellowship in His sufferings. As I ponder the story of Mary, the feeling of my heart is that I would rather be in succession to her, than the whole company of the apostles.

XXXI

THE YOUNG RULER

THE picture presented to us in this story is that of a young man in virile life, confronting Jesus. He was a Ruler, and that means that necessarily he had passed thirty years of age. The fact that he is referred to as a young man, however, proves that he had not long held that office. He was probably about the same age as our Lord Himself at that time.

We are at once arrested by the contrast. On the one hand a young, virile man, the owner of great possessions; on the other, Jesus, a man of about the same age, having no possessions, being homeless. The story in itself is a most familiar one, and I suppose every preacher sooner or later has dealt with it. It is now about four years ago since I preached on the subject under the title of " Life a Quest, and the Way of Conquest," which sermon was published in pamphlet form. Necessarily, therefore, in going over the ground again, much the same things will be dealt with; and yet it is perfectly true that however often one returns to these stories, there is still fresh light to break forth therefrom.

As I have been pondering the story again I have to repeat what I have often said about it, that in my judgment it is one of the most surprising in the series we are following. Indeed, in the reading of it I go through a series of surprises. The first is that there could be any man to whom Jesus could say that he only lacked one thing. The fact that it was so compels closer attention to the man; and the second surprise follows, which is that it could be said that he lacked anything. Then, when following carefully the whole story, I come to the third surprise, and it is a surprise that I was ever surprised; because I see the supreme importance of the thing he lacked.

Looking at the man, and beginning on the lowest level, we remember that he had great possessions. He was a wealthy man. That fact in itself speaks of great opportunity, and grave peril. This is always so. There is no need to argue as to the opportunity created by the possession of wealth. One out-standing word of our Lord will be sufficient in this connection:

" Make to yourselves friends by means of the mammon of unrighteousness; that, when it shall fail, they may receive you into the eternal tabernacles."

The Revised Version has accurately rendered the word. It shows how the measurement of the ages that lie beyond the earthly life may be put upon the use of earthly possessions. We are to use our possessions so that when they fail, or it, the mammon fails, they, the friends we have made by the use, shall greet us on the other side of life. The young man's great possessions created great opportunities.

It is equally true that great possessions create grave perils. As we look at him it would appear as though they had not had an evil effect upon him, except in the deepest things of his spiritual life. Wealth is always perilous. To quote again the words of our Lord:

" A man's life consisteth not in the abundance of the things which he possesseth."

That great saying of Jesus shows that if a man has great possessions it is not only true that they do not constitute his life, but that they may stifle it, may ruin it. Therefore, this young man had grave perils.

It is evident that he was a man of fine temperament. This is seen in the fact that he was discerning. The people of his class, that is, the rulers, by this time were hostile to Jesus. Quite evidently he had been watching Him, and listening to Him, and in so doing he had seen Goodness. When he approached Him, he addressed Him as " Good Master."

By Matthew, and Mark, and Luke, this account of the young ruler is placed in close connection with the occasion when they brought the children to Jesus. I have often wondered if that had particularly impressed this man. Necessarily I do not know that it was so, but it is at least a permissible speculation. In the case of that incident he had seen in Jesus two things quite clearly, namely, anger and infinite tenderness. Mark tells us distinctly that when our Lord uttered the words which have become the

242

very charter of child life, He was moved with indignation. It is well for us to remember this when we read the gracious words. As they were uttered they were vibrant not only with the infinite pathos and tenderness of God towards the child, but with anger against any who could, for a moment, look upon children in such wise as to prevent their reaching Him. This young ruler heard these words, and how they were spoken. Moreover, he saw our Lord take these children in His arms, lay His hands upon them, and bless them.

It was then, as moving on His way, the young ruler ran, and fell at His feet, and said, " Good Master." He was a discerning man.

Moreover, he was courageous. As we have said, the rulers by this time were hostile to Jesus, and it was a daring thing for him thus to go to our Lord, and address Him, as revealing the fact that he was conscious of His goodness.

Yet again, he was characterised by humility. When coming into the presence of the Lord, Whose goodness he had seen, he knelt. It may hurriedly be objected that that is merely the record of the fulfilment by this man of the Eastern custom. It is well for us to remember, however, that it is not now, nor was it then, the custom for rulers to kneel to peasants. He had seen something which brought him to a consciousness of the truth concerning himself, and of that superior greatness of goodness which he had seen in Jesus.

When presently our Lord flashed upon him the six commandments written upon the second table of the Law, quickly, rapidly in condensed form, making to shine upon him the light of the commandments which condition relationships between man and his fellow-men, we hear the young ruler replying:

" Master, all these things have I observed from my youth."

Now it is quite true that it has been the habit with some expositors to treat that as an empty boast. It is certainly remarkable that at the point when he had uttered these words, Mark tells us:

" Jesus looking upon him, loved him."

I pause to say that that should not be misunderstood. If he had broken all the ten commandments voluntarily, Jesus would still have loved him. It is nevertheless a significant fact that it was at that moment that the statement is made. The one thing that is definitely proven is that of his perfect honesty, and that implicated the fact that he was a man of clean record. It is well to remember in passing that such a thing is of great value. A depraved condition is not primarily a ground of acceptance with God.

Then we face that which was the supreme thing in the life of this man. Something was lacking, and he knew it. He had great possessions, occupied a high position among his people, was a man of fine natural temperament, had a clean record, but was conscious of lack. That is why he came to Jesus. Matthew in his story tells us that as he came, he employed the very word as he said to Jesus, while claiming to have a clean record:

" All these things have I observed; what lack I yet? "

Moreover he had revealed the thing he lacked by using the term " eternal life." He did not say he lacked eternal life, but he had admitted he lacked the secret of it. Hence his enquiry.

" What shall I do that I may inherit eternal life? "

Thus in his own thinking he felt that he did not possess life in its fulness. It is most important that we remember the real significance of the phrase, " eternal life." Necessarily when we use the phrase we are inclined to think of life that never ends. Now, whereas that is not inaccurate, eternal life is far more than that. Indeed it is never ending, because of what it is in itself. We might with perfect accuracy render the question of the young man:

" Good Master, what shall I do that I may inherit the life of the ages? "

Now that is much more than life that continues. It is life that contains, that is, life which in itself belongs to the ages, breathes their atmosphere, enters into their realisations. It is full-orbed life. Thus this man, with the tremendous advantages that he had, realised that he was not living in the full sense of the word. He wanted life, and wanted it more abundantly.

Though at the moment almost certainly he did not realise it, the cry of his heart was the cry of his spiritual nature after God. He certainly believed in God. He was a ruler, and believed in the Law of God, and had been obedient to that part of it which had affected his relationship with his fellow-men. Nevertheless he knew in the centre and core of his personality that he lacked something.

We turn, therefore, to consider carefully what Jesus had to say to such a man. The matter is of commanding interest because we meet this kind of man over and over again, both in the universities and in business. They are men, it may be of great possessions or not, that is secondary, but men of position, men of fine temperament, men with a clean record. Sometimes we find them inclined to say that because of what they are, they do not need Christ or Christianity. Therefore we watch this story with very keen interest.

Let us notice first that our Lord precipitated a problem in his thinking. He had seen goodness in Jesus, and had confessed it by the way in which he had addressed Him. Immediately our Lord said to him:

"Why callest thou Me good? none is good save one, even God."

Here let us for a few moments dispossess our minds of everything except that of a cold, logical attention. By that I mean let us ask ourselves what can be the meaning of such a question and statement? The answer is inevitable. We are shut up to a sharp alternative, which we may state bluntly thus. He either meant, I am not good, or, I am God. I repeat, there can be no escape from this alternative. Quite a number of years ago now there was published the *Encyclopædia Biblica*. In that an article on Jesus Christ by a German scholar, Schmiedel, declared that five sayings of Jesus recorded in the Gospel narratives might be depended upon as accurate. On examination it was found that these five sayings were those in which Schmiedel understood Jesus as denying His divinity, and His sinlessness. Of the five, this saying of Jesus to the young ruler was the one that he specially dealt with, and declared that our Lord meant by it that He was not good, and therefore not God. I am not proposing to argue about it. To do that would involve the consideration of the whole and continued attitude of Jesus, and the claims that He unvaryingly made. The point at present is that the question would precipitate as we have said, in the mind of this intellectual man a definite problem. The sequel of the narrative does not suggest that he either understood it, or ever returned to it. That does not necessarily mean that he did not do so. Personally I think probably he did, but more of that anon.

Then our Lord in clear-cut brevity, flashed upon him the light of the commandments on the second table of the Decalogue. It is observable that He did not quote the first. As a matter of fact it was in relation to these that he was failing. He quoted the applications on the level of inter-relationship among men, of those four. It was when the light of these six fell upon him, and he had claimed that he had been obedient to them, that he enquired, "What lack I yet?" and it was at this point that our Lord definitely said to him, "One thing thou lackest."

This brings us to the point where superficial reading and thinking may lead us astray. The question arising necessarily is as to what this man did lack. With almost monotonous consistency it has been declared that he lacked poverty. That view contradicts everything we find in the teaching of Jesus. He never suggested that poverty was a necessity of life. On the other hand, as we have already seen, He told men to use their wealth in the right way, by putting the measurement of eternity upon the activities of time, and by employing the balances of eternity for the weighing of temporal possessions.

As a matter of fact we stopped too soon in examining our Lord's answer. Let us hear it once more in full.

"Go, sell whatsoever thou hast, and give to the poor, and thou shalt have treasure in heaven; and come, follow Me."

Two distinct words of command were thus uttered, "Go," and "Come." Which was the essential and ultimate word? It is quite evident that it was "Come, follow Me." "Go" was preliminary, and commanded such action as should prepare for the fulfilment of the "Come." He was commanded to go and clear out of the way the things that were hindering him in discovering the secret of life, and so finding it in its eternal value.

He was commanded to sell what he had, and give to the poor, because in his case his possessions were standing in the way of something which was supreme. It is important that we should understand that the command to go has many applications in many differing cases. Everything depends upon that which is, in the person being dealt with, the supreme hindrance; and that, whatever that may be, it must at all costs be cleared out of the way, so that there may be obedience to the supreme matter.

What then was the one thing? We may reply with perfect accuracy that it was that of following our Lord, only in doing that if we are not careful, we still miss the supreme thought. This man was commanded to put his life under control, to submit to authority, to bend the neck, kiss the sceptre, and crown the King. The central lack of his life was this very fact of submission to authority. That, moreover, is always the case. However the

" Go " may vary, the " Come " remains the same, and that because no man is equal to the management of his own personality, without submission to authority external thereto. When the poet said:

> " There is a divinity that shapes our ends,
> Rough-hew them as we will,"

it is well that we remember that he revealed the fact of all that man can do, and that is " rough-hew." The whole folly of our life is that we continue rough-hewing, and fail to make personal relationship with the Divinity that shapes our ends.

Our Lord is seen, then, standing in front of this young man in the place of, as representing, as actually being God to Whom the human soul must make its submission. He was calling him to submit himself to the only Control to which any man has any right to submit his life, that of God, and that of God as revealed in Christ.

We enquire, therefore, what is the message of this great story for us? It is first a revelation of the fact that life needs control external to itself if it is to find perfect peace, perfect satisfaction, perfect power and poise. A human life can only be controlled in a Wisdom that knows it perfectly, in a Power that is equal to dealing with it, and by a Love that cannot be called in question. That is what we all supremely need, and the reason is that of the greatness of personality. Man is too marvellous, too majestic, to be able to arrange for and govern his own being, in order to the full realisation of its capacities and possibilities. He needs an authority greater than himself, Whose knowledge is profounder, Whose ability is transcending, and Whose love is certain.

Where shall we find any to whom we may thus submit ourselves? Certainly not on the human level. No man has any right to submit his life completely to the authority of any other human being. Such authority can be found only in God. He alone has perfect knowledge and sufficient power, and equal love to be able to govern.

Naturally the question then arises, how can we find God, and establish such relationship with Him? And here the answer of the story is unequivocal. In Christ God is found, and it is as we obey His " Go," and remove everything that interferes, and then obey His " Come " and submit to Him completely, that we have made the true relation of submission to the supreme authority of God.

247

The story ends on a sad note, and yet on a note in which, for me, there always shines a gleam of hope. The sadness is found in the statement:

"He went away sorrowful, for he had great possessions."

The note of hope is found in that word "sorrowful." Great possessions are not supposed to make a man sorrowful, and indeed, in themselves, they do not do so. But when a man is called upon to put them against life itself, they certainly do so.

Watts' picture of the young ruler is a very remarkable revelation. Watts dared to give us nothing more than a portrait of his back. We cannot see his face. We do get a glimpse of a profile, but it is the back turned on Jesus that he has represented. Nevertheless Watts has put into that back everything that speaks of dejection. He is seen, magnificently robed, the turban round his head sparkling with jewels, and his hand hanging listlessly by his side.

In that sorrowfulness there is hope. If he had gone away angry we might have wondered and been hopeless. But he went away sorrowful. We have no record of the ultimate result. We may be certain of the alternative. Either he went back to his wealth, and presently perchance persuaded himself that he very nearly had done a foolish thing, until at last he might be able to laugh at his folly; or else, going home, he pondered further his meeting with Jesus, until the moment came when rising he obeyed completely the "Go" as he dispossessed himself of the things that hindered; and the "Come" as he submitted himself to the full authority of his Lord.

XXXII

ZACCHÆUS

IT is arresting to go through the full account of our Lord's ministry, and to observe how ever and anon in connection with some apparently casual event He uttered some great word which we have no record of His having repeated. In the case of Nicodemus He said:

"Except a man be born from above, he cannot enter into the Kingdom of God."

The truth is of universal application, but was once uttered. On another occasion He said to His disciples:

"The Son of man came not to be ministered unto, but to minister, and to give His life a ransom for many."

In these words we have a revelation of the underlying principle of all His life and work.

So in the story we are now to consider, that of Zacchæus. In connection with that He uttered words which reveal the meaning of His mission in the world:

"For the Son of man is come to seek and to save that which was lost."

The story ends with this great declaration, and illuminates it in a remarkable and perhaps unexpected way. In the story we discover what our Lord meant by seeking and saving. We glory in the declaration, and it is well to have it thus interpreted by the incident which called it forth.

Moreover, the story of Zacchæus is the more interesting because it is the account of one of the last men that Jesus gathered to Himself before His Cross. That He was on the way to the Cross now definitely and positively, and very soon to reach it, is self-evident. In subsequent studies we shall meet with Bartimæus and the dying thief. It is evident, therefore, that this was among the very last.

The events recorded took place in Jericho, that great city as it was at the time of at least one hundred thousand inhabitants, that city which still in the thinking of the Jew remained under the curse of God which had long rested upon it. The city had become, strangely enough, a dwelling-place for priests and Levites, who travelled up and down the road constantly between it and Jerusalem. On His way to Jerusalem our Lord passed through that city. Taking all the narratives and combining them, we may see Him approaching the city, entering into it, staying for a little while, and then passing out of the gate that led to the road for Jerusalem, all the way moving towards His Cross.

We begin by looking at this man Zacchæus. The story is a very old and familiar one, and we all seem to know him. It is important, however, that we should look carefully at him. His name Zacchæus was purely Jewish, and unquestionably he was a Hebrew. In passing it is at least interesting to observe that his name meant Pure. One wonders whether in the early days, on the occasion of his circumcision, his mother and father had given him the name expressive of their hope and desire for him. That, of course, cannot be proven, but it is interesting, for these Hebrews gave names generally for some reason.

Luke tells us that he was a chief publican, and it is of the utmost importance that we should understand what is meant by that definition. We all know that a publican was a tax-gatherer. There were many such, and the rank and file of them were under the direction of chief publicans. Zacchæus was one of these. The district was under Roman rule, and over the tetrarchy Herod was king. The method of taxation would be Roman. That method was that of placing a whole district under a chief publican. It was, to use a very modern term, that of farming out a district to someone thus definitely and imperially appointed for gathering therefrom the taxes. Rome fixed the rate of taxation, and handed the schedule of the same to the man so appointed. Rome fixed the rate *per capita*. The chief publican was required to remit according to that regulation the amount represented by the population. Then Rome closed its eyes. So long as the chief publican rendered the right amount, that is all the imperial government asked. He was left free as to his method of gathering. The rank and file of the publicans acted under his direction. He was supreme in authority and in responsibility.

It is self-evident that these men, both the chief publicans and those who served under them, were in disfavour with the Jewish people. For this there were two reasons. The first was that in many cases the men themselves were Hebrews, and yet were representing the Roman power. The Hebrew people hated that power, and never willingly surrendered to it. This in itself would create a feeling of resentment against the publicans as a class.

But there was another reason for that resentment. It is notorious that these men in collecting the taxes, extorted more than was due, and so enriched themselves. We remember when the publicans went to John the Baptist and said to him:

" Master, what must we do? he said unto them, Extort no more than that which is appointed you."

That is exactly what they were all doing. For those two reasons they were held in contempt. Whenever a man hired himself to Rome he was banned by his fellow-religionists, and disliked because of the method of extortion by which they gathered the taxes.

It is interesting to observe as a sidelight in this connection that the Talmud declared that there were three persons to whom it was perfectly legitimate to lie; a murderer, a thief, and a publican. In the application to the publican we are not yet entirely free from guiltiness. Having crossed the Atlantic fifty times I have been amazed to see people who otherwise were perfectly honest, resorting to all sorts of tricks to dodge the Customs.

As we look at Zacchæus we discover in the light of all these facts that he was a rogue. That declaration will very possibly be challenged. My reason for saying so is found in the statement of Luke:

" He was a chief publican, and he was rich."

That settles it. Now let it be carefully observed I am not declaring that because a man is rich he is a rogue. But no chief publican farming an area on the basis of the Roman arrangement, could possibly become a wealthy man. If he simply gathered what was due, and received his commission, he was well cared for, but he could not amass wealth. All those who in the course of this function became wealthy, had extorted more than was their due. Such was the case with Zacchæus.

Turning to look at him very carefully, we discover that he was a man mastered by curiosity, and therefore a healthy-minded man. Curiosity and investigation are of the very essence of sanity. His curiosity is revealed in the declaration:

> "And he sought to see Jesus, who He was; and could not for the crowd, because he was little of stature."

That statement has often been too hurriedly read, and the revealing nature of the phrase " Who He was " has been lost sight of. It has been said that he was an enquirer, one waiting for Jesus to come along, wanting to see Him, having heard about Him. Such, indeed, was the case in many instances, but not here. A great crowd was surging down the streets of the city, and Zacchæus, keen to find out its meaning, and who it was that was thus attracting attention, climbed the tree for the very purpose of seeing " Who He was." This is evidence of his curious and enquiring mind. He ran on before the crowd, and climbed the tree in order to have that healthy curiosity satisfied.

It is evident, therefore, that he was a man of determination. He was little of stature, and could not see over the heads of the thronging multitudes; but he overcame this physical disability by climbing. Here was evidence of his determination.

The next revelation of the man is found in the statement made about him after the invitation of Jesus had reached him. Luke says that when he heard that, " he made haste and came down, and received Him joyfully." He did not know Him, but something in the look of Jesus, and in the tones of His voice, and in the very invitation itself arrested him, and in his quick response we discover him to be a hospitable man. Thus the man is seen to be an interesting personality, curious, determined, hospitable.

Is that all? No, there is much more, and the more is the supreme thing. He was lost! Nothing he said suggested that condition. No one in the crowd would have used such a word concerning him. They might have described him as a sinner, for it was their habit to link publicans and sinners. When presently however our Lord had dealt with him, and interpreted what He had done, He said:

> " The Son of man is come to seek and to save that which was lost."

In that declaration we have the truth concerning Zacchæus. It is an arresting word that is here employed and translated " lost." It does not merely mean lost in the sense of being mislaid. Something lost in the sense in which the word is used here may still be possessed, but be of no value. That is exactly its intention. Zacchæus as he was living, in his outlook on life, in his habits, in his character, was of no value to God in this world. Moreover, he was lost in that sense as to his fellowmen. It may be that I have possessed a watch of real value, but its main-spring is destroyed; then it is lost. It is impossible to tell the time by it. It is valueless. That is the sense of the word here employed concerning Zacchæus. This man, named Pure, with a lapse of years had become a tax-gatherer for Rome, which was a perfectly legitimate calling, in spite of objection to it; but in carrying out his work he had employed methods which had destroyed his honesty. He had no vital interest in righteousness, but a great interest in revenue. He was lost, of no value, I repeat, to God, of no value, to man; contributing nothing having purpose and power in the procedure of life, contributing nothing to the well-being of his fellow-man; and so by the calculations of eternity, he was spiritually, morally lost.

It is well now to remind ourselves that when we speak of a lost man or woman, the final emphasis in our thinking should not be on the lost person, but on the one who has lost that person. When we speak of a man being lost, do we think most about his suffering, or of the suffering of God? The tragedy of a lost soul in the last analysis, is that God is robbed. In this connection I have sometimes used a very simple and personal illustration. Many years ago when my youngest boy was about four years old, he was out one day with his mother in a London fog, travelling in a bus. When they got to the neighbourhood of Victoria, mother got out, and for some reason the bus moved on into the fog and darkness before the boy alighted. For the moment the boy was lost to the mother. Who suffered most in those moments? There is no doubt that the boy was frightened, but it was the mother, left for a few moments standing there, and unable to do anything, who knew most of suffering. Let us remember this when we think of any man as lost, and think of it so as we look at Zacchæus.

Turning to the contemplation of our Lord's dealing with this man, we are first arrested by a very simple phrase, and it is that as Jesus passed by, He looked up. On the human level, if you are walking along, in the midst of a procession, a man in a tree looking down, may easily be missed. But not by those eyes. He was watching, and watching as He ever did for lost things.

Then He called him by name, as He said:

"Zacchæus, make haste, and come down; for to-day I must abide at thy house."

He knew him, and all about him. That statement carries us back to our earliest study, when John tells us that He knew all men, and needed not that any should tell Him what was in man.

Nevertheless on the human level it is interesting to notice that He did know him and named him; and I am going to tell you of a legend which I do not, of course, suggest for a moment has any historic accuracy, but to me it was, when I heard it, at least full of beauty. When conducting meetings at Birmingham, in Alabama, for Dr. George Stuart, a great Methodist preacher and saint, he and I were sitting together one day, and talking about these Bible stories. In the course of conversation Zacchæus was referred to, and George Stuart said to me:

"You know, Zacchæus was a publican, and so was Matthew. When Matthew began to follow the Lord, one of the first things he did was to gather together those of his own class. I often think that probably he said to his Lord, Master, if one day You should happen to be passing through Jericho, I wish You would find a man named Zacchæus."

That legend can be forgotten, but it is at least an interesting one.

Then observe that our Lord commanded this man's hospitality. Of course, it would be perfectly accurate to say He asked for it. There is only one other occasion on record when He did so, and that was in the case of the woman of Samaria. Here, however, we see Him seeking hospitality from a man who was a notorious rogue.

When I said a moment ago He commanded it, I did so, recognising the Kingliness of our Lord. Kings do not ask for hospitality, but command it. That is so even in our own country to-day. It was equally true in the East, and therefore I look upon the word of Jesus to Zacchæus as the command of a King.

Moreover, the command was issued in the terms of necessity. Said Jesus, "I must abide at thy house." That "must" is revealing. We remember the word is used about Him on other occasions. It was used before He asked hospitality of the woman as it is written, "He must needs pass through Samaria." In dealing with that story we considered the meaning of the "must." The surroundings are different. Here we have a man, not a woman. Here we have, not a woman outside the covenant, but a man failing within it, and lost. We enquire, why must He abide at the house of this man? And the answer is found in the great statement to which we have referred at the end of the story:

"The Son of man is come to seek and to save that which was lost."

In spite of all adverse opinion concerning Zacchæus, Jesus must carry out His mission, and so find His way into this man's house.

We glance for one moment at the house. It would almost certainly be on the Eastern pattern, with its rooms gathered round a central court. If one entered by the principal entrance right opposite to it, perhaps elevated a few steps, would be the guest chamber. There is no doubt that Jesus entered by that door, and found His way into that guest chamber. As He did so we hear the voices of His critics saying:

"He is gone in to lodge with a man that is a sinner." The word "lodge" is arresting. It is a verb derived from a noun. We find that noun in one place in the New Testament where it is said there was no room for Him in the inn. That word for "inn" is *kataluma*, a sheltering place, a lodging place. From that noun this verb is derived. He has gone in to the shelter and the lodging place of this notorious rogue.

The next statement is that "Zacchæus stood," found in verse eight. Between the end of verse seven and the beginning of verse eight there is an interval. How long it lasted we have no means of knowing, and what happened in that guest-chamber has not been told us. It is quite certain that in that interval, while the people waited outside, Jesus and Zacchæus had a private interview.

After that interview, Luke says, "Zacchæus stood." That means that he came into visibility, standing in the court where the people were, and then saying something to Jesus, but saying it publicly. This is what he said:

"Behold, Lord, the half of my goods I give to the poor; and if I have wrongfully exacted aught of any man, I restore fourfold."

It is of the utmost importance that we understand that in these words Zacchæus was not telling the Lord what had been the habit of his life, but what he was now about to do as the result of that interview. Something had taken place in that period of personal dealing between himself and Jesus. A radical change had taken place in the man. The habit of his life might have been expressed in the words, "I get." He now is saying "I give." He had entered, mastered by greed. He came out, mastered by grace. Had he been honest, he would have spoken of the past by saying "I rob." He is now saying, "I restore." He went in, in the grip of roguery. He came out, possessed by righteousness.

What, then, had happened? The answer is found in the declaration of our Lord.

"To-day is salvation come to this house."
This is the true interpretation of salvation. During recent years we have heard men very often declare that the next revival would be an ethical revival. My objection to that statement is that it suggests that previous revivals have not been ethical. Yet look back for a moment. The revival under Whitefield and Wesley was evangelical, but it was ethical. Indeed, if the evangelical be absent, the ethical never results. The ethical change in Zacchæus was wrought by a spiritual change by grace. This is of the very essence of the Gospel.

This, then, is salvation, and this is what our Lord came to do, to seek and to save that which was lost.

That was His mission. It is still His mission.

"Down in the human heart, crushed by the tempter,
    Feelings lie buried that grace can restore;
Touched by a loving hand, wakened by kindness,
    Chords that were broken will vibrate once more."

Jesus entered into the house of Zacchæus, and laid His hand upon the broken chords, and they vibrated with the music of a restored soul.

Thus salvation is the word that tells the whole meaning of the mission of Christ. He has come to proclaim the possibility of the salvation of the unfittest, in order to the survival of the fittest. There is no room in the enterprise of Christ for unfit men. But His mission is to take the unfit, and make them fit. To lost Zacchæus salvation came, and expressed itself in the complete revolution of his life, for:

"The Son of man is come to seek and to save that which was lost."

XXXIII

BARTIMÆUS

IN considering the story of Bartimæus we find ourselves still in the company of Jesus on His way to His Cross. It is set in the same geographical surroundings as that of Zacchæus, that is to say, the events recorded took place in connection with His visit to Jericho. In the story of Zacchæus we saw our Lord entering the city, and then within the city dealing with Zacchæus. Matthew and Mark refer to things that happened when He was leaving the city. It is in itself a matter of great interest that on this final journey our Lord took His way to this city.

We halt for a few minutes with a matter which is not of supreme importance, perhaps, but is at least of interest to the Bible student. The majority of harmonists attempting to set out the story of Jesus in chronological sequence, have confused similarity with identity. The story which we have in Mark is treated as a variant of that found in Matthew, giving an account of the healing of two blind men, and with the story in Luke of the healing of one. Now let me repeat what I have already said that the matter is of no really serious importance, but I may state at once that I believe that these are distinct stories. We must bear in mind that Jericho at the time was a great city of at least a hundred thousand inhabitants, and at its gates, whether on the one side or the other, and clustered upon the wayside near the gates, would always be a multitude of beggars. Moreover unquestionably at this time many of them would be blind.

Luke tells us of our Lord's meeting with one blind man, and is very careful to say, " As He drew nigh unto Jericho." His dealing with this man took place as He was entering the city. Mark tells us the story of Bartimæus, and distinctly says that He met him as He was going out of the city. Matthew tells us of two that He encountered as He went out. Possibly Bartimæus was one of the two Matthew refers to, although he does not name him. I admit that there is a great similarity in the details of these stories, but there is no reason to think they are identical.

We confine ourselves to Mark's story of Bartimæus. The account is brief and dramatic in itself, and is very full of value when considered in the atmosphere of the time when it occurred.

If we begin our reading with the statement made in x, 32, " And they were in the way, going up to Jerusalem," we shall find that everything in the paragraph there beginning, circles around one verse, the forty-fifth. The Lord was speaking to His disciples, and in so doing in that atmosphere He made this tremendous and overwhelming declaration:

> " For verily the Son of man came not to be ministered unto, but to minister, and to give His life a ransom for many."

In our consideration of the story of Zacchæus we noticed how upon that occasion He uttered another of His supreme sayings:

> " The Son of man came to seek and to save that which was lost."

We saw how the story of Zacchæus illustrates that saying, showing us at once in the case of the man, the real meaning of being lost, and revealing by Christ's action what it is to seek and save the lost.

Here again we have apparently incidentally a great and inclusive word of our Lord. While we are familiar with it in the form in which we find it in our versions, it may be well slightly to change the wording in order to emphasise the sense. We may read it therefore:

> " Verily, the Son of man came not to be served, but to serve, and to give His life a ransom for many."

The saying is startling because, and of necessity, we are constantly serving the Son of man; yet here He said that the purpose of His coming was not to be served, that is, not for personal aggrandisement in any form. The purpose of His coming into the world was that He might serve. Now all that must be borne in mind as we come to this story of Bartimæus, and Christ's dealing with him, as passing from the city, He met him.

This man was evidently well known, for Mark names him, Bartimæus, and then repeats the naming by translating, " the son of Timæus." The natural deduction from this method of introduction is that the man and his father were well known in the circle of the disciples. The story is not merely that of the opening of the eyes of the man, but of the beginning of his definite discipleship. Very probably his father also had been, or became a disciple of Jesus. Here, however, he is first seen as blind, and withal a blind beggar, living upon the charity of the casual passer by, sitting by the wayside, receiving gifts, unable to see anything that was going on around him; but as blind people so constantly are, acute in hearing and understanding as he listened.

One day he heard unusual sounds, that is the sound of an unusual crowd, the tramp of a great multitude passing by the place where he sat begging. Undoubtedly he enquired the meaning of this, and received the answer. Here, of course, is the origin of the great hymn with which Ira D. Sankey made us so familiar in bygone days:

"What means this eager, anxious throng,
    Which moves with busy haste along—
These wondrous gatherings day by day,
    What means this strange commotion, pray?
In accents hushed the throng reply,
    'Jesus of Nazareth passeth by.' "

We can imagine Bartimæus asking this very question, and receiving this answer.

Now fastening our attention upon the man in action we notice first that directly he knew that Jesus of Nazareth was passing, he made a direct appeal to Him. Still sitting in the place where he had been a beggar, living on alms, he cried out:

"Jesus, Thou Son of David, have mercy on me."

This method of appeal makes it perfectly clear that he had some previous knowledge of Jesus, that he had heard of Him. He designated Him in words that were equivalent to a confession, or at least an admission of His Messiahship, "Jesus, Thou Son of David." Whether it was a venture made half in the darkness it it impossible to say, but it is quite evident that this man, trusting for a living to the charity of the casual passer-by, was now reaching out after some gift other than any he had ever received, because possibly that this Prophet, of Whom he had heard so much, was indeed the Messiah; and he sought His compassion as he said: "Have mercy on me." It is clear that he was not asking for alms of Jesus in the usual sense of the word. He recognised the special meaning in the moving of that crowd when he found Who it was that was at its centre; and we have this vision of him rising above

259

material necessity in a certain sense, and seeking the one inestimable gift he lacked, that of sight. Moreover, his appeal was made to the compassion of Jesus.

The next impression made upon us is that of his persistence. Mark says, "Many rebuked him." He does not distinctly say that the disciples did so, but in all probability they did. If so, their rebuke, as on other occasions, was a part of their solicitous care for the Lord. There rested upon our Lord at this time the shadows of His coming suffering, and undoubtedly, they were conscious of this fact. He had been in the city of Jericho, and in the home of Zacchæus. They knew He was leaving the city, and more than ever stedfastly and definitely setting His face towards Jerusalem. What more natural than that they should think that as He started out on this final stage of the journey, He must not be disturbed by the plea of a blind beggar. We remember how not long before this, these disciples endeavoured to prevent children coming to Him, and undoubtedly it was for the same reason. Therefore they attempted to prevent Bartimæus disturbing the Lord.

Then his persistence is seen in the declaration that " he cried out the more a great deal." We can hear the voice of this man in his earnest desire, rising above the tramping of the crowds. He repeated the same words over and over again:

"Thou Son of David, have mercy on me."

Then in looking carefully at Bartimæus, we have to remember in advance that Jesus stood still and commanded His disciples to call the man. When He did so we read that "casting away his garment," he "sprang up and came to Jesus." We see him acting with promptness and decision. Possibly now the disciples, or some others standing by, would guide him as he approached the Lord; but his own action in flinging away the garment that might impede his progress, was made.

Then when our Lord asked him:

"What wilt thou that I should do unto thee?"

the definiteness of his reply is marked:

"Rabboni, that I may receive my sight."

Quite literally what he said was, Rabboni, that I may look up. Asked what he wanted, he knew at once and declared it, the blessing of being able to lift his eyes, and lifting them, to see. He declared the supreme consciousness of need without hesitation and without qualification.

Then once more, after he had received his sight, we are told as the final thing concerning him that " he followed Him in the way "; which means infinitely more than that he joined the crowd. The following of Jesus in the way was his acceptance of the logical issue of the thing that had happened to him. He had flung himself out on the compassion of the Son of David. He had received his reply in all fulness. He could see. He had looked into the face of Jesus by this time, and I dare venture to affirm that he had eyes at first for no other Face. Then he had seen Jesus begin to move away, along the way, with His face stedfastly set towards Jerusalem. He then did the only logical thing, " He followed Him in the way." He was nearly the last disciple of whom we have any account won by the Lord to discipleship; and discipleship is the meaning of the statement, " He followed Him in the way."

It is here that the attitude and activity of Christ is seen set in relation to the circumstances of the time.

" They were in the way, going up to Jerusalem."

They had been in Jericho, the city still under the curse of God from the standpoint of Jewish opinion, the city which at the time was nevertheless full of beauty in all material ways. In that city He had found Zacchæus, and had revealed the meaning of His mission as the Son of man, seeking and saving the lost. Now leaving the city behind them, they are travelling to Jerusalem. At this point Mark makes the illuminating statement, " Jesus was going before them; and they were amazed." We see the Lord then moving forward in loneliness. All the ineffable sorrows of His passion were with Him, and He walked alone. The disciples loved Him, but none of them understood Him. For six months they had walked in a mystery ever since He had told them at Cæsarea Philippi that He must go to Jerusalem and suffer, and be killed, and rise again.

And not the disciples alone, but the crowds were evidently impressed by something full of mystery. They were afraid. He was alone. His disciples were amazed, and durst ask Him no questions. The multitudes seeing something of all this, were filled with fear. It was a silent and hushed movement. Then it was that He took the twelve alone, evidently away from the crowd, and repeated to them the things He had been telling them for these past six months. Indeed, upon this occasion He referred to it all with tremendous and awe-inspiring particularity. He declared that He was going up, and that they would spit on Him

261

and mock Him and scourge Him and kill Him. But He did not end there. He added:

"And the third day He would rise again."

It is a matter that one has often referred to, though it cannot be too often insisted upon, that from the moment when He first revealed to these disciples at Cæsarea Philippi the necessity for His Cross, He never made reference thereto, but that at the same time He foretold His resurrection.

It was now that James and John came to Him with their request. Let us be careful that we do not join the ten apostles who were angry with them. In the very hour when He was insisting afresh upon the coming of His Cross, they preferred their request. We learn from another of the evangelists that the request was made through their mother, who said:

"Command that these my two sons may sit, one on Thy right hand, and one on Thy left hand, in Thy Kingdom."

The request made by the mother was undoubtedly that of the sons themselves, and it is of the utmost importance that we recognise that in spite of what He was now telling them about coming suffering, which they could by no means understand, they still believed that it was inevitable that He was coming into His Kingdom.

Moreover, if we are inclined to criticise them, it is well to remember that Jesus did not do so. Looking at them, He enquired:

"Are ye able to drink the cup that I drink? or to be baptised with the baptism I am baptised with?"

They replied, "We are able." They meant what they said. They were quite sincere, and it is arresting that our Lord told them they should drink His cup, and be baptised with His baptism. How little they understood of how they would fail Him directly; but how perfectly He understood that ultimately they would indeed be partakers of His sufferings.

The story reads on naturally. The ten were angry with these men for seeking positions of power; and He rebuked not the two, for the request; but the ten, for their criticism. He then declared to them the very genius of His Kingdom, that it was not one to be established by force of compelling men to serve. It was rather one that inspired men to the service of others. Positions of power in His Kingdom are not opportunities for the exercise of mastery, but for the rendering of service. Here it was that He said:

"The Son of man came not to be ministered unto, but to minister, and to give His life a ransom for many."

It was in this atmosphere that He came to Jericho, passed through it, won Zacchæus, and departing, responded to the cry of this blind man.

He heard the cry of anguish, and knowing all that lay behind it, He stood still. He stood still on His way to the Cross. We remember the occasion upon which in Tyre and Sidon He had entered into a house, and would not that any man should know He was there; and He could not be hid, when a woman in her agony appealed to Him. So now, He Who was on His way to the Cross for the fulfilment of His mission in the world, to give His life a ransom for many, in answer to the cry of a blind beggar, He stood still. He halted the procession to the Cross in the spirit of the Cross.

When He told His disciples to call the man to Him, they, addressing Bartimæus said, "Be of good courage." That is the one occasion when we have a record of His disciples using that expression. On the other hand we have five occasions recorded when Jesus employed it, facing conditions of human need and dereliction. The disciples had caught, if I may venture so to state it, the trick of His speech, and said to Bartimæus the thing they had heard Him say to others, "Be of good courage."

When the man came, and the Lord had enquired:

"What wilt thou that I should do unto thee?"

and received with quick directness the answer:

"Lord, that I may receive my sight,"

the word of Jesus was uttered:

"Go thy way, thy faith hath made thee whole."

At once his eyes were opened.

The whole story is speaking to us a message larger than that of the merely historic incident. The miracle is a parable. As Dr. Arthur T. Pierson said long ago:

"Every parable of Jesus was a miracle of wisdom; and every miracle of Jesus was a parable of teaching."

This miracle was most certainly a parable of teaching. Bartimæus and his circumstances were local, and the incident is definitely historic; but as we look we see him representing humanity on the highway, blind and begging. We look over the world to-day, and that is exactly what we see, humanity going hither and thither, blind to all the highest facts of life; and always begging, seeking something to satisfy their deepest need, which they never find.

Moreover the story illuminates the Cross. He had said:

"The Son of man came not to be ministered unto, but to minister; and to give His life a ransom for many."

Here was a man in need, a soul in agony, seeking His compassion; and that was exactly what filled His heart; and His purpose in the world was to serve humanity in that way. He was on His way to give His life a ransom, and therefore I say with great reverence, and with tremendous conviction, He could not help stopping when He heard that cry.

Thus we are warranted in putting together two sentences from the whole paragraph:

"He was on His way, going up to Jerusalem,"
and

"he followed Him in the way."

We have no further details, but we know that in the story we see Jesus, with all the shadows gathering about Him, and the sorrows of His passion surging in His soul, carrying out the very intention of His going as He paused and answered the cry of the blind beggar.

The whole thing is the revealing of the facts still abiding. To-day any human soul, conscious of need, of spiritual sight, and of moral cleansing, who will make his or her appeal to Jesus of Nazareth, as He passeth by, that same Lord will pause and give that soul what it needs.

XXXIV

THE WIDOW AT THE TREASURY

IT is at least possible that some surprise may be created that we should include this story in the present series. In it we see a woman and Jesus. The woman, however, is nameless, and we have no record of any word she uttered, and our Lord did not speak to her, but only about her. It would seen to be most likely that she did not know what He said concerning her. She simply passed along, and carried out the intention of her heart as she went through the Temple courts, and proceeded on her way in loneliness and absolute poverty. There seems to have been no contact between her and the Lord. Moreover, what He did say was said to His disciples, and apparently semi-privately, because we are told that He called His disciples to Him to say what He had to say.

In this sense, then, the case is peculiar. Nevertheless, here we have the one woman of whom no record has been preserved save this, who evidently with absolute truth could have sung the lines from Frances Ridley Havergal's hymn:

" Take my silver and my gold,
Not a mite would I withhold."

We have often sung that, and I am not saying untruthfully, but here is a case where it is the simple and actual truth concerning one woman.

Mark tells us that our Lord was seated " over against the treasury." The treasury in the Temple courts was situated in the Court of the Women, which was flanked by the Court of the Gentiles. It occupied a vast space. In that one Court alone fifteen thousand worshippers could be accommodated, so great and vast was the Temple area. It was there that this thing took place. In that Court there were placed thirteen *shopharoth*, which means simply trumpet-shaped receptacles. As the people passed through the Court they placed their gifts in these receptacles. At the time many were doing so, and among the rest this woman passing along, placed her gift therein. Jesus sat watching, and the whole incident is the more arresting because it is the last but one recorded in the life of Jesus ere He left the Temple, never to return to it again. The other was that of the coming of the Greeks, of which John gives us an account.

It is well to observe carefully the attitude of our Lord by combining the stories of Mark and Luke. Mark immediately preceding his record of the incident says:

> " And in His teaching He said, Beware of the scribes, which desire to walk in long robes, and to have salutations in the market-places, and chief seats in the synagogues, and chief places at feasts; they which devour widows' houses, and for pretence make long prayers; these shall receive greater condemnation. And He sat down over against the treasury, and beheld how the multitude cast money into the treasury; and many that were rich cast in much. And there came a poor widow."

Having uttered the words of condemnation He evidently took up His position, and sat down where He could see the treasury.

Luke records the same things as he writes:

> " And in the hearing of all the people He said unto His disciples, Beware of the scribes, which desire to walk in long robes, and love salutations in the market-places, and chief seats at feasts; which devour widows' houses, and for a pretence make long prayers; these shall receive greater condemnation. And He looked up, and saw the rich men that were casting their gifts into the treasury. And He saw a certain poor widow."

It will be observed that Marks says that sitting there Jesus " beheld," and the imperfect tense employed suggests not a passing glance, but careful watching.

Luke says " He looked up, and saw." If we put the two things together we have a vivid picture of the attitude and action of our Lord. Let it be remembered that it took place at the close of a day in which He had been confronted with the criticism of the clever, cynical and sinister opposition of the religious rulers. It had been a day in which we see Him triumphing with august majesty over every attempt to entrap Him. But with weariness He sat, and Luke tells us that " He looked up." It is evident that sitting there, He had not at first been watching the passers-by, but looking down, probably in profound thought concerning the day through which He had passed. The last words He had spoken were those of denunciation of the false religious leaders who,loved pre-eminence; and among others things He had uttered His severe indictment of them that they devoured widows' houses.

Then, as Luke tells us, He looked up, and Mark tells us that He " beheld how they cast into the treasury." There is almost certainly a link between the final denunciation of hypocrisy in the persons of the rulers and the thought of the watching of Jesus. As He watched He saw the multitudes, and among them the rich who as they passed, " cast in much." The Greek word which we have rendered " much " is literally " many," that is, they cast in a handful of coins. Then He saw this one lone woman coming along in the crowd, garbed unquestionably as she inevitably would be in the habiliments of her lonely mourning and widowhood. As she passed, she also cast something into the treasury.

We pause then to look at the woman. Very little is told about her, and yet what is told is very revealing. She cast in two mites, which is described as " all her living," and the word " living " there may be correctly rendered livelihood.

It is difficult, and perhaps finally impossible to state in the terms of our own times the value of the gift intrinsically. Our translators say " two mites," that is, two perutahs. Of course, values now are different from what they were at that time. The one certain fact is, however, that the perutah was the smallest copper coin, and that two of them equalled a quadrans. The quadrans was one-ninety-sixth of a denarius. When we ask the value of a denarius, we learn that in our present currency it was worth sixpence. Necessarily we cannot thus measure exactly with accuracy the value of the denarius, but the gift certainly reveals the appalling poverty of this woman. We are distinctly told that it was all she had. This woman had nothing else at the moment upon which to depend for her very existence. She had no means put away, and these were the last two coins she possessed. Looking at her, then, we see a woman in abject poverty.

But as we watch her act we recognise necessarily that she was a daughter of Israel, and a worshipper of the living God. That was why she was in the Temple courts at all. In spite of her condition, in spite of her abject loneliness, in spite of her appalling penury, she still believed in the God of her fathers, and in her personal relationship to Him. This she expressed as she cast her gift into the treasury.

Jesus was watching. I do not think she saw Him. In all probability she did not know Him. She was one of the thronging crowd of worshippers, and yet remarkably separated from that crowd. She was a true worshipper of the God of her fathers, believing in Him, she realised her obligation to make her contribution in material things to that great and glorious Temple.

All the gifts put into the treasury were divided between the priests and the poor. One wonders whether as she cast in the two mites, one was devoted to the priests and one to the poor, in her mind. Be that as it may, we see a recognition of responsibility in her worship. To the ordinary onlooker she was one of the crowd, and to herself unquestionably inconspicuous, probably hoping that she was unnoticed, wanting no one to see what she gave, but giving as a worshipper to God.

Her gift was far more than a symbol of her attitude. It was the totality of her life, all her livelihood, all that she had. She would indeed have passed unnoticed and unknown but for those watching eyes of Jesus. He saw in her unquestionably a member of the elect remnant which had ever been true to the God of Israel, in spite of the general failure and deflection of His people.

We remember that Jesus was greeted as He came into the world by such; His Mother Mary was of that number, Joseph also. Simeon and Anna were of the elect souls, faithful and true in the midst of declension. This woman was, I repeat, of that company.

Now we turn to consider carefully our Lord's words about her. Weary after the day of conflict, knowing the depth of the hostility stirred against Him, suffering not so much because they were hostile to Him, but because their hostility was reacting upon themselves for their own inevitable destruction, He saw the action of that woman.

We are arrested by the significance of one little word used by Mark in his account of the watching of Jesus. He says that He watched " *How* the multitude cast money into the treasury." We miss the whole point of the statement if we omit that word " how " in our thinking. It is not merely a statement that He beheld the fact that the multitude were casting in money; but

He was watching how they were doing it. He was not so much concerned with what they gave as with how they gave it.

He saw the rich casting in much. He saw one woman casting in all; and in each case He saw how they gave. Goethe tells us that Lavater once said he always watched the hands of people giving as he held the offertory plate before them; and he claimed that he was able to tell the kind of person from the way in which the hand was opened. Of course that may be a mythical story, but in this case it may be said that it was literally true. The Lord saw the hands, but behind them the attitude of the soul. We may say that He was not concerned to add up the collection, although He did this, too, presently in a remarkable way. But He saw what this woman gave, as undoubtedly He did in the case of all the rest; but it was the spirit of the giving that He was observing.

Having done this He spoke to His disciples, and in doing so He first appraised the giving, and then interpreted the reason of His appraisal.

In appraising the gifts He held the balances in one hand, and in the one side of them He put all that was cast in that day, except the gifts of the woman. These He put into the other scale. Then He drew His disciples' attention to what He had seen, and declared that in the scales which He held, the gifts of the woman out-weighed the rest. We must carefully observe that He said she had cast in more than they all. That was much more than saying she had given more than anyone else that day. That would have been a remarkable and arresting thing; but what He said was that her gift amounted to more in the balances of heaven than all that had been put in by the whole crowd. He knew how much those money-chests contained as the result of the giving of the day. The incarnate eternal Son of God in human form knew without any question exactly the amount that would presently be found in those thirteen chests. He knew also that when the money was taken out there were two small coins, two mites, which almost certainly the collectors would hardly notice; and He declared that in value they outweighed all the rest. What an appraisal!

We pause a moment to think of this appraisement as being in a sense literally true. All the gifts which they had cast in were presently made use of, some devoted to the poor and some devoted to the priests. The Temple treasury was really a wealthy thing. When presently Pompey came, he found, using our coinage as expressing value, two millions sterling stored away in riches. We ask what became of these gifts, and we cannot answer. We do know, however, what became of these two mites. The appraisement of Jesus lifted them into a realm of active value which through the centuries which have follow~d, have produced an amount which would out-weigh all that was put into the treasury that day.

Thus He took the two sacred and sacramental mites, the copper coins, and kissed them into the infinite and multiplied gold of the sanctuary of God. Herein a great principle is revealed. When Mary anointed His feet He declared that what she had done should be told in all the world as a memorial of her. So it has been. That alabaster cruse of ointment has inspired the giving of untold wealth, consecrated to Him. So with the gift of this woman, who had slipped away from sight unnoticed, but great in heart and loyalty and devotion. Her gift became the inspiration of a new and multiplying value of giving.

It was immediately connected with this appraisal our Lord gave His reason for making it, as He compared the underlying motive of the giving in each case. They cast in of their " superfluity." She put in " all her living." The difference is the difference between " superfluity " and sacrifice.

Superfluity refers to something which is easily spared, in all probability never missed. Such giving was, therefore, a gesture of formalism, a conforming to a ritual, a doing of the supposedly correct thing. Jesus, with fine, infinite, and appalling scorn, gathered up all such gifts, and said, " superfluity." On the other hand He selected the two mites of the widow, which constituted all her living. The principle behind her giving was that she was enduring " as seeing Him Who is invisible." Her action was her response to her belief in God, and the carrying out of the deep feeling that such vision had produced. She only had two mites. By the traditional law of the time no one was allowed to cast into those chests less than two mites. She possessed that amount. She had on the material level enough to do the smallest thing that she was permitted to do. Human wisdom would have declared that if that were all she possessed, prudence would demand that she certainly had better keep them. But her vision of God, her faith in God, and her emotion toward God demanded that she devote it to Him.

In the Old Testament Scriptures over and over again it is declared of some offering provided for, that it created " a sweet savour" unto God. What this woman on that day did created a sweet savour to Christ.

Following the chronological sequence, in an examination of the narratives of the evangelists we find that our Lord immediately afterwards uttered His eight-fold Woe against the Pharisees. Then the disciples as they were leaving the Temple, drew His attention to its glory, and the beauty of the stones. Whereas our Lord told them that all that was nothing, and that the time was coming when one stone should not be left upon another, this little narrative of the woman shows us that in the midst of all the terrible failure of the nation as centralised in that Temple, He had something which was a sweet savour. It was that of this one lonely soul, who without compromise, without halting, had devoted everything to the God of her fathers.

The whole story is its own vindication to its place in the series we have been considering. As we said at the beginning, we have no record of any word our Lord spoke to her at the time. It is probable that she knew nothing about it. But the thing He said was so significant, and the comparison between the two conceptions of life manifested in the gifts placed in the treasury, warrant our consideration of the story.

It is inevitable that we should remind ourselves of the great facts revealed, and their perpetual value. He is still watching. It may be that someone is lost in the crowd, but everyone is seen by Him. As He watches He sees the gift which is supposed to be the sacramental symbol of our attitude. What a great thing it would be if all the givers in the House of God for ever bore this in mind.

Moreover thus still watching, He still registers according not to amount, but to the motive that prompts the giving. It is really arresting how that in looking over subscription lists, when some enterprise is on hand, and subscriptions are being sent in, we find the gifts are arranged according to amounts, and then very often at the end of the list we have the words, "Amounts under £1," so much, no names being given. Nevertheless it is true over and over again within that sum total of small amounts with no names attached there is more sacrificial giving than in the totality of the larger sums. Too often the large amounts may be dismissed under Christ's word, "superfluity"; and within the small and apparently unimportant section, described as "Amounts under . ." may be found the gifts which are of infinite value.

In the case of this woman no provision was made for the morrow. By all the standards of human wisdom it was an unwise action; but by the standards of eternity it was of the essence of wisdom. She had no other livelihood. Nevertheless to the God of her fathers she must leave the future, and acting in the present, devote that which was a symbol of her faith and her devotion. In the measure in which we act in the spirit of this unknown and poverty-stricken widow, we shall reach the Divine appraisement, which will describe our action as other than the devotion of superfluity, being sacrificial, and so reaching the highest possible level.

XXXV

ANNAS AND CAIAPHAS

IN this series of studies on the Great Physician we have seen His mighty power in the healing of humanity, and watched the varying methods of His wondrous wisdom. On one or two occasions we have had to leave the story unfinished as to the result of what He did, as in the case of the young ruler.

We come to-night and for the next two considerations to the tragic side of our subject. We have to watch Him in the presence of what seems to be incurable humanity. I am referring to the story of Annas and Caiaphas, to that of Pilate, and to that of Herod. We have these three illustrations of men who came into contact with our Lord, but did not seem to have been healed.

We take the story of Annas and Caiaphas together because they were so intimately related in their contact with Jesus. Indeed, this is the only way in which we see them in the New Testament. We may pause, however, by way of introduction to note certain facts with which we are familiar from sources outside the Biblical revelation. Josephus and other historians give us these particulars.

Let us first of all remember that at that time the priests of the Jews were appointed by Roman procurators. That in itself is a revelation of the appalling degeneracy of the faith of the Hebrews. The high priest, the successors of Aaron, were being appointed by an alien and pagan power. Annas had been made high priest by Quirinius, who was the governor of Syria. Taking our dating, we find that he was made high priest in A.D. 7. He was deposed from his office in A.D. 15 by Valerius Gratus. Thus the period of his high priesthood lasted for eight years. A revelation of how remarkable a man he was is found in the fact that although thus deposed from holding the actual office, he remained the dominant member of the priesthood. So much was this so that five of his sons and then his son-in-law, Caiaphas, held the position of high priest. During the whole period he was associated with them, and was the dominant power. Moreover, he retained the title long after he was officially deposed. At the beginning of the Book of the Acts we read:

> "And Annas the high priest was there, and Caiaphas, and John, and Alexander, and as many as were of the kindred of the high priest."

As a matter of fact, the historic fact was that he was not then holding the office of the high priesthood, but he was still so referred to. In the Gospel according to Luke, when referring to the coming of the Word of God to John, he says:

> "In the priesthood of Annas and Caiaphas."

I repeat, these facts do reveal the remarkable influence of this man.

Caiaphas we need not tarry with, because we have said all there is to be said concerning him. He was a son-in-law of Annas. He held the position of high priest by Roman appointment from A.D. 18 to A.D. 36. He was ultimately deposed by Vitellius.

Thus we see these two men, and the position they occupied. This accounts for what we find in the New Testament references to the priesthood of Annas and Caiaphas. While Caiaphas was the titular priest, Annas was the active priest. This double priesthood covered the whole period of the ministry of our Lord, and, indeed, the previous period of the ministry of John the Baptist.

These men were of the Sadducean party. We remind ourselves of that with which we are familiar, that there were two Schools theologically, that existed and were active all through the ministry of John and of Jesus, that of the Pharisees and that of the Sadducees. These were bitterly opposed to each other theologically and religiously and politically. At last they formed a coalition in order to encompass the death of Jesus, but there was a very radical difference between them. The Sadducees were the rationalists in religion. They believed neither in angel, nor spirit, nor resurrection. These two men, Annas and Caiaphas belonged to that party. From the very beginning of the ministry of Jesus they were evidently definitely opposed to Him. They were exerting a remarkable power over the people, and by employing certain methods they had become enormously wealthy. From Roman history we learn that when the Romans seized Jerusalem they found over two and a half million sterling, stored by Annas. Our Lord's denunciation applied specially to these men, when He said:

" Is it not written, My house shall be called a house of prayer for all the nations? but ye have made it a den of robbers."

In that connection we are told:

" And the chief priests and the scribes heard it, and sought how they might destroy Him; for they feared Him, for all the multitude were astonished at His teaching."

Annas was behind all this gathering of money, and he had amassed his wealth by the sale of requisites for Temple sacrifice. Caiaphas was his partner in the business, and these were those centrally denounced in the scathing terms employed by our Lord. They had made the house of God " a den of robbers."

Turning from these historic facts gathered outside the New Testament let us glance for a few moments at the occasions where they appear in the New Testament in chronological order. Annas is referred to four times, Caiaphas seven.

Annas is first named when Luke was dating the coming of the Word of God to John. He is never referred to again in chronological sequence until we see Jesus led before him after His arrest in the Garden. There we see Him causing the binding of Jesus, and sending Him to Caiaphas, who was the titular high priest. We see him next in the Acts with the Sanhedrim, when the apostles were arraigned before that body, after the resurrection of our Lord. These are the appearances of Annas.

When we turn to Caiaphas we find him at the beginning with Annas, named as one of the high priests, when the Word of God came to John. The next reference to him is to an occasion perhaps two or two and a half years later, when we find him addressing the Sanhedrim concerning Jesus, on an occasion when they were consulting as to what could be done to silence Him. We hear Caiaphas deliver one of the most polished, finished, clever and damnable addresses that politician ever uttered, and that is saying much. Reduced to its simplest meaning he declared that there was only one way to deal with the situation, and that was to bring about the death of the Lord. This the Council decided to do, postponing His arrest until after the feast.

Our next view of Caiaphas is in the darkness of the early morning when he received Jesus as a prisoner, as He was sent to him by his father-in-law, Annas. Following that he is seen

275

presiding over the illegal trial of Jesus; and finally sending Him to Pilate. The last glimpse we have of him is when he is present with Annas in the Sanhedrim, when the apostles were arraigned before him after the resurrection.

Thus these men appear before us always acting together, and Annas as the inspiring genius, if we may debase a great word by calling him a genius. It was Renan who said if guilt is to be attached to anyone on the human level, it must be to Annas. Nevertheless, they were acting together in consort and in agreement.

We ask, then, what are the facts revealed concerning these men as we see them in the light of history outside the Bible, and in the revelation of them we have in the passages we have referred to ?

We see them first as two religious degenerates, men who were prostituting a Divine office to personal ends. They were men of remarkable worldly wisdom, as witness the speech of Caiaphas, to which we have referred. In that speech Caiaphas had introduced what he said by the statement to the whole Sanhedrim, " Ye know nothing at all." He then went on to declare that it was expedient that one man should die rather than that a nation should perish. His meaning was perfectly clear, that unless Jesus was compelled to cease His teaching, and in order to that end, put to death, Rome would take away the nation from them, that is, from the influence exerted by this high priestly party. The speech was characterised by worldly wisdom. It was the language of the astute and clever politician. I repeat what I have said, they were religious degenerates, prostituting a Divine office for personal ends.

They were spiritually moribund, or dead, for moribund means dying, or near to dead. It would be more correct to say that they were dead. They had no understanding of God; they had no sense of the Divine activity in the midst of which they were living. Jesus, the Son of God, was acting for God, and God was acting through Him. As Peter declared on the day of Pentecost:

> " Jesus of Nazareth, a Man approved of God unto you by powers and wonders and signs, which God did by Him in the midst of you."

God was acting through Him, but these men had no consciousness of the fact. Intellectually they believed in God, in the living God, but practically they were unconscious of His nearness and His activity. Their constant and consistent hostility to Jesus resulted from this blindness in the presence of Divine activity. By His teaching and His actions He was necessarily interfering with their earthly interests, and therefore their opposition. In them we have an appalling picture of what humanity may come to.

We now turn to watch our Lord dealing with them as He came into contact with them. There may be a slight difference in the matter of interpretation at this point, because the passage in John which declares that the high priest asked Him of His disciples and of His teaching, is believed by some to refer to Annas, and by some to Caiaphas. It is possible that one cannot be finally dogmatic concerning the matter. Yet I want to say definitely that to me there is no difficulty at all. I have no doubt whatever that when they arrested Jesus they brought Him first to Annas, and that seems to be borne out very clearly by the fact that it is declared in that connection that Annas sent Him bound to Caiaphas.

It was Annas, therefore, who asked Him concerning His disciples and His teaching. The statement is a very simple one, but it is quite evident what it intended. He was enquiring from Jesus inferentially as to what His purpose really was, what it was that He was seeking for Himself and through the disciples He had gathered about Him. He was at least suggesting that there was something seditious, something secret in the methods of Jesus, that He was disseminating teaching which might bring insurrection and trouble. That is what the enquiry meant. There is no doubt that he said more than is reported, but the report covers the whole of the investigation.

We are first impressed by the fact that when Jesus answered, He made no reply about His disciples. That fact may have many meanings. We are bound to admit that there was nothing very good to say about them at that moment. One of them was betraying Him. Another would presently declare he did not know Him. Nevertheless it seems to me the fact that He did not reply to the enquiry about His disciples was rather that He would not involve them in trouble. Already in the Garden He had charged those about to arrest Him, not to arrest His disciples.

" If therefore ye seek Me, let these go their way."

The only reference He made to them in His reply to Annas was a reference to their witness. He declared that what He had taught had been taught in the synagogues and in the Temple courts where all the Jews gathered. There had been nothing clandestine about His teaching. Said Jesus to Annas, " Why askest thou Me? "

One is inclined to wonder where the emphasis lay in that question. Perhaps on the " Why," as though He should tell Annas that he already knew what His teaching was. Be that as it may, He denied emphatically the suggestion lurking in the question of Annas.

Evidently He had spoken with sternness, for someone standing by, struck Him, and asked Him how He dared to speak thus to the high priest. Our Lord made no reply to the question, but reaffirmed the truth of what He had declared concerning His teaching; and enquired why if He had told the truth, He was thus smitten. Annas had gone as far as he dare, and therefore he sent Him to Caiaphas.

Thus we see our Lord now in contact with Caiaphas. We start by remembering that the intention of Caiaphas had already been clearly revealed in the speech before the Sanhedrim. His opportunity had now come to see the intention carried out, and it had come in an illegal assembly. That it was an illegal assembly we cannot stay here and now to argue; but as a matter of fact, everything in the trials of Jesus, both in the priestly court of Caiaphas and presently in the civil court of Pilate, was distinctly illegal. Every principle of law was violated. I may say in passing that those who care to go fully into the matter may profitably consider a booklet published by George Newnes and Co., by Lord Craigmyle, on the matter. Caiaphas had waived the technicalities of the law which provided that no man might be put on trial on the day of his arrest, and at last had Jesus arraigned before him.

As the trial proceeded, witnesses were called, but they were false witnesses, and not one of them was able to contribute anything that could help Caiaphas to formulate a charge against Jesus which would ensure His death. One alleged that He had said:

" I am able to destroy the Temple of God, and to build it in three days."

The falsity of the declaration is at once proved by reference to what He had really said. He had declared that they would destroy, and that He would raise it again. Nevertheless when these false witnesses were heard, our Lord made no reply. He had no answer to give to lying lips.

Then driven to desperation, Caiaphas put Jesus on oath. It is of the utmost importance that we notice this carefully. The words which Caiaphas used were of the nature of a legal formula:

" I adjure Thee by the living God, that Thou tell us whether Thou be the Christ, the Son of God."

Thus we see them face to face, Caiaphas the representative of the priesthood of the Hebrew people, appointed by Rome, the titular head of the priesthood, and the Son of God, ostensibly arraigned before him. Caiaphas adopted the legal phraseology of the Hebrew people, introducing the supreme fact of the Hebrew faith, in the term "the living God." What he asked was that on oath Christ should declare whether or no He was the Messiah, the Son of God. Thus Jesus is seen standing before this representative of the Hebrew people, this degenerate, steeped in selfishness, now rich by the robbery of the poor, and He hears this man take upon his lips the name of the living God, as he adopted the formula of the oath.

Then occurred that which must for evermore be an amazing and never to be forgotten thing. Right there, at the end of the ministry, close to the end of His life, Jesus replied, and He did so by accepting the form of the oath. His answer was a formula, as was Caiaphas' adjuration. He replied, " Thou hast said." The form to us is somewhat different to our own manner of speech, but it was exactly the language of one who claimed to answer the enquiry by an affirmation. Said Caiaphas, in effect, I put you on oath, are you the Christ? Are you the Son of God? And Jesus replied at once, accepting the terms of the oath, and claiming that He was the Messiah, and the Son of God, as His followers had already confessed.

But He said more:

" Nevertheless, I say unto you, Henceforth ye shall see the Son of man sitting at the right hand of power, and coming on the clouds of heaven."

The word " Nevertheless " is arresting. Expositors seem to have found some difficulty in explaining the meaning. I suggest that He had seen something in the face of Caiaphas, something of incredulity manifesting itself. They did not believe Him, notwithstanding the fact that He had made His affirmation on oath. If that were so, we have a natural explanation of the " Nevertheless." Nevertheless, in spite of your incredulity, you shall see the Son of man coming in His glory. Thus before that court He reaffirmed the declaration He had made at Cæsarea Philippi to His disciples when He had declared to them that Peter had made the confession that He was the Messiah, " the Son of the living God," that He was going to the Cross, but that He would come in His glory, and the glory of the Father, and of the angels.

It is at least possible that Caiaphas knew of that confession of Peter, and the answering affirmations of Jesus had become the common conviction of the disciples. It is possible that he knew that they believed Him to be the Christ, the Son of the living God. Therefore, on this occasion, he put Him on oath on that matter; and our Lord had replied, and had declared there, as He did at Cæsarea Philippi, that henceforth, that is, at some future time, the Son of man would come in His glory. Then Caiaphas had done all that he could in his own court, and in the morning he sent Him to Pilate, and so passes out of the picture.

This is indeed a terrible picture. It is that of two men prostituting a Divine office for personal enrichment, and to the enslavement of their fellows. We remember how constantly in the course of His teaching our Lord had denounced such action, how He had pronounced unutterable woes upon them for doing these very things, binding heavy burdens upon men's shoulders that they themselves were not lifting with their little fingers, that for a pretence they were making long prayers while they devoured widows' houses. In Annas and Caiaphas we see these men finally prostituting a Divine office; and our Lord's action in connection therewith. He asserted on oath the truth concerning His mission and His nature, declaring there in the hour when everything seemed closing around Him, the certainty of His ultimate victory.

Thus the story of these two men ends, and we stand face to face with the awe-inspiring fact that it is possible for the human soul to come into such condition that it remains unmoved in the presence of the most stupendous spiritual truth. We learn also that to such attitudes of life issuing, and persisted in, the Christ has nothing to say.

XXXVI

PILATE

PILATE finds his place in the historic records of the New Testament, and by threefold reference in the Acts of the Apostles. We see him most clearly in the Gospel of John. He owes his fame, such as it is, to contact with Christ. Had it not been for this contact, we should probably have known nothing of him. He is placed in contemporary history, and we learn some little concerning him from this source. He is named as procurator of Judæa. We know that he occupied that position for about ten years, during the whole of the ministry of John the Baptist, of the ministry of our Lord, and at the beginnings of the Christian movement. He was the representative of the Roman government. As procurator, he held civil and military authority, which means, of course, that as representing Rome, the power of life and death was vested in him. When Pilate spoke in that area, Cæsar spoke through him.

We now turn to the New Testament revelation of him found in the references already referred to. As we do so we discover that the revelation exactly coincides with the statements concerning him made in history outside the New Testament. He was a man known everywhere as of haughty disposition, fully realising his authority, and glorying in it. His whole bearing towards Judæa and the Jews was that of scorn, and indeed, that of hatred. In his exercise of authority he was cold and dispassionate, and quite unperturbed by scenes of blood or riot. We have one glimpse of him incidentally in the New Testament in that regard. Some came and told Jesus of certain Galileans whose blood Pilate had mingled with their sacrifices. That statement can, of course, quite easily be filled in. The Galileans were hot-headed. They constituted the greatest political trouble to the authority of Rome in that area. Evidently somewhere, in their religious practices, they had been offering sacrifice after some political outburst. While they were so occupied Pilate sent down a punitive expedition, and slew them. The man is revealed in that story.

He was, moreover, a contemptuous man. That is proven by his attitude towards the Jewish priests. The first thing that he asked them when they brought Jesus to him was evidently a question marking his contempt for them.

" What accusation bring ye against this man? "

The question in itself may not suggest his contempt, but it is revealed in the answer which the priests made to him:

" If this Man were not an evil-doer, we should not have delivered Him up unto thee."

The answer reveals the very tone in which Pilate had asked his question. The final evidence of the same attitude is discovered when with his own hand, he wrote the accusation to be placed over the head of the crucified Jesus:

"JESUS OF NAZARETH, THE KING OF THE JEWS."

It is impossible to read this without seeing his contempt for the Jews, and especially for the priests.

When we examine the story carefully we find that Pilate was actuated by a sense of justice. We are perfectly familiar with the fact that in that regard he utterly broke down. The whole story, however, reveals that his attempt was to be just. He had a passion for justice, a Roman passion, a passion for the observance of Roman law. He did everything he could, except the one final thing, to save Jesus. I have sometimes, perhaps a little daringly, said what I still believe to be true, that Pilate would have much preferred to crucify Caiaphas than to crucify Christ.

Yet once more it is impossible to read the story, and arrive at the moment when, after the brutal and bloody scourging which Pilate had been compelled to watch, for it was the law that he should do so, and not to believe that when he led Jesus forth and showed Him to the people, exclaiming, " Behold, the Man," that he himself was moved with a sense of pity, and desired if possible to inspire that feeling in the crowd.

Yet again, he was a man of enquiring mind; a man attempting to investigate things. The question which we so clearly remember that he asked Jesus, " What is truth? " supremely reveals this. To that we shall return presently. But we hear him asking questions throughout. " Art Thou the King of the Jews? " " Art Thou a King then? " " Whence art Thou? "

All these things being observed it yet stands out clearly that the one over-mastering characteristic of Pilate was that of a self-centred diplomatist, an astute politician. A man, naturally cold, haughty, oppressive, contemptuous, having a sense of justice, a capacity for pity, and a spirit of enquiry; but all these subservient to the one fact that he was a diplomat, a politician.

Here it may be enquired as to whether diplomacy is in itself, wrong, and whether politicians are to be looked upon with contempt or suspicion. Let it at once be said there is nothing wrong in diplomacy, and nothing wrong in being a politician, unless the diplomat or the politician is self-centred, and all the forces of personality are employed in the interest of self.

Now let us turn to see him in contact with Christ. The first appearance of Jesus before him, possibly the first time he had ever seen Jesus, was in the early morning. The procurator thus disturbed, met the situation with the enquiry of the priests to which we have already referred:

"What accusation bring ye against this Man?"

With the authority of Rome vested in him, he was compelled by Roman law to appear when a prisoner was brought to him. His first glance was not so much for Jesus, though he saw Him, as for these troublesome Jews. Hence his question. When they, evidently recognising his annoyance, replied:

"If this Man were not an evil-doer, we should not have delivered Him up unto thee,"

he yet further manifested his annoyance and contempt, as he said:

"Take Him yourselves, and judge Him according to your law."

It was then that Pilate heard these priests say something which revealed the situation in a clearer light. They said:

"It is not lawful for us to put any man to death."

In a moment Pilate saw that with them it was not a question of seeking for justice, but an attempt to encompass a death. They had made their minds up that He must die. I think it was at that point that he began seriously to look at Jesus, and I believe he was startled and arrested. Often enough they had brought someone to him for a decision in the civil courts that would have no validity in the priestly courts.

That he was arrested and even startled is proven by the fact of the private interview between him and Jesus that immediately followed. Pilate took Jesus into the Prætorium or palace, and we have a graphic description of what there took place in general. When they were thus alone Pilate said to Him, "Art Thou the King of the Jews?" and Jesus replied to him with that very searching question:

"Sayest thou this of thyself, or did others tell it thee concerning Me?"

Now if we read that with real care we at once recognise that it was a curious question. Let us remember that up to this point they had not yet told him what was the accusation they were bringing against Jesus. It is quite evident, however, from Pilate's question that he had heard something. The question of Jesus was as to whether he was asking this question as the result of some private information that he had received, or was he indeed asking the question out of his own personal wonder. The subject is full of interest, and may have many applications which it is not now our business to make. We may say, however, that it is a question that Christ ever asks in the presence of enquiring unbelief. He has no answer to a second-hand agnosticism.

It is quite evident that the question somewhat annoyed Pilate as he said in reply:

" Am I a Jew? Thine own nation and the chief priests delivered Thee unto me; what hast Thou done? "

Thus dismissing the subject he asked Jesus Himself to state the reason why He was arraigned before him. " What hast Thou done? "

To this our Lord replied:

" My Kingdom is not of this world; if My Kingdom were of this world, then would My servants fight, that I should not be delivered to the Jews; but now is My Kingdom not from hence."

Again Pilate found himself confronted by a remarkable statement, involving a claim to Kingship on the part of Jesus. This drew from Pilate the question, " Art Thou a King then? " At first he had asked Him, " Art Thou the King of the Jews? " Now recognising a claim to Kingship in some form, came the simpler question, " Art Thou a King then? "

" Jesus answered, Thou sayest that I am a King. To this end have I been born, and to this end am I come into the world, that I should bear witness unto the truth. Everyone that is of the truth heareth My voice."

Thus in reply to Pilate's question our Lord claimed Kingship in the realm of truth, and affirmed that His purpose in the world was that of witness to truth.

When Pilate heard this, he exclaimed, " What is truth? " Bacon in his essay on Truth commences what is certainly a great writing, with the words:

" ' What is truth? ' said the jesting Pilate, and did not wait for an answer."

Admitting the greatness of Bacon's essay, I join issue entirely with the suggestion of that opening sentence. Pilate never felt less like jesting than when he asked that question. It was a cry wrung out of the centre of his personality. He was conscious that he was living in a world largely under the domination of that which was untrue. Perchance there was a touch of mockery in this question, but it was a wail rather than a jest.

It was at this point that he sent Jesus to Herod. He desired to be rid of Him. He was seeking to shirk all responsibility. That first interview had shaken him to the foundations of his life. He would fain wipe his hands of the whole business, and therefore sent Him to Herod. Herod could do nothing, and sent Him back to Pilate. I think it was at this point that he received a message from his wife:

"Have thou nothing to do with that righteous Man; for I have suffered many things this day in a dream because of Him."

We are not told of any effect produced upon Pilate by this message, but we do see him in difficulty and in turmoil, created by the strangeness of the Prisoner arraigned before him.

Now Pilate proposed to chastise Him and let Him go. It was an irregular and illegal proposition. Nevertheless he carried it out so far as the scourging was concerned. He had given the people a choice between Jesus and Barabbas. In doing that he had been attempting to find a way to release Jesus. He was offering them a choice between a man who had been the scourge of the countryside and One Who had been going about everywhere doing good. When instructed by the priests, the crowd clamoured for Barabbas, Pilate said:

"What, then, shall I do unto Jesus which is called Christ?"

and the answer came:

"Let Him be crucified."

That is the point at which the ultimate crisis arose for Pilate. He had found and publicly uttered his verdict, for the words, "I find no crime in Him," constituted a legal verdict.

The priests later said to him:

"If thou release this Man, thou art not Cæsar's friend."

That unquestionably was in his mind in this hour of crisis. He realised that these priests might report him to Rome, and charge him with setting at liberty One claiming to be a King. Eventually, the priests definitely said, "We have no king but Cæsar," thus revealing their determination to secure the death of Jesus, even though they made an acknowledgment of loyalty to Cæsar, which they by no means felt.

As things proceeded, Pilate called for water and dipping his hands in the water, said:

"I am innocent of the blood of this righteous Man; see ye to it."

There was yet another private interview between Pilate and Jesus. In that interview, strangely perplexed unquestionably, Pilate asked Him, "Whence art Thou?" To that enquiry our

Lord vouchsafed no reply. When Pilate, astonished at His silence, said to him:

> "Speakest Thou not unto me? knowest Thou not that I have power to release Thee, and have power to crucify Thee? "

To this our Lord replied with a dignity that is almost appalling:

> "Thou wouldest have no power against Me, except it were given thee from above; therefore, he that delivereth Me unto thee hath greater sin."

At last, in answer to the machinations of the priests and the clamour of the crowd, he violated justice as he delivered Jesus to be crucified.

Thus we see Pilate arrested by the purity of Jesus, by the patience of Jesus, by the power of Jesus, in strange perplexity, not knowing which way to turn. I watch the processes of his mind. First, his contempt for the priests and for any prisoner they brought before him; then a sudden arrest in the Prisoner Whom he had to face; then a growing fear as to who it was Who was thus arraigned before him. Finally we see him driven to choose between obedience to conscience and a sense of right, and expedience in the interest of policy. He made the fatal choice. He then attempted to relieve the anger of his mind as he wrote the superscription:

> "THIS IS JESUS, THE KING OF THE JEWS."

Two other, who were malefactors, were crucified with Him. When presently those in charge of the crucifixion came to Pilate to ask permission, according to Roman law, to break the legs of the crucified, he granted them their request. When, however, they came to the three crosses, they found Jesus was dead already.

Presently there came to Pilate those who begged the body of Jesus, and he granted them their request. After that the rulers came and asked for a guard to be set over the tomb, for they declared that they desired to make it certain that no one should steal the body, and so assert that Jesus was risen. We can hear the infinite scorn and anger of Pilate as he said to them:

> "Ye have a guard; go your way, make it as sure as ye can."

There would seem to have been lurking in his own mind a suspicion that there was about this Prisoner something supernatural, and that it would prove itself stronger than all their hostility.

As we survey this whole story of the contact of Pilate with Jesus we see that in its process the bad in Pilate was weakened and the good strengthened for a time. He was a man of swift brutality, but he did not manifest it towards Jesus. He was a man of haughty indifference, but he was not indifferent in the presence of Jesus. He was a man exercising an arrogant authority, but there is no arrogance manifested in his dealing with Jesus. His sense of justice was roused, and became active. His pity for pain overwhelmed him, and made him present Jesus to the clamouring crowd, bruised and wounded, in the hope that the vision might appeal to their pity. His desire for right drove him to the employment of sundry expedients, some questionable, and yet all pointing to his desire to set Jesus free. Thus our Lord, to use a modern literary illustration, in the case of Pilate put Dr. Jekyll and Mr. Hyde face to face, and made them look at each other.

When Matthew records the story he says, " Jesus stood before the governor." It is a perfectly accurate legal announcement. Actually, spiritually, morally, finally, we may say that the governor stood before Jesus. In the last analysis not Jesus but Pilate, was on trial. Through all the processes of that eventful day a choice was being forced upon him. Through all the tempest of those stormy hours there was one clear issue before him, and he himself expressed it when he said:

" What then shall I do unto Jesus? "

Not to dwell upon it at length here and now we may nevertheless declare that in that day the whole Roman Empire stood arraigned before Jesus. Religion was arraigned there also in the person of the priests, and democracy had come to judgment in the crowds. It is true that He was led as a lamb to the slaughter, and as a sheep before its shearers is dumb, so He opened not His mouth; but He was the Arbiter, the Judge, and compelled the making of a definite choice.

As to the ultimate history of Pilate everything is shrouded in mystery. It has been declared that he committed suicide. On the other hand there is a legend that presently in Rome, after he had been deposed from power, he found himself in the Catacombs where Christians were gathering together, and yielded himself to the Lord. It is a legend only. One thing we know, and that is that if it be true, he was received and pardoned by Christ.

I think one of the most terrible stories I know in literature is that of Anatole France in his " Mother of Pearl," where he attempts a picture of Pilate at the end, which is purely imaginary, and yet profoundly philosophic. He depicts him living in lust and luxury in a villa on the shores of Italy. Many years had passed when one day a visitor from Rome, conversing with him said to him, " By the way, Pilate, were you not procurator in Judæa when they put to death that Man Jesus? " Anatole France makes Pilate look at this visitor through bleary eyes and say, " Jesus, Jesus, I don't remember the name ! "

I am not saying that this is history, but it is a terrible revelation of what may happen to a man who violates his conscience. The whole thing may seem to leave no mark behind, and he may even forget the hour when it took place.

Certain it is that contact with Christ always creates an issue. We have never been able to analyse and finally classify Christ, but He always analyses and classifies us.

Thus we learn from the story that the battle between expedience and obedience is the utterest folly. To lose the central principle of loyalty to conscience is sooner or later to find the whole super-structure of life lying in ruins.

From the story we also learn that responsibility cannot be transferred. Pilate attempted to transfer it to the priests and then to Herod; but the personal element in his question, "What shall *I* do with Jesus?" was supreme.

> "Though some of you, with Pilate, wash your hands,
> Showing an outward pity, yet you Pilates
> Have here delivered me to my sour cross,
> And water cannot wash away your sin."

Shakespeare understood.

So also did Russell Lowell when in a couplet which may lack elegance, but has the element of eternal truth, he wrote:

> "An' you've gut to git up airly
> Ef you want to take in God."

No man will ever be up early enough for that.

XXXVII

HEROD

IT is impossible to approach the story of Herod, and to have to consider our Lord's dealings with him without a sense of dread, and almost appalling solemnity. One is almost tempted to wish that the story could be omitted, but to do so in such a series would be singularly to fail, for it emphasises certain truths of the most solemn nature. Throughout the series we have been constantly in the presence of the amazing love and patience of Jesus; but it is impossible to forget that there is such a thing as the wrath of the Lamb, and it is an illustration of that to which we come in this study.

The story is startling in that it has no parallel in the records of the life and ministry of our Lord. We may say at once that the story of the dealing of Jesus with Herod can be told in three brief sentences; He avoided him; He sent him a message of stinging satire; and He refused to speak to him. When we compare the facts revealed in these statements with all the stories we have been considering, the difference is arresting. How far He travelled to reach men, rather than sought to avoid them. How tender were the words He spoke to them constantly, rather than words of rebuke and satire. How ready He was to talk to men, to answer their questions, even when they were hostile to Him, rather than refusing to speak at all.

Now it will be admitted at once that such an unusual attitude on the part of our Lord demands careful consideration and explanation. As we seek that explanation, we inevitably do so, remembering the usual habit of the Master, and this makes this story all the more arresting and solemn, and shows that it must yield some message of vital importance. We come to it in that spirit. We shall seek the explanation by endeavouring to see Herod as he is revealed to us on the pages of the New Testament, and from such contemplation we shall endeavour to deduce the warning which the story conveys.

When we turn to consider Herod we find how seldom he appears. Indeed, there are but three references to him in detail, one in Matthew (xiv, 1, 2, 13) and two in Luke (xiii, 31, 32; xxiii, 8, 9). To these we will return.

We may, however, go outside the revelation of him in the New Testament, for he is placed in other history quite definitely, and, indeed, much has been recorded concerning him. The outstanding facts are that he was the son of Herod commonly called the Great, and of Malthake, who was a Samaritan woman. That is to say, he was not a Jew, but half Edomite and half Samaritan. He came to be known as the King of the Jews. That was a title that he personally coveted, and which was granted to him by Rome.

His contemporaries have described him by words which I will quote directly from them. They said he was:

" Cruel, scheming, vacillating, utterly evil."

It is well that we bear in mind these words are not those of the New Testament writers concerning him. They came from his pagan contemporaries who knew him well. This fact makes even more arresting the description of him as " utterly evil."

We know, too, that he was sensual in the most daring and flagrant way. At the time when he crossed the pathway of Jesus indirectly, he was living in incestuous adultery.

Then we know also from our records that he murdered the greatest of the prophets in response to the request of a dancing wanton, when he was drunk. It is by no means an attractive picture of a man. The picture is dark, it is sinister, it is repulsive; but all this does not account for the attitude of Jesus towards him. Not a thing we have said about him would have prevented Jesus loving him, delivering him, saving him. As a matter of fact, all these things were the incidental revelations of something else, which created the attitude of our Lord towards him.

We turn, then, to look very carefully at Herod as he is revealed in his attitude toward John the Baptist. The story of the murder of John is told parenthetically both by Matthew and Mark. In each account the writer had been declaring the attitude of Herod when he heard about Jesus, that he was alarmed, and said:

" This is John the Baptist; he is risen from the dead."

Then to account for that saying of Herod they told the story of the murder. They went back in the history to the point when this happened. In that connection Mark gives us some details which Matthew omits, which are very revealing. He tells us that Herod had been evidently deeply impressed by John. These were the days when all Judea was going out to the ministry of John, and there can be no doubt that Herod was one among the number who went to hear him. This does not necessarily mean, of course, that Herod travelled with the crowds; but he sought him, and went to hear him. This contact with John convinced Herod that the prophet was righteous, and was holy. Moreover it aroused serious questionings within him, for we are told he was strangely perplexed, and Mark says, " he heard him gladly," which is a most significant statement.

As, then, we look at Herod at that time we see a man arrested by the voice of John the prophet, having heard of it from others, and learned what a tremendous influence it had exerted through all the countryside, himself seeking John, and passing in a remarkable way under the influence of his preaching. To repeat, he was convinced that John was right, was convinced that John was holy, was perplexed, that is, disturbed in his mind, and was evidently ploughed to the very depths by the preaching of John, and yet further, was attracted thereby, for " he heard him gladly."

In this connection it is more than interesting to notice that the words used to describe the way in which Herod heard John, namely " gladly," is found again in the Gospel according to Mark, in its twelfth chapter and thirty-seventh verse, when the writer declares that " the common people heard Him gladly." Thus the very effect produced upon the crowds that were thronging upon Jesus is here declared to have been produced upon Herod himself.

Thus we see the man of whom his contemporaries said, he was " cruel, scheming, vacillating, utterly evil," listening to the voice of the prophet, attending to it, being convinced that he was right and that he was holy, being stirred to the depths in his own personality, and attracted moreover, for he heard him gladly. There had come to him moral illumination, and moral arrest, leading to moral reconsideration, and he had almost consented to the issues. "He heard him gladly."

At the same period while thus impressed, his vacillating nature is revealed in the fact that fighting against the conviction that had come to him, he had committed open and flagrant sin by taking his brother's wife, and making her so far as he could his wife by marrying her. Quite evidently he was still seeking opportunities of listening to John, for John, learning this fact, sternly rebuked him. The prophet who had impressed him, whom he had heard gladly, whom he knew to be holy and righteous, in the presence of his sin denounced it, declared to him its unlawfulness. In all this story, between the lines it is quite evident that a strange intimacy had sprung up between the prophet and Herod. John had access to the king, and so definitely denounced the sinfulness of his action.

But he continued in his sin. He stifled the voice that had sounded so clearly within his own soul. He refused to conform to those moral principles that had been so definitely enunciated to him by the prophet. We see him here still having respect for John, but persistently continuing in his sin.

This is revealed in the fact that when, because he had been sternly rebuked, and his marriage with Herodias declared illegal, the hatred of Herodias was stirred against John, and she was determined to bring about his death. It is here that the action of Herod is significant and revealing. He imprisoned John, not with any intention of sacrificing him to Herodias' hatred, but rather to keep him safe from the wrath of this infuriated woman.

Having done this, Herod yielded himself to his passion, answered the calls of the animal side of his nature. In doing so he negatived the pure voice that had been speaking clearly to him. This respect for John caused him to put him in prison for safe keeping; but he persisted in his course of evil. So righteous impressions were sacrificed to the clamant cry of animalism.

Then came the occasion of the final catastrophe in a night of carousal. We are not told in the records in so many words that he was drunk, but only a man whose senses for the moment were corrupted by drink could have done the things he did that night. The daughter of Herodias danced before him, and this passion-mastered man, his passion inflamed by drink, told her that he would give her anything that she demanded. He repeated the offer with emphasis, in the words:

"Whatsoever thou shalt ask of me, I will give it thee, unto the half of my kingdom."

Thus the voice that had warned him was silenced for the moment, and he uttered this rash word. If it should be said that a man is not responsible for what he says under such influences, it should at once be answered he is responsible for being in such circumstances and consequently, is responsible for whatever takes place.

Thus the voice of conscience was silenced, and he made the unutterably foolish and wicked offer. When after consultation with her mother, the dancing maiden said:

"Give me in a charger the head of John the Baptist," it is evident his conscience awoke, and "he was exceeding sorry." Nevertheless, even then, he persisted in the course of evil, and for his oath's sake was guilty of the murder of John.

In this connection we may suitably remind ourselves of words written by Paul in his letter to the Romans.

"Know ye not that to whom ye present yourselves as servants unto obedience, his servants ye are whom ye obey; whether of sin unto death, or of obedience unto righteousness."

Herod had yielded himself a servant to sin, to lust, to animalism. He had allowed the transient, triviality of a sensual excitement to silence the voice of God in his soul. A careful consideration of the whole story will help us to understand the attitude of Jesus.

In considering this we notice that Herod had heard about Jesus. The context reveals that Jesus had sent out His twelve apostles, and as they had gone about upon their mission, marvellous things had transpired. The work of Jesus was multiplied by these men, and Herod heard the account of it, and knew that everything resulted from the teaching and the work of Jesus Himself. He heard of the wonders, and was filled with perplexity and with terror, and he desired to see Jesus.

This desire was based upon that perplexity and that terror. Here we must remind ourselves that Herod was a Sadducee. He belonged to the party which, among other things, did not believe in resurrection. But in the presence of this crisis, and when conscience was speaking, he declared, "John the Baptist is risen from the dead." He was terrified. He had brought about the death of John, and as we hear this cry we find far more in it than a superstitious fear of a ghost. It revealed the fact that he had memories of what John had meant to him, and of how he had hardened his conscience against him. His terror was that of an arrant coward, and out of it there was created a desire to see Jesus.

When Jesus heard it He went into Galilee. Jesus did not see him. He avoided him. It is to be noted that when He did so, He departed into the tetrarchy over which Herod ruled. It is evident that Herod's fear was of a personal nature, and had no element in it of repentance. As a matter of fact he continued in coming days in courses of evil more flagrant than those of the past. Jesus knew all these facts concerning him, and, therefore, did not grant his desire to see him, but departed into Galilee.

Later on there came a day when the Pharisees came to Jesus for some reason, and said, " Herod would fain kill Thee." There can be no question that the report they thus brought was a true one, or He would not have acted as He then did. Their advice really was that He should escape from Herod. There can be no doubt whatever that Herod, frightened by the memories of the past was determined to do with Jesus what he had caused to be done with John.

It is in this connection that we read the sentences which are appalling, and yet the rightness of what Jesus said, and the justice of it no one can for a single moment call in question. The authority and dignity of His action are amazing. He sent Herod a message, and this fact makes it evident that He knew that what the Pharisees had reported was true. Seeing that He thus knew, He commenced His reply by saying, " Go and say to that fox." This is the one occasion upon which a biting, contemptuous word passed the lips of Jesus about a human being. Indeed, it is more contemptuous than it appeared, for He used the feminine word, and we may render accurately, " Go and say to that vixen." The message that He sent was:

" Behold, I cast out demons and perform cures to-day and to-morrow, and the third day I am perfected."

The message was a declaration that all Herod's attempts at hostility would be futile. The Lord was marching along the pathway of purpose, and moreover, that must continue until His appointed work was completed. Then, on the third day, which by all seeming would be the day of His defeat, He would reach the day of His perfecting. Thus He forecast His pathway to the end, and spoke of it in the terms of absolute confidence and victory. That was the message which He sent to Herod.

At last there came a day when they actually met. It was a day when Pilate sent Jesus to Herod, and it is an appalling story. We read Herod was glad when he saw Him, but the word " glad " used to describe his state of mind is not the word that was used in the past when it is declared that he had heard John gladly. It simply means that he became cheerful. The sight of Jesus cheered him. We stand appalled, and wonder what such effect meant. We are not left to speculation, for we are told:

" He hoped to see some miracle done by Him."

This man, utterly corrupt, hoped for some new thrill as he watched Jesus work some wonder. He saw no wonder wrought. Then it is recorded that he asked Jesus many questions, and that Christ gave him no answer. He had nothing to say to him.

What a revelation all this is of the inevitable hopelessness of the case of Herod. Who was this Who stood silent before him? It was the Law-giver. Who was this Who was silent? It was the King. Who was this Who was silent? It was the Saviour. There was no question among those which Herod asked that day, any sincere enquiry concerning the law. There was no question among those put to Jesus by him that had anything of sincerity in it with regard to authority. Certainly there was no question which was the equivalent of, What must I do to be saved? Had there been he would have been answered. In the appalling silence of Jesus we have a revelation of Divine retribution, necessary but not capricious. Our Lord could do none other with this man. Herod had silenced John's voice not only literally and physically, but within his own soul. He never heard the voice of Jesus.

It is impossible to read this story without recalling the words which our Lord uttered upon another occasion, but certainly had their application and illustration here:

" Give not that which is holy unto the dogs, neither cast your pearls before the swine."

Herod had returned to his vomit, and his wallowing in the mire, and Christ had nothing to say to him.

The whole story startles and appals. We are so familiar with the readiness, and even eagerness of Christ to answer the call of the sinner. Herod never called. He became curious and desired to see Jesus. When he could not do that, he tried to kill Him. When at last he did see Him, he was cheered, because he expected a thrill, a sensation; but the moral sense was dead. There are conditions to which Christ has no message, remorse without repentance, blasphemous curiosity in the presence of His power. Then His silence is his sentence. It is just, it is inevitable, it is irrevocable. Light disobeyed wilfully, becomes darkness.

In the presence of that solemn consideration we conclude by quoting from the Roman letter, a continuation of the quotation already given.

> " Thanks be to God, that, whereas ye were servants of sin, ye became obedient from the heart to that form of teaching whereunto ye were delivered; and being made free from sin, ye became servants of righteousness."

That quotation reveals the alternative, and shows how it is possible to be delivered from the power of sin, and become servants of righteousness.

XXXVIII

THE DYING THIEF

THE story of the dying thief shines with a wonderful radiance amid the most appalling gloom. During the ministry of our Lord, as we have seen, many had committed themselves unto Him, some unworthily, as John points out, when he said that many trusted to Him, but He did not trust Himself to them. Many had committed themselves with full purpose of heart, and He had responded to them by committing Himself to them completely.

The story of the dying malefactor is the last we have of any committing himself to Christ prior to His death. It gives the account of one who committed himself to Christ completely, and of one, therefore, to whom Christ immediately committed Himself in all fulness.

It was indeed a lonely hour in the history of our Lord. There are senses in which His had been a lonely pilgrimage throughout, while in other senses He had never been alone, as He Himself said:

"I am not alone, because the Father is with Me."

On the level of human friendship and companionship, however, He had been strangely lonely. Even those who had committed themselves to Him sincerely, those nearest to Him, that little band of chosen men, never really came close to Him in the days of His flesh. They were unable either to understand or to follow. In this hour Jew and Gentile had united against Him. His disciples had all forsaken Him, and fled. Round about that lifted Cross priests, elders, scribes, and impaled thieves were mocking Him. Matthew and Mark distinctly tell us that at first both these malefactors railed on Jesus.

So as we reverently watch in this hour of strange and awful loneliness, something happened in a most remarkable way. A man on one of the crosses first spoke for Him, defending Him, and then spoke to Him, committing himself to Him. He on the Cross, in the midst of all the ribaldry of the surroundings, answered that man in language full of august majesty and authority. It was a remarkable breaking in upon the loneliness, a happening of radiant beauty.

As we look at this dying malefactor we have to say that we know practically nothing about him, except what is revealed in the story. Legendary lore has been busy with him, but we know nothing of his parentage. Two things which resolve themselves into one, are revealed. Matthew and Mark describe him as *leistes*, that is, a robber, or in other words, a brigand, or bandit, or outlaw. Luke uses another word, which nevertheless exactly covers the same ground. He speaks of two *kakourgoi*. The *kakourgos* was a criminal, a man of the criminal order. How long this man had been so living we cannot tell. It may be that he had passed into this class as the result of training, or lack of training. It may be that some mother's heart had been broken over him. All that we do not know, but we are face to face with him in the hour when he is seen, one of the marauders prevalent at the time in the district. This is the man we see hanging by the side of Jesus. He was a man who ignored God. I am not prepared to say he denied God. Indeed, presently we see he referred to Him; but in the practices of his life he had put God out of his mind. He had dared the laws and had broken them. He had no regard for his fellow-men. The central principle of his life was that he was self-centred.

We recognise at once that it is a terrible condition. When a man sinks so low as to ignore God, and exploit his fellow men in order to enrich himself, he is certainly in a terrible situation. In passing I may say I am inclined to think there is a yet more terrible condition. There are men who are self-centred just as much as the bandit is, but who use God and man in their own interests. They do not ignore God. They may even go to Church. They do not rob men by open violence, but they rob them in sweated labour. I sometimes wonder which is the most despicable. I think I would rather be the bandit.

But to return. We have seen all sorts and conditions of men as we have followed the story of our Lord's contact with them. Here we are in the presence of a man who, from the human standpoint is in the most hopeless condition in that he has not only broken law, but the law has now broken him.

The marvel of the story is that of its revelation of Christ's contact with this man. So far as we know, his only contact with Jesus was made in this hour. It is impossible to say that he had never seen Jesus, or that he had never heard Him; but we have no evidence that he had done either. He had been caught, condemned, crucified. So had Jesus. That, of course, is to speak in the terms of the time and occasion on the human level.

As we read the story of the crucifixion it is quite evident that Jesus was the first one they nailed to His Cross. What, then, we enquire, had this man probably seen or heard before he spoke? Undoubtedly he had watched the crucifixion, perhaps his own heart filled with terror as he looked forward to his own experience. Watching, he had seen the One Who was being crucified, pass through the excruciating agony without any complaint, without any word of angry protest; led as a lamb to the slaughter, and as a sheep before her shearers is dumb, He opened not His mouth.

Then he had heard Him speak once, saying that amazing thing,

" Father, forgive them, for they know not what they do."

I cannot read this story without feeling that both these facts had their bearing on this man's attitude toward Jesus. Not immediately, because as we have seen, in the earlier part of the tragic and dreadful hours, he, in company with the other of the malefactors, railed upon Jesus. He had seen Him then, in awful silence, suffer without a complaint, and had heard that cry escape Him, uttered to the God of the universe by the name Father, asking Him to forgive the men who were causing His suffering.

We now remember that after our Lord was crucified these malefactors suffered the same fate; and in the midst of the terror and agony they joined with the ribaldry of priests and soldiers, and mocked Him.

Then something happened in the soul of this man, and in his next speech we find evidence of a most remarkable upheaval and revolution, and contradiction of all he had been, and all that had brought him through the processes of law to the cross. Suddenly he ceased his railing, and addressed himself to the man on the other side of Jesus, saying:

" Dost thou not even fear God, seeing thou art in the same condemnation? And we indeed justly; for we receive the due reward of our deeds, but this Man hath done nothing amiss."

299

These words were spoken not to Jesus, but about Him, and they reveal the fact that suddenly his whole attitude toward life was changed. He had ignored God. He now remembered Him, " Dost thou not even fear God? " He had wronged his fellow-men, pitilessly, heartlessly, and he now said, We are suffering as we ought, for this is the just reward of our deeds. The final note of revolution is his confession there and then of the sinlessness of Jesus as he said, " This Man hath done nothing amiss."

It is a perfect example of repentance. Repentance is infinitely more than sorrow for sin. A man may be sorry for his sin, and yet never repent. The Roman theologians insisted that the chief element in repentance was sorrow, while the Protestant theologians claimed that its chief element is that of a changed mind. There is no doubt that this latter is the true meaning of the word. And this is exactly what did happen in the case of this man. He had changed his mind concerning his attitude towards God, and concerning his attitude to his fellow men.

Perhaps at this point we may pause to say that the question may be asked as to why the other malefactor did not repent. The answer is that here we are face to face with the mystery of the human soul. Both had the same truth before them. Both had the same Christ in the midst. Both had seen Him submitting to His Cross. Both had heard His prayer. One repented, and the other did not; and so it has ever been, and still is.

He then spoke to Christ directly:

" Jesus, remember me when Thou comest in Thy Kingdom."

Familiar as we are with this story, it abides as a most arresting utterance. The very words prove a recognition on the part of the man, that the One hanging by his side, crucified as he was, numbered with transgressors, was nevertheless a King. He realised that the inscription written over Him meant more than it seemed to do. His cry, moreover, revealed a conviction that in spite of the fact that He was impaled upon the Cross, He was coming into His Kingdom.

I claim that in all this I am not drawing on my imagination. To take that sentence in all simplicity is at once to recognise that this dying malefactor saw the One by his side as a King. There had come to him the profound and absolute conviction that in spite of His apparent defeat as He was impaled upon a Roman gibbet, He was inevitably passing to a Kingdom. Suddenly, this dying malefactor is seen as having a grasp of spiritual verities, seeing through the blood of the Cross to the gleaming glory of the crown. That unquestionably is the meaning of his cry:

"Jesus, remember me when Thou comest in Thy Kingdom."

It follows necessarily that it was far more than a recognition of Kingship. It was submission thereto. Said he, "Remember me," bear me in mind, think of me. He was not asking for pardon, though that undoubtedly was included in his thinking. He was not seeking for reward. He knew that he was going to die. He knew also that Jesus would die. Following upon the revolution which was repentance, there came the sense of eternity. He saw things lying out beyond the present, "when Thou comest in Thy Kingdom." It was a singularly remarkably correct apprehension of the nature of His rule. Confessedly he was justly condemned. He now made his appeal to the One Whom he had heard pray for His murderers. He had come to a conviction that there was a realm beyond that in which he was suffering the just rewards of his deeds, and that there was another tribunal other than the one that had condemned him. He had heard Jesus appeal to a Throne higher than Cæsar's and now he made an appeal to Him. What he said may be described as the gasp of a dying man, but what a gasp it was. In it he gathered up his own personality, nailed to the cross as to bodily presence, and flung himself out into the realm of the spiritual, and asked to be remembered there.

That was indeed an act of faith, and speaking without dogmatism, and merely from personal conviction, I do not find in all this New Testament record any faith that to me is more arresting, more amazing, more triumphant, more complete, than that of this dying malefactor.

Then we turn to consider how Christ dealt with this man, and we hear one sentence uttered:

"To-day shalt thou be with Me in Paradise."

That was first of all response to faith, and involved within it there was the answer of repentance.

It was response to faith. It was the word of the King. It was the word of One speaking with authority in the realm of the life that lay beyond. Presently the malefactor will be dead. Presently Jesus will be dead on the earth level. Presently evil will seem to have triumphed over good. The word of Jesus assumed the place of authority in the realm of life that lies beyond the earthly. "To-day shalt thou be with Me in Paradise," was His answer to the faith and the repentance of the malefactor.

We pause for a moment with the phrase, "In Paradise." The Hebrew people spoke of the world of departed spirits as Sheol, or Hades in the Greek. In all their thinking they divided this place of departed spirits into two realms, first that in which the unjust were imprisoned, and secondly, that where the just were existing. This was ever referred to as Paradise. Thus Jesus adopted the language of their own theology as He addressed the dying malefactor. He declared in effect that this man should be with Him in the realm of the departed spirits, and in that realm where are the spirits of the just made perfect. In the language of to-day the declaration meant, To-day you shall be with Me in heaven.

We now go a step further and enquire what happened presently? Jesus died before the malefactors. According to the custom of Roman law, they came towards sunset to break the legs of those who had been crucified. Different reasons for this could have been given. There are those who think that the breaking of the legs was an element of pity for the hastening of the end. Perhaps it was rather a brutal means of preventing their escape when taken down from the cross. In this connection we are distinctly told that when they came to break the legs of the crucified, Jesus was dead already.

What had taken place between the moment in which Jesus had spoken to this dying man, and His death? The dying thief had heard Him almost immediately speak to His own Mother, and commit her to the care of John. He had hung there by the side of Jesus through three hours of darkness and of silence, when suddenly he had heard escape the lips of Jesus the words:

"Eloi, Eloi, lama sabbacthani, My God, My God, why hast Thou forsaken Me?"

It is impossible to attempt to interpret what he felt as he listened to that. Directly afterwards he had heard Jesus say, "I thirst." Then further, he heard Him say with a loud voice, "It is finished." He heard Him thus refer to some transaction that had been going forward in the darkness, when he heard Him declare that whatever it was, was now accomplished. It was the cry of a great victory. Still, hanging there, he heard Jesus say:

"Father, into Thy hands I commend My spirit."

One can almost imagine, and I think the imagination is warranted, that so far as he was able, he turned to watch this dying One. Presently he saw His head fall, His eyes close, and knew that on the human level, He was dead. Presently there came the soldiers, and brake his legs, and then he, too, was dead.

Then we may still watch. He passed across the borderline. He left the earthly scene. He entered into that spiritual realm which is ever near, and yet of which we seem so little conscious. What happened then? There can be no doubt that the answer is that Jesus met him, and he found himself with his King in Paradise.

I repeat, there is no more remarkable instance of faith on record. Its opportunity was created by Christ. In this connection we remember with all solemnity that there was another malefactor. He had the same opportunity, but he did not respond. This man might have continued his railing, but he did not. Thus we see the Cross dividing, ratifying the judgment which falls upon a man who lacks repentance, and cancelling that judgment in the case of a man who repented and believed.

This story is full of value in many ways. It proves that nothing more must be superimposed upon repentance and faith as necessary to salvation. He could not be baptised. He could not observe any rite. He could do no good works. He could not serve in any way. He had no opportunity of a period of holy living. All this simply means that however sacred these things may be, none of them constitutes a right of entry to the Paradise of God. That right is created only by that action of the soul in which in repentance and faith, it commits itself to the Lord.

Such a meditation cannot close without our being reminded of things which our fathers so constantly said about the story. We have here the account of repentance and faith exercised in extremis. It is given in order that none may despair, but it is the only such story that none may presume.

We need not despair. That couplet:

" 'Twixt the saddle and the ground,
    Redemption sought, redemption found,"

is more true than we are inclined to think. At any rate it is well that we bear in mind that at the end we shall enter into the presence of the Lord having still to say:

" Nothing in my hands I bring,
    Simply to Thy Cross I cling."

If we pass below all the accidentals of this story, using that word accidentals in its highest sense, we may be inclined to say we are not criminal. Let us make no mistake. In the presence of the holy God, in the spiritual realm we are all criminal. There is only one way of deliverance, but thank God, there is one way.

" Ere since by faith I saw the stream
His dying wounds supply,
Redeeming love shall be my theme,
And shall be till I die."

XXXIX

MARY OF MAGDALA

IN many ways there is no story in the New Testament more radiantly beautiful than that of Mary of Magdala. We observe in passing that the New Testament always speaks of her as Mary Magdalene, which, of course, means simply Mary of Magdala. The word Magdala indicates the city in which she dwelt.

Through some strange and unhappy confusion of the women of the New Testament, Mary Magdalene has been looked upon from medieval times in such a way as to cast a stigma upon her that has no right to be there. She is confused with the woman in Simon's house, and at times with Mary of Bethany. There is no warrant for any such confusion. The stigma to which I have referred is wholly due to her having been confused with the woman in Simon's house. It is interesting to refer to two definitions in a modern dictionary of the word Magdalen. The first definition reads:

" Magdalen. By confusion with the unnamed penitent of Luke vii, 36-50, represented as a fallen woman raised to saintship."

The second definition reads:

" Magdalen. A reformed prostitute."

These are remarkable definitions for a dictionary, showing as they do, correct Biblical intelligence on the part of the lexicographer. That idea has fastened upon this woman of the Gospels, and Churches have been named with that in mind. I suppose we shall never overtake this false use of the term, based upon this unhappy confusion.

Let it, therefore, in our present consideration, be immediately recognised, and throughout borne in mind that she was not a woman of that order. Incidentally I may say that had she been so her name would not have been given, for no New Testament writer gives the name of any woman of that kind. Each preserves in such references a tender and gracious anonymousness, necessarily for the sake of the times in which they were written.

As we consider her story we find five pictures of her contact with Jesus in the New Testament. These we will follow, endeavouring to see her as she is revealed in them; and then to watch our Lord's dealing with her.

The first occasion hardly constitutes a picture, but is a statement clearly revealing her first contact with Jesus. Then we have statements revealing her relationship with Him during His life. We see her also in connection with His resurrection. Lastly, she is seen on the day of Pentecost.

As to the first occasion, Mark and Luke state the fact that Jesus had cast seven demons out of her. Luke tells us this in connection with his statement that she was one who helped to support our Lord in material matters; Mark mentioning it in connection with the fact that she was present at the Crucifixion.

There is no need to stay with the statement at any length save to emphasise the fact of how tremendous and superlative a revelation it is. Unfortunately, our Revised Version throughout has failed to make a distinction between devils and demons, uniformly rendering the word which should read demons, devils. There is a very great distinction which ought to be remembered. Into that matter it is not necessary now to enter in any detail, but recognising it, we realise that a demon was a spiritual personality, and in the New Testament, always evil in nature. Outside the New Testament we find the recognition of demons who were not, according to the writers, necessarily evil. As we have said, this is not the case in the New Testament.

These evil spirits are referred to as possessing men and women. We come across it constantly, and have had occasion to refer to it several times in the present course of studies. The declaration that she was possessed by seven demons may be a superlative and intense way of making a statement. Taking the general conception as revealed in the New Testament, we find that demon possession resulted sometimes in physical disability and material suffering. It also issued in mental trouble, as with the man possessed with a legion of whom it is said he was exceeding fierce, and a dweller in the tombs. Moreover, it resulted in moral failure and depravity. It is to be observed carefully that our Lord and His apostles in all their dealing with, and their references to demon possession, treated it as a disease rather than as moral obliquity. This is not to say that there were no immoral results from demon possession. It is quite certain that there were. There must ever remain much that is mysterious about the matter. Indeed, we may be inclined to ask the question which the disciples asked Jesus concerning the man born blind, Who did sin, this woman or her parents, that she was possessed with demons? There is no doubt that if we did so, the Lord would give us the same answer, namely that He was not dealing with such problems. His business was to cast the demons out. That indeed is a complete philosophy of the work of Christ. His mission was not that of solving problems, but dealing with human dereliction, and that in such a way as to put an end to it.

Demon possession meant irresponsibility in the moral realm. There can be no doubt that in some cases demon possession was the result of immorality. In that case there was necessarily responsibility, for it is always so. By way of illustration, if a man commits murder when he is drunk, he is responsible for the thing he did under the influence of drink, because he had committed the sin of putting himself in such a condition. So if a person became mastered by evil spirits as a result of sin, such a person was responsible. In the case of Mary of Magdala, however, there is no reference whatever of any connection between demon possession and immorality. However the fact may be accounted for it remains a startling truth that here was a woman so mastered by evil spirits that the account refers to them as " seven demons." We are not told anywhere of how, or when, or where Jesus met her. The fact is, however, recorded that He did meet her, and set her free from this demon possession. He set her free from the awful domination, and thus consecrated her to His own Lordship. It is quite evident that she answered the action by the dedication of herself completely to Him in the most remarkable way.

As we observe her during the life of our Lord we are again in the presence of a very brief statement. Both Mark and Luke reveal the fact that she was a woman of wealth and substance, and declared that she, in company with a group of such women, followed our Lord during the days of His public ministry, and ministered unto Him. Thus we see her. She had met Him. He had freed her from demon possession. She recognised Him as her Master, and she was eager to serve. She travelled with Him, and dedicated her wealth to His service. Together with this honourable company of women, for two years at least she ministered to His physical necessities, and to those of the apostles. As I have said, the statement is a simple one, but it is twice made by the two evangelists, and as we watch her thus following Him and ministering to Him in the commonplaces of life, travelling on those journeys over the hills, and along the valleys, into the cities, and into the villages, we see the loyalty with which she rendered a sacred service to Him.

But Mary of Magdala comes out into clearest relief in the stories of His death and resurrection. We may summarise first quite simply. First let it be observed that Matthew, Mark and John all tell us that she watched at His Cross. When all the disciples forsook Him and fled, possibly she was among the number at first. John, however, returned, and in doing so joined the little group of women, and Mary of Magdala was one. This woman whom He had set free from demon possession, who had loved Him and followed Him, and cared for Him in the days of His public ministry, now saw Him nailed to the Cross. If there were any who might have been excused from standing there in the presence of the appalling and awful tragedy, it surely would have been the women. The proportion in which we are able imaginatively to put ourselves in her place is the proportion in which we may come to some understanding of the suffering she endured in that dark and appalling hour.

Mark, in a brief sentence, tells us something which is very significant. He tells us that Mary of Magadala, in company with another Mary, watched His burial, and " beheld where He was laid." The word that Mark uses in this connection is a strong word, and means more than that she merely saw, conveying the idea that she carefully observed it, and took note of it. Thus she is seen standing by. Jesus was dead, but she could not go away. She watched Nicodemus and Joseph of Arimathea as they wound the body, and laid it in a tomb. She saw the rolling of the great stone to the entrance to the tomb, and she knew that His body had been laid therein.

Here I want us very carefully to notice a statement by Matthew. He says:

" Mary Magdalene was there, and the other Mary, sitting over against the sepulchre."

In close connection, he continues:

> "Now on the morrow the chief priests and the Pharisees were gathered together unto Pilate, saying, Sir, we remember that that deceiver said, while He was yet alive, After three days I rise again. Command therefore that the sepulchre be made sure until the third day, lest haply His disciples come and steal Him away, and say unto the people, He is risen from the dead; and the last error be worse than the first. Pilate said unto them, Ye have a guard; go your way, make it as sure as ye can."

The words " on the morrow " reveal the fact that Jesus lay in the grave one whole night before the guard was set, and Mary of Magdala stayed by all night, watching that grave. When the guard came and took charge she went away, but not for long.

Thus we see Mary of Magdala in her deep sorrow standing by the Cross until her Lord was dead, carefully familiarising herself with the place of the grave, watching as He was buried there, seeing the grave stone rolled to the opening of the sepulchre, and staying there all night. There were no Roman soldiers there during that night. There were no disciples there.

Her experience must have been one of terrific fear. Her freedom from demon mastery had been due to Him, and He was dead. I believe that during that night all hell got up and looked at Mary of Magdala. She, however, felt safer by His dead body than anywhere else. She could not tear herself away. He had set her free from the intolerable agony of demon possession, but He was dead. Inevitably she must have questioned whether she was safe any longer. She might almost have imagined that she heard the mockery of laughing fiends waiting to come back and take possession of her. Mary felt that she had lost her Lord, and yet she could not leave the place where His body had been laid in the tomb.

When she did leave the sepulchre she hastened to buy spices, and so we are to see her in connection with His resurrection. She brought those spices in company with others, very early. As they were coming back to the sepulchre with these costly spices which they had bought in love, symbols of their devotion, they were conscious of their weakness. They had seen the massive strength of the stone rolled to the opening of the grave, and the question now arose, Who would roll away that stone?

The sequel, of course, is well known. When they arrived, the stone was already rolled away. Then Mary of Magdalene's agony became greater than ever. She now felt she had lost even the dead body of her Lord. She had left it only for a little while, and now returning, desiring to show her love and devotion, as she brought her spices, even His body was gone. The story goes on with great natural beauty as it tells how she immediately ran to find Peter and John, and to them pour out the agony of her heart in the words:

"They have taken away the Lord out of the tomb, and we know not where they have laid Him."

The result was that these two started at once for the tomb. Evidently they outran Mary, and John arriving first stood with reticence gazing into the empty tomb. Peter upon arrival, went into the tomb, and saw the amazing sight of undisturbed grave clothes. Thus emboldened, John entered, and he saw and believed. When this had taken place we are told that the disciples, that is Peter and John, "went away again unto their own home," "wondering at that which was come to pass."

By this time evidently Mary had arrived. Peter and John do not seem to have thought of her. When she came, looking into the tomb, she saw what it is not recorded that they saw, namely, two angels:

"One at the head, and one at the feet, where the body of Jesus had lain."

As she peered into the tomb, and saw the vision, she was weeping. An angel enquired, "Woman, why weepest thou?" The sorrow of her heart was such that she seems not to have been at all startled by the vision of the angels, or by the voice, but immediately poured out her deepest agony in the words:

"They have taken away my Lord, and I know not where they have laid Him."

Notice carefully she still called Him "my Lord," though He was dead. She was true till death, aye, and beyond death.

When the angel enquired, Why are you seeking the living among the dead? and declared that the Lord was risen, Mary became conscious of a person standing behind her. Turning to see who it was, she imagined that it was the gardener. He asked the same question which the angel had asked:

"Woman, why weepest thou? whom seekest thou?"

Then carefully observe how the love of her heart expressed itself in what she said:

> " Sir, if thou hast borne Him hence, tell me where thou hast laid Him, and I will take Him away."

The suggestion was that she, a woman, should carry a dead man. She felt equal to that, if only she could regain the body of her Lord.

Then took place that which can be read with reverent imagination, but which defies interpretation in some senses. Jesus uttered one word, and that her name, " Mary."

Then Mary stood in the presence of the miracle of all the ages. She did not understand it, but she knew it as a fact that her Lord was not dead, but alive. Then from her heart which had been well-nigh breaking, she uttered words which mark the complete surrender of love, " My Master." It was indeed a beautiful thing to say, but she had not grasped the significance of the thing at which she was looking. She realised that He Whom she had thought to be dead and lost, was there before her. He was near to her. The demons would not have power over her. She wanted to be close to Him, to have Him as in the olden days as Deliverer and Teacher and Master.

He held her away. Very beautifully He proceeded to transfigure her conception of their relationship. We have translated what He said by the use of the word " touch," " Touch Me not." The word is a far stronger one than that. It is the same that He used on the occasion when the woman in the crowd had grasped the *kraspedon* on the hem of His garment. We might render the word of Jesus then as, Do not take hold on Me. Her Lord intended to show her at once that everything was changed. She would not be able to hold Him in the old way, but in a new way. He intimated to her that presently He would be ascending to His Father, and that not until that ascension could there be the complete understanding and realisation of the new relationship. He charged her to go and tell His disciples that He was so ascending. Thus Mary is seen in the early light of the garden scene knowing that she had recovered her lost Lord, and standing in the presence of something which must wait for further explanation.

As we follow the narrative carefully we find that Jesus appeared to her again a little later in the same day. Not long after, the group of women came, and they worshipped Him.

We see her once again on the day of Pentecost. She was with the company on whom the Spirit fell, and was filled with the self-same Spirit. She who had been possessed with seven demons of evil was filled with the seven-fold Spirit of God. So He had met her. So He had dealt with her. So He had led her, and at last, having responded to His mastery, she was brought into closest association with Him in the gift of the Spirit.

Here was indeed a consecrated life. When I use the word *consecrated*, I do so carefully, referring not to her attitude, but to His action. He consecrated her by freeing her from false possession, and provided for her the true possession. She answered His consecration by dedication of herself to Him in the commonplaces of the days when she ministered to His earthly needs; and then at last, as she yielded herself to Him as she cried " Rabboni."

Thus in looking at Mary of Magdala we are looking at a great soul, but we are seeing that her Lord was greater. He is still able to cast out every evil thing that holds and masters and blasts and ruins human life, and to introduce such as are thus set free from evil into the power of His own risen and glorified life by the Holy Spirit.

XL

CLEOPAS AND ANOTHER

THIS is the story of the appearing of the Lord to two disciples
on the day of His resurrection. Luke is careful to point
out that it was on the same day in which, in the morning,
He had appeared to Mary and others, as he writes, " that very day."
Mark tells the same story, but in a very abbreviated form. It should
however, be read because it gives us two details. In the sixteenth
chapter of his Gospel, at the twelfth verse, he writes:

> " And after these things He was manifested in another
> form unto two of them as they walked on their way to the
> country. And they went away, and told it unto the rest;
> neither believed they them."

The two things in this account to be observed are, first Mark
distinctly says He appeared " in another form." That fact will
account on the human level for what we read in Luke, namely,
that they did not know Him. It was characteristic of these post-
resurrection stories that He was not at first recognised. Mary
did not know Him when in the garden she supposed Him to be
the gardener. These two men, familiar as they must have been
with Him, did not recognise Him. It is quite evident that He, of
His own choice, appeared in different ways, and then made Himself
known, so that there could be no mistake as to His identity. Then
Mark tells us the startling thing that when these men returned
with their news, even though before they told it, the eleven declared
to them:

> " The Lord is risen indeed, and hath appeared to Simon,"

these, the eleven, did not believe. We can only say how slow they
were.

Now, whatever this story has to reveal is concerned with the
two disciples, otherwise quite unknown. Mark does not name

them. He uses the expression "two of them." Luke also says "two of them," but he names one. It is quite evident that they were not apostles, because Luke tells us that when they went back they reported to the eleven. The apostles were still in Jerusalem. One of the two is named, Cleopas. Now who was Cleopas? It has been suggested that this person may be identified with Clopas, the husband of one of the Marys who was standing by the Cross, but the suggestion seems very unlikely. As a matter of fact Clopas, the husband of Mary, is an Aramaic name. Cleopas is a Greek name. It is perfectly true that these Hebrews sometimes gave the Greek form to their own names, but it seems to me there is no warrant whatever for this identification. I think rather that the beauty of the story arises from the fact that we do not know who they were.

Looking, then, at these two, it is evident that they were disciples by the phrase used by Mark and Luke "two of them." They were two of that company which was much larger than the number of the twelve. We remember that on the day of Pentecost one hundred and twenty were gathered together, and Paul tells us in his Corinthian letter that our Lord appeared to about five hundred brethren at once when He went into Galilee. We have, then, here two of that nameless crowd.

As we see them, they were travelling towards Emmaus. To me there is a fascination in the way in which Mark puts it, as he says they were going "to the country." Thus we see them leaving the crowded city where things had recently taken place. They were setting out on a seven and a half mile walk, getting away from everything, going into the country together, as it seems to me to be away from these scenes, and away from men. They were even getting away from the apostles. This does not need labouring, but it is a vivid touch, showing two unidentified disciples, endeavouring to escape, and yet communing with each other. Luke interprets the communion by his use of the word "questioned," which means discussed. Quite evidently they were conscious of bewilderment, and in going away were attempting to talk matters out.

Imagination may help us here. If we put ourselves into the position of these men, we can understand how they were anxious to get away from the city, and all its surroundings, and all its people; but they did not want to get away from the things that had happened. They were puzzled, they were communing together, and they were discussing things. Then we read that they were

314

sad. This, of course, was inevitable. That which had happened at the moment to them was a supreme tragedy. They were walking in a great gloom as they took that journey of seven and a half miles to Emmaus.

Why were they sad? We ask the question in order to discover the answer in the narrative itself. When our Lord addressed them, and they replied, they revealed the whole reason of their sadness. We may summarise by saying they had lost their prophet. They had seen Him caught, condemned, crucified, dead. As they told the story the fact is revealed that in losing Him Whom they described as:

" A prophet mighty in deed and in word,"

they had lost their hope. Their love for Him had not perished. Their faith in Him personally had not perished, but their hope had. Said they:

" We hoped that it was He which should redeem Israel."

This was the line of their thinking. They had become His disciples, had received His teaching, had been filled with hope as to the ultimate of His mission. Then their rulers had condemned Him, and had crucified Him. Therefore they lost all hope that through Him redemption was coming to Israel.

Let it be at once noted that their idea of redemption was faulty as the fact emerged later in the story told by Luke in the Acts of the Apostles. They hoped that He was going to restore the Kingdom to Israel, and free them from the tyranny of Rome. All this was now to their thinking impossible, in view of the fact that He was dead.

Continuing their story they told Him something further. There was a rumour that He was alive. It is quite evident, however, from the way in which they told it they did not feel there was any proof of this fact. They said:

" Yea, and beside all this, it is now the third day since these things came to pass. Moreover, certain women of our company amazed us, having been early at the tomb; and when they found not His body, they came, saying, that they had also seen a vision of angels, which said that He was alive. And certain of them that were with us went to the tomb, and found it even so as the women had said; but Him they saw not."

Thus both the women and others had seen nothing but an empty grave and angels, " Him they saw not." It is impossible to watch these two, and to consider the whole situation from their standpoint without finding the heart going out to them in very real sympathy. The one thing that possessed them was the fact of the death of their prophet, and they found no certain proof that the reports that He was alive, were true.

Then we come to the point in the narrative when our attention is fixed upon the Lord. The opening words are arresting, and full of beauty:

" Jesus Himself drew near, and went with them."

The statement is indeed full of suggestive beauty. The risen Lord is seen following upon the highway of that lonely, desolate pilgrimage with two of the company of the disciples. He understood those sorrowing hearts, and drew near to them. Moreover, He recognised their foolishness. He addressed them as " foolish ones," literally senseless. Knowing this, and recognising their slowness in believing their own Scriptures, He nevertheless drew near to them. In spite of all this dullness of apprehension He joined Himself to them, but did not immediately reveal His identity to them. It was necessary that they should have their slowness and dullness corrected and illuminated. There was certain teaching it was necessary that they should have. The point of their failure must be dealt with, and He must show them why He had described them as foolish. These men had lived all their lives in the atmosphere and the light of the Holy Scriptures, but had never understood them. This was the first reason why He drew near them.

Then we observe closely, and listen as we read of how He drew them into conversation. Whereas the phrase is perhaps an unworthy one as applied to Him, I cannot refrain from referring to His method as illustrating a fine art. We are often in danger of doing harm, because our approach to men and women is wrong. Now one can imagine that as He, an apparent stranger, drew near, they might even have felt something of annoyance that anyone should intrude upon them as they were getting away from the city, and desiring to think and talk of the strange things that had taken place.

As He approached, not to quote the exact words, but to catch the sense of them, we find Him asking them what they were talking about. Luke tells us that when He asked the question they were looking sad. As we read their reply we find a touch of amazement in it. Once more, not to quote their exact words, they said in effect, Who are you, and what do you mean by asking such a question? They were astonished and suggested that He was only a sojourner in Jerusalem. Even if this were true, it seemed strange that He was not acquainted with the things that had happened.

Then we listen almost with amazement as He said, " What things? " Necessarily He knew better than they, but it is evident that He wanted them to state their view of things, that they should naturally expose themselves to Him. This they did in words that we have already largely quoted. Glancing at them again, we see at once that their love for Him continued as they described Him as:

" Jesus of Nazareth . . . a Prophet mighty in deed and word."

The description is a demonstration of the fact of the effect which had been produced upon them both by His deeds and His teaching, in His acts and His ideals. It was in this connection that they revealed the death of their hope. In effect, they told Jesus that He had been defeated. They had seen Him done to death, and they told Him that. They thus exposed to Him their own state of mind. He knew it perfectly, but it came into yet clearer view to themselves in the very fact of their statement.

Then follows the account of what He did with them. He first gently but definitely rebuked them:

" O foolish ones, and slow of heart to believe in all that the prophets have spoken."

As He said this they would naturally wonder what He could mean. They knew their prophets, and there can be no question that they felt they understood them and believed them. Nevertheless He declared that they were slow of heart to believe.

Then He opened to them all the Scriptures as they applied to Himself. From their standpoint we see these two, then, listening to a stranger interpreting to them the Scriptures which they thought they knew, but the deep meaning of which they had never apprehended. Moreover, they were listening to this stranger interpreting to them the events through which they had recently passed in the light of Messianic foretelling.

Here I propose to indulge myself for a moment and say I never read this story without feeling that I would have given anything to have walked down that road, and heard Him open the

Scriptures. He began with Moses, and then went through all the prophets. I dare not trust myself to attempt to dwell on that at any length, but we may reverently survey the field.

He began with Moses, and the reference was to the books which we call the Pentateuch, their own Scriptures, the first five books, the Torah, the Law. He showed them how all types, all ritual, all ceremonial, were fulfilled in Him. He passed from that to the prophets, and if we take the reference as applying to those prophetic writings which we find in our Bible, there are certain things which are perfectly plain. From the stately language of Isaiah, through all the minor and major of the music of the prophets, to the teaching of the seers and psalmists, all was moving towards Himself. He is David's King, fairer than all the children of men; and in the days of Solomon's well-doing, He it was that was " altogether lovely," " Chiefest among ten thousand." He was Isaiah's Child-King, with a shoulder strong to bear the government, and a name " Emanuel," gathering within itself all excellencies. He was Jeremiah's " Branch of righteousness, excuting judgment and righteousness in the land." He was Ezekiel's " Plant of renown," giving shade, and shedding fragrance. He was Daniel's Stone cut without hands, smiting the image, and becoming a mountain, and filling the whole earth. He was the ideal Israel of Hosea, " growing as a lily," " casting out His roots as Lebanon." In Joel He was " the Hope of His people, and the Strength of the children of Israel." He was the Usherer in of the fulfilment of the vision of Amos, of " the plowman overtaking the reaper, and the treader of grapes him that soweth seed." He brought about Obadiah's vision of " deliverence upon Mount Zion and holiness." He was the Fulfilment of that of which Jonah was a sign; the " turning again " of God of which Micah spoke; the One Whom Nahum saw upon the mountains " publishing peace "; the Anointed of Whom Habakkuk sang as " going forth for salvation." He it was Who brought to the people the pure language of Zephaniah's message. He was the true Zerubbabel of Haggai's word, rebuilding the city and house of God. He was the Dawn of the day when " Holiness unto the Lord shall be upon the bells of the horses," as Zechariah had foretold; and He the Refiner, " the fuller's soap, the Sun of righteousness," of Whom Malachi had spoken. On that Emmaus road these two unknown disciples heard Him at least show them that these things were so. He thus brought them back to their own Scriptures, the Scriptures they thought that they understood so well, and gave them the key to the true understanding of them.

318

At last they arrived at Emmaus, and we get another of those statements which perhaps are a little difficult at first seeming. It is said that " He made as though He would go further." That is to say, He seemed to be walking on past the place where they were going to stay. He seemed as though He were about to continue His journey along the robber-infested road. We have other instances of this kind in the story of Jesus. When the storm was sweeping the lake, and He approached them, He made as though He would have passed them by. So now. He Who on the highway had acted as Host, appeared to be leaving them. It was then that they said to Him:

" Abide with us; for it is toward evening, and the day is now far spent."

It is important that we should recognise what they really meant. We are all familiar with the great hymn of Lyte's:

" Abide with me, fast falls the eventide."

That hymn is indeed full of beauty, and is warranted in all its teaching, but what it suggests is not what these disciples meant. That hymn means, Stay with us; we are in danger. We shall fail if Thou art away. These men on the other hand were thinking of Him. They knew that the road ahead was a dangerous road, and they were attempting to persuade Him to remain with them, for His protection. He accepted their hospitality, and entered the house.

Then, although they had invited Him as their Guest, He at once assumed the attitude of the Host, and sitting with them took bread, gave thanks, and brake it. It was the action of a host, and as He did it, there came to them illumination. They saw Who it was Who had been talking to them on the highway. His very action was reminiscent of another occasion. Possibly these two men had not then been present, but undoubtedly they had heard of it from those who were there, and they saw Him do exactly what He had done on the betrayal night. He took the bread and He blessed and brake. Then as their love-lit eyes fastened upon Him, He was not there. He had passed out of their sight. This vanishing was part of His method with them. It ever seems to me as I read these post-resurrection stories that His disappearing was ever as valuable as His appearances. During these forty days and nights He was repeatedly appearing and disappearing. The accounts of His appearances show that they were supernatural, and that when they first saw Him they did not know Him. Then when He had demonstrated the fact of His identity, He disappeared. Thus He was training them to do without the visible upon which they had depended through all the days of their discipleship. He was proving to them that when they could not see Him, He was still there, and might at any time appear to them.

As we read the story we do not wonder that these men immediately hurried back. They arrived at eventide, and found the eleven gathered together. We have no account of that journey back, save the statement of the fact of it, but it is quite certain that they travelled, now convinced that He was alive, even though that might still be beyond their understanding. Thus our Lord, dealing with these two slow of heart, had brought them back to their own Scriptures, and given them interpretation; and then had ratified all by proving that He was the living One.

What wonder that they exclaimed presently:

" Was not our heart burning within us, while He spoke to us in the way, while He opened to us the Scriptures? "

There is nothing the Church of God needs more than this rekindling of fire. We have become altogether too:

" Faultily faultless, icily regular,
Splendidly null."

In the case of these men, the fire was rekindled, when they took time to listen to Jesus. It was not as they talked to Him, but as He talked to them that they were conscious of this burning. The fire begins to burn when we cease our discussions, and listen to the voice of the Lord.

XLI

THOMAS

A VOLUME full of interest, and I think of instruction, might be written on the misunderstood men and women of the Bible, misunderstanding arising, I have no doubt, through faulty exposition at some time or another. To me among the most conspicuous of such is Thomas. We ever associate him with one word in our mind, and that is the word doubting. It is not long since a man of somewhat cynical and critical attitude of mind on things generally, said to me, " I am a bit of a Didymus." I think I astonished him when I said, " Where is the other? " He asked me what I meant, and I reminded him that Didymus meant Twin, just as Thomas means twin in our language.

Now, as a matter of fact, this man was a man to be thankful for as a friend. Do not let us forget that Jesus appointed him an apostle, and that therefore he was in that inner company to whom our Lord said at the close of His ministry:

" No longer do I call you servants . . . but I have called you friends."

We admit, however, at once that there are senses in which Thomas was a difficult man, but the only thing that proves is that he was worth while. The dealing of our Lord with him is a radiant example of His perfect understanding and His perfect method.

We ask, then, what do we know about Thomas? As in the case of Philip, Matthew, Mark and Luke name him once, and once only. Luke names him in his Gospel, and in his Second Treatise. He is named by these evangelists as being of the number of the twelve. This was, of course, necessary, because he was thus chosen and appointed by our Lord. If, however, we want to know anything of Thomas, as in the case of Philip, we have to turn to John.

We have six occasions when Thomas is referred to. Five of these are in John, and one in Luke. There are three principal occasions upon which he is seen, and it is at least suggestive that every time we see him, the day is one of almost appalling gloom. We have no picture of Thomas, or account of anything he did or said in the day of sunshine. In this case it will be well for us to pause long enough to read the actual statements as they occur.

In John xi, 16, we read:

"Thomas, therefore, who is called Didymus, said unto his fellow disciples, Let us also go, that we may die with Him."

In John xiv, 5, we read:

"Thomas saith unto Him, Lord, we know not whither Thou goest; how know we the way?"

At chapter xx, 24, we read:

"But Thomas, one of the twelve, called Didymus, was not with them when Jesus came. The other disciples, therefore, said unto him, We have seen the Lord. But he said unto them, Except I shall see in His hands the print of the nails, and put my finger into the print of the nails, and put my hand into His side, I will not believe."

In the same chapter (26-28):

"And after eight days again His disciples were within, and Thomas with them. Jesus cometh, the doors being shut, and stood in the midst, and said, Peace unto you. Then saith He to Thomas, Reach hither thy finger, and see My hands; and reach hither thy hand, and put it into My side; and be not faithless, but believing."

The twenty-first chapter opens with these words:

"After these things Jesus manifested Himself again to the disciples at the Sea of Tiberias; and He manifested on this wise. There were together Simon Peter, and Thomas called Didymus, and Nathanael of Cana, in Galilee, and the two sons of Zebedee, and two other of His disciples."

Luke tells us in the Book of the Acts (i, 13), that Thomas was among the number of those who foregathered in the upper room. There is yet another reference, Revelation xxi, 14:

"The walls of the city had twelve foundations, and on them twelve names of the twelve apostles of the Lamb."

Of these Thomas was one.

As we glance over these references we see three outstanding occasions upon which this man is revealed, and as we have already said, in each case it was a day of gloom. The first is in the story connected with the death and raising of Lazarus. He was on the other side of Jordan in the company of Jesus and the other apostles, when the message came that Lazarus was sick. He was there also when the further message came, declaring that Lazarus was dead. When this news came, our Lord turned toward Judæa, and His disciples unquestionably did their very best to dissuade Him from going. They knew perfectly well the attitude of the Jews, and that if He went back into Judæa, every human probability pointed toward His arrest and even His death. It was then that Thomas said:

" Let us also go, that we may die with Him."

We see him next in the hour when Christ was giving to that group of His disciples His final instructions. The story occurs in those marvellous chapters which record the intimate conversations that our Lord had with these men. The first part of His instructions to them consisted of His dealing with difficulties raised by His disciples. In every case they were the expression of difficulties showing how perplexed these men were by the circumstances in the midst of which they found themselves. Peter, Philip, and Jude, and also Thomas spoke on that occasion.

Peter had asked Him, " Whither goest Thou? " He had replied to him, and the last thing He said in the reply was that declaration that in His Father's house there were many abiding places, and indicating that in His going, He was not leaving the Father's house, but only passing to another abiding place. He told them that He was going to prepare a place for them, and said, " Whither I go, ye know the way." Then the voice of Thomas was heard, literally contradicting the Lord, as he said:

" Lord, we know not whither Thou goest; how know we the way? "

There can be no doubt that Thomas, in common with the others, had grasped the fact that when our Lord spoke of the Father's house He had referred to the whole universe, and he realised that He was passing out in that universe to some realm, in order to prepare a place for them. Thomas then said:

" Lord, we know not whither Thou goest; how know we the way? "

and his statement meant that they were ignorant of the facts concerning that larger spiritual world, and therefore they could not know the way to any sphere therein. To me it was a great word that he uttered, and probably was expressive of much in his own mind. The one fact was that they had no certainty concerning the worlds or the abiding places lying beyond the earthly.

Foregathered with the apostles, we find that Thomas was not there. It is at this point that he is criticised, and I think probably justifiably. Nevertheless, it may be well for us to attempt to understand the real reason of his absence. I believe the only answer can be found in the fact that he was so appallingly perturbed by the horror of the thing he had seen, he had no desire to talk to Simon or John, or any of the company. He wanted to escape from the old associations. I do not think there was any intentional disloyalty revealed in his absence. I think it was the outcome of an appalling agony.

Then eight days after, Thomas is found in the company. Somewhere in the interval he must have returned to them, because we have the record of the fact that they declared to him, " We have seen the Lord "; and it was then that he revealed the whole agony of his soul as he said:

" Except I see in His hands the print of the nails, and put my finger into the print of the nails, and put my hand into His side I will not believe."

I cannot read that saying as the revelation of cynical unbelief. It was rather the outpouring of the heart of a man who had been so filled with horror at the sight of the wounds of Jesus that he declared he would not believe that He was alive, until His identity was demonstrated by those very wounds.

We see him next on the shore of Tiberias listening to Jesus. John names him as being present, but not a word is recorded beyond that. He was there a silent listener as the Lord talked to Peter.

The next place in which we see him is in the upper room at Pentecost, waiting for, and in the Temple courts presently receiving, the baptism of the Holy Ghost. Thus he passes from our view.

There are many legendary stories, undoubtedly many of them well founded as to where he went and what he did. The ultimate picture, as we have seen, is that of his name inscribed on one of the foundation stones of the city of God.

What sort of man was this? First of all, quite evidently he was practical. That is evidenced by his revelation of a sense of hopelessness as Jesus had decided to go into Judæa. He had calculated the situation carefully, and knew perfectly well, and he was quite right on the human level, that if Jesus went there, they would apprehend Him and kill Him. Equally we see the practical side of his nature when he dared definitely to contradict the Lord, saying when Jesus told them that they knew the way, that they did not know where He was going, and consequently could not know the way. He was not going to pretend to understand that which to him was fraught with mystery. The demand he made to the other disciples after his absence on the first resurrection day also shows his practical outlook on life.

The same set of incidents show him to be a man of perfect honesty. He would not affect a faith which he did not possess. Thomas was not the kind of man who would profess approbation and understanding of something that baffled him.

And again his loyalty shines through all the story. It is, perhaps, most clearly seen in the account of his words, " Let us die with Him." The intention was good. If his Lord was going into Judæa to certain failure, then he wanted to be associated with Him in that failure. It was an expression of extreme loyalty. We know that in the sequel he broke down and fled with the rest, but at the moment, when he contradicted Jesus, he did it in the profoundly respectful words, " Lord, we know not whither Thou goest." Confused and bewildered, he still spoke to Jesus as to his Lord.

It is, of course, equally evident that he was a man of courage. That courage necessarily flames into clearest vision in the great confession which he ultimately made, " My Lord and my God."

As we have twice already said, the supreme revelation of the man comes in the midst of circumstances of gloom and of darkness. In such we see him a man moved to the depths of his soul in each case, and blurting out the truth concerning his consciousness at the moment. He was a great emotional soul. He is spoken of as being sceptical, and there is no doubt that it is true. It is well, however, that we ask ourselves what we really mean by that word. We have used it for a generation and more as applicable to flippant unbelief, but the flippant man is never truly a sceptic. He lacks the sceptical ability. The sceptic is one who looks carefully into things, determined to enquire as to their deepest meaning.

We now come to the great subject of how our Lord dealt with this man. In order to discover this, we pass over the same stories again. We may remind ourselves that we have no account of how Christ first met him, or of how he came to be a disciple of Jesus. His introduction to us is found in the fact that our Lord selected and chose him among others from the larger company of His disciples to be with Him, and to serve Him in a special way.

The method of Jesus with him was wholly that of adopting such means as would strengthen him at the point of his weakness. When he said, Let us go up with Him and die with Him, Jesus allowed him to go, and in Judæa gave him, of course in company with the rest, the supreme revelation of His mastery over death. Our Lord had said to him, again necessarily to the rest also, concerning the death of Lazarus:

" I am glad I was not there, to the intent ye may believe."

Thomas then travelled with his Lord to the grave, and saw the One with Whom he had come up to die, Master of death. Standing at the tomb of Lazarus, he heard Him speak to the world that lay beyond, and call a spirit back. One wonders if Thomas did remember that when a little later he declared that he had no certainty concerning the world beyond, that Jesus had proved Himself to have knowledge and certainty as He addressed that world, and called the spirit of Lazarus back.

When he had declared that he did not know whither the Lord went, and could not know the way, Christ answered him with infinite patience, and uttered a word in the midst of his doubting and questioning, which had in it an element of revealing light, as He had said:

" I am the Way, and the Truth, and the Life."

When Thomas, gathered on the second first day of the week it is, I think, perfectly clear that our Lord's appearing was specially on his behalf. As He had done on the resurrection day, He greeted the company with the words, " Peace unto you," and then, addressing Himself directly to Thomas, He offered him the demonstration of His identity, which he had declared to the disciples that he must have. Personally I do not believe for a moment that Thomas stretched forth his hand, but the offer was made. In connection with it our Lord spoke to him, " Be not faithless, but believing." These words would be more accurately rendered, Do not be unbelieving, but be trustworthy.

It is very arresting to notice the different method our Lord employed with Thomas and with Mary of Magdala. When she would have taken hold on Him, He told her not to do so. She had been satisfied with the earthly presence, and she had to learn that there would be a new relationship, independent of earthly contact. Thomas on the other hand, questioning the supernatural, and only able to find it through the natural, was offered this contact. Our Lord's method depended entirely upon the character of the person He was dealing with. Mary of Magdala had to be taught the reality of the spiritual, even when there was no possibility of physical contact. Thomas needed the demonstration of the spiritual in the realm of the natural, and Jesus offered it to him.

We may summarise the method of Jesus by saying He had confidence in Thomas; He believed in him; He chose him for an apostle; and proved His faith in Thomas all the way through. Secondly, He corrected each blunder with infinite patience. Thirdly, He gave him opportunity for advance. At last His victory was complete when He received the great confession: " My Lord and my God."

The story is full of value for all, but of especial value to some. It teaches us that firm foothold for faith has often to be found by fighting. There are those who seem never to have difficulty. They may be happy, and thank God. There are others who cannot avoid the critical and sceptical spirit.

Such an attitude produces a great seriousness of mind which is always sad. It is the attitude of a man who wants to believe, and yet must be true. Almost inevitably we recall the words of Tennyson about Arthur Hallam:

" He fought his doubts and gather'd strength,
        He would not make his judgment blind,
    He faced the spectres of the mind
        And laid them; thus he came at length
    To find a stronger faith his own."

Any merely flippant person in these curious days in which we live, who imagines he or she has some relationship with Thomas, and says smilingly, " I am an agnostic," is not for a moment to be considered in the same category.

We, then, remind ourselves of that to which we made earlier reference, that Thomas made his gravest mistake when he was absent from the assembly of his comrades on the resurrection day. I think the reason of his absence, as we have already referred to it, was true, but it was a mistake. In the hour of darkness we should never forsake the assembling of ourselves together.

The whole story appeals to the faith-assailed man to deal with the Master directly. There may be varied methods of making that personal contact, but it is the secret finally of full assurance of faith. In this connection I call to mind an incident in my ministry here at Westminster in the olden days. There came to see me on some matter of Christian service a Christian Jewess.

In the course of conversation I said to her, " Do you mind telling me what led you to Christ? " and she replied, " Oh, yes, it was a novel, called ' The wide, wide world.' " She said, " There is a girl in that novel named Ellen, a Christian, and I felt I wanted to be like her. When I told my father he was furiously angry, and at his command, I burnt the book. Years passed over my head, but I never forgot Ellen. Then someone introduced me to Emerson's Essays, and I found that in dealing with Jesus he spoke of His excellencies, while denying His Deity. That led me to further investigation. I bought a New Testament. I read through the stories of Matthew, Mark, Luke, and John, and when I had reached the culminating point in the story of Thomas, I knelt down and I said, ' My Lord, and my God.' "

I am not recommending novel reading, or Unitarian literature as a way to Christ, but I am attempting to emphasise the fact that there may be very many ways of reaching Him. The great value is that we are honest, and following through, get into close contact with Him.

Let those who find faith easy rejoice, and live in that last beatitude of Jesus:

" Blessed are they that have not seen, and yet have believed."

It is well here to remember in saying that He was not speaking of the other apostles. They had seen. He was rather referring to all who believed, without the vision of the physical.

Let all such, however, wait patiently for Thomas. Upon one occasion, Dr. Simpson, referring to this subject said, the blame for his absence was not wholly on him. If Thomas was not there on the first occasion, they ought to have gone out and found him. Well, perhaps they did. In any case the whole truth is this, when this man arrives by whatever means, his confession will not be behind any made by those who have had no struggle in faith. He is the man who at last will say, " My Lord and my God."

XLII

THE ETHIOPIAN EUNUCH

SO far our studies in the work of Jesus as the great Physician have all been selected from the account of His earthly ministry.

We are now crossing over into the Acts of the Apostles, and the apostolic letters, in order to look at some illustrations to be found therein, but under new circumstances.

We find ourselves in an entirely new age, but with the same Lord. Mark, at the close of his narrative, in a paragraph, concerning the genuineness of which doubts exist in the minds of some, but concerning which I personally have no question, referring to the period beginning with the resurrection, speaking of the disciples, says:

"And they went forth, and preached everywhere, the Lord working with them, and confirming the Word by the signs that followed."

We are now, then, in the period when His mystical Body, the Church, had been created as to its beginning. The Church is seen moving out into the world indwelt by the Holy Spirit, and the Lord is seen continuing through the Church and the Spirit His own work.

To use Luke's expression found in the commencement of the book of the Acts, we have been watching Him in things which He began to do and teach. We are now to watch Him still doing and teaching, carrying on His work as the great Physician, but operating by the Spirit through the members of His Body, the Church.

The story of the Ethiopian eunuch is pivotal, because it begins that particular story of the ministry of Christ towards the ends of the earth. He has recorded the fact that our Lord had

329

charged His disciples that they were to be His witnesses in Jerusalem, in Judæa, and Samaria, and unto the uttermost part of the earth. Thus the ever widening circles of His work were indicated. As we follow through the book we shall find that they are clearly marked. Their work in Jerusalem occupies the first five chapters. Then we see them scattered by persecution, passing out into Judæa, and on through Samaria. Then beyond these circles the first story of the movement towards the uttermost part of the earth is this of the Ethiopian eunuch. We may remind ourselves again in passing that the book of the Acts is evidently an unfinished fragment. It carries us so far as to show us Paul in Rome, a prisoner, but announcing the great message of the Kingdom of God through Christ.

The story of the Ethiopian eunuch is the account of the movement towards Africa. In this movement the instrument of the Lord, a member of His new mystical Body, was Philip. It is important that we remember this was not Philip the apostle, but Philip the deacon. He evidently had received the call and the equipment to become an evangelist. It is impossible to be definite, but the probability is that when this call came to him, and he answered it, he gave up his work as a deacon. The last we see of him in the story is that from Azotus he passed on, preaching through all the cities. He, then, is the instrument through whom the Lord operated in the case of the Ethiopian eunuch. The great Physician is brought into living touch with this man through a member of His Body, the Church, Philip.

Following the custom we have adopted throughout, we will attempt first to see the man. He is described as a man of Ethiopia. The statement is perfectly simple and straightforward, and can mean none other than that he was a negro. We are then told that he was a eunuch of great authority under Candace, and that his position entailed that of having authority " over all her treasures." We remind ourselves in this connection that Candace may be the name of a particular queen, or it may be a title, as Pharaoh was a title. It is, however, quite definitely established that these people were ruled over by queens, and that in this connection the reigning queen is referred to.

Necessarily the background, then, of the narrative is that of conditions obtaining at the time. Three centuries before Christ, Greek literature and thought had penetrated Africa, and there can be no doubt whatever that at the time a very remarkable civilisation existed there. This man, therefore, was an eminent man in his own country, as he held this position of authority at the court of Candace.

A sidelight in the story shows that he was not an uneducated or ignorant man. He was a man of the Ethiopian race, but when we see him we find him with a Hebrew scroll in his hand. I do not mean that it was necessarily in the Hebrew language. In all probability it was a copy of the Septuagint Version which was then being used. Moreover, he was reading this scroll, and reading aloud, all which, as we have said, proves that he was an educated man.

At this point one is tempted to turn aside, but it must only be for rapid reference. Ethiopia to-day is admittedly the home of a backward people. Let us never forget that when that fact is in mind, that it has been the place of great and remarkable civilisations; and, moreover, history shows that it became the home of a remarkable branch of the Christian Church. As we face these facts we are inevitably compelled to ask wherein lay the cause of this appalling failure? I reply without any lengthy argument to that question by declaring that the Church of God failed in Africa because it did not give its members its Holy Writings in their own language. Wherever that has been the case, the testimony of the Church has failed. That necessarily is an aside, but it is an arresting fact.

Looking, then, at this man we see him a man of education, a man of eminence, but we see more. He had come to Jerusalem to worship. Out of that African civilisation, with all its wealth as it existed at the time, and all its civilisation, this man had been to Jerusalem for the distinct purpose of worship. What may lie behind that statement who can tell? Certainly he knew of the Hebrew religion, for he had not only gone to Jerusalem to worship; he took with him, or had obtained there, a copy of at least a part of the sacred writings of the Hebrew people. The possibility is that he was a proselyte which means necessarily a proselyte of the gate only. He could not be received into full standing of the Jewish nation by reason of the fact that he was a eunuch. That excluded him from full communion with the Jewish people. Nevertheless he had been to Jerusalem to worship, and one can easily imagine the one thing that had attracted him to the Hebrew religion. They were the people of one God, and that fact was ever an attractive one to sincerely seeking souls.

Again, looking at him ere Philip joined him, we see a man questing after truth, and yet conscious that he had not grasped it.

When presently Philip said to him, " Understandest thou what thou readest? " he replied:

" How can I, except some one shall guide me? "

He was a man of remarkable intelligence, and that is revealed in the fact that in his reading in the prophet Isaiah, he found himself face to face with a definite difficulty.

I pause here to remark that it is a remarkable illustration of his intelligence that he was perplexed at that particular point. The question he asked was:

" Of whom speaketh the prophet this? of himself, or of some other? "

The arresting fact in this man is that this is a question even now being debated in what are called scholarly circles. Men of investigation,—I speak with great respect for them,—along critical lines, and sometimes in the atmosphere of a naturalistic philosophy, are still making that same enquiry. Sometimes the answer is given that the prophet was referring to himself, and others suggest his reference was to Jeremiah. We find as we read on that Philip had no doubt about the matter. Our point at present, however, merely is that this man was sufficiently intelligent to feel he could not grasp the significance of that tremendous passage revealing some one, some servant of the Lord, suffering on the way to triumph.

Thus, when we look at the Ethiopian eunuch, dismissing for the moment all the things we referred to at first as to his position and scholarship, we see a man who was a seeker after truth, a man evidently dissatisfied with everything he had so far found, even though he was a worshipper at Jerusalem; a man who was returning from that visit to Jerusalem still questing.

Now we turn to watch our Lord's dealing with this man through Philip who was a member of His Holy Body the Church, and who was operating under the direction of the Holy Spirit.

We are first of all arrested by the man who thus became the instrument of Jesus. In the sixth chapter of the book of the Acts we find that he was one of those elected to the diaconate, and of them it is said that they were to be " full of the Spirit and wisdom." The description unquestionably, therefore, applies to Philip. The description in itself is valuable. The two things for ever go together, fulness of the Spirit and fulness of wisdom. Whereas wisdom may mean much more, it certainly does mean among other things, commonsense and tact. It must be admitted that we have heard people claim to be full of the Spirit whose activity towards others was utterly foolish. Philip because of this equipment, was a fitting instrument for the Lord Himself, and thus knew how to handle a human soul.

Moreover, as we first see him we see an evangelist engaged in a great and mighty work in Samaria. His preaching there had stirred that capital of the Northern Kingdom. Multitudes had gathered round and listened, and believed. Observe carefully that as the instrument of his Lord, while in the midst of this most successful work, he was suddenly commanded to leave Samaria. Much of the man is revealed in the fact that he immediately obeyed. The command gave no programme, and declared no ultimate purpose. It was simply, " Arise, and go toward the South." He was told to travel by the way of Gaza, and the way is described in the significant words, " The same is desert."

Thus Philip is seen as a member of the mystical Body of Jesus, in such close and happy fellowship with his Lord, that he yielded immediate obedience, although the command contained no word of explanation as to its meaning and issue. Therefore he left the busy and populous centre, and the rejoicing crowds to follow the lonely trail across the desert, with no apparent objective.

Now let us carefully observe that before we see him in contact with the eunuch there was a preparation for that contact. There was the preparation of the eunuch. There was the preparation of Philip. The preparation of the eunuch is discovered in the fact that as he travelled back to fulfil his duties in the place of responsibility which he held, he was studying the scroll of the prophet Isaiah. In the possession and the reading and the pondering of that writing we see the preparation for all that was to follow. The fact of preparation is still further emphasised by his honest sense of ignorance and incompetence to understand the things he was reading. If a man possess these writings, and gives himself to their study, it is a great thing when he recognises his own inability, without a guide of some kind, to interpret to him the meaning of the things read. That sense of inability is in itself a preparation.

Now as to Philip, what was his preparation for his meeting with this man? He also had the prophetic writings, but he had more. He knew their historic fulfilment. Possibly he had been brought into contact personally with Jesus, but even if that were not so, spiritually he had knowledge of the One referred to by the prophet in his great foretelling. He knew Who it was Who had been wounded for our transgressions. The eunuch was prepared by the foretelling of Isaiah. Philip was prepared by the fulfilment in Jesus. In the eunuch the sense of ignorance was preparation. In Philip the Spirit of knowledge and understanding was preparation.

Then we observe the contact, and in doing so we mark carefully the method of Philip's approach. First he saw the man driving in his chariot, and then he heard the command of the Spirit, " Join thyself to this chariot." His response was immediate. He " ran to him." One may reverently imagine that the chariot was travelling faster than he, but he was determined to make contact. As we watch this man we see, then, a member of the Body of Jesus through whom the Lord was acting, and all that happened was the result of this action of the Lord Himself through Philip.

He began by asking him, " Understandest thou what thou readest? " It must have been a somewhat strange if not startling experience to this nobleman of Ethiopia thus to have an unknown man approach his chariot and ask him a question like that. The word rendered " understandest " is the word *ginosko*. We might render it with perfect accuracy, Do you know what you are reading? The word " understandest," however, is preferable, because it reveals the true value of reading. The word for reading is, in itself, a remarkable one, for it simply means, knowing again. All reading should be of that nature. Something has been written, because some one knew it. In your reading you are finding that knowledge, you are knowing again. The question Philip asked this man was, therefore, almost a play upon words, Do you know what you are knowing again? It is a simple but a vital question. How often in our reading we have found that having read a paragraph or a page or a chapter, we suddenly discover we do not know what we have been reading. If, therefore, it be true that that is the secret of all reading, it certainly applies to the reading of the Holy Scriptures. It was, indeed, a simple question, but a most profound one. Approaching this man of eminence and learning, Philip asked him if he really knew what he was reading, if he understood. It was a question, therefore, which reached the very centre of the man's intellectual life. It was a question characterised by great wisdom; and this, as we have seen, was the result of the fact that he was full of the Holy Spirit; and consequently was an instrument of the great Physician, Who ever knows what is in man, and needs that none shall tell Him. Thus through Philip, that Physican was handling the soul of this negro nobleman.

Then it was that the eunuch said:

"How can I, except some one shall guide me?"

In this enquiry he recognised the depth of the thing he was reading, and with an honest and magnificent confession of ignorance he revealed a profound necessity. The words he used to describe that necessity were "Some one shall guide me." The word he used means, quite literally, Some one who knows the way and can lead. He had the scroll in front of him. He could read it, but he needed some one to interpret.

Then he told Philip the point where his intellectual power had broken down. He could not understand to whom the prophet was referring:

"Of whom speaketh the prophet this? of himself, or of some other?"

We remind ourselves for a moment of the poignant power and pathos of the things he had been reading.

"He was led as a sheep to the slaughter;
    And as a lamb before his shearers is dumb,
  So He opened not His mouth;
    In His humiliation His judgment was taken away;
  His generation who shall declare?
  For His life is taken from the earth."

The eunuch was seeking to know who it was that was thus described. I think we may fairly assume that he was familiar with the movement of the prophetic writing. He had seen the figure of a servant of Jehovah who was to make the wilderness blossom as the rose, and then he had reached this chapter, with its revelation of travail, leading to triumph, and he said, Who is this?

Then, beginning at that Scripture, "Philip preached unto him Jesus." For the man there was a great hiatus, a sense of lack, and consequently a quest that only left him in an agony of suspense. The answer to all these things was found in Jesus. Philip would tell this man the story of Jesus as we know it, the story of the life and death and resurrection and ascension of the Lord.

The eunuch heard, and it is quite evident that he had understood, and far more, that he had yielded himself to the One Who fulfilled the prophetic foretelling. Moreover, it is evident that

335

Philip had told him of the necessity for making confession of his submission. Therefore, at his own suggestion, he proposed to make that very confession as he said:

"Behold, here is water; what doth hinder me to be baptised?"

Philip responded, and the two passed down into the water, and the eunuch's confession was made in the act of baptism. That was then, as always, an outward and visible sign that this man was also baptised by the Holy Spirit into living membership with the living Lord.

The end of the story is full of beauty. Philip was caught up of the Spirit, and the eunuch "went on his way rejoicing." We are supremely interested in what is said about the eunuch. Philip had gone. The Spirit needed him in some other place. The eunuch, however, was not depressed because Philip had departed. He had found Philip's Master. He had made contact with the great Physician Who had answered all his questions, and satisfied the deepest desire of his heart.

Thus we have a glorious unveiling of the victorious Christ in the new age, still carrying on His healing work. He is seen using His own man, Philip, to run on His errands, to deliver His message, to fulfil His purpose. The whole thing speaks to us of the responsibilities of those who are members of the Church of God. They are ever to be ready to obey, and as they do obey they become the media through which the great Physician deals still with the spiritual and moral necessities of the soul of man.

XLIII

SAUR OF TARSUS

THE story of Paul is found in the records of his friend
Luke, that is, in those preserved for us in the book of
the Acts. Much concerning him is also discoverable in his
own writings. Moreover, Peter referring to him, called him " our
beloved brother Paul," and declared that he was not always easy
to understand. That is a comforting admission.

No writer of the New Testament has unconsciously, or shall
I say, unintentionally, yielded up his own personality more
completely than has Paul. I have in my possession a small booklet
which I find is now out of print, entitled, " Saint Paul, an
Autobiography, transcribed by The Deaconess, a Servant of the
Church." I never have been able to discover who this Deaconess
was, but she has made a list of Paul's references to himself in his
speeches and letters, which selection is most illuminative. Whole
volumes have been written concerning this man, and more than
once he has been a veritable storm centre of theological controversy.
I remember how, in my youth, there was a popular cry, Back to
Christ, which meant, Back to Christ from Paul. The phrase is
not so often heard now, and yet even to-day a popular novelist
undertakes practically to dismiss him.

In history, however, Paul stands out, a pioneer missionary,
fundamental theologian, and an ecclesiastical statesman in these
records greater than all the apostles, and standing above any other
than has arisen in the history of the Church. In this study, however,
we must religiously limit ourselves, excluding the wider facts of
his life and service, endeavouring to see him as a man, and observe
our Lord's dealings with him.

We begin with him as Saul of Tarsus. In doing this we
consider briefly his national placing, his religious background, his
moral outlook and practice, his position, and his general
characteristics.

Racially he was a Hebrew, and withal, a Jew. He spoke of himself as being " A Hebrew of Hebrews," which is not an intensive way of emphasising the fact that he was a Hebrew merely, but which meant that his father was a Hebrew, and his mother was a Hebrew. He declared that he was of " the tribe of Benjamin," which marked him as belonging to Judah, the Southern Kingdom.

When, however, we have said that Paul was a Jew, we cannot dismiss him as Voltaire attempted to do by describing him as " that ugly little Jew." He declared, concerning himself:

" I am a Jew, of Tarsus in Cilicia, a citizen of no mean city."

On another occasion, referring to the same fact, he said he was " born in Tarsus." Tarsus at that period was the second educational centre in the world, from the standpoint of Greek culture, Athens being the first. This man was born there. If a boy is born in Tarsus, and remains there during the early years, the very atmosphere of Tarsus will enter into his mental make-up. Tarsus with its Greek outlook, its Greek thinking, its Greek schools, its Greek atmosphere was where unquestionably he spent the earliest years of his life, probably until he was twelve years of age. Therefore we have in him a man not only a Jew, but a Greek in his outlook. This fact is evident in the whole of his writings as they have been preserved for us.

But there is still another fact that must not be lost sight of. He was a Roman citizen. He had the right to employ that talismanic sentence as it was at the time, *Civis Romanum sum*. In the story of the Acts we find a moment when he did so to protect himself from subsidiary officers who were troubling him.

These three elements then merged in the personality of Saul. He was a Jew by blood, a Greek by earliest influence, and a Roman by citizenship.

Then, as to his religious background, we know that he was a Pharisee, and that he had studied in the School of Gamaliel. That means that in all probability he would have been placed in that School after his barmitzvah, or Jewish confirmation, and so would be sent from Tarsus to Jerusalem. The course in the School of Gamaliel covered eight strenuous years. It was the great Pharisaic School of the time, presided over by Gamaliel, who was the grandson of Hillel. In that School, therefore, he received his religious training.

His moral outlook and practice at the time we learn from a remarkable sentence from his own pen, written when he was a

Christian apostle. Looking back to those years, and looking back in the full light that had come to him in Christ, he said that he was:

" As touching the righteousness which is in the law found blameless."

This statement clearly means that he had obeyed with meticulous attention all the details of the Rabbinical interpretation of the Law as he had learned them in the School of Gamaliel. According to those standards he was upright, straight, moral, or to repeat his own word, " blameless."

Then we see him, after he had been at the School of Gamaliel, and find him a member of the Sanhedrim. No man occupied that position before he was thirty years of age, and no man gained that position unless his record was satisfactory to the authorities.

Thus we see a man, a Jew, a Greek, a Roman citizen, trained in the School of the strictest Pharisaism, clean in all moral observance on the side of human inter-relationship, elected to membership of the Sanhedrim, and so having the right to vote thereon. In passing we may remind ourselves that the statement made in connection with the death of Stephen, " Saul was consenting unto his death," means far more than that he agreed. It indicates the casting of a vote. We see him directly after this, sent forth as an officer of the Sanhedrim with letters of high priestly authority, to stamp out what he honestly then believed was the Jesus heresy.

These details help us to see the man, and how unusual and remarkable a personality he was. Necessarily we look at him now in his relationship with Christ, and yet in doing so we may discover his characteristics. He may be described then first as honest. As a matter of fact he was as honest when persecuting the Christians as when prosecuting the enterprise of Christ.

Again it is self-evident that he was intense. He could do nothing by halves. The Lord could never say to Paul, I will spew thee out of My mouth, because thou art neither cold nor hot. In his great autobiographical passage in Philippians, already referred to, he spoke of himself as " persecuting the Church," and later in the same passage, he said:

" One thing I do . . . I press on toward the goal unto the prize of the high calling of God in Christ Jesus."

Mark those two words, " persecuting," " I press." The verb in the Greek is the same. It marks intensity of life and action.

It is equally clear that he was a dominating personality. He was capable of anger and of biting sarcasm. These things are perhaps pre-eminently manifest in his Galatian letter, in which he referred to certain authorities in Jerusalem who he saw were putting the whole Church in danger, and said, " who were reputed to be pillars." It is impossible to read that description without catching its satirical note. Moreover he revealed himself as he told of the attitude he took up towards Peter.

He is also clearly revealed as a man of sensitive disposition, a man of great heart, and tremendous emotion. When we get such a combination in a man of honesty, intensity, dominating power, sensitiveness, we certainly have a great personality; and this is the man at whom we are looking, and attempting to see the method of our Lord's dealings with him, the question arising, What can Christ do for such a man?

As we approach the story we must bear in mind that we are still observing the great Physician Whom we watched in the days of His flesh, handling men personally with such marvellous ability. He is still doing the same work, dealing with men through the members of His mystical Body, the Church, by the Holy Spirit. We see Him, however, in this case, dealing at certain points with this man directly. We follow the line, then, by observing these two personal appearances to Paul, one on the Damascene road, when He arrested him, and one much later, in a dark and desolate hour, when Paul was in prison. Saul saw Jesus on the Damascene road. Paul saw Jesus when he was imprisoned. We also watch our Lord dealing with him immediately through Stephen and through Ananias.

We first of all see our Lord dealing with him mediately, that is, through another, through Stephen. The story of his conversion is told three times in the book of the Acts, once by Luke, as historian, and twice in addresses which Paul himself gave. In considering Luke's account of it, it is necessary that we remind ourselves of what had happened immediately before. We have the account of Stephen. Saul was a member of the Sanhedrim on the occasion of the trial of Stephen. He saw the face of Stephen as it appeared to those who were watching as " the face of an angel." Moreover, he listened to Stephen's defence, that defence which is recorded for us in the seventh chapter, a defence, not of himself, but of his Lord as Messiah. Tracing the whole course of Hebrew history, he argued for the Messiahship of Jesus. Having thus seen the face of Stephen and heard his defence, Saul voted for his death Being a member of the Sanhedrim he could not cast stones at Stephen personally, but he was so much to the front that he guarded the garments of the stone-throwers. As he did so, he watched, and he heard Stephen pray for the forgiveness of the men who were stoning him.

Without the slightest hesitation I declare that what Saul saw in Stephen, and heard from his lips that day, had challenged his deepest convictions, and compelled a reconsideration of his whole position. The thing evidently began to goad him, and yet he continued in his opposition. That opposition was fierce as is revealed in the words used presently, he was " breathing threatening and slaughter." It may be objected that that does not seem to suggest that he was being goaded by a demand for reconsideration, and yet how often it occurs that when a conviction is clamouring for consideration, attempts are made to drown the voice by increased opposition. That is exactly what Saul did. Determined to silence these voices, he sought the position of authority from the high priest, and gained it in the form of letters to the synagogues, providing that if he found any that were of the Way, he might summon them to appear before a tribunal in Jerusalem. Thus he became the public prosecutor of the Christian religion. As we watch him starting on the Damascene road we know what he was doing was not easy. He had looked at the face of Stephen. He had heard from his lips the history of his own people, and the claim that his hope of the Messiah had been fulfilled in Jesus. He had seen Stephen die, and heard him declare that in his dying he saw Jesus. He had heard him pray for the men who killed him.

It was while he was thus travelling that, to use his own great word, he was apprehended by Christ Jesus. The word suggests an arrest laid upon liberty, and capture. Suddenly a light above the brightness of the noon-day sun shone round about him, and he heard a voice calling him by name, and making a strange appeal:

" Saul, Saul, why persecutest thou Me? it is hard for thee to kick against the goad."

In that word we have a clear revelation of Saul's state of mind. A goad was pricking him, piercing him, a goad that demanded a reconsideration of the Nazarene teaching in the light of Stephen's witness and death. The very intensity of his passion at the moment was carrying him along. He was not having an easy time; he was kicking against a goad.

Immediately, Saul, not knowing who it was that spoke to him, but recognising that whoever it may have been, he knew his condition of mind, said, " Who art thou, Lord? " In the implication of that word " Lord," he recognised the superiority of the One Who spoke, Whomsoever that One might be.

Then came the answer:

" I am Jesus, Whom thou persecutest."

It is impossible to realise what that meant save as we remember who this man Saul was, and what he was doing at the time. The shattering declaration was now made to him that the One Who now arrested him was the very One Who had been put to death, and yet the One Whose followers claimed had risen from the dead. In that moment of discovery the whole superstructure of the man's religious convictions lay in ruin about him. With remarkable immediateness he said " What shall I do, Lord? " He had already addressed the One Who had spoken to him as Lord, but now knew Who He was. Now that the amazing revelation had come to him, in a moment Saul handed in his resignation to all the past, and put himself under the authority of Jesus. As I once heard that remarkable preacher of a previous generation, T. de Witt Talmage say, " He went over at once, horse, foot, and dragoons into the army of the Lord." The crisis of conviction had come, and he immediately obeyed. There came a moment when talking to Agrippa he said:

" I was not disobedient unto the heavenly vision."

Thirty years after he wrote:

" What things were gain to me, these have I counted loss for Christ,"

and in that same passage he brought the experience which commenced in that surrender up to date as he said:

" Yea, verily, and I count all things to be loss for the excellency of the knowledge of Christ Jesus my Lord."

Having thus made his great surrender we learn from what Paul himself said after, that he was at once told that he was appointed to special service.

The first command laid upon him was that he was to enter the city of Damascus and wait. Now our Lord is seen dealing with him through Ananias. Concerning him the Lord said to Ananias, " Behold, he prayeth." The human element in the story is very valuable, for we find Ananias evidently somewhat perturbed, and telling his Lord who this man really was. The Lord then declared to Ananias concerning Saul, " He is a chosen vessel unto Me."

Then we see Christ acting through His servant as Ananias went to him, and his first words of greeting were a revelation, " Brother Saul." Then we are told that scales fell from the eyes of Saul, and he was filled with the Holy Spirit. Moreover he took food, and was strengthened.

Here occurs something of great interest in the narrative. In that chapter nine, verse nineteen reads:

" And he took food and was strengthened."
" And he was certain days with the disciples which were at Damascus."

The revisers have divided the verse, making the second part begin a new paragraph, and in so doing, they were drawing attention to the fact that there was a gap between, " He took food and was strengthened," and " And he was certain days with the disciples." Now as a matter of fact in that gap there were at least two whole years. We learn this from the letter to the Galatians. He went away after his apprehension to the loneliness of Arabia, probably under the very shadow of Sinai. It is, I think, easy to imagine what those two years of reconsideration meant to him. After them he came back to Damascus, and the opposition which followed him throughout life began.

Finally, we have the glimpse of our Lord's second personal appearance to him. The story of the intervening years is told, and in the twenty-third chapter of the Acts we find Paul in the midst of hostility which was brutal and determined. He was rescued from the mob by Romans. We can follow him into the prison, and be conscious of the weariness that fell upon him. Looking out upon the circumstances, it must have appeared as though everything was drawing to an end.

Then " the night following," that is, following the day of turmoil and arrest, Lo, in the prison a radiance, a glory, and the Presence. The Lord stood by him. He heard a voice, and the voice was uttering words which His first disciples had often heard fall from the lips of the Lord. " Be of good courage." This charge was followed by the clear declaration:

" As thou hast testified concerning Me at Jerusalem, so must thou bear witness also at Rome."

In other words, our Lord told him in the hour which naturally was one of dejection, when it seemed that everything was closing in upon him, that his programme was in the hands of his Master. All around seemed to be against Paul. It looked as though he would never leave Jerusalem alive. He was assured by his Lord that he would come to Rome, and bear witness there. That is the end of that particular story, but it is impossible to escape from the conviction that with that vision and voice, all depression passed from the soul of Paul, and he lay down and rested.

Many years ago someone wrote to me and said, " If I had Paul's experience I would yield Paul's obedience." I replied then, and still would reply to anyone who takes up that position, by saying that we have far more than Paul ever had. The one thing that brought full and overwhelming conviction to him was the fact that Jesus was alive Who had been dead. That is what he meant when in one of his letters he said He was:

> " declared the Son of God with power, according to the spirit of holiness, by the resurrection of the dead."

That is what happened in the case of Saul on the Damascene road. It was the risen Christ that brought him conviction.

Now the whole Christian age is the full and final demonstration of the fact of that resurrection. It remains central to Christianity, and the Christian Church in itself is proof of what Paul saw was no mirage of the desert, and no hallucination of a lonely road. A would-be clever writer of some years ago, said what happened in the experience of Paul was that in a thunderstorm he had an attack of epilersy. If it were possible to persuade me of the truth of so stupid a declaration, I should immediately give myself up to prayer that God would send us thunderstorms and epilepsy. The supreme evidence, therefore, is the resurrection, and the words of Paul himself have tremendous significance:

> " If thou shalt confess with thy mouth Jesus as Lord, and shalt believe in thy heart that God raised Him from the dead, thou shalt be saved."

That is exactly what happened to Paul. 'He confessed Jesus as Lord, because he believed in his heart that God had raised Him from the dead.

XLIV

CORNELIUS

A S to actual happenings, the story of Cornelius occupies the tenth chapter of the Acts, and the first eighteen verses in chapter eleven. The results of the events recorded run on to the end of the book. Necessarily the chief interest of the story is discovered in the effect which the things that happened produced on Peter, and the way in which it prepared for the wider work of the Church of God. The conversion of Cornelius produced nothing short of convulsion in the Church as it then existed. This is shown by the fact of the account which Luke gives of how Peter, when he arrived at Jerusalem, had to enter into a very full explanation of all that had happened.

Our present study, however, is necessarily confined to the story of our Lord's dealing with an individual. We are still following the line of our meditation upon the great Physician at work, now seeing how He continued that work, operating through members of His mystical Body, which is the Church, by the Holy Spirit. It is the same Lord. He is still seen as the great Physician confronting human needs, and meeting them in varied ways.

So far as our records reveal Cornelius was the first Gentile, entirely separated from Hebraism, to be admitted to the Christian Way. It goes without saying that there may have been others, because we have by no means a complete record of all that was transpiring in those wonderful years. It is true we have had the story of the Ethiopian eunuch, but he was a proselyte to the Jewish faith. That was not so in the case of Cornelius, although, as we shall see, he was undoubtedly a man who had been influenced by that faith.

His very name, Cornelius, marks him as a Roman. It may leave us a little in doubt as to what was his status in the Roman empire. He may have belonged to the patrician people, or the plebian. There was a great patrician family of the Cornelians. On the other hand there was another large family, slaves freed by the edict of an emperor, known as the Cornelii. This man may have belonged either to the Cornelians or the Cornelii, but the name does mark him as definitely a Roman. Such was his race.

His calling in life is distinctly told. He was a centurion, which means that he was commanding a hundred soldiers in the interests of Rome, under the government of Herod Agrippa, who at that time had been given, by courtesy of Rome, the title of king. We are told, moreover, that he was a centurion of the Italian band, which means that the hundred soldiers under his command were all of them Romans. Thus we see that he was a man exercising authority, ultimately under the mastery of the emperor. Thus he and those closely associated with him, were entirely outside anything like direct relationship with the Hebrew people.

When we come carefully to look at the man we find that we have a remarkable and arresting portraiture. He was not a proselyte, but I think there can be no question that he had been brought under the influence of the teaching of the Hebrew religion, at least concerning the fact of there being one God. Undoubtedly he did entertain the Hebrew view of God, and unquestionably was thus a monotheist.

Here, then, we find a Roman, resident for the time being in a country far removed from Rome, who had almost unquestionably been brought up in paganism, and had known of the gods of the Roman people. Perchance he was familiar with the fact that there was an approach on the part of the emperor to a claim to deity, which the empire eventually accepted, and offered him worship. Nevertheless, here he is seen believing in one God, and that so sincerely that his faith is expressed in three ways that are named. First of all in the behaviour of his life, he was devout; secondly, he gave much alms, that is he was a man moved with compassion; and finally, he was a man of prayer. The statement of this last particular is remarkable, in that Luke says he " prayed to God alway."

Thus we see a man outside the Hebrew economy, but who most probably, through Hebraism, had learned of the fact of the one God, and accepting it, acted in accordance with it. It is probable that there were many in that strange, wild, weird, pagan world, driven by the surfeit of deities to the quest for the one God. Be that as it may, it was certainly true in the case of Cornelius that he was devout. Moreover, he expressed his belief in the one God in his love of his fellowmen. He gave much alms to the people.

The story reveals a further fact concerning him. Believing in one God, expressing his belief in a devout life, in the giving of alms, in constant prayer, he was yet seeking something which he did not possess. This is made clear by the story of the visit of the angel to him, who in answer to prayers that he was offering, commanded him to send men to Joppa and fetch one named Simon, who would give him instruction. Then we have further light as we see him immediately obeying the command, personally responding to the light that came to him. This is really manifest in all his story. He had been responsive to the light that had dawned upon his soul concerning the falsity of all other gods save one. And now notwithstanding the fact that the vision had filled him with fear, he recognised it as a Divine message, and immediately obeyed.

As we look at Cornelius, then, we see everything that seems to be admirable, and we are inclined to ask what more was necessary. As in the case of Nicodemus and the young ruler, Cornelius was a man of excellent character. It is well, however, to remember that neither of them was satisfied. Each was seeking for something, not knowing what it was. What that something was, in each case was revealed in contact with the Lord.

The commencement of our Lord's dealing with Cornelius is very full of vital interest, and more than that, it is full of beauty. Two things were happening at a distance of thirty miles from each other. In the one case a man received an open vision, that is, a vision in the daylight, not one when he was asleep. Thirty miles away, on the sea-coast at Joppa there was a man named Simon Peter. He also received a vision, but in a state of trance, that is, in a condition of high ecstasy. To Cornelius there came an open vision and an angel of God. To Peter, a strange vision of a vessel let down out of heaven. Thus two men were prepared by visions, of a different nature, for making contact with each other.

The story, therefore, is definitely a supernatural one, and we may at once say that to eliminate the supernatural from Christianity is to have nothing left that is vital.

The speech of the angel of God to Cornelius was a revelation first of the fact that his life was acceptable to God. He was told:

" Thy prayers and thine alms are gone up for a memorial before God."

This declaration was a ratification of all the past in his own experience. The word told him that in his attitudes and activities he had not been wrong, but rather right, and taught him that whatever it was he was seeking at the time, he must not undervalue the experiences through which he had already passed.

Then came the command which must have been to Cornelius a very strange one. He was to send to Joppa, and was told that there by the sea shore, in the house of a man named Simon, who was a tanner, he would find lodging another man named Simon, who would give him the instruction for which he was waiting. Thus Cornelius was prepared for the contact with Simon Peter.

The story of Peter's preparation is equally remarkable. There is a human touch in it which arrests us. He had gone on to the house-top; and was hungry, and being hungry, was waiting for his meal. On the human level there is no question that the trance resulted from the hunger. He became, on the human level, semi-conscious, possibly bordering on the realm of sleep. In that condition he saw strange things. A sheet was lowered from heaven, and as he looked into it, he saw all manner of animals, and unquestionably among them animals which were forbidden in the Hebrew economy to be used as food. Looking at them he heard a voice saying:

" Rise, Peter, kill and eat."

Instinctively and immediately all the Hebrew within him revolted against the idea. The prejudices of the years expressed themselves. A literal rendering of what he then said is:

" By no means, Lord. I have never eaten anything that is common or unclean."

The only reply that he received was that startling statement:

" What God hath cleansed make not thou common."

It is quite certain that the ultimate meaning of the vision did not come to him then. He learned it afterwards; but recognising that he had received a communication from God, he was obedient, and presently, travelled the road commanded him, towards the house of the Gentile Cornelius.

Then followed the events which resulted from the vision of Cornelius and the trance of Peter. The men Cornelius had sent arrived at the house in Joppa, and were enquiring whether Simon was there. At once the Spirit spoke to him. The trance itself had vanished, but the memory of it was still with him. While he was undoubtedly wondering what was meant by the declaration concerning things God had cleansed, the Spirit commanded him to accompany these men. Thus we see him starting upon that journey in the company of these men, in simple obedience to the command that had been laid upon him. Ten of them travelled together, Simon and six brethren from Joppa, and the three men who had come from Cæsarea. The brethren who accompanied him were of the circumcision, that is, they were Hebrews by race. There can hardly be any question that he took that journey trembling as he went, because it must have seemed to him that he was crossing a boundary line. Nevertheless he was doing so in obedience to what he was convinced was the command of his Lord. Thus we see the Lord Himself acting through a member of His mystical Body, and reaching Cornelius through him.

Having arrived, Peter went immediately to the case in hand, as he said:

"I ask, therefore, with what intent ye sent for me?"

I repeat that he was certain that he was there by Divine authority, and in obedience; and even yet probably perplexed, he asked Cornelius that simple, direct, immediate question.

We remember how in one of the earliest stories of the work of the great Physician, that of His dealing with Andrew and John we listened to the Master as He said to them, "What seek ye?" That is, What do you want? Why are you coming after Me? The question that Peter asked was, in effect, the same question, though in another form. To what intent did you send for me?

Now from Cornelius' answer we take the central declaration. He told him that he had sent for him:

"To hear all things that have been commanded thee of the Lord."

Thus in effect Cornelius said, You ask what I want, for what intent I sent for you? The answer is that I am seeking God, and to know things which I do not know. There are things which perplex me, and I need light. An angel visitor commanded me to send for you. You have done well to come; and now that you have arrived, I want to hear the Word of God from your lips. Thus Christ through His intermediary said to Cornelius, What seek ye? And Cornelius answered, expressing the quest of his soul which was already remarkably illuminated by contrast with the darkness in which he had been born and brought up. I seek the Word of God to me. I desire to know what God has to say to me.

Then Peter answered him. We cannot attempt to go over all the ground of his wonderful address. It is, however, arresting to notice how all these early messengers of Jesus, again and again put into brief statements all the cardinal facts of their faith. Reverently we may epitomise the answer of Peter thus. He first declared to him that Jesus is Lord of all. He had declared that Jesus had come to the people of Israel, and evidently revealing the new conviction that was coming to himself as the result of all that was taking place, he thus declared the Lordship of Jesus over all, not over Israel only, but over all. He then told him that this Lord had been crucified by His own race, but that He had been raised from the dead. The proof of this was to be found in the fact that he and others were witnesses of the resurrection, for they had eaten and drunk with Him after the resurrection. Thus the declaration made to Cornelius was that of the Lordship of Jesus over all, and of the fact that He had been crucified and raised from the dead.

The ultimate meaning of the great facts declared was that of the possibility of the remission of sins. That was exactly what Cornelius needed, something he had never found. He had obeyed the measure of light that had come to him, and heaven had accepted his alms and his prayers. There had remained something, however, in his life not dealt with; and the message of God to him through Simon Peter concerned One Who is Lord, and Who, by the way of His death and resurrection, was able to give to the human soul cleansing and the remission of sins.

As I read this story I am always inclined to the conviction that Peter had not finished his discourse to Cornelius. I am convinced that at this point his speech was interrupted by the great thing that happened. The Spirit fell upon all who listened:

"While Peter yet spake these words, the Holy Ghost fell on all them which heard the Word."

Notice carefully it was while he, Peter, "yet spake." Quite evidently as Cornelius listened, he had made definite contact with Christ, and accepted Jesus as Lord. He had trusted his soul to Him as his Saviour by the way of His Cross and resurrection. In answer to his faith he received that which his heart had been seeking, the remission of sins; and in that moment as he yielded to the evangel declared, he was born again, receiving the Holy Spirit.

The wonder of the occasion and the evident power of the apostolic message is seen in the fact that not only Cornelius, but that all that heard the word shared the experience.

Observe carefully that the Spirit fell before baptism, and without the laying on of hands. Undoubtedly we have occasions on record when the Spirit fell after baptism, and after the laying on of hands. That which happened, however, to these Gentile souls, who had been born and brought up in the darkness of paganism, and who had been obedient to the light that had come to them when they heard and accepted the great declaration of the apostle, was that immediately they became new creatures, old things passed away; all had become new.

We may safely make the affirmation that if Cornelius had been writing about his own experience thirty years later, he might have written in the very language of Paul, and declared that with regard to the righteousness which had been revealed to him, he was blameless; but that having found Christ, and Christ having found him, he counted all the past as loss.

And then followed the open confession of that great change which had come to him. Having received the Spirit, he made his confession of allegiance in the solemn act of baptism.

We ask what this story really has to say to us, and the first thing is that it reveals the fact that all Cornelius had was not enough. There was something lacking in his life, and he was conscious of it. This was true, as we have said of Nicodemus, and of the young ruler. Nevertheless all that he had already was preparatory to what he was to receive. The picture of Cornelius before this contact with Christ is in itself a very arresting one. Convinced of the existence of one God, he had so far as he was able, squared his life with that conviction. Because he walked in the light as he had received it, he was led into fuller light, and at last found his own life incorporated into the very life of Christ. This is still the one thing lacking in multitudes of lives which otherwise appear and are admirable. But this lack makes all else valueless.

The great fact revealed to Peter and the rest, as the result of the experience was that God is no Respecter of persons.

Looking at the story again, we see the living Lord acting through His intermediaries. He employed the open vision, the trance, the angel, and supernatural voices. Necessarily these were subsidiary and incidental things, and we must be careful not to put an undue emphasis on such things. The central verity is that a man, Peter, was ready though imperfect, obedient though not understanding, and so became the medium for the carrying out of the will of his Lord, and for the exercise of His power. Though still unquestionably perplexed, he was obedient, and therefore capable of hearing the voice of the Spirit, and ready to obey, even though he could not at the moment see the issue of the thing he was called to do.

But after all, the supreme revelation is not that of angels and voices and utterances and visions, or even that of a man, but rather that of the Holy Spirit of God Himself acting for the Lord, and the Lord acting through that Spirit in reaching the enquiring soul in Cæsarea, and employing the obedient man in Joppa. Thus it is the same great Physician Who is revealed to us in this matchless story.

XLV

LYDIA

THE story of Lydia does not, in itself, occupy many sentences, but it is full of simple beauty, and, in its setting, full of significance.

We have been following our Lord, first in the days of His flesh as the great Physician, observing Him dealing with individual souls. We are still watching Him, no longer limited, no longer restricted, to use His own word, no longer " straitened," but having risen, ascended, and by the baptism of the Holy Spirit having united to Himself those who believed on Him, He had created for Himself a new Body, a spiritual Body, and yet very definitely a material one in the members of the Church. We are now watching the same Lord carrying on the same work through these members of His Church.

As we do so I think we must be impressed with what for the moment we may describe as the irregularity of it all. Necessarily we use that word irregularity in a particular sense. The whole book of the Acts of the Apostles manifests the regular irregularity of the Spirit's action. Incidents are recorded one after another, seeming to have very little connection with each other, and yet being vitally connected. As in the days of His flesh our Lord is seen meeting with individuals apparently casually. He went about doing good, and this still tells the story. Yet there is a tremendous significance in each incident which may appear to be almost trivial; because all the while we see how through His Church His sphere of operations is being enlarged. In the days of His flesh He was largely confined to Jewish territory, except when upon occasion He crossed the borderline and visited Tyre and Sidon. Before He left His disciples however, He had charged them to be His witnesses in Jerusalem, in Judæa and Samaria, and to the ends of the earth. We now see Him, then, moving forwards as, to quote from Mark, they went out, the Lord working with them. Thus He is seen working through these witnesses, being members of His Body, and He the supreme Worker.

The story of Lydia must be taken in connection with all that lies round about it. Paul had been passing through what I venture to say were among the strangest experiences of all that came to him in his pioneer apostolic work. He was forbidden of the Holy Spirit to preach the Word in Asia. Necessarily the word there refers to Pro-consular Asia, as it existed at the time. This must have been a somewhat strange experience for him. As we read these stories we are growingly impressed by the familiarity of these early witnesses with the will of God, made known through the Holy Spirit. They knew when the Spirit spoke to them, and Paul knew that he was forbidden of the Spirit to preach in that district. It is evident, however, that he thought if so forbidden, he might cross the borderline, for we are told he "assayed to go into Bithynia." Once more he was prevented:

"The Spirit of Jesus suffered them not."

I repeat, that it must have been a strange experience for the man whose very watchword was the regions beyond, to be thus prevented from carrying on his work in certain regions.

If we look at the picture with the map in our mind we can see him travelling on, forbidden to go north, until he reached the land's last limit at Troas. There he slept, and there came to him a vision of a man of Macedonia, "Standing, beseeching him," and calling to him:

"Come over into Macedonia and help us."

It was a call to cross from Asia into Europe.

The apostle was evidently working in fellowship with Luke and the others who were with him, for Luke says that they concluded that God had called them to preach the Gospel unto them. The word "concluding" employed by Luke is a very suggestive one, meaning that they put this and that together. Evidently in consultation they considered the combination of their situation and this vision, and became assured that it was a Divine leading.

They acted at once, and Luke says, "We made a straight course to Samothrace," which literally means that having entered into the boat, the wind was with them. The result was that the voyage was accomplished in two days. It is interesting in passing to remember that Paul took the same journey later, and it took five days, because the wind was against them. Thus all these matters were working together to a definite end; the call, the obedience, and the wind.

Having arrived at Samothrace, they still travelled on until they came to Neapolis, the port of Philippi, and thence still on, until they arrived in Philippi, eight miles beyond Neapolis.

Luke says of Philippi that it was the first city of that district, and it was a colony. It is important to a correct understanding of the story that we realise what was meant in the Roman empire by a colony. The colonies were points fixed by Rome on the frontiers, and the colonists were sent directly from Rome to occupy these positions. They reproduced at the point of settlement the Roman order of life. Their magistrates were not elected from the populace, but were sent from Rome. Philippi was indeed an important city, for it was there that a tremendous battle was fought between Brutus and Mark Antony. Philippi therefore was in closest touch with Rome and its government.

Paul, who was himself a Roman citizen, came at Philippi perhaps more into the Roman atmosphere than he had ever been before. He was born in Tarsus, and brought up there until he was twelve years of age, or thereabouts. He had been at least eight years in Jerusalem at the School of Gamaliel, a Hebrew of Hebrews, but all the while a Roman citizen. He now stood in a city wholly Roman in its government and value.

But he was there as the ambassador of his Lord, and as the messenger of the new Kingdom and the new Empire. It was there that Lydia was found. She was the first convert, then, of whom we have any personal record, in Europe. We may now attempt to see her, and watch our Lord's method with her.

Lydia was a business woman. She belonged to Thyatira, which was the home of the purple industry, and was herself a dealer in purple. She had her house, and doubtless her business in Philippi. Evidently she was a woman of wealth, for her house is revealed as large enough to be capable of entertaining Paul and the group associated with him. These are the material facts.

Turning to the more important matters we learn that she was " one that worshipped God." That form of speech reveals the fact that she was a proselyte to the Hebrew faith. From the standpoint, therefore, of her conviction about God, she was already one at heart with these messengers of Christ. We see her resorting on the Sabbath to the place of prayer, and that in itself throws light on the state of affairs. Evidently there was no synagogue in Philippi, but there was a *proseuche*, or place of prayer. These were found scattered in many places where synagogues did not exist. Where there were ten Hebrew men it was by law necessary to form a synagogue. This reveals the fact that there were not ten such men of the Jewish faith in Philippi, and the only persons that Paul found were a group of women, groping in the darkness, dissatisfied with the diffusion of devotion by the multiplicity of gods, having found the one God, and gathering together for the purpose of worship. It is clear that before Paul arrived, the religion of Lydia was far more than mere intellectual interest. It was active; it was obedient. She observed the day set apart by the law of God, and found her way to the place of prayer. These places of prayer were often simply enclosures, constantly found by the side of rivers, that is in the interest of washings and ablutions made necessary by the rites of the Hebrew faith. Thus we observe a rallying centre in a Roman colony around the religion of one God, and this woman is seen among others, as yielding to the demands which such convictions produced.

I have no doubt that there were very many in those days who had found some answer to the quest of their restless souls in the monotheistic religion of the Jew. They had found one God. This is all we know concerning Lydia. We see her outside the territory of Judaism, in the midst of pagan Rome, but a worshipper of God. The very fact that she resorted to the place of prayer would suggest that she was still seeking for fuller knowledge, more complete understanding, making time for these holy exercises.

We now turn to examine Christ's method with this woman. In doing so we find that the arrival of Paul was not the beginning. When Christ is seen at work He is seen first acting directly, and then mediatorially. This is markedly so in the case of Lydia. To emphasise the fact let us remind ourselves once more of her position, and the attitude of her soul. Undoubtedly clever and successful in business, and yet at the very centre of her life a hunger after reality, she had found a doctrine of God that unquestionably had brought her some measure of quietness and peace and satisfaction. Of her the simple and yet sublime statement is made, " whose heart the Lord opened." That is how it all began. Paul might have preached, and with no effect, had this not been true. It is a mystic sentence, and it is conceivable that there may be clever people who would smile at it. Nevertheless I cannot but feel that the ribald jesting of some writers of this age constitutes a minor obligato to the infinite music of the Gospel. No amount of cleverness can finally explain what is meant by the statement as to the processes of that opening of Lydia's heart. It is, however, worthy of note that Luke uses a word here which no other New Testament writer ever uses. We find it in his Gospel in several places. It is a Greek verb which means literally to thoroughly open up. Indeed, we should get to the very heart of its thought if we rendered it, disentangled. The probability is that every woman will understand that illustration better than a man. I have often seen a skein of tangled wool. I never disentangled one, but I have seen my mother do it many times. That is the word telling of what the Lord did, and it reveals also the condition of the mind of this woman. Great things were mixed, and lacked clarity in her thinking, and the Lord opened them up, and prepared her for what was to follow.

Luke uses the same word of the two men who walked to Emmaus, as he says, " Their eyes were opened," and yet again when he speaks of the Lord opening the Scriptures, and once more, opening their understanding.

He " opened her heart," He created her capable of hearing, and hearing intelligently. He brought to bear upon her a constraint to attention, a desire to attend, to these things of the heart.

We have seen in other connections the word *heart* is used in different ways, but it often stands for the whole of personality, with a special emphasis upon the emotional nature. Here undoubtedly the word refers to far more than the emotion, and includes the whole personality of Lydia. Let it at once be said that He was opening up the way into Europe, and thus directly brought to this woman some preparation of personality so that she was prepared for His mediatorial activity through Paul.

As we now read the story it is arresting to observe that Paul and the rest of them tarried two or three days before doing anything. They waited for the Sabbath, and when that came they made their way down to the banks of the river where they supposed, and correctly, they would find a place of prayer. On arrival they found only women assembled there. Someone has recently remarked in disparagement of the work of the Church, that it is largely now attended by women. In reply to any such criticism we have to say, God have mercy on the nation when women cease to worship.

To this company Paul, the Pharisee, the Hebrew of Hebrews, the man brought up at the feet of Gamaliel, came. As a Pharisee through all those years of his life until he was apprehended on the Damascene road, he had uttered a form of thanksgiving, which every Pharisee employed every day:

" Oh God, I thank Thee that I am not a Gentile, I am not a slave, and I am not a woman."

Here we find him in a Gentile city, and when he came to the place of prayer he found himself there confronted by women. In Christ he had found the contradiction and correction of the thinking expressed in that formula of thanksgiving. It was Paul who wrote that in Christ:

" There can be neither bond nor free; there can be no male and female; for ye are all one man in Christ Jesus."

Therefore, when he came into the midst of that worshipping company of women he preached the Gospel. As his custom constantly was, his first action in Philippi was that of seeking those of his own nation. As he preached the Gospel, and Lydia listened, Christ was operating through him. He had opened her heart, and there was now to be brought to her knowledge and understanding through the preaching of Paul.

Then Luke puts the result in one sentence characterised by directness and great simplicity:

" She gave heed to the things spoken by Paul."

That means infinitely more than that she listened. To heed them was to accept them. She yielded her personality, which had been strangely and supernaturally moved before Paul began his story. There had been an unloosing of the heart, an opening up of the tangled web of her strange conflicting quest; and in that condition she heard Paul tell the story of Jesus. We have no reason to speculate as to what were " the things spoken by Paul." Unquestionably he had told her of Jesus as the Son of God, how He had lived, how He had died, how He had risen from the dead, how that He was then at the right hand of God, anointed to be a Prince and a Saviour, and to give remission of sins. Lydia listened; she gave heed; and then by the river side in Philippi, in the place of prayer, she was won for Christ. She immediately carried out her belief in confession as she was baptised. She joined that company of the disciples of the Lord. In her yielding she was

358

baptised in water as the sign and symbol of the baptism of the Spirit.

At once we see Lydia beginning to act in fellowship with the enterprises of the Lord. She became hostess. She opened her house, and Luke says she constrained them to enter into her home, and make it the base of their operations. The word " constrained " is essentially the word of hospitality. We find it in one other place in the New Testament when it is used of the two men who had walked to Emmaus in the company of Jesus, that they constrained Jesus to abide with them. Paul made her house the base of his operations for the period of his sojourn in Philippi. Thus when the Lord opened this woman's heart, He found vantage ground for the carrying on of His work in Europe.

Then directly we see Satan at work, and that through another woman. Whereas the story of this damsel of divination is not our special theme, it is arresting to notice the method of Satan. He always has two methods with the Church. The one is that of alliance, and the other is that of antagonism. He tried alliance. He sent this damsel forth declaring that what Paul said was true. Paul would have none of it. Like his Master, he would receive no testimony from the underworld, even to the truth of his Gospel. The demon was exorcised.

Then antagonism manifested itself. As persecution began in Europe, it changed its note. The persecution which the witnesses of Christ had found in Asia had always arisen from religious opinion. In Europe it resulted from commercial disaster. " The hope of their gain was gone." As a result Paul was put in prison. In our next meditation we shall be dealing with the story of the Philippian jailor. We now observe that when presently Paul was brought out of prison, it was to Lydia's house that he went, and she opened it and received him.

All this is a very simple story. It is interesting however to know what Paul thought of it. Years after, writing to these people in Philippi, he said:

> " I thank my God upon all my remembrance of you, always in every supplication of mine on behalf of you all making my supplication with joy, for your fellowship in furtherance of the Gospel from the first day until now."

That is how Paul remembered Lydia, and the house of Lydia, and the action of Lydia.

Again in that same Philippian letter he referred to the matter at the close, as he said:

> " And ye yourselves also know, ye Philippians, that in the beginning of the Gospel, when I departed from Macedonia, no Church had fellowship with me in the matter of giving and receiving, but ye only."

Thus the story is seen in its beauty and its grace. Lydia's opened heart was the Lord's vantage ground for a forward movement. Through that opened heart He passed into Europe. The whole thing is seen in its greatness. An opened heart, an opened house, an opened continent. However apparently unimportant it may seem when the message of the Lord is given to one woman, to one man, it is well to remember that when we deliver that message He Himself has ever been ahead of us, preparing the ground, and that the apparently simple may be, and constantly is, sublime in all the results that follow.

XLVI

THE PHILIPPIAN JAILOR

WE may remind ourselves once more of the reference made by Mark to the fact that the witnesses of the Lord went forward, " the Lord working with them." The door of entrance into Europe had been found in the open heart of Lydia, a woman, a seller of purple, and her home was the temporary base of operations for Paul and Silas and others in this forward movement.

It is quite evident that they tarried there for some time. It was during this period that the soothsaying maid followed them as they were on their way to the place of prayer. Such a reference may, of course, refer to a Sabbath activity when they would naturally assemble in the *proseuche*. If that were so, it would seem as though some weeks had passed, because the writer says that " this she did for many days." On the other hand it is quite possible that Paul, and those associated with him, made the place of prayer the gathering ground to which they went daily, to give their teaching. In either case, the story shows that a considerable period of time was spent in Philippi.

It is further evident that results were following their work, for we are told that after the imprisonment, and the story which occupies our attention now, they tarried long enough to see the brethren, and to comfort them ere they passed on their way.

At last the definite antagonism of the underworld of evil manifested itself. The whole story reveals the method of these evil spiritual forces. They first attempted co-operation, and that failing, they adopted the definite method of outward opposition. The co-operation attempted was that of an evil spirit entering into a maid, who following the apostle and those who were with him, declared:

> " These men are servants of the Most High God, which proclaim unto you the way of salvation."

It is most significant to observe that Paul acted exactly as the Lord ever did as he refused to accept testimony borne by this underworld of evil. Indeed we are told he was " sore troubled." The word employed is a strong one, and shows that he was troubled to the point of anger. He knew what is constantly true, that anything in the nature of co-operation offered by the underworld of evil is sinister, and compelled ultimately to do harm. Therefore, he charged the evil spirit to come out of the damsel, and immediately it did so.

This method of co-operation being defeated, there began at once that of definite and hostile opposition. As we have seen in our last study, the opposition in Europe took on an entirely new form. In the Asian cities it had been religious. Now it became commercial. When the masters of this maid saw that because her soothsaying had ceased, their gains were going, they protested, the protest being made not on religious grounds, but rather upon civil and national. They declared that these men were teaching things in that city which were causing a disturbance, and that what they were teaching, the citizens had no right to observe, because they were Romans. Paul and Silas were seized, and brought before the magistrates. They were roughly used, for they tore the clothes off Paul and Silas, and the lictors rained blows upon them. Having done so, they handed them over to a jailor, and commanded that he keep them safely. Being so handed, he thrust them:

" Into the inner prison, and made their feet fast in the stocks."

The story presents to us a picture which is really radiantly beautiful of these two men in the inner prison, the dark dungeon in which was no light at all, their feet fast in the stocks, their backs broken and bloody from the lictors' rods, and they:

" Were praying and singing hymns unto God."

The statement does not mean that they were asking anything, but rather that they were worshipping, and their worship took the form of praise. In passing we may say it is a picture of Christianity. Anyone can sing when he gets out of prison. These men sang in prison. There was no human possibility of leaving the prison, at least until the morning. In that connection we are told the remarkable fact that the prisoners were listening, and once again the word " listening " is an arresting word. It means listening with pleasure.

Then as Mildred Cable has so beautifully said, " Something happened." While they were thus worshipping in praise, the

Lord touched the land, and it trembled, and the prison doors were flung open. The word indicates the fact that the doors were set wide open, not ajar.

All this leads to our actual story, that of the Philippian jailor. Our first business is to attempt to see him. He was a Roman official, and the title which in our translations we render jailor means quite simply the guardian of the shackles. His business was that of taking charge of the prison and the prisoners in such wise as to ensure their appearance before the tribunal. Thus he is seen as eminently concerned about his duty. Moreover, in the discharge of his duty he resorted to the utmost severity in the case of these men. He was not content with putting them into one of the ordinary cells, but cast them into the inner prison, dark and damp, as those inner prisons ever were. Even there he attempted to make assurance doubly sure by fastening their feet in the stocks.

All this reveals concerning him more than that he was a man doing his duty. He was evidently a man brutalised in nature. He had no concern whatever about their wounds. Having assured, as he thought, their security, he went into his own house, and went to sleep. Moreover, we may say that the story reveals the fact that he slept soundly. He did not hear the singing. He was comfortable, and asleep, nothing waking him but the earthquake.

The development of the story further reveals that he was a man influenced by the fatalistic courage which marked the age. When he discovered that the prisoners whom he had been charged to keep safely, and others with them, were probably escaped and gone, he was prepared to kill himself. It is a well-known fact that Roman officials answered with their lives for the escape of the prisoners. The law demanded that they should do so. This man realising it, was mastered by courage of a brutal and fatalistic kind, and was prepared to take his own life, rather than face the authorities. This, then, as he is revealed in the process of the story, is the man. In passing we may note how different is the type of personality from that of Lydia.

We now come to watch the method of the great Physician with him. We once more emphasise that which we have been insisting upon that the Lord was still at work, working now largely through His new mystical Body, the Church, breaking in ever and anon with some direct contact. This was so in the case of Lydia, and in a different form is repeated here. His direct action here, of course, was that of His supernatural intervention through the earthquake. How tremendous this was is revealed in the fact as stated:

"The foundations of the prison-house were shaken . . . the doors were opened, and everyone's bands were loosed."

This surely was a supernatural breaking through. The Lord Himself Who came and opened a woman's heart, now to reach this man and this city, convulsed Nature in a touch of mighty power that produced the earthquake.

When the jailor awoke and found the prison doors thus open, he naturally surmised that the prisoners had gone, and he was terrified, and taking his sword, prepared to take his own life. Then out of the darkness of that inner prison he heard a voice. It was a reassuring voice. It was the Lord speaking through Paul:

"Do thyself no harm; for we are all here."

We can only appreciate what this meant to the jailor as we resolutely attempt to put ourselves into his place. He suddenly discovered that in spite of open doors the prisoners were still there. One was speaking, and one of those in the inner prison, and he declared that they were all there. The man who had been terrified by the upheaval of Nature, and more terrified because he thought his prisoners had escaped, now heard this reassuring voice and message.

Now it is evident that a new terror seized him. Calling for lights he leapt into that inner prison, and there he saw Paul and Silas. He had bound them safely, putting their feet fast in the stocks. Now he looked upon them free, the stocks open and the staples and chains wrenched from the walls. The sight brought from him the exclamation:

"Sirs, what must I do to be saved?"

The title he employed as he addressed them marked his consciousness of their superiority, and these were the very men whom he had treated with such brutality but yesterday.

Many evangelistic sermons have been preached on the enquiry of the jailor, and that quite rightly. It is, nevertheless, important to recognise that it was a cry coming out of his sense of necessity, and referred to what appeared to him as his immediate peril. It was the cry of a horror created by all the circumstances by which he found himself surrounded; and it was a cry addressed to men who, undoubtedly, he felt had something that was different from other men, something strange, something supernatural. Indeed, we may say that the earthquake might have been a natural thing, but that these men were still in the dungeon, and addressed him in terms of such astonishing comfort, revealed the presence of forces that could only be accounted for as being supernatural. A little while ago he was so much afraid that he would have killed himself. Now, with a new fear born of this consciousness of the supernatural, this cry escaped his lips:

" Sirs, what must I do to be saved? "

We ask, What was in his mind? What was it from which he desired to be saved? I do not think had he been asked, he could have answered that enquiry. He was conscious of danger, and in that consciousness he was coming to a new consciousness of himself which was beyond his understanding.

Paul's answer was immediate, and most remarkable:

" Believe on the Lord Jesus, and thou shalt be saved, thou and thy house."

I have said it was a remarkable answer to the enquiry, and that is especially seen if we keep ourselves conscious of the mind of the jailor. Whatever that cry may have meant, out of confused sense of terror, the answer of Paul was given on the level of its deepest meaning, even though, perchance, the jailor himself did not understand that meaning. " What must I do to be saved? " was the cry of agony, and Paul confronted that agony with an answer that went to its very heart, and dealt with the condition in which the man was, even though he himself did not perfectly understand it. We as Christian people are so familiar with the answer that we may fail to recognise that to the Philippian jailor it must have been a more amazing thing even than the earthquake. He cried to be saved, delivered from peril, hardly knowing what the peril was, and he had presented to him the one way of complete escape and freedom, " Believe on the Lord Jesus and thou shalt be saved." I recognise that it may be at times a dangerous thing to build a doctrine on a preposition, and yet every student of the New Testament must recognise oftentimes the profound significance of a preposition. Paul did not say, Believe in the Lord Jesus, and thou shalt be saved; but " believe on." Not *en*, in; but *epi*, upon. Belief in, might refer to an intellectual consent. To believe upon, suggests complete surrender. Paul was calling upon this man to yield himself to the Lordship of Jesus, and declaring that as he did so he would be saved. The jailor understood later what

365

Paul really meant, but for the moment the statement was really an amazing one, that whatever the perils were that threatened, there was deliverance in the surrender of the life to the Lord Jesus. The lines of an old hymn occur:

> " Venture on Him, venture wholly,
> Let no other trust intrude."

Believing in Jesus never brings salvation to the human soul. It is possible to believe in Him, in His idealism, in His intention, and yet still be in the place of peril. It is when the soul of man steps off and trusts Him wholly that he finds perfect safety.

It is interesting in this connection to observe that Paul did not tell this man to repent, and if we ask the reason why, the answer is to be found in the fact that he was already a repentant soul, that is, his mind was changed. The very question he asked showed this. Paul's own formula later for salvation is expressed in the words, " Repentance toward God, and faith toward our Lord Jesus Christ." This man, however, had already given evidence of a complete revolution, a change of mind. Last night they were prisoners, and he had bound them, and put their feet in the stocks. To-day they were addressed as " Sirs," there, by a man with a changed mind, and a changed attitude; that the apostle was able to say, " Believe." The command was that he should obey the state of mind produced by the terror of his soul, and cast himself out upon the Lord Jesus, and there find deliverance.

That, of course, is not all that Paul said to him. Luke gives us no details of what followed, but he does say that:

> " He spake unto him the Word of the Lord."

That evidently means that having called him to complete surrender on the basis of his change of mind, he then interpreted to him what he meant by salvation. There can be no doubt that he told him about Jesus, and how His Lordship was based upon His teaching and His atoning death. Thus Christ, the great Physician, was approaching the Philippian jailor with healing.

The result is revealed in the account of what happened immediately. The man is seen as an entirely changed being. This is evidenced by the fact that he brought Paul and Silas into his house, and washed their stripes. Last night we saw him a man so hard, so callous that he had no thought for their wounds and their sufferings. But now he is seen mastered by a great tenderness, so that with his own hands he is attempting to remedy the brutality of the night before, and washing their stripes.

Moreover, we see him making his confession, as the whole effect was so great that all in his house joined with him. He was baptised and all his, immediately. Thus they were enrolled among the company of those who, having believed on the Lord Jesus, were saved.

Then Luke adds another touch, full of suggestive beauty, "he set a table before them." This man, unquestionably a Roman, would in all probability be entirely ignorant of the Old Testament, but I cannot read this statement without being reminded of the great singer who speaking of God said, "Thou preparest a table before me." This very thing this man is now seen doing for others. He had become God-like, having washed their stripes, he spread a table before them.

How beautiful is the final scene. He:

"Rejoiced greatly, with all his house, having believed in God."

Paul had said, "Believe on the Lord Jesus," and he had done it, and that meant he had believed in God, the God of the earthquake, the God of the supernatural actions, and the result of this belief in God was the banishment of all fear and terror, and the coming to him of a great rejoicing.

The sequel is full of interest. We are told that the jailor still kept them, and kept them safe. He produced them in the morning when they had to appear before the tribunal. He was still carrying out his duty, but he was in himself an entirely new man. It is noticeable, necessarily, that being thus free, Paul and Silas remaining with him was voluntary on their part.

Then comes the account of Paul's magnificent independence in the presence of violated justice. He stayed with the jailor so that the jailor was able to produce his prisoners, but as the representative of his Lord, he made his protest against the unjust action of the Roman authorities.

Thus the great Physician is seen on His way into Europe. He opened a woman's heart, and He shook the earth to reach the soul of the jailor. The contrast in types between these two persons is outstanding, a woman, and a brutalised man.

The contrast in method is equally arresting. He opened the heart of the woman mystically, but definitely. He shook the earth to arouse the man. Whether it was Lydia or whether it was the jailor, we have exactly the same result, that of a new creation in Christ Jesus. In the case of Lydia we see humanity healed in answer to the quest after truth, which until Christ came through His messengers, she had not been able to find. In the case of the jailor we see humanity aroused from carelessness and brutality, and changed into a man of compassion and tenderness.

Thus He passed on His way into Europe, the great Physician, meeting the woman, meeting the man, and through the members of His Body, dealing with each in healing and saving.

XLVII

FELIX

FELIX appears on the inspired page only in connection with his relation to Paul. From other histories we learn certain things about him. He was a freed-man of Antonia. Of him Tacitus said that:

> " He exercised the authority of a king with the disposition of a slave, in all manner of cruelty and lust "

His personal character may be gathered from the fact that he had persuaded Drusilla, a Jewish princess, to leave her husband, and become his wife. All we know of his subsequent history is that he was recalled to Rome.

The picture we have in the narrative of Luke is chiefly psychological. It is evident that somehow he had been brought into close contact with the Christian propaganda, and that it had produced certain effects upon him. He passed through a period of unrest and disturbance, which created for him a great spiritual opportunity. What the ultimate issue was we are not told.

The different stages of his experience are clearly marked. We may select the four statements that reveal him.

> " Felix, having more exact knowledge concerning the Way."
> " Felix . . . sent for Paul, and heard him concerning the faith in Christ Jesus."
> " Felix was terrified."
> " Felix left Paul in bonds."

The statement that he had more exact knowledge concerning the Way is arresting in the expression " the Way." This expression was often made use of by Luke. Saul had letters of authority to act against any that were of " the Way." The damsel at Philippi referred to " the Way " of salvation. Apollos, the eloquent Alexandrian, was instructed " in the Way " of the

369

Lord. In Ephesus the Jews are reported as having spoken evil of " the Way." In this same city it is said there was no small stir concerning " the Way." Later, Paul in Jerusalem declared there had been a time when he persecuted " the Way." Before Felix Paul declared he had served the God of their fathers, according to " the Way."

Most evidently, therefore, the phrase described the whole Christian movement as to its doctrine and its practice. Perhaps it resulted from the language of the Lord Himself when He had said, " I am the Way, the Truth, and the Life."

Of this Way we are told Felix had more exact knowledge, that is, more than Paul's accusers. It is evident that he based his decision and his action not upon what these accusers said, but upon what he knew. This knowledge resulted in his adjournment of the case, in his kindness to Paul, and in the fact that he sent for him. Thus we see a man of whom Tacitus said that he reigned as a king with the disposition of a slave, a man of whom we know he gave his passions full play, somehow having come into contact with Christianity, and being so impressed by it that he declined to listen to the clamour of the Jews, treated Paul with kindness, and presently sought a personal interview with him.

That leads us to the second declaration that Felix heard Paul concerning the faith in Christ Jesus. Whatever emerges in the narrative presently, there is no evidence that his sending for Paul was born of any spirit of cupidity. That motive certainly entered into his dealings with Paul later; but for the moment we see a man who had felt the power and appeal of the Christian " Way," and knowing that he had near him its most illustrious exponent, sent for him to hear about " the faith in Christ Jesus."

All this is sure evidence of a mental activity along the line of enquiry and investigation. Somewhere, as we have said, his path had crossed " the Way." Christianity had touched him, and he was desirous of seeing what more he could discover about it.

We remind ourselves once more of the facts concerning Felix. He was the governor, which reveals his official position. The woman who sat by his side, listening to Paul, reveals the manner of man he was as to moral character; but the deeper fact of his personality, and his consciousness of those deeper facts are seen in his action, in sending for and listening to Paul. There are spiritual and moral facts in every human personality from which none can absolutely escape. They may be ignored, and actually forgotten during certain courses of life, but they will recur, and that without exception, when man is brought into contact with Christ in any way. Thus in sending for Paul it is quite evident that for the moment he was following the gleam, pressing a little nearer to the light, to find out what it really meant for him.

The next plain statement concerning him is that he was terrified. Necessarily that brings us to the enquiry as to what it was that terrified him. Luke tells us that he heard Paul reason concerning " righteousness, temperance, and judgment to come." He had sent for him to hear more of the Way. Paul spoke to him " concerning the faith in Christ Jesus," and he did so by thus reasoning. Paul gave to this man, therefore, a reasoned application of the faith in Christ as it applied to him. This is of such tremendous importance that we are compelled to pause to consider the three matters referred to.

The first was that of righteousness. There is very little need that we tarry to define that. If we shorten the word by omitting its central syllable we have rightness; and if we enquire what rightness is we may find an answer by omitting the last syllable—right. Right ever means a recognition of final standards, and the conforming of action thereto. Holiness is a condition of character. Righteousness is the conduct that springs from holiness. Holiness is what a man is in himself if he be a good man. Righteousness is the activity that springs from that condition. Thus in dealing with the faith that is in Christ Jesus, Paul first dealt with this matter of doing right, and the importance of the standards of life and the sanctions of life, and conduct conformable thereto. Paul declared to Felix therefore in effect that the faith that is in Christ Jesus insists first of all upon the supremacy of righteousness. It is not merely the declaration of a method, but the application of it in actual conduct.

Then he reasoned with him concerning temperance, and we are halted again by this word. Much modern use of the word temperance entirely misses the mark as to its value in this connection; and it is of the utmost importance that we understand it.

There are four Greek words which are suggestive. The word *sophron* referred to a man who was master of his passions. The word *egkrates* referred to a man who, fighting and struggling, was nevertheless gaining mastery over his passions. The word *akrates* described a man who was losing the mastery over his passions. The fourth *akolastos* was used of a man who had lost the mastery over his passions. The word that is used in describing the reasoning of Paul is a verb derived from the second of these words. Not *sophron* which refers to one who has mastered his passions. It is very significant that Paul did not use that word. He did not reason of him as to the necessity of a man being perfectly master of his passions. The word he used referred to the necessity for a conflict in order to gain mastery over the passions. Thus he reasoned with him first of righteousness as the standard of human conduct, and secondly of temperance, that activity of personality necessary to achieve mastery over the passions of life.

I cannot ponder this without feeling that there was a touch of tender solicitude in the reasoning of Paul. Righteousness, yes, there must be, and no lowering of that standard, no accommodation. The faith that is in Christ Jesus never makes any compromise at that point. It recognises, however, the conflict that is necessary, and reminds us that there shall be that temperance which is the effort to gain the mastery over passion. Thus the faith that is in Christ Jesus declares to a man that however far he may have gone wrong, however paralysed his powers may be, however he may have wrecked or weakened his own will, he may enter upon a new struggle, and so gain the mastery of his passions.

And once more, he reasoned concerning " judgment to come." Thus Paul reminded Felix that the final fact in every human life is not reached in the passing moment, but lies over the borderline, in the beyond. In effect, he said to him, Life is not to be measured by the present, but by the future. Every human life must pass out to the place of judgment where there will be the finding of the true verdict, and the passing of the true sentence; and, moreover, the carrying out of that sentence by the action of inexorable law. Paul said to Felix in effect, What you do to-day as governor, what you do in your private habits of life are coming up presently for review. You will have ultimately to report to a higher Throne than that of Caesar. Thus the faith that is in Christ Jesus declares to every human life that the ultimate meaning of life is to be found beyond the span of earthly probation. There is a judgment to come.

He reasoned with Felix of righteousness, and that reasoning touched all his activity in his official position as governor. He reasoned with him of temperance, and that touched all his personal habits of life. He reasoned with him of judgment, and this reasoning placed his official responsibility and his personal life in the light of a final Tribunal from which there can be no appeal.

Thus he "was terrified." He was terrified by the truth, the light, the larger outlook on life. For a moment this man, who had reigned as king, with the disposition of a slave, whose despotic and cruel rule brought him presently to Rome to report for judgment; this man who had given himself up so completely to the passions of his life, saw everything in the clear light of the faith that is in Christ Jesus. That faith, thus interpreted, tore the veil from his eyes, and he was terrified.

That was the hour of opportunity. His terror was the touch of God's infinite grace upon his soul. It was God's gentleness giving him an opportunity of a new way of life.

The last statement sounds almost commonplace. "He left Paul in bonds." Looking back we find that his first act was that of postponement. He said to Paul:

" Go thy way for this time; and when I have a convenient season, I will call thee unto me."

He made the wrong answer to terror. That was the vital mistake. That postponement led him to the admission of other motives. Two years passed. It is evident that the terror faded, and the suggestion arose that possibly he might make some material gain out of Paul. Luke tells us that "he sent for him the oftener." I think it is impossible to read this without seeing that the terror was passing until he allowed cupidity to gain the upper hand. Then, also, as he was being recalled, he desired to please the Jews, and so left Paul in bonds. That is the end of the story as Luke tells it.

In the presence of this story one wonders whether there is any need to point the moral, or adorn the tale. It may be well, however, to gather up some of the things which this story seems to teach.

First, we have a revelation of the influence of the Way, that is, of the action of Christ as the great Physician in the presence of the human soul. Secondly, necessarily, we have a revelation of human responsibility in the presence of Christ.

The story of Felix shows how Christ arrests the soul, and recalls it to the consideration of forgotten things. All the facts of life, whether official or personal, are placed in the light of spiritual and moral verities. Christ ever says to man that his life cannot be ultimately, and therefore is not now, wholly conditioned by the things of daily calling and personal habits, by the immediate. There are such things as righteousness, a struggle for the mastery of passion, and judgment to come. Christ ever arrests the soul, compels it to put known things in the light of forgotten things. That is His first appeal. He says to man that if he be exercising his authority officially in a wrong way, if he be allowing his passions to hold revel, he must not forget that his action does not destroy essential and eternal things. Thus Christ arrests the soul. He does more than make the soul conscious of these things, He reasons with it concerning them. In doing so He ever presents Himself as at once the Pattern of righteousness, and the Power, when He is submitted to, for its realisation.

Moreover, He reasons with man concerning getting the victory over his passions. In doing so it is well to remember that He Himself could never be described as *egkrates*, a Man gaining mastery over His passions. He was ever *sophron*, One Who had complete mastery over them. But He ever presents Himself to every other man as Saviour, that is One Who is mighty to deliver and to help in the struggle to obtain such mastery on the part of others.

Moreover, finally, without any qualification, Christ insists upon the fact of the judgment to come. He declares to His own followers that they must all appear before His judgment seat. In that connection we remind ourselves that the statement came from the inspired pen of the apostle:

" We must all be made manifest before the judgment-seat of Christ."

The reference there was to the *Bema*, where all Christians are to appear that they:

" May receive the things done in the body, according to what he hath done, whether it be good or bad."

The principle is of wider application, and applies to all men. This is revealed in the pictorial beauty of the declaration in the Apocalypse:

" I saw a great white throne, and Him that sat upon it, from Whose face the earth and the heaven fled away; and there was found no place for them. And I saw the dead, the great and the small, standing before the throne; and books were opened; and another book was opened, which is the book of life; and the dead were judged out of the things which were written in the books, according to their works."

This is indeed the ultimate judgment, and it is to be noted that before that great white throne men will be judged by the things written in the books. Those whose names are in the book will have appeared before the Bema or judgment-seat of Christ.

The story reveals the fact, moreover, that Christ not only arrests, not only reasons, He terrifies. No man can possibly come face to face with Christ without a sense of terror. If righteousness is interpreted by Him, then we are conscious of our lack. It is quite true that the first effect produced may be that of attraction, because of His winsomeness. When, however, we press nearer to Him, while the consciousness of winsomeness will not depart, we stand in the presence of a light that reveals the darkness of our own character. The only man for whom we need entertain fear is the man who is not afraid in the presence of Christ.

Finally, He not only arrests, reasons, and terrifies, but by that very process He opens the way of escape. In this sense also the fear of the Lord is the beginning of wisdom. There is, indeed, a matchless beauty in the prophecy of Hosea where, in declaring the method of God to apostate Israel, he said:

" I will allure her, and bring her into the wilderness . . .
And I will give her her vineyards from thence."

The significance is patent. Fruitfulness gained in the wilderness of desolation; and then the prophet added:

" And the valley of Achor for a door of hope."

Achor means troubling, and when God deals with a soul, troubling is the opening of the door of hope. It was when Felix was terrified that that door swung open before him. If he then had yielded to that new sense of fear, he might indeed have begun to hope.

Thus the narrative necessarily reveals the responsibility which Christ creates for the soul of man. He knows as the great Physician, arrests, reasons, terrifies, and so opens the door of hope, and shows the way of escape. As He does so, our responsibilities are clearly revealed, and illustrated in the case of Felix. He is first seen upon right lines. He stopped, he waited to consider, he investigated. All this is exactly what Christ demands that the soul shall do.

Then the negative revelation of the story is graphic. We see Felix proceeding upon wrong lines. In the presence of the terror he postponed decision. That is always a perilous action.

The word of the Gospel with which we have long been familiar is indeed significant, "Now is the day of salvation." God has given man no promise for to-morrow. All the revelation of the activity of Christ, and all human experience points to the fact revealed in the story of Felix, that if we postpone until to-morrow, the danger is that terror will weaken, and opportunity pass. Some day we shall see the things on the earthly plane from the heavenly heights. Great spiritual tragedies are ever taking place, which cannot be reported by the press of earth. A man trembles in the white light of the glories and the power of Christ because he becomes conscious of his own failure. If he then will answer his terror and yield himself to Christ, he can be delivered, he can be healed. Men tell me that procrastination is the thief of time. It is, but it is also the burglar of eternity. As to the story of Felix we repeat that we do not know the ultimate issue. History says that Drusilla and the son of Felix were swept out by the fires that destroyed Pompeii. This we know that if ever the moment came when he returned to Christ and yielded to the early terror, then he, too, was received.

XLVIII

AGRIPPA

AS we have taken our way through this series of studies one very solemn thing has been occasionally revealed, namely that notwithstanding His almighty skill as a Physician, there were some who came into contact with Him who by reason of their own attitude did not gain His healing power. It would seem that this was so in the case of Agrippa. It is unquestionably a sad story, and we want to endeavour to see it as it is presented to us on the pages of the inspired narrative.

I should like at the very beginning of our study that we disabuse our minds of the false conception, so widespread, that Agrippa nearly became a Christian. This view is based upon an undoubtedly mistaken translation of something he said, to which we shall return presently.

Herod Agrippa II, to give him his full title, crosses the page of New Testament history suddenly, and passes away with equal suddenness. He is only seen in his connection with Paul. Here, as in some other cases, we may make reference to certain facts concerning him which are not recorded in Luke's narrative. We find Agrippa both in pagan and Jewish history, and there can be no doubt that he was a very remarkable person. Descriptions of him reveal him as a man of fine physique and of magnificent presence. It is also true that he was a man of wide education, and of great natural ability. Born in A.D. 27, he lived to be 73 years of age, dying in Rome in A.D. 100. He received his education in the palace of the emperor. As a politician, he espoused the cause of the Jews, claiming through the early years that he himself was a Jew. When the Rebellion broke out, as the result of which the Jewish nation fell, he completely joined the Roman power, and fought against the Jews.

377

His relationship with Bernice was a scandal both to the Jews and to the Gentiles, as the writings of Josephus and Juvenal very clearly show. This, then, is the man as revealed from sources outside the New Testament narrative.

In order to see him as revealed in the narrative of Luke we need to remind ourselves of certain circumstances and events. Felix had left Paul a prisoner. He was succeeded in the Roman governorship by a Roman named Festus. He, desiring to gain favour with the Jews, and at the same time to administer Roman law, found himself placed in a strange dilemma in the case of Paul. While he was facing the situation, Agrippa appeared upon the scene. Whereas he was called a king, and Paul addressed him in that way, it is well to remember that it was a title of courtesy. He was in effect, a vassal under Festus, and came to Cæsarea to pay his respects to his superior, the Roman governor. Knowing his intimate acquaintance with all Jewish matters, Festus felt he had an opportunity to gain some light on the problem confronting him concerning Paul. Agrippa responded that he was anxious to hear Paul. A formal occasion was arranged.

Now we see him, and his contact with " the Way," that is with Christ, through Paul. We are first arrested by the simple historic statements made in the record concerning him. The narrative tells us that he and Bernice came together to what was certainly a formal and even a pompous occasion, with the military leaders, and others around him. Agrippa and Bernice were central to the group. We may remind ourselves here that he was the great-grandson of the Herod who had murdered the innocents at the birth of Jesus. His great-uncle had murdered John at the request of a dancing wanton. His father had murdered James. That gives us his family background.

When we look at Bernice the whole outlook is full of shame. She was Agrippa's sister, the sister also of Drusilla, who was the wife of Felix. She had been married to her uncle, Herod of Chalcis, until she abandoned him, and consorted with Agrippa. After a while she married Polemo of Sicily, but stayed a very little while with him, and then went back to Agrippa. Finally, she went to Rome with him, and then pagan history tells us that she figured shamefully in the lives of Vespasian and Titus, father and son. That is the woman who was sitting by Agrippa's side. Everyone knew of his incestuous connection with his own sister. He did not attempt to hide it, but flaunted his shame and her shame in the sight of Festus, the whole assembly, and Paul.

The other brief historic revelation is contained in what he said to Festus when told the story of Paul.

> " And Agrippa said unto Festus, I also could wish to hear the man myself ";

a suggested rendering in the margin of the Revised Version is unquestionably correct and important. What Agrippa really said was, " I was wishing." The very form of the statement reveals the fact that he had some previous interest in, or curiosity concerning Paul. He knew something about him. The probability is that he had never seen him, and was glad of the opportunity offered when Festus told him that he held him as a prisoner. It will be remembered that Paul's presence there was due to the fact that he had used the proper Roman formula, " Cæsarem appello," I appeal unto Cæsar. It was a legal formula, and when once a Roman citizen, which Paul was, had employed it, no other tribunal could deal with his case. On the other hand when a governor sent a prisoner to Cæsar, it was necessary for him to make a formal charge against him. That was Festus' difficulty. He did not know with what to charge him. The people at whose instigation Paul had been arrested were unable to make a charge of sedition, the whole question being one about their religion, and concerned the declaration that Jesus Who had been put to death, was affirmed to have risen, and to be alive. Festus, knowing Agrippa's knowledge of these turbulent Jews, felt that he might help him in the matter.

It was then that Agrippa said:

> " I also was wishing to hear the man myself."

It is, therefore, quite evident that he had some previous knowledge, and now he had his chance of meeting, seeing, and hearing the man himself.

Our next revelation of Agrippa is discovered as we read Paul's address to him. He declared that he was:

> " Expert in all the questions and customs which are among the Jews."

Whatever Agrippa knew about Paul, Paul knew this about Agrippa. Paul would not have said this if it had not been true. He was not employing the language of courteous flattery. That is the man that Paul saw.

Later in the same address he said, still concerning Agrippa, " For the king knoweth of these things," and the reference was to all that he had been telling him, that is, the story of Jesus. Paul declared that he was persuaded that none of these things were hidden from Agrippa. Thus he is seen, a man expert in all the questions and customs of the Jews, and a man having knowledge of the Christian movement.

And we have still a further revelation in this address of Paul. Festus had interrupted him, and Paul having replied to the interruption, again addressed himself directly to Agrippa, and he said:

"Believest thou the prophets? I know that thou believest."

This is a remarkable addition, showing that Paul saw him not merely as a man clever, expert, learned, highly trained, not merely as having knowledge of the fact of the Christian movement, but familiar with the Hebrew writings, and in some sense believing in the prophets.

To summarise. Agrippa was flagrantly sensuous, a slave to his passions. He had become quite careless about public opinion. Jewish opinion was against him, and so was pagan, but he cared nothing as is evidenced by the fact of his bringing Bernice with him. He was, moreover, a man careful about Roman law, as well as expert in the customs of the Jews. His finding about Paul was strictly accurate.

"This man might have been set at liberty if he had not appealed unto Cæsar."

He knew, however, that the appeal to Cæsar was irrevocable, and that Paul must be sent to him.

The last revelation of Agrippa found in the narrative is that of a man contemptuously dismissing a possibility. The possibility, to use his own expression, was that of becoming a Christian. We are familiar with the story of that word "Christian." It only occurs three times in the New Testament, and was at first undoubtedly a name applied to the followers of the Way by those who were outsiders. There are those who think it was a term of contempt. Personally I think it meant simply that those so named were recognised as followers of Christ. At any rate Agrippa's use of the term shows that it was a familiar one. He said to Paul quite literally, With a very little are you trying to make me a Christian? There is no doubt that we understand the question if we place emphasis on two words, the words "me" and "Christian." With a very little thou wouldest fain make *me* a *Christian*. He accurately interpreted Paul's intention to make him a *Christian*. He contemptuously referred to the method as of very little value as he said "With a very little." He was dismissing Paul and his arguments as being of little weight with him. The door of opportunity opened in front of him. It had been opened by a man whose mind was equal to Agrippa's intellectually, and indeed greater. The offer grew out of the fact that Paul had shown the relationship between the things of which Agrippa had knowledge, and those customs and prophetic writings of the Hebrew people. He saw that the door was open, but had no desire to enter in. The last thing we see of him, then, is his act in this contemptuous dismissal of opportunity.

So far as Paul was concerned, his method was a serious attempt to gain the soul of Agrippa. As we watch, let us remember that our chief interest is in Christ, as He was dealing with the human soul through His messenger. When Agrippa attempted thus to dismiss Paul and his arguments, Paul had one more method of appeal. As we have seen, he first approached Agrippa with great courtesy by recognising his expert knowledge of the customs of the Jewish people, of the facts of the Christian Way, and of the prophets. It is well that we bear in mind that this man Paul was equally expert in all these things, and indeed more so than Agrippa. He had been brought up at the feet of Gamaliel, and if any man would be an expert in these matters of Jewish belief and custom, it was such a man as Saul of Tarsus.

Paul, however, saw all these things irradiated, illuminated, interpreted in Christ. He had seen the history of the Hebrew people, and all their literature leading to Messiah, and in the light that had shined about him on the road to Damascus he had found that Jesus was that Messiah. There can be no doubt whatever that in all his dealing with Agrippa Paul was supremely desirous of leading him to the point of a like conviction, with his consequent surrender. He was saying as within himself in desire, If this man Agrippa could see these things of which he has expert knowledge, as thus interpreted, illumined, explained, it would be a way for him into life.

There was nothing in his address to Agrippa of the nature of an explanation of the doctrines of the Faith. In all probability by this time he had already written his letter to the Romans, but he did not suggest to Agrippa any of its massive arguments. The interpretation of Salvation is found in that letter, but an intellectual grasp upon its arguments is not the way of Salvation. Therefore Paul did not give him an argumentative statement of the doctrines of the Faith, but rather, gave him a testimony, thus acting as a witness. Agrippa had said, " Thou art permitted to speak for thyself," and Paul evidently fastened upon that permission, and said in effect, I will speak for myself. Leaving out all argument, I will tell you my own story.

This he did in a remarkable way. He first referred to his past as he declared that he was of the straitest sect of the Pharisees. That meant among other things that he claimed to have been trained in a School where most meticulous attention was paid to every detail of ceremonial and ritualistic religion. Referring to his attitude of mind under those conditions he said that the result of that training was that he thought that he ought to do many things contrary to the name of Jesus of Nazareth. It is well to remember that he was never more sincere than when he thought that. Sincerity is not an evidence of accuracy. A man may be very sincere and at fault at the same time. He emphasised the sincerity that had characterised him in that conviction by a declaration that he had put into the business of opposition all the passion of which he had been capable.

He then told the king of what had happened to him on the way to Damascus, of the light that had shined around him of such brilliance as to bring himself and the company travelling with him to their faces on the ground. He then told him how that he had heard a voice which had said to him, " Saul, Saul, why persecutest thou Me? " and that recognising the authority of the voice he had enquired, " Who art Thou, Lord? " and received the amazing answer, " I am Jesus Whom thou persecutest." What that fact that Jesus was alive and speaking to him had meant to Paul he was telling Agrippa, giving him the opportunity for the same experience. To Paul it had meant the reconstruction of his theology, and a new interpretation of Hebrew history and the Hebrew Scriptures. There had come to him a light which, after two years of consideration under the shadow of Sinai in Arabia, had made it necessary for him to recognise the triviality of even a Divinely ordained ritual when the full spiritual realisation had arrived.

In effect, therefore, he said to Agrippa, After that light upon the Damascene road I had to go back to all the things with which I was familiar, back to Moses and his writings, back to the prophets, and I found they were all foretelling the things which now were realised. He then said to Agrippa:

" I was not disobedient unto the heavenly vision."

I think the whole emphasis of the declaration, as Paul spoke to Agrippa was on the personal pronoun " *I.* " As though he would say, When conviction came to me, I was obedient. How wilt thou act?

He accompanied the story of his own experience by two final home-thrusts as he addressed the king. The king knoweth, the king believest. It was then the answer came to Paul to which we have already referred. " With but a little persuasion thou wouldest fain make me a Christian."

Then Paul made his final appeal, and there is exquisite beauty in it. He said:

" I would to God that whether with little or with much, not thou only, but also all that hear me this day, might become such as I am, except these bonds."

The sweep of his desire included Bernice, Festus, and those present. I venture to declare that there is nothing in human history more dramatically magnificent than the vision presented to us at this point. Agrippa in his robes of royalty, Bernice bedecked with her jewels, Festus in the scarlet of the Roman governor, the military leaders in their garments of magnificence, as Luke has said, " great pomp." Before them a prisoner, formally arraigned, and therefore wearing chains that marked his position. Yet this prisoner, looking into the faces of these royalties, said that he would to God they were such as he was. There was a royalty, and a dignity, and an august majesty in this outlook upon his position, all Christian experience flaming into a glory that put the tinsel and the gaud of earthly splendour into darkness, and made them even disreputable.

But the final touch is in that little phrase, " except these bonds." There the Christ was speaking in fulness of power through His servant. Paul stood, his wrists and his ankles manacled, and perhaps lifting those manacled hands he declared that whereas he desired that those whom he addressed should be such as he was, he exempted from that desire the chains of his bondage. In that phrase there flashed the very genius, the very spirit, the very heart of Christ. There was a passion to win Agrippa and the rest for the freedom that was his in Christ, and a desire that they might be exempt from the bondage in which he found himself. In effect he said, Agrippa, I would give you my freedom, the franchise of the ages, but not my bonds. I would give you all the joy of my heart, but not my pain. I would wish you to be exempt from suffering. That is Christianity, and with it he flooded the soul of Agrippa.

As we close we ask, Where does it all end? We read the story, and it is perfectly clear that Paul's interpretation of the prediction of the past in the sacred writings, and the history of their fulfilment in his own experience, produced for Agrippa a point where he must consent, or definitely refuse.

We ask, Was Agrippa convinced? If not, the reason was undoubtedly to be found in the fact that he had not been honest with the logical argument, for it was unanswerable. If he were convinced, still that conviction did not make him a Christian. Being convinced never makes a man a Christian. Conviction must be carried out by submission. So far as we know, Agrippa never submitted. At the moment, and perhaps eventually he was disobedient to the heavenly vision, and therefore, in spite of Christ's activity through His chosen servant Paul to reach the citadel of his soul, and capture it for high things, he said No. It is a story of the most solemn import and warning.

XLIX

DEMAS

A S we have been following our course of studies, watching the great Physician at His work, we have seen some cases in which His healing power was frustrated by certain conditions and attitudes of human life.

In the case of Demas the possibility of relapse after healing by the great Physician is revealed. His name is three times mentioned by Paul, and in each case when Paul made the reference to him, he, that is, Paul, was in prison. In the first imprisonment, that during which he wrote his letters to the Colossians, the Ephesians, the Philippians, and Philemon, Demas is seen as one of a faithful group, joining with them and with Paul in the salutation which was sent to the Colossian Church. Moreover, Paul speaks of him at that period as he wrote to Philemon, as " a fellow worker."

In his second imprisonment from which he wrote this letter to Timothy, the last letter from his pen that has been preserved for us, Demas is once more referred to, but as having forsaken Paul and gone to Thessalonica. The reason for his defection is clearly stated:

" Demas forsook me, having loved this present age, and went to Thessalonica."

It is with that story of relapse that we are now concerned. Let us bear in mind—and I want to emphasise this at the very beginning of our study—that of the ultimate history of Demas we have no record. We have no right to say that Demas was ultimately an apostate. It may be true, but to repeat what I have said, we have no knowledge of the matter. That he had been definitely committed to Christ his association with Paul clearly

385

proves, for he was with him during the period of his first imprisonment in Rome, and as Paul referred to him as one among his fellow-workers, there can be no doubt that he was one whom Christ had met and had healed. Somewhere he had come into contact with the great Physician. We have no means of knowing where. We are not even told his citizenship. The probability is that Christ had reached him through Paul. He had been spiritually healed, and received the gift of life.

Our story, then, is not that of a final apostacy, but it is that of a definite relapse. The whole story of this relapse is contained in the paragraph at the end of this second letter of Paul to Timothy, written at a time when Paul was evidently conscious that everything, on the human level, was closing in around him, and the end was near. His first trial was over, and the second was anticipated. In Roman jurisprudence the second trial was not for investigation, but for the promulgation of sentence. Paul knew what that sentence was going to be. In the story there are human touches full of revelation. He felt the cold, and charged Timothy to bring his cloke with him. He was evidently, however, mentally alert, for he told Timothy to bring the books with him. That alertness was principally concerned with spiritual things as his words, " especially the parchments " prove. There is a touch of ineffable tenderness in his reference to his loneliness. A little group had been with him, but they had all gone, some of them on the Master's business. Crescens had passed on into Galatia. Titus had gone to Dalmatia, and Tychicus had been sent elsewhere. He was not absolutely alone, however, as the sentence so full of meaning reveals, " Only Luke is with me." It was in that connection that he referred to one whom he had numbered among his fellow-workers, who had shared in his sufferings and in his service, but of whom he now had to write:

" Demas forsook me, having loved this present age, and went to Thessalonica."

This study, therefore, has in some senses a very special message to those who are followers of the Lord. The possibility of having met the great Physician, of having been brought into living contact with Him, having received from Him the healing of our sin-sick souls, and yet of a relapse, of a going back, of a forsaking of the Lord.

When we take the story as told in that simple sentence by Paul there are three things which are self-evident. The first is that of the alluring forces which had led him astray. They were those of " this present age." We then see the soul of Demas yielding and assenting to the appeal of those forces until, by a decisive act, he chose them, " having loved." Finally, therefore, we have the record of the act, " Demas forsook me." Although we are going to attempt to examine all this carefully, it may be well to briefly epitomise the story once more. Demas had left Paul and gone to Thessalonica. Why? Because the alluring forces of the present age had proved too strong for him. We then ask, Why did they prove too strong for him? Paul says the reason was that he had " loved " them. That needs fuller interpretation, to which we are coming back.

What, then, were the forces that lured Demas? And here it is really important that we should correct a possible mis-apprehension of the story as it is revealed in an oft-times mis-quotation thereof. Again and again I have heard the story quoted thus, Demas forsook me, having loved this present evil world. Now Paul did not write that, and there are two things that it is important that we remember. The first is that the word " evil " is not in the statement, and the second is that the word " world " should be rendered " age." If by the use of the word " world " we are led to think of the cosmos on its material side, this is not what proved the alluring force. It was rather the age, and that sounds so harmless, and I think accounts for the popular misquotation. Somewhere, somewhen, perhaps a per-fectly sincere soul felt that the story needed the introduction of a word revealing the wrong of it all, and so employed the word *evil*.

What was it, then, that Paul referred to? The present age, that is, the *zeitgeist*, the time spirit, the spirit that dominated the age. The phrase of the apostle apparently so innocuous and harmless is in fact an arresting revelation of the reason why so often in Christian life there is relapse. There is something in the time spirit which makes its appeal, and Demas had felt this. He had felt the enticement of its nearness, the enticement of its method, and the enticement of its gifts.

We remind ourselves again that this man had been with Paul in Rome, and there had seen the age in which he was living. He had travelled with Paul almost certainly for a time. In Rome, however, he was in a great city, pulsing and palpitating with its own conceptions and consequent conduct. As Demas observed all this, he felt the enticement of the seen as against the unseen, the tangible as against the intangible, the sensual as against the spiritual, the present as against the future.

In this same letter, just before referring to the case of Demas, Paul had said:

"I have fought the good fight, I have finished the course, I have kept the faith; henceforth there is laid up for me the crown of righteousness, which the Lord, the righteous Judge, shall give to me at that day; and not only to me, but also *to all them that have loved His appearing."*

Mark the contrast. Paul and those associated with him, and all the followers of Christ were living in the power and passion of the unseen. To them the goal of everything was the appearing of Jesus. They were those who loved that appearing. As a matter of fact there was hardly a beam of light upon the sky in those days which suggested the ultimate victory and appearing of Christ. But these men knew its inevitability, and were sustained by their love of it. Demas had been among their number, but had failed. All round about him were the near things, and these were so real, while the unseen were nebulous. The things occupying the mind of the age were such as could be touched and handled. The things occupying the thought, and creating the inspiration of Paul and those with him could neither be touched nor handled. The near things appealed to sensibility, that is, to the sensuous nature. The other things were spiritual. The things of the age were near. The things which Paul loved appeared to be far in the future. Demas felt the enticement of the near things, the seen, the tangible, and the sensual, the present.

Moreover, he had seen the method of the age in which he lived, and we see it by placing it in contrast with the method of the followers of Christ. The method of the age was that of self-gratification, rather than self-sacrifice, mastery over others instead of service rendered to others, possession here and now instead of the constant necessity for renunciation. These things of the spiritual world were those which Paul had taught, and by which men and women associated with him in loyalty to Christ, were living. Self-denial, self-emptying, self-sacrifice constituted the very heart and soul of Christian experience. Looking round about him Demas saw the contrast. The way of the age was not that of self-sacrifice, but that of self-gratification. It was that of compelling service, rather than that of impelling sacrifice. That was the spirit of the Roman empire. It still is the spirit of the age. Demas felt the enticement of these methods.

It follows, therefore, necessarily that he was allured by what the present age offered him, wealth, pleasure, liberty, as freedom from all restriction. It was in that atmosphere that Demas had lived.

The question arises as to whether it is necessary to yield to such allurement. The reason is that Demas had done so, and evidently there came a moment when he came to definite decision in the presence of the contrast. This is revealed in Paul's pregnant phrase, " having loved."

It is a remarkable thing that at this point Paul used the highest and most noble word for love. It is a word that describes love not merely as an emotional attraction, but rather as an intellectual, informed decision. Moreover, it was a definite act. Demas did not come to it at once. No man ever does. He had listened to the voices sounding round him, telling him of the apparent liberty of the age, speaking to him of the foolishness of self-sacrifice and self-denial. Having listened to these voices, at last he came to a decision. He fixed his love and affection upon the present age.

In this connection we notice that Paul merely states the fact, and we may ask, quite properly, how it came to pass that Demas thus succumbed; and a reference to the writings of Peter will help us to find an answer to the question.

> " For this very cause adding on your part all diligence, in your faith supply virtue; and in your virtue knowledge; and in your knowledge temperance; and in your temperance patience; and in your patience godliness; and in your godliness love of the brethren; and in your love of the brethren love "

That is unquestionably one of the greatest passages in the New Testament in its unveiling of the development of Christian life.

It begins with faith. It ends with love. Love is the full-orbed result of faith, but there is a process of development from faith to love, and this is what Peter is pointing out in his teaching. The passage may really be likened to a description of the growth and opening out of all the life forces obtained in faith, until the ultimate fruitage is reached in love. In an aside we may say that if this be carefully pondered we may turn from it to Paul's great passage on " the fruit of the Spirit is love," with its analysis of love, which immediately follows. Now we have turned to this teaching in Peter, note that he said immediately afterwards:

" If these things are yours, and abound, they make you to be not idle nor unfruitful unto the knowledge of our Lord Jesus Christ. For he that lacketh these things is blind, seeing only what is near."

Thus we have revealed the inwardness of the story of the deflection of Demas. The hour had come when he saw only what was near, and the reason was that, in the past, he had neglected to give diligence for the development of his Christian life from its root of faith to its ultimate fruitage of love.

Arrested development always means deterioration. We have met Him, the great Physician. He has healed our sin-sick souls. Then our duty is that of giving diligence to the cultivation of the life resulting from faith until it reaches its ultimate fruitage. If we fail to do that, the result is inevitably that of arrested development, which ever means deterioration.

It is self-evident, then, that the final assent of the soul marked by the expression, " having loved," followed a period in which Demas had been making his comparisons between the near and the far, between the sensual and spiritual, between the the advantages of the immediate, and the apparently questionable nature of the ultimate. He had been considering and as he did so, the distant became more distant. Prayer unquestionably became irksome. The Word of God, and the teaching of the apostles became dull as the near became nearer, more to be desired, and apparently, better; until at last he fastened his affection upon the present age.

The next step was easy, though it was tragic. Paul speaks of it from the personal standpoint as he says, he " forsook me." Whether this forsaking took place during Paul's first imprisonment, or during the interval between the first and the second, we cannot tell. Enough to know that Paul was now in prison for the second time, and Demas was not with him. He had left Paul and the experience of prison, and all the difficulties of Christian service. He had departed from fellowship with those like-minded, from Luke who stayed by to the end, as well as from Paul and from all the persecuted saints. He declined their way of life. In thus forsaking Paul and that fellowship he forsook the hope, the love of the appearing of Jesus. This means that he left his Lord.

When a man has taken up that position, and come to that decision, what will he do, where will he go? Of Demas it is written, he went to Thessalonica. Thessalonica was then one of the great cities in the empire. It stood on a hill of beauty, sloping to the sea. It was guarded by mountains on both sides. It was a great commercial centre. It was a city of wealth, of luxury, of pleasure, of idolatry. It was the embodiment of the age. Thessalonica is always near at hand for Demas. When he turned his back upon the love of the appearing of Jesus he found himself in a city thus embodying the conceptions and conduct of the age. There we leave the story of the relapse.

It is self-evident that this story makes its appeal to those who have been with Jesus, have had fellowship with His followers, have been workers together with Him; and it compels the asking of certain questions with regard to our own position. These questions may be personal. Where are we now? Are we with Paul, like Luke still standing by, still helping? Then let us see to it that we give diligence to add to our faith all those things that mark its true development, and come at last to the perfect fruitage of love. Do not let us rest satisfied with our present position.

Or are we perchance even now making a comparison? Has the age been forcing itself upon our attention, this present age? Do we feel the lure of the near, and the apparent advantages of the methods of the age? Perhaps we have not yet come to a definite decision. We have not yet parted company with Paul or Christ, but we are making the comparison. Let us bear in mind, then, that if we are inclined to the decision of Demas, faith is against us, history is against us, science is against us.

That faith is against us goes without argument. It is equally true that history is against us. All those things that have been wrought by men and women down the ages that have been of real value to the world, have been accomplished by those who have believed in the unseen, those who have endured, as seeing Him Who is invisible. It is equally true that science is against us. In the early years of my own life it did seem as though science was contrary to faith. That is not so to-day. Science in its own way is definitely declaring the ultimate reality of the mystery that lies behind phenomena, the reality of the unseen.

Or have we already made our choice in favour of the present age, and find ourselves in Thessalonica? Have we broken with our Lord? Have we forsaken Paul, leaving the company and the fellowship? If so, the question that forces itself upon us is, Are we at rest? Are the near things we are grasping satisfying us?

Are there not haunting memories following us? I am putting these things in the form of questions. They might be put in the form of definite affirmations. Demas went to Thessalonica, but he did not get what he went for. No man ever does.

As we close this meditation let us at once say Demas might have come back. Perhaps he did. The certain thing is that if he did, he was received and restored. That needs no argument.

It may be that some one will say, Yes, we believe it to be true that Christ would take us back, but would the group of people whom we left, be willing to receive us? Well in that connection we may say that Paul would. We have a remarkable illustration of that in this very same letter. Writing to Timothy, he said:

"Take Mark, and bring him with thee; for he is useful to me for ministering."

So far as Paul was concerned, Mark was a man who at some point had gone back, with the result that Paul refused to have him associated with him for the time being; but years had passed. Mark had gone on his way with Barnabas, and now toward the end, evidently even from Paul's standpoint, Mark having returned to his loyalty, Paul was eager to receive him. If peradventure we are inclined to make the comparison, let us make it beneath the Cross. If we do so, we shall be compelled to exclaim:

"Were the whole realm of nature mine,
That were a present far too small.
Love so amazing, so Divine,
Demands my life, my soul, my all."

L

ONESIMUS

OF all the stories we have been considering, in certain ways there is no more radiant revelation of the power of the great Physician than the one of Onesimus. His name only appears in a reference found in the letter to the Colossians, and the details given in the letter to Philemon. In passing we may say that in the King James' Version the name appears in two other places. It is found in the subscription to each of these two letters. At the close of the letter to the Colossians these words occur:

"Written from Rome to the Colossians by Tychicus and Onesimus."

At the close of the letter to Philemon we find:

"Written from Rome to Philemon by Onesimus a servant."

These are, to say the least, interesting references. The Revisers have omitted these subscriptions from all Paul's letters, because they form no part of the inspired Word. As a matter of fact they are ascribed to Euthalius, and are not to be found in MSS. earlier than those of the Fifth Century. In some cases examination shows that they contradict the contents of the epistle. In others they were evidently true to the facts, as I think they are in the Colossian and Philemon letters. The references, however, add nothing of value to our study of Onesimus.

Let it be remembered that this story of Onesimus has as its background the pagan world, with all its laws and its customs, into which Christ, as the great Physician, was moving out through His new mystical Body, the Church. As we read the letter we notice the scene shifts from Rome to Colosse. If that fact be examined, it will be discovered that the distance which Onesimus had to travel with that letter was close upon a thousand miles. That journey he took in the company of Tychicus. In itself it is a very revealing fact.

In order to an intelligent consideration of the account of Onesimus, it is necessary that we bear in mind the story that lies behind the letter. The certain fact is that he was a fugitive slave, the property of Philemon; he had left his master, and in all probability had robbed him. There is a reference to him, however, the interpretation of which may possibly be open to question. Let me say at once, however, that to me it is a fact that Onesimus was a brother of Philemon. Referring to him Paul said:

> "No longer as a servant, but more than a servant, a brother beloved, specially to me, but how much rather to thee, both in the flesh and in the Lord."

It is somewhat interesting to discover how all sorts of expositors seem to be in a difficulty in interpreting the meaning of that reference to him as a brother in the flesh to Philemon. The difficulty evidently consists in the fact that he was certainly a slave, and there seems to be doubt in the mind as to whether a brother could be a slave. Here it is quite necessary that we bear in mind that to which we have already referred, that here the background of everything is the pagan world. In that world slavery was prevalent. In all those cities there were found those who were born in slavery. There were also hundreds of slaves who became such as children, having been sold by their parents into slavery, that they might be freed from responsibility for them. There were also those who became slaves through poverty, and sold themselves. There were debtors who were made slaves. There were those who became slaves through capture in war. There were slaves from piracy and kidnapping. There were slaves as the result of offerings made to the temples. If we take the case of Athens, which then was at the zenith of its fame, Pausanias tells us that it had twenty-one thousand free citizens, ten thousand foreign residents, and four hundred thousand slaves. Now the fact is that blood relatives were sold into slavery. Here, I believe, then, we have a case of a brother who was a derelict, and who had robbed Philemon, and so had been doomed to slavery. From this he had fled, and had put a long distance between himself and Philemon, a thousand miles at least.

In Rome, somehow, he made contact with Paul. Seeing the relation that Paul bore to Colosse and Philemon, it may have been that he had known Paul, and so, perhaps in need, sought him out in Rome, where he was a prisoner. Of these things, of course, we have no definite statement. The one thing certain is that he did make that contact, and through it that he was led to Christ. As Paul says, " I have begotten him in my bonds."

It is also clearly evident that he had stayed with Paul, and had ministered to him in his imprisonment, making things easier for him. Then there came a day when Tychicus was to take a letter from the apostle to the Church at Colosse. It was then that Paul decided that this man Onesimus must put to the practical test his relationship with Jesus Christ. He must go back to his master. To refer again to the subscription in the Authorised Version, if it is to be trusted, Onesimus wrote it himself at the dictation of Paul. Again we reach the point of certainty when we say that he travelled with Tychicus over the distances until he came to Philemon.

In this little letter we have two remarkable groups of portraits, and in addition, a central portrait. To see the groups we take first the names that we meet with at the beginning of the letter, and then those found at the close thereof. Seven are named as being in Rome: Paul, Timothy, Epaphras, Mark, Aristarchus, Demas, and Luke. Three of them are named as being in Colosse: Philemon, Apphia and Archippus; and these are surrounded by a larger and nameless group consisting of the household. At the centre of everything is the portrait of Onesimus. The portrait is that of one man, and as a matter of fact, there are two portraits of him. The one is contained in the words, " Who was aforetime unprofitable to thee "; the second in the words, " Now is profitable to thee and to me."

We may omit all the words of those verses except two, which reveal the striking contrast. They are the words " unprofitable " and " profitable." In each case the word presents a picture. By the use of them it was quite evidently Paul's intention to create that very contrast, and to present it to the mind of Philemon.

Imaginatively we can look at the scene when Onesimus arrived, and Philemon saw him, received the parchment, and then read it. It must have been for Onesimus an hour of trial as he came back into the presence of one whom he had wronged. It was equally an hour of trial for Philemon as he looked at the man who had wronged him. Then as he read the letter, these two words must have arrested his attention, the one describing Onesimus as he had been, " unprofitable," and the other describing him as he then was in the view of Paul, " profitable."

Now here we are in the presence of a matter of arresting importance. In making his contrast between the past and the present in the case of Onesimus, he did not do so in the accidentals of material things, nor in the essentials of spiritual experience, but in the matter of his relationship to his fellow-men.

There can be no doubt that the contrast might have been made in many ways. It is conceivable, and almost inevitable that when, having run away, he reached Rome, he came presently to the place of hunger and destitution. Now standing before Philemon -he was neither hungry nor destitute.

It is equally true that in the old days he had been dead in trespasses and sins, and that now he was alive unto God. Paul, however, did not draw attention to these contrasts. The word " unprofitable " marks relationship to others. So also does the word " profitable." It is in that way that Paul directs the attention of Philemon to the change wrought in this man Onesimus.

This matter is so supreme in this story that we will take time to examine the two pictures before applying the principles. In passing we may note the fact that the man's name, Onesimus, means one who gave pleasure, or gave advantage, and so one who was profitable. However it does not suggest itself to me that when Paul made use of the word " profitable " he was in any sense referring to his name. Let us examine these two words in themselves. The word " unprofitable " is the word *achrestos*. The word " profitable " is the word *euchrestos*. In both words there is the root idea found in the word *chrestos*. In the one case the prefix is *a*, which is the negative. In the other the prefix is *eu* which is a superlative. The simple meaning of the root word *chrestos* is useful. When Paul says that in past days Onesimus was *achrestos*, the prefix cancels the value of the root idea, and simply means not useful, or of no use. We are further arrested by the fact that when Paul turned to describe his present position, he was not satisfied with dropping the negative, and using the word *chrestos*, he prefixed it with the *eu*, which marks completeness, so that now he declared this man was completely useful. It will be seen, therefore, how the words themselves constitute graphic portraiture, and reveal a striking contrast.

The root idea, then, is that of usefulness. That necessarily involves a sense of inter-relationship, the fact that no man liveth unto himself, an idea of the commonwealth in which every man gives and gets; the recognition of the fact that every man is either profitable or unprofitable to his fellow-men. The fact, therefore, that confronts us in the story is that a man's value is not that of his own personal perfection, but that of his usefulness to others.

Norman Macleod once wrote a little book called " Character Sketches." In that he has one entitled " T. T. Fitzroy, Esq." He pictures T. T. Fitzroy from his babyhood, through all his boyhood, surrounded with nurses and tutors and valets, all of them ministering to the needs of T T. Fitzroy! Norman Macleod then describes an old cobbler working as a shoemaker, who has taught a starling to speak. This starling talks as the people pass by, and amazingly but definitely cheers the heart of those who hear him. Norman Macleod says that that cobbler making shoes for other men, and that starling, perhaps all unconsciously ministering some cheerfulness to the passer-by are worth more to God and man than T. T. Fitzroy, who has always received, but never given.

We are, therefore, touching here the very central value of Christianity. It is that of being of service to others. I repeat, then, that the contrast created is sharp, decisive, and final. Unprofitable is the highest condemnation of a man. Fully profitable is the highest commendation of a man. The unprofitable man is the man whose motive is selfishness, whose method is robbery. The profitable man is the man whose motive is love, and whose method is service.

The claim for Christ, therefore, made inferentially in this two-fold description, is that He had found him unprofitable, and had made him profitable. He had transformed him from waste into wealth in the interest of the community.

When we enquire, as necessarily we are bound to do, how this transformation had been wrought, we find the reply in the words of Paul, " Whom I have begotten in my bonds." It was a great claim, for it is ever a great thing when one man can say this about another. Paul certainly considered it of great value, for once when writing to the Corinthians, he said:

> " For though ye should have ten thousand tutors in Christ, yet have ye not many fathers; for in Christ Jesus I begat you through the Gospel."

That tells the secret of the transformation. Christ, the great Physician, had met Onesimus mediately through this member of

His mystical Body, and Paul had been the means through whom the contact was made. The fact, however, is that he had been born anew, and in the miracle of that new birth he had been transformed. The evidences of the transformation are discovered in his recognition of responsibility, and his immediate surrender thereto, which things made him willing to travel with Tychicus over a thousand miles, to go back to the man whom he had wronged and robbed. We gather also from the Colossian letter that he was travelling in perfect fellowship with Tychicus, and with the band of Christians surrounding Paul, as Paul described him as " Onesimus the faithful and beloved brother."

Thus as we come to this final study in our series we ask what it really has to say to us. Necessarily it first of all brings us back face to face with the fact of humanity's need of Christ as the great Physician. Humanity as it is self-centred and depraved, is waste. Christ meeting man in that condition, creates out of the waste one who becomes wealth in the sense of being a blessing to the community. The story finally reveals the method of Christ, that, namely, of the impartation of new life.

The appalling fact of waste is surely self-evident. The man who hates instead of loves, he who looks upon his brother in contempt, and calls him Raca, or with malicious intent and calls him fool, is waste. According to the teaching of our Lord there is only one fitting place for such a man, and that is Gehenna, the refuse heap consumed by fire. Equally men are waste who are liars, for the man who lives except upon the basis of simple truth is ever robbing the community. The man, too, who is a thief, and that not according to our ordinary use of the word, but according to the New Testament. It was Paul who wrote:

" Let him that stole steal no more; but rather let him labour, working with his hands the thing that is good, that he may have whereof to give to him that hath need."

An honest reading of that reveals the conception that any man who is not working is a thief. He is either contributing to the common wealth, or he is robbing the other man.

It is from such attitudes of life that all false social conditions arise, carelessness and cruelty, slander and deceit, coercion and war; and, moreover, any attitude that consents to the victory of wrong on account of cowardice. That is waste.

But this story of Onesimus reveals in microcosmic manner the great and glorious fact that Christ is able to deal with that condition of waste, and to transmute it into that of profit; creating men to whom love is the inspiration of all action, truth the method thereof, and service its expression. In the fellowship of such men we have compassion and care, straightness and security, freedom and peace.

When we enquire as to how that transformation takes place we face once again the fact already declared, only now we will employ the very words of Christ, " Ye must be born from above." There is no way into new life, there is no way into true value or worth in the community but the way of the new birth, in which the spirit is changed, the mind is renewed, and the whole life, spent in the same circumstances, changes them. It is the old, old story of how the potter takes the marred vessel, and makes it again, so that it passes into the realm of beauty and utility.

Once again the story reveals the fact that our relationship to God creates our values to our fellow-men. The other side of that law is that our value to our fellow-men is the test of our relationship to God. If we are really right with God we shall be profitable men and women to our fellow-men. If, on the other hand, we affirm that we are right with God, and love not our brother, and fail to serve him, and be profitable to him, we lie, and the truth is not in us.

Necessarily the whole significance and beauty of the story of Onesimus is that which we have seen all the way in our study, namely the power of Christ to transmute waste to wealth. It is a good many years ago now since I was in Bradford, conducting a series of meetings, and I was taken one day to Saltaire. Many of you will be familiar with it. On that day, however, I learned its history, and I have never forgotten it. The whole thing arose out of the fact that a business man named Titus Salt was on the dockside watching men unpack machinery, and he looked and saw wrapped round the machinery stuff that he did not know. Being curious, he picked it up, and he wondered where it came from, and what it was. Taking it with him, he investigated matters, and so found alpaca. The machinery had been packed in it in South America, as being mere waste. There is no need for me to tell at length the story of what happened. Suffice it to say, the day that I was at Saltaire there were five thousand persons employed in the manufacture. On the dock side in Liverpool there was waste. One man discovered its value, and transmuted it into wealth.

The illustration is admittedly on a somewhat low level, and yet it does illustrate the truth that the great Physician saw in the waste of the world potential wealth. He still sees it, and is able to take that waste and transmute it into wealth.

It was Luther who said:

" We are all the Lord's Onesimi ",

that is, we are all the Lord's profitable servants. Let us never forget that we were all unprofitable. It is the great Physician Who, taking hold upon us in our worthless condition, has made us of use to our fellow-men.